Best
Newspaper
Writing

Best Newspaper Writing

2008–2009 Edition

American Society of Newspaper Editors
Award Winners and Finalists

Edited by Tom Huang
and Steve Myers

The Poynter Institute for Media Studies
and

CQ PRESS

A Division of SAGE
Washington, D.C.

CQ Press
2300 N Street, NW, Suite 800
Washington, DC 20037

Phone: 202-729-1900; toll-free, 1-866-4CQ-PRESS (1-866-427-7737)

Web: www.cqpress.com

Cover design: Auburn Associates, Inc.
Cover photos: front, clockwise from top: Michel du Cille/*The Washington Post,*
Gus Chan/*The Plain Dealer,* Grace Beahm/*The Post and Courier;* back: Mona
Reeder/*The Dallas Morning News*
Composition: Auburn Associates, Inc.

⊗ The paper used in this publication exceeds the requirements of the American
National Standard for Information Sciences—Permanence of Paper for Printed
Library Materials, ANSI Z39.48-1992.

Printed and bound in the United States of America

12　11　10　09　08　　　1　2　3　4　5

ISBN: 978-0-87289-612-3
ISSN: 0195-895X

This book is dedicated to the journalists
whose passion, commitment and excellent work
inspire us to persevere through turbulent times.

Contents

PART 1 Reporting on Deadline   1

PART 2 Column Writing   87

PART 3 Investigative Journalism   151

PART 7 Looking Beyond Conflict: Reporting on Human Connections

Foreword: Courage, Determination and Sacrifice

BY KAREN BROWN DUNLAP

Remember the news stories of 2007: killings at Virginia Tech University, climate change concerns that helped former Vice President Al Gore earn two Academy Awards and a Nobel Peace Prize, a Minneapolis bridge collapse, a baseball home-run record set by Barry Bonds, genocide in Darfur, wildfires in California, the legal entanglements of U.S. Senator Larry Craig of Idaho and NFL quarterback Michael Vick, and the assassination of former Pakistani Prime Minister Benazir Bhutto.

We saw the presidential campaigns begin, a home mortgage crisis mount and war in Iraq continue.

We recall the stories but seldom think about the work of the reporters, photojournalists, editors, producers and other news personnel who were there when we needed them.

In January 2007, *Newsday* reporters told readers of a monumental problem in their midst that had continued for nearly three decades. Gaps between Long Island, N.Y., trains and passenger platforms caused over 800 injuries and contributed to a death. During one 90-minute period in 1996, three people fell through gaps at the Syosset station in unrelated incidents. One man broke his back. A woman fell all the way between the train and the platform until her briefcase broke her fall. Commuters pulled her out. Between 1989 and 2007, at least 39 others fell at the same station.

The *Newsday* series prompted other victims to tell of their injuries and fears. The stories led to changes in the Long Island Rail Road system.

In August 2007, Oakland, Calif., residents learned that Chauncey Bailey, editor of the *Oakland Post,* had been shot to death on a city street. A journalist for 37 years, he was working on a tough investigative piece on an Oakland business. A young man employed by the business later confessed to the shooting. During his career, Bailey had been a reporter for *The Detroit News* and the *Oakland Tribune*. After his death, journalists came together to continue his investigation into the business and find the whole story behind his murder.

Bailey is on a list of 65 journalists killed in 2007, as confirmed by the Committee to Protect Journalists. He is the only one killed in the United States. All over the world, journalists are killed, injured and jailed. Some disappear as they courageously report the news.

In December 2007, the staff of *The Chronicle* helped guide the people of Centralia, Wash., when major storms led to flooding. Newspaper reports led the community through the confusion and loss, including two deaths. The staff tracked the closing and reopening of a 20-mile stretch of Interstate 5, explained government assistance and provided tips for cleaning flooded homes. More than that, it acted as a neighbor in a grieving community. As the long rebuilding began, *The Chronicle* advised "caution, patience and community service."

The stories of 2007 show journalists at work. They lift communities during disasters, build the case for needed changes and take the risks needed to reveal truth. In pursuit of truth, some die in war, under repressive regimes or while uncovering corruption. Reporting the news requires skills, but also courage, determination and sacrifice.

This book presents shining examples of journalists at work. It includes widely acclaimed stories, including the Walter Reed Army Medical Center series by *The Washington Post*. It also includes portraits of everyday people and glimpses into situations that didn't draw national attention but affected local communities.

That leads to the underreported story of 2007: the story of how much citizens need quality reporting in a democracy. Reports told of declining newspaper sales, a fragmenting audience and a grinding challenge to the business model of traditional news organizations. But much less was said about the importance of credible news reports in society.

With compelling prose and stunning visuals, through familiar media or creative new uses of multimedia, journalists tell the stories that guide communities. Where would we be without them?

Take time to salute them and learn from their good work.

Karen Brown Dunlap is president and managing director of The Poynter Institute, as well as a Poynter trustee and a member of the board of directors of the Times Publishing Company. She is co-author of The Effective Editor *with Foster Davis and of* The Editorial Eye *with Jane Harrigan.*

Links to Material Mentioned Here

- *Newsday*'s series "Investigating the Gap":
  www.newsday.com/news/specials/nyg-gap-sg,0,6256927.storygallery
- The Chauncey Bailey Project:
  www.chaunceybaileyproject.org/

Preface

In *Best Newspaper Writing,* The Poynter Institute, a school for journalists in St. Petersburg, Fla., explores the work of winners and finalists in the annual contest sponsored by the American Society of Newspaper Editors (ASNE).

This 2008–2009 edition features outstanding journalism in these categories: the Jesse Laventhol Prizes for Deadline News Reporting by a team and by an individual; the Freedom Forum/ASNE Award for Distinguished Writing on Diversity; Distinguished Writing Awards for nondeadline writing, commentary/column writing, editorial writing and local accountability reporting; the Community Service Photojournalism Award; and the Batten Medal, which celebrates the values of "compassion, courage, humanity and a deep concern for the underdog." The selected stories include two 2008 Pulitzer Prize winners and three Pulitzer finalists.

In this edition, we have created two new special sections: "Covering Diverse Communities: Immigration, Race and Ethnicity," which focuses on covering immigrant communities and race relations, and "Looking Beyond Conflict: Reporting on Human Connections," which focuses on covering the quiet stories that don't often get media attention. We present interviews with journalists who were recognized by ASNE for their work and offer insights into what it takes to cover these important areas of journalism.

How to Use This Book

In *Best Newspaper Writing 2008–2009,* readers will find these resources:
Behind the Story

- **Winner's Q&A:** conversational interviews with the winning journalists about their craft, focusing on news judgment, reporting strategies, collaboration and source development.
- **Lessons Learned:** essays by the finalists about the trials and tribulations of producing their honored work and what they learned in the process.
- **Online Journalism:** Matt Thompson of StarTribune.com interviews Web site staff about how their work is presented online.
- **Sources Say:** a feature that allows sources to talk about their experience being part of a story. We hope their feedback offers journalists another frame through which to see how their work affects others.
- **Ethical Reporting:** Pulitzer Prize–winning journalist Louise Kiernan of the *Chicago Tribune* tackles the ethical challenges that arise in reporting on ordinary people with troubled backgrounds.

Learning Tools

- **Narrative Strategies:** Pulitzer Prize–winning journalist Thomas French of the *St. Petersburg Times* examines the narrative techniques of some of the reporters featured in *Best Newspaper Writing*. He explains how the narrative style captures color and action and advances each story, and he highlights the portions of the writing that show narrative tools at work.
- **Writer's Workshop:** discussion questions and assignments—ideal for classrooms—that provide an opportunity to analyze and emulate winning work.
- **X-Ray Reading:** Ben Montgomery of the *St. Petersburg Times* deconstructs the writers' language and offers a toolbox of techniques for reporting and writing.

Web Resources

The complete series for the stories in this book, as well as multimedia, can be found online at www.poynter.org/bnw2009/resources.

Readers will see that the book has been broken into eight parts that represent different types of newspaper writing and photojournalism. The book was organized this way to better follow the structure of classroom teaching and the professional writer's desire to focus on particular genres. The eight parts are: Reporting on Deadline; Column Writing; Investigative Journalism; Feature Writing; Editorial Writing; Covering Diverse Communities: Immigration, Race and Ethnicity; Looking Beyond Conflict: Reporting on Human Connections; and Community Service Photojournalism. The structure makes it easier to learn more about a particular form and to compare different forms of journalism.

About the Interviews and Other Material

Poynter faculty and fellows interviewed ASNE winners by e-mail and by phone. The interviews have been edited for clarity, flow and brevity. Faculty, fellows and editors wrote winner and finalist biographies from information provided by the journalists and their news organizations.

News organizations provided Poynter with electronic versions of the winners' and finalists' stories for publication in this book. They may differ slightly from the stories that originally appeared in print. *Best Newspaper Writing* editors made minor changes for spelling, grammar and Associated Press and Poynter style. But wherever possible, the newspapers' original styles remain.

Photos have been reprinted as they originally appeared, with captions edited for clarity, length, spelling and grammar.

Reporting and writing can be messy. Once writers know the rules, they sometimes choose to break them for effect. In this book, some writers use the passive voice, and some sentences begin with a conjunction. Some writers use language that may be offensive. Based on their experience and comfort, writers and editors may make choices that would not be allowed elsewhere. We have preserved those choices so readers can learn the rules and learn from those who know when and how to break them.

About the ASNE Contest

The goal of this book is to help students of the craft become better journalists. We have selected award-winning work honored by ASNE that we believe will help teach craft and values. Links to many of the multipart series can be found at www.poynter.org/bnw2009/resources. Unfortunately, we could not reprint all the work of the 2008 ASNE contest winners and finalists:

Batten Medal
- Kevin Cullen, *The Boston Globe* (winner)
- Rubén Rosario, *Pioneer Press*, St. Paul, Minn. (finalist)
- Howard Witt, *Chicago Tribune* (finalist)

Distinguished Writing Award for Commentary/Column Writing
- Leonard Pitts Jr., *The Miami Herald* (winner)
- David Sarasohn, *The Oregonian*, Portland, Ore. (finalist)
- Connie Schultz, *The Plain Dealer*, Cleveland (finalist)

Community Service Photojournalism Award
- Mona Reeder, *The Dallas Morning News* (winner)
- Gus Chan, *The Plain Dealer*, Cleveland (finalist)
- Karen Ducey, *Seattle Post-Intelligencer* (finalist)

Jesse Laventhol Prize for Deadline News Reporting by an Individual
- Todd C. Frankel, *St. Louis Post-Dispatch* (winner)
- Jeff Coen, *Chicago Tribune* (finalist)
- Dan Shaughnessy, *The Boston Globe* (finalist)

Jesse Laventhol Prize for Deadline News Reporting by a Team
- Staff, *The Post and Courier*, Charleston, S.C. (winner)
- Staff, *Omaha (Neb.) World-Herald* (finalist)
- Staff, *The Washington Post* (finalist)

Freedom Forum/ASNE Award for Distinguished Writing on Diversity
- David Gonzalez, *The New York Times* (winner)

- Christine Evans, *The Palm Beach (Fla.) Post* (finalist)
- Monica Polanco, *The Hartford (Conn.) Courant* (finalist)

Distinguished Writing Award for Editorial Writing
- Marie Dillon, *Chicago Tribune* (winner)
- Ruben Navarrette Jr., *The San Diego Union-Tribune* (finalist)
- Linda Valdez, *The Arizona Republic* (finalist)

Distinguished Writing Award for Local Accountability Reporting
- Anne Hull and Dana Priest, *The Washington Post* (winner)
- Binyamin Appelbaum, Lisa Hammersly Munn, Ted Mellnik, Pam Kelley, Liz Chandler, Stella M. Hopkins, Gary Schwab, Patrick Scott, Peter St. Onge, *The Charlotte (N.C.) Observer* (finalist)
- Pamela Gould, *The Free Lance-Star*, Fredericksburg, Va. (finalist)
- David Josar, *The Detroit News* (finalist)

Distinguished Writing Award for Nondeadline Writing
- Lane DeGregory, *St. Petersburg (Fla.) Times* (winner)
- David Finkel, *The Washington Post* (finalist)
- Louise Kiernan, *Chicago Tribune* (finalist)

Acknowledgments

We want to thank the many people who helped make this book possible, beginning with the journalists whose work is featured in these pages. Without them, we would know less about reporting and writing.

Many others also helped. We want to thank ASNE, its executive director, Scott Bosley, and his associates Suzanne Martin and Cristal Williams for their work on the contest, and the judges for the 2008 ASNE Awards. Here are the judges' names and affiliations at the time the judging took place:

Andrew N. Alexander, Cox Newspapers
Jim Amoss, *The Times-Picayune*, New Orleans
Gilbert Bailón, *St. Louis Post-Dispatch*
Peter K. Bhatia, *The Oregonian*, Portland, Ore.
David Boardman, *The Seattle Times*
Charlie Borst, *The Free Lance-Star*, Fredericksburg, Va.
Neil Brown, *St. Petersburg (Fla.) Times*
Milton Coleman, *The Washington Post*
Michael K. Connelly, *Sarasota (Fla.) Herald-Tribune*
Manny Crisostomo, *The Sacramento (Calif.) Bee*
George de Lama, *Chicago Tribune*
Gregory Favre, The Poynter Institute
Pamela B. Fine, *The Indianapolis Star*
Kenneth F. Irby, The Poynter Institute

Mike Jacobs, *Grand Forks (N.D.) Herald*
Pamela J. Johnson, Missouri School of Journalism
W. Martin Kaiser, *Milwaukee Journal Sentinel*
Suzanne Kreiter, *The Boston Globe*
Carolyn Lee, New York
Wanda S. Lloyd, *Montgomery (Ala.) Advertiser*
Akili-Casundria Ramsess, *Orlando (Fla.) Sentinel*
Sharon Rosenhause, *South Florida Sun-Sentinel*
Mark E. Russell, *Orlando (Fla.) Sentinel*
Carlos Sanchez, *Waco (Texas) Tribune-Herald*
Cynthia A. Tucker, *The Atlanta Journal-Constitution*
Michael E. Waller, Hilton Head Island, S.C.
Patrick A. Yack, Jacksonville, Fla.

The following people at CQ Press made this a better book with their creativity and enthusiastic support: Aron Keesbury, Christina Mueller, Dwain Smith, Anna Socrates and Anne Stewart.

We are indebted to Kenny Irby, Poynter's Visual Journalism Group Leader and Diversity Program Director, for the talent, wisdom and expertise he brought to editing the photojournalism in this book.

We would like to thank the Poynter faculty and fellows who contributed to this volume: Roy Peter Clark, Karen Brown Dunlap, Rick Edmonds, Tom French, Jill Geisler, Bill Mitchell, Chip Scanlan, Mallary Tenore, Al Tompkins, Butch Ward and Keith Woods. Thanks also to Ben Montgomery of the *St. Petersburg Times* and Matt Thompson of StarTribune.com for their significant contributions. Special thanks to Sandy Johnakin, Kelly McBride, Jessica Sandler, Rick Scheuerman, David Shedden and Maryanne Sobocinski for their support and counsel—and especially to Julie Moos for her guidance throughout this project.

—Tom Huang and Steve Myers

About The Poynter Institute for Media Studies

The Poynter Institute is a school dedicated to teaching journalists, educators, media leaders and aspiring journalists. Through its courses, publications and Web site (www.poynter.org), the Institute promotes excellence and integrity in the craft of journalism and in the practical leadership of successful news businesses. Poynter stands for a journalism that informs citizens, enlightens public discourse and strengthens ties between journalism and democracy.

The Institute offers a combined curriculum of seminars and conferences at its St. Petersburg, Fla., campus, along with Webinars, online programs and a wealth of self-directed courses through its e-learning portal, News University (www.newsu.org). Poynter faculty and staff also work with journalists at various locations across the nation and around the world.

The Poynter Institute was founded in 1975 by Nelson Poynter, chairman of the *St. Petersburg Times,* and its Washington affiliate, Congressional Quarterly. Poynter, who died in 1978, willed the controlling stock in his companies to the school. As a financially independent, nonprofit organization, The Poynter Institute is beholden to no interest except its own mission: to help journalists seek and achieve excellence.

About the Editors and Contributors

About the Editors

TOM HUANG is ethics and diversity fellow at The Poynter Institute and assistant managing editor for Sunday and enterprise at *The Dallas Morning News*. On a yearlong fellowship at Poynter, he is teaching ethics, diversity and leadership issues and coaching journalists on writing. He has worked at *The Dallas Morning News* since 1993, first as a feature writer, then as features editor, and now as the Sunday Page One editor. His reporting has taken him from Bosnia and Vietnam and the Athens Olympics to the aftermath of the Oklahoma City bombing and the 9/11 attacks in New York. Before moving to Dallas, he worked at *The Virginian-Pilot* in Norfolk. He is a member of the Asian American Journalists Association and the American Association of Sunday and Feature Editors and serves on the national advisory board of the Knight Center for Specialized Journalism.

STEVE MYERS is news editor of Poynter Online (www.poynter.org). Before he joined Poynter, he spent 10 years as a newspaper reporter, focusing in his last several years on government accountability. He has worked for the *Press-Register* in Mobile, Ala., *The News & Observer* in Raleigh, N.C. and the *Charleston Daily Mail* in West Virginia. He was a 2006 fellow in The Ohio State University's Kiplinger Program in Public Affairs Journalism and followed that with a Katrina Media Fellowship from the Open Society Institute. He has reported on sexual abuse in the Catholic Church, illegal court expungements, Gulf Coast hurricanes and disaster preparation, religion's role in politics, labor unions and coal mining. He completed Poynter's college fellowship program in 1997.

About the Contributors

ROY PETER CLARK is vice president and senior scholar at The Poynter Institute, where he has taught writing since 1979. He founded the Writing Center at Poynter, lending support to the writing coach movement. He is a distinguished service member of the American Society of Newspaper Editors and was inducted by the American Association of Sunday and Feature Editors into its Features Hall of Fame. He is the author of *Writing Tools: 50 Essential Strategies for Every Writer* and is at work on a new book, *The Glamour of Grammar*.

KAREN BROWN DUNLAP is president of The Poynter Institute as well as a Poynter trustee and a member of the board of directors of the Times Publishing Company. She is also on the boards of the Newspaper Association of America Foundation and Eckerd College. She is co-author of *The Effective Editor* with Foster Davis, co-author of *The Editorial Eye* with Jane Harrigan and was editor of the Institute's *Best Newspaper Writing* series. She has served as a Pulitzer Prize jurist three times.

RICK EDMONDS is media business analyst at The Poynter Institute. His work centers on the future of the newspaper business and measurement of newsroom capacity. Earlier in his career, he was editor and publisher of several magazines for the *St. Petersburg Times* organization and managing editor of the paper's Tampa edition. Before that he worked as a reporter and editor at *The Philadelphia Inquirer* and was a finalist for the Pulitzer Prize for national reporting in 1982.

THOMAS FRENCH, The Poynter Institute's first writing fellow, began work as a *St. Petersburg Times* reporter soon after his graduation from Indiana University. His first newspaper series, "A Cry in the Night," is an account of a murder investigation and trial that French turned into the book *Unanswered Cries.* A year spent reporting in a public high school produced the series and book *South of Heaven.* His series "Angels & Demons," about the murder of three women visiting Florida, earned him a Pulitzer Prize for feature writing.

JILL GEISLER heads the leadership and management group at The Poynter Institute. She was the country's first female news director of a major market network affiliate, WITI-TV in Milwaukee, where she worked for 25 years. As news director, she coached a team of award-winning, enterprising journalists. She is the author of Poynter Online's "SuperVision" column and the author of many articles on journalism and leadership, as well as the book *News Leadership: At the Head of the Class.*

KENNY IRBY, visual journalism group leader and diversity program director at The Poynter Institute, is the founder of Poynter's photojournalism program. Before joining Poynter, Irby worked as a photographer and deputy director of photography at *Newsday* and contributed as a photo editor to three Pulitzer Prize–winning projects there. In 2007 he chaired the Pulitzer Prize judging in the photography categories, lectured at the World Press Photo's buddy-training program and was awarded the National Press Photographers Association's Sprague Award, the organization's highest honor.

BILL MITCHELL is director of Poynter Online (www.poynter.org). Before joining Poynter in 1999, he was editor of Universal New Media (1995–1999) and director of electronic publishing at the *San Jose* (Calif.) *Mercury News* (1992–1995). Mitchell also has worked as a reporter, editor, Washington correspondent and European correspondent for the *Detroit Free Press* and as Detroit bureau chief for *Time* magazine. He served as a juror for the Pulitzer Prizes in 2002 and 2003.

BEN MONTGOMERY is a general assignment reporter at the *St. Petersburg Times*. He grew up in Oklahoma and schooled at Arkansas Tech University, where he played defensive back for the Wonder Boys. He worked for *The Courier* in Russellville, Ark.; the *Standard-Times* in San Angelo, Texas; the *Times Herald-Record* in New York's Hudson River Valley and the *Tampa Tribune* before joining the *Times* in 2006.

CHRISTOPHER SCANLAN is a senior faculty member in the reporting, writing and editing group at The Poynter Institute and journalism adviser to NewsU (www.newsu.org), Poynter's e-learning portal. Scanlan joined the Poynter faculty in 1994 from the Knight Ridder Newspapers' Washington bureau, where he was a national correspondent. From 1994 to 2000, he edited the *Best Newspaper Writing* series. Scanlan is the author of *Reporting and Writing: Basics for the 21st Century* and co-editor of *America's Best Newspaper Writing: A Collection of ASNE Prizewinners.*

MALLARY JEAN TENORE is The Poynter Institute's copy editor. A 2007 graduate of Providence College, Tenore has spent the past year working as the Institute's Naughton fellow, reporting, editing and producing content for Poynter Online. She edited her college newspaper, *The Cowl,* and has written for a variety of publications, including the *St. Petersburg Times, The Boston Globe* and *The Dallas Morning News.* She is especially interested in reporting on diversity-related issues and Hispanic affairs.

MATT THOMPSON is a deputy Web editor at the Minneapolis *Star Tribune* and a 2008–2009 Reynolds Institute Fellow at the University of Missouri. A former online reporter/producer at The Poynter Institute and *The Fresno Bee,* he currently sits on Poynter's national advisory board.

AL TOMPKINS is The Poynter Institute's group leader for broadcasting and online. Every weekday, thousands read his online journalism story idea column, "Al's Morning Meeting," on www.poynter.org. He has taught writing and storytelling seminars and workshops in 43 states, five countries and dozens of newsrooms over the last 10 years. Tompkins is the author of the book *Aim for the Heart: A Guide for TV Producers and*

Reporters, which was adopted by more than 70 universities as their main broadcast writing textbook. He co-authored three editions of the Radio and Television News Directors Foundation's *Newsroom Ethics* workbook and was a consulting contributor to the NPPA national code of photographic ethics. Tompkins joined Poynter's faculty from his job as news director at WSMV-TV in Nashville, Tenn. For 24 years, he worked as an 18-time Emmy Award–winning photojournalist, reporter, producer, anchor, assistant news director, special projects/investigations director, documentary producer and news director.

BUTCH WARD is distinguished fellow at The Poynter Institute. He joined the staff of *The Philadelphia Inquirer* after working at *The News American* in Baltimore. At the *Inquirer* he was New Jersey editor, assistant managing editor for the Sunday paper, assistant managing editor in features, metropolitan editor, assistant to the publisher and managing editor. He left the *Inquirer* in 2001 and spent three years as vice president for corporate and public affairs at Independence Blue Cross.

KEITH WOODS is dean of faculty at The Poynter Institute. In 16 years at *The Times-Picayune* in New Orleans, he worked as a sportswriter, news reporter, city editor, editorial writer and columnist. He joined Poynter in 1995 and led the institute's teaching on diversity and coverage of race relations as part of the ethics faculty; he then served as reporting, writing and editing group leader. Woods is a former editor of the *Best Newspaper Writing* series. He is a co-author of *The Authentic Voice: The Best Reporting on Race and Ethnicity*.

Introduction: The Perfect Line

BY ROY PETER CLARK

When I add this edition of *Best Newspaper Writing* to my shelf, it will complete a set of 30 volumes, three decades of winners of the contest that my mentor Gene Patterson built. As the president of the American Society of Newspaper Editors (ASNE) in 1977, Gene and his colleagues created a contest that would come to define the best practices in the field of newspaper writing. Gene also hired me as a writing coach for the *St. Petersburg Times* and assigned me the task of creating a book that would showcase the winners.

I wanted to title it *Top of the Craft*. The old man pulled out Occam's Razor and shaved it down to *Best Newspaper Writing*.

That first book is a collector's item. (If you happen to own a copy, I'd happily give you five bucks for it.) On the outside "it's not much of a book," William Zinsser wrote for the *Columbia Journalism Review.* But Zinsser appreciated what was on the inside and the spirit behind it, a sense that over the generations the best newspaper writers held a torch high. That torch has been passed on now for three decades, an era in which newspapers have changed in a thousand ways.

What has not changed is the power of the story, told not only in words but, in recent contests, in great photographic images as well.

To prepare for writing this introduction, I went back to year one to examine what I had written then. What shocked me was the currency of some of those original ideas, including the sentence, "Distracted by the new newspaper technology, editors have abdicated their responsibility to train and encourage good writers." Distracted by technology, indeed! I continued:

> Why are these stories so good? They are written by gifted storytellers who are also careful, thorough reporters. The writers share a sense of style and structure. And they all write about people.
>
> This book should help dispel persistent myths about newspaper writing in America: that there is no room in newspapers for good writing; that reporting and writing are mutually exclusive skills; that deadlines make good writing impossible; that governmental or international news is, by definition, unreadable; that good writing can only be found in powerful papers with enormous resources.

These stories prove that if articles are well-written, newspapers will find room for them. They show that good reporting adds the detailed description, the anecdotes, the quotations that bring stories to life. Most of these stories were written quickly, some in "the white heat of frustration," as one writer puts it.

That writer was Richard Ben Cramer, who was just 28 when he won an ASNE award for his dramatic dispatches from the Middle East, including this one published in *The Philadelphia Inquirer* on March 15, 1978:

> The Hadani family was sitting shiva. The house was filled with family and friends observing the ancient Jewish custom, a custom that surrounds the bereaved with the living so they will not dwell morbidly on the dead.
>
> In the 48 hours since their daughter, Na'ami, who was 9, died in the Palestinian commando raid on the highway between here and Tel Aviv, Joseph and Levana Hadani have not been alone.

Since he wrote those words, Cramer has become one of America's most important writers, the biographer of Joe DiMaggio and Bob Dole. His profile of Ted Williams was judged one of the best stories ever to appear in *Esquire* magazine.

Cramer was joined on the medal stand that first year by Everett S. Allen, a silver-haired essayist for *The Standard-Times* of New Bedford, Mass. He received his prize at the age of 63, and after a 41-year career at his newspaper. For the book, I paid Allen a visit and wrote this description:

> An old elevator rattles up to the fifth floor of the *Standard-Times* building in New Bedford. Like other antique newspaper houses, the place carries an air of functional decay, best symbolized by the only sign on a Men's Room door. It reads FIRE ESCAPE. Nearby, overlooking the harbor, is a crow's nest of an office occupied by Everett S. Allen, the great white father of iambic journalism.

That last phrase was inspired by the acceptance speech offered by Allen at the ASNE convention. He said:

> I believe that I am the only newspaper reporter who deliberately and successfully inserted in a general-alarm fire story a perfect iambic line. I was so titillated at being able to do it…that even though it was something like 38 years ago, I remember it perfectly.
>
> The line was, "Ten pumpers roared throughout the night in Sawyer Street." Now, if 13 pumpers had shown up at the fire, or if

the fire had been, let us say, in Brock Avenue, I would have had to either a) change the meter of the line, or b) respectfully decline to cover the fire.

Thoughts of iambic journalism may seem quaint or self-indulgent in an era when reporters are dumping stuff onto Web sites and the foundations of newspaper journalism are crumbling. But I bet if you read carefully, you'll be able to find somewhere in this book a perfect iambic line. That line is not as important as the powerful reporting and storytelling that make these stories standards of excellence. But that perfect iambic line is still important. It will prove that when the reporter's eye teams up with the writer's ear, the result can be magic.

Roy Peter Clark is vice president and senior scholar at The Poynter Institute, where he has taught writing since 1979.

Best
Newspaper
Writing

PART 1

Reporting on Deadline

Winner: Individual Deadline News Reporting
Todd C. Frankel

ST. LOUIS POST-DISPATCH

Reporters love autonomy, the freedom to identify and develop stories of their own choosing rather than following the dictates of an assigning editor. That's the tension that goes on in daily journalism—my story or your story? A few gifted reporters find a way to do both. They take the editor's suggested topic and find a better way to tell it.

Todd C. Frankel's work demonstrates that talent of doing both. Frankel has been a general assignment reporter at the *St. Louis Post-Dispatch* since 2003. His passion is finding the story on the margins of the one that everyone else sees. One of this year's ASNE judges called his talent "Seinfeldian," in that he can take ordinary events and find meaningful stories within. That's how gawkers, nondescript apartments and people choosing not to participate in ceremonies drove Frankel's award-winning work.

Frankel graduated from the University of Delaware in 1997, where he wrote for the student publication, *The Review.* Following graduation, he took part in a six-week summer fellowship at The Poynter Institute. His roommate and colleague in the program, Steve Myers (co-editor of *Best Newspaper Writing*), says of him: "Even when Todd got to Poynter, he had developed an appreciation of good writers and he studied good writing. He often parked himself at one of the computers in the library and printed out stories from Nexis. He may have printed out every Rick Bragg story he could find."

Myers recalls: "He seemed to look out for small things and focus on them. I remember one of his college clips was about which coffee cup lids were better than the rest."

Frankel worked as an assistant city editor and general assignment reporter at *The Herald* in Everett, Wash.; a city hall and statehouse reporter at the *Charleston Daily Mail* in West Virginia; and a cops reporter at *The Gleaner* in Henderson, Ky.

In 2002, while at *The Herald,* Frankel won a Society of Professional Journalists Sigma Delta Chi award and a Casey Medal for Meritorious Journalism for "Day Zero," the story of 3-year-old Sebastian Marat, a child fighting cancer, and his family's struggle. The wrenching story, one without a happy ending, became a 12-page special section in the paper.

Frankel and his wife, *Post-Dispatch* photographer Stephanie S. Cordle, became parents at the same time Frankel received news of his ASNE award. Their firstborn is named Eli.

—Jill Geisler, Leadership and Management Group Leader,
The Poynter Institute

Among These Honored Dead, Fresh Graves in Section N

MAY 29, 2007

By Todd C. Frankel

The latest troops to die in combat come here, to section N.

The section is small and sits on a sloping hill behind an administration building, beyond a fence. It is tucked in a corner, so close to the main entrance of Jefferson Barracks National Cemetery that it is easily over-looked, potentially lost among the 166,000 graves spread over 333 acres.

It was Memorial Day, and a grand ceremony was taking place about a quarter-mile away in another part of the cemetery. The annual event featured speeches, honor guards and a crowd of hundreds.

From section N, the one set aside for active-duty deaths, it was possible to hear only the faintest sounds of music.

"Too bad they don't have a microphone, a sound system," Marie Costello said.

"It's OK," her husband, Jim Costello, responded. "We're here."

They sat in folding camping chairs next to a grave marker bearing the name "James F. Costello III," their son. They called him Jamie. He was a 27-year-old Oakville native. An Army soldier. He died April 11, 2006, when an improvised explosive device detonated in Iraq.

Jim Costello wore his son's dog tags around his neck. He watched his wife place flowers at the graves of others killed in action.

"We're kind of a community," Marie Costello said, clutching red and peach roses. "So I try to share the flowers."

They have gotten to know the other families who have lost sons and daughters in the ongoing wars. Jim Costello knows that the father of Riley E. Baker, a 23-year-old Marine sniper killed on June 22, 2006, in Iraq, likes to leave a bottle of Wild Turkey whiskey at his son's grave, located one row behind Jamie Costello. The two fathers sometimes share a swig.

Jefferson Barracks is both a quiet, respectful place and a bustling center. About 20 funerals take place at the cemetery every day, mostly for World War II and Korean War veterans who pass away in old age.

The cemetery does not keep a count on the number of Iraq and Afghanistan active-duty troops buried here. Officials estimated the number

Friends of Brandon L. Wallace, a Jefferson County native who was killed in Iraq, visit his grave at Jefferson Barracks National Cemetery, where Memorial Day services were held. From left are Abby Wynn, Jeff Wynn, Joshua Axtetter and David McKinney. (Photograph courtesy of Sam Leone/*St. Louis Post-Dispatch*)

A Memorial Day procession marches to the Old Flag Circle in Jefferson Barracks National Cemetery. (Photograph courtesy of Sam Leone/*St. Louis Post-Dispatch*)

is fewer than a dozen. But the number is growing. Jim Costello could tell you that just from the frequent visits to his son's grave.

"Riley wasn't here yet. Nor was Russell," Jim Costello said, twisting in his chair to count the graves added since his son's. "One, two, three.... At least five new ones since we've been coming out to see Jamie."

There is Russell Makowski, a 23-year-old Union resident who died Sept. 14, 2006, in Iraq. And Matthew Clark, a 22-year-old Ladue High graduate and Marine who was killed in Iraq on Dec. 14. And Milton Gist Jr., 27, a former St. Louis resident killed on Jan. 30 in Iraq.

And Ryan Garbs, 20, an Edwardsville man who was one of eight soldiers killed Feb. 18 in a helicopter crash in Afghanistan.

The latest arrival is Brandon L. Wallace, 27, a Jefferson County native who was killed April 14 in Iraq. His marker is just a few down from Jamie Costello's.

Jamie Costello grew up about three miles away in Oakville. He went to grade school just up the street. Father and son used to drive by the cemetery all the time.

Now it is the father who comes, sometimes with his wife and sometimes alone, to spend some time with his son, in section N.

Boys Were Hidden in Plain Sight

JAN. 14, 2007

By Todd C. Frankel

It is an anonymous place in the middle of St. Louis' comfortable suburbs. Hidden, yet right there.

Apartment D, the one that held the two kidnapped boys, sits on the ground floor of a two-story brick building. Seven identical buildings surround it. The '60s-era complex has no name. The only distinguishing detail is the color of the doors: one building has black, another green, then white. And orange. Apartment D has an orange door.

The man inside Apartment D kept to himself. Not unusual, residents say. They thought the teenage boy with him was his son. The boy didn't seem to go to school, but they didn't want to ask any questions. Really, no one thought to. The second boy? No clue he was even there.

People come and go here, some staying for just a few months in the $495-a-month units. The entire complex, sitting in a valley next to the road, can escape notice as people drive by on busy South Holmes Avenue. "They pay no mind," said Rob Bushelle, 29, who has lived here for 1^1/2 years.

Maybe it is a fact of modern life that something like this can happen—that two boys kidnapped four years apart can be kept in an apartment by a man who is not their father and no one knows. Investigators and the victims' families have marveled at how the alleged kidnapper hid what he had taken in plain sight.

"It goes back to everybody minding their own business, not wanting to get involved, not paying attention and putting their blinders on and worrying about themselves and themselves only," Craig Akers said Saturday at a news conference, a day after being reunited with his son Shawn Hornbeck, who disappeared in 2002. "We've lost a lot of our sense of community. We've lost a lot of our neighbor-helping-neighbor."

But the Holmes Avenue apartments do not seem remarkable in that regard. The complex is not on the wrong side of the tracks but literally in between: freight trains run close by just to the north and south. This is the edge of affluent Kirkwood. The historic train station at this suburb's heart is a half-mile up the road. Just 500 yards away is a sprawling $1 million house with a tennis court and crushed-stone driveway. But the apartments

"It's scary. You never think it could be your neighbor. It could have been one of my kids," said Krista Jones, 25, who lived across from Michael J. Devlin's apartment, where Ben Ownby, 13, and Shawn Hornbeck, 15, were found. (Photograph courtesy of Laurie Skrivan/*St. Louis Post-Dispatch*)

also are neighbors to bland warehouses and Interstate 44, which leads southwest to the rural spots where the boys were kidnapped.

This is where Michael J. Devlin, the 41-year-old pizza parlor manager accused of taking the boys, chose to live. He was surrounded by people, yet insulated from them. He could have picked a more isolated location. But here he blended in.

Bushelle, who works as a landscaper, knew Devlin only at a distance. Last fall he had a confrontation with Devlin over a parking space. But that was it. Bushelle saw the boy who lived with Devlin. But he never suspected he was a kidnapping victim.

"How am I supposed to know?" Bushelle asked. "It's a total cliché, but you never think it is going to happen in your neighborhood."

A mile away sits a Schnucks supermarket with a bench featuring a missing poster for Shawn Hornbeck. It contains an age-progressed photo. Akers said his son saw the poster at the supermarket before he was rescued, and his son called the guesswork at what he might look like "insulting."

But it was haunting.

Karen Mooney works at that Schnucks selling lottery tickets and renting videos. She sits just a few feet from the poster, near the automatic doors. She has worked here 16 years. Mooney said she has a good mind for faces—she once identified a store thief by his gold-capped teeth. She is friendly with customers, saying "hello" as they walk in and offering comments like how fast a son is growing up.

She had studied that poster of Shawn Hornbeck. She is stunned that he might have walked into the store, past her desk, maybe even responding to her offer of "hello." And she never knew. Never suspected a thing.

"You'd think I would have noticed him," she said, with a shake of her head.

But she was not the only one.

Crowds Gather to Catch a Glimpse

OCT. 10, 2007

By Todd C. Frankel

It was on the second stop of Michael Devlin's whirlwind tour of the region's courthouses that three school-bus drivers showed up.

The women stood outside the old brick courthouse in Potosi, their Tuesday morning routes complete, angling for a glimpse.

They wanted to see Devlin for themselves, to judge him, to lay eyes on him in the flesh. Devlin was a curiosity. He was a celebrity. He was a ghoul who has dominated the imagination since being caught in January after kidnapping two boys, having held one boy for four years.

One of the bus drivers, Melissa Thompson, stood on her tiptoes in her white sneakers, sunglasses pushed back on her head, trying to get a better look. She peered over the broad shoulders of police officers and the yellow tape holding back a small crowd of onlookers.

"I've just got to see what such a monster looks like," said Thompson, 38, a mother of three.

A circuslike atmosphere has enveloped Devlin's trips to four courtrooms in four cities, spread over 150 miles and three days this week. Court in Union. Potosi. Clayton. His guilty pleas and lengthy sentences, including life terms, in those courts are done. The last stop is expected today with federal court in St. Louis.

The settings were often dramatic: Devlin escorted by flak-jacketed SWAT members at one stop, a police helicopter hovering low overhead. Devlin changed outfits with each venue—orange prison garb, then green, then brown. A thick moving mass of cameras and reporters tracked it all. People with no connection to the case showed up. They snapped photos. They craned their necks. They offered their views.

In Union, a truck circled the courthouse square carrying a giant metal claw and a sign reading, "Pedophile Terminator II: I'll be Back." And a woman reached into a trash can to grab the chipped, red coffee cup discarded by one of Devlin's attorneys after he dropped it. She joked that she would sell it on eBay.

But for many others, there seemed to be a genuine desire to understand Devlin, to glean from a glance some sense from the horrific situation. They wanted to see in Devlin some clue that might keep their family safe, might give away someone who managed to elude authorities for so long.

Some approached the topic with blunt humor.

"I want to see what a real pervert looks like on the streets," said Diane Price, 36, sitting on the stone stoop of an appliance store across from the Potosi courthouse.

"Oh, Diane," admonished Rosemary Smith, 50, sitting next to her.

"Well!" Price said. "You could be sitting next to a pervert and never know. So I want to know what one looks like."

In Potosi on Tuesday, Devlin walked out in a green shirt and black track pants. His hearing was over. Escorted by SWAT team members, he walked from the courthouse toward a hulking, black armored vehicle. Someone booed. The state police helicopter swooped down. The three bus drivers stood together.

"There he is," said Jane Ruble, 60.

"Oh, gosh," said Janet Bettis, 55. "I've never seen anything like this."

"He does look different," Ruble said, noting how Devlin had dropped weight and shaved his beard and head since his capture.

"This makes me nervous," Bettis said. "Look."

She held out her arms, showing her twitching fingers and goose bumps heading under her shortsleeves.

As school-bus drivers, they felt a deep connection to Devlin's case. He is accused of snatching his last victim after the boy was dropped off by a school bus in another county. After the abduction, the bus drivers were told to watch for suspicious vehicles as they traced their rural routes.

With Devlin gone, Bettis and Ruble headed off. But Thompson stayed. The mother of three walked across the courthouse grass to where the county prosecutor talked before a bank of microphones. Reporters and cameras surrounded him. Thompson nudged her way in and listened. She heard the prosecutor describe the terror of Devlin's first victim. She hung on every word, pushing deeper into the ring of media to hear over the roar of passing trucks.

"It's like an education for your kids—how to stop this," Thompson said. "Devlin is a monster no matter what. But my initial thought was that he was a deviant-looking guy. But he looks like the normal guy walking down the street."

From Potosi, Devlin and his entourage of law enforcement traveled to Clayton. Another swarm of onlookers and reporters awaited. Jurors on lunch break milled about.

"It's like we're waiting for a rock star," said Tammy LePage, 24, of Florissant, "but he's a creep."

But the office towers of the St. Louis County Circuit Court provided no opportunity for the public to see Devlin outside.

And when that hearing ended Tuesday afternoon, as the victims' families and the prosecutor walked out, Devlin seemed to have disappeared, like a ghost.

BEHIND theSTORY

An Interview with Todd Frankel

This edited e-mail interview was conducted by Jill Geisler, Poynter Leadership and Management Group Leader, with Todd C. Frankel, winner of the Jesse Laventhol Prize for Deadline News Reporting by an Individual.

JILL GEISLER: In these winning stories, you invite readers to look past the core events everyone's covering—Memorial Day services, the processing of a prisoner—and see them through new eyes. Please describe how and why you select those vantage points.

TODD FRANKEL: I try to follow my own curiosity and trust my instincts that perhaps the best story is not the obvious one. If something bores me, it likely will bore readers. Like the Memorial Day story or the sentencings of a notorious child kidnapper—these were highly scripted events. The outcomes were pretty well-known. There were plenty of other media there—cameras and reporters standing pretty much shoulder to shoulder. So I looked for other possibilities. Sometimes, at the edges of highly choreographed events, the truly interesting occurs. And events at the periphery can provide a new understanding of what is happening at the center. This is what I was looking for.

Your stories are rich with detail, something that's challenging to accomplish when you're racing against the clock. How do you harvest so many fine points to illustrate the people and places in your stories?

I write everything down—not just names and dialogue, but color, smells, impressions and themes that I might want to pursue. I strive to lead readers into these places, and if something sends a shiver down my back or makes me choke up or makes me laugh, I need to write that down. Because there is likely something there. Something I might want to use later.

And when you're on deadline, your mind is racing and you might forget that fleeting feeling you had at the scene. Plus, writing it down makes it more concrete and helps me look for other details in a similar vein.

Like in the story about the apartment where a kidnapper held two young boys, I was immediately struck that he hid in plain sight, in an upper-middle-class suburb. I wrote down that feeling, and I think that helped me notice another detail that I really liked—how the apartment was located not on the proverbial wrong side of the railroad tracks, but literally between two sets of train tracks.

Your Memorial Day story is haunting. Section N of the cemetery seems a world apart from the "grand ceremony" nearby. Why did you focus on section N instead of the "speeches, honor guards and a crowd of hundreds"?

Honestly, because I didn't want to cover the ceremony. That was my assignment. I tried dodging it. That didn't work. All reporters have to work the occasional weekend shift and mine happened to fall on that holiday weekend, which usually means covering a parade or a ceremony. So I decided to look for something different.

Around this time the number of military deaths in Iraq was in the news. So I went out to the cemetery with no story in mind, just curious where they buried those killed-in-action from Iraq and Afghanistan.

The first clue that I might have a story came when a cemetery worker tried giving me directions to section N. It was hard to find. And everyone heading to the Memorial Day ceremony was walking in the opposite direction. When I did find the section, I was struck by the handful of people milling about. Their grief was so fresh. It was hard to see. And I knew this is where I needed to be.

Your writing is authoritative and at the same time conversational: "The boy didn't seem to go to school, but they didn't want to ask any questions. Really, no one thought to." How did you develop this technique and why do you think it works?

It is a balancing act. I try to avoid newspaper-speak—the suitcase leads and multiple clauses. But at the same time, I don't want to sound too informal. It also is about trying to digest the reporting, to give it context and texture, rather than just parroting the people I've interviewed and writing a story that is essentially just a string of set-ups for quotes.

What is your approach to organizing your stories?

Haphazard. I've tried to get disciplined with outlining my stories. When I'm writing a nondeadline story, I can do that, structuring the story from beginning to end. But on deadline, I try to think of the major points or themes and just begin writing. Knowing my lead before I sit down to write helps. But sometimes I just go through my notes, rereading, looking for the right starting place. I tend to write from beginning to end, although I try to know my ending before I get there. On deadline, my writing process is more fluid and less deliberate because it has to be.

How many drafts did you do on these deadline stories?

I'm not a fast writer. It actually takes me a painfully long time to write a story—or at least it feels like it. So I don't usually have time to go through drafts. I spend the most time searching for the right lead and everything tends to flow from there. But it is also a good sign if I know my ending before I sit down to write. Once I have a finished draft, I usually read it through two to three times for pacing, tone and wording. I'm constantly tinkering with my stories. It is not unusual at all for me to be driving home after deadline and calling my editor to see if we can change a single word or two.

What role did your editors play before, during and after your reporting and writing?

These stories were unusual in that each had a different editor. One story broke on a Saturday and I was called in to write. Another was a part of a regular weekend shift. And the last one occurred during the regular work-week. Also, I was between editors for part of the year.

But one thing all of the editors did was allow me to take risks—and to fail. And that takes trust on their part. There was no guarantee there would be an interesting story about where a kidnapper lived or the crowds that gathered to watch a court hearing. And when it comes to line editing, there were discussions about word choice or perhaps pacing in a particular paragraph. Those talks are always helpful.

If you had all the time in the world to develop these stories, would you have wanted to do anything differently?

I can always find problems with my stories. Always. But I'm fairly happy with the way these stories turned out, although there are phrasings and wordings I might want to play with. I tend to have more regrets with my nondeadline work because the parameters of what is possible are so much greater. On deadline, you've got to focus your stories to write them quickly.

Did you face any ethical challenges in reporting these stories? If so, how did you handle them?

Not ethical in the traditional sense, but because most of my stories center on ordinary people (the non-celebrities and never-public officials among us) I sometimes encounter the challenge of doing right by someone unaccustomed to being in the news.

In the Memorial Day story, especially, I was sensitive to tromping up on families standing graveside. They were not expecting to be interviewed or observed. So the couple I did end up talking with, I tried to make clear what the story was and why I wanted to talk with them.

I probably spent an hour just watching them and others before I got up the nerve to approach them. And in the story where I followed the school bus drivers, I had to overcome their initial reaction of "why would you want to talk to us?" I wanted them to be comfortable allowing me to essentially eavesdrop on their reactions. And I did not want them to feel that I was taking advantage of them, either.

How, if at all, did the print and online versions of your stories differ? Were you able to add any other dimensions to the stories online?

There were no differences between the print and online versions, and nothing extra online. But I think the Web changed these stories—because the news behind the stories was pretty well-known by the time I came upon them.

The child kidnapper had been caught and his hideaway had long been on our Web site and on TV by the time my story appeared. When the kidnapper was sentenced to multiple life sentences, it was part of a plea bargain that was announced days previously.

And Memorial Day festivities had been covered online before my story hit. So I knew going in to all of these stories that straight copy would not be enough. And that was freeing. I could explore other angles. The immediacy of the Internet took the pressure off. The news was already out there. But I could still deliver the story.

Writer's Workshop

Talking Points

1. Memorial Day stories are often about the organized events: parades, speeches, wreath-laying. Todd Frankel's story about section N has no ceremony attached to it. What gives the story its power?

2. When you read the Frankel story about the boys hidden in plain sight, you learn a good bit about the lay of the land. But this story also raises questions about civic life. What questions do you hear? What answers?

3. People who gather at the scene of news events are sometimes dismissed as rubberneckers, but in the story about Michael Devlin's court appearances, Frankel makes the onlookers his focus. What do we learn about the story by looking at it through their eyes? What do we learn about the onlookers?

Assignment Desk

1. The power of the "Section N" story comes from its contrast to the day's ceremonial events. A small human drama is playing out in the shadow of ceremony. Go to your preferred news Web site and find a public event that's been covered. Think about that event. Now, write five possible story ideas you might find if you turned your back on the main action and looked all around you.

2. Frankel's "Hidden in Plain Sight" story is rich in detail. You can visualize the apartment complex, right down to the color of the doors. Identify a place that you often see, perhaps even drive by. Go to that place and imagine what details you would most want to include if that place became the location of a news event.

3. In Frankel's story about the Michael Devlin watchers, he made the crowds his focus. How do you feel about shifting the lens from Devlin to the crowd? Write a paragraph about the challenges of working the crowd for a story.

Winner: Team Deadline News Reporting

Staff, *The Post and Courier,* Charleston, S.C.

The Post and Courier

When firefighters showed up at the Sofa Super Store in Charleston, S.C., that Monday evening in June, big news was nowhere in sight.

Just a trash fire. Just an everyday event unlikely to generate much more coverage than a brief inside the paper. Then flames began to spread up the sides of the showroom and warehouse buildings.

The resulting inferno would kill nine of the firefighters, jolt the city and test its journalists.

Billing itself as "the South's oldest daily newspaper," *The Post and Courier* has chronicled Charleston's storied past through the Civil War, the great earthquake of 1886 and Hurricane Hugo in 1989. The coverage of the Sofa Super Store fire followed an arc that reporter Tony Bartelme characterizes as "shock, grief, anger and then lots of questions."

That first night, Night City Editor Cleve O'Quinn recalled that "Nadine Parks, our night cops reporter, and I put together the story mostly from her eyewitness accounts." He added: "In hindsight, we should have thrown more at it, but I'm pretty sure we wouldn't have ended up with much more than we did. Authorities all evening were not answering our questions."

O'Quinn stayed with the story all night, updating the paper's final Tuesday editions with information provided by

The Associated Press that Charleston Mayor Joe Riley had confirmed the deaths of at least two firefighters.

When O'Quinn awakened City Editor Rick Nelson at 6 a.m. Tuesday with word that the death toll had apparently grown to nine firefighters, he set in motion a string of decisions that would win the paper the Jesse Laventhol Prize for Deadline Reporting by a Team.

The paper won the award not for its first-day story, or for its subsequent investigation of how the deaths might have been prevented. It won for its second-day coverage, a classic journalistic form rendered all the more critical in the Internet Age.

As reporter Glenn Smith points out in the accompanying Q&A, the paper's 100,000 subscribers had already learned—from TV, from the Web, from their neighbors and co-workers—that nine firefighters were dead. Given the way news cycles work in a digital world, the print edition of the paper had already been badly beaten on the basics of the story.

The paper's opportunity, of course, was to provide readers with coverage of the fire they couldn't get anywhere else: an intimate glimpse inside the fire and well-reported profiles of each of the men it killed.

The work by *The Post and Courier* team provides a useful case study for other newsrooms that, sooner or later, will face their own high-stakes challenge to serve their communities in times of disaster or other deadline news.

Of particular significance are the ways the paper's second-day coverage built on the work of colleagues from the night before, and how the winning entry established a foundation for the watchdog work to come in the weeks and months ahead.

In the Q&A, several staff members address a tension of particular import in this sort of coverage, perhaps especially so for newsrooms serving smaller or mid-sized communities: paying appropriate respect to victims and their families while pursuing often unpleasant truths about what happened and why.

About *The Post and Courier* team:

Tony Bartelme, 45, is a senior reporter who joined the paper in 1990 and is responsible for investigative reports and feature projects. He is the co-author of *The Bridge Builders,* a book about the construction of a large bridge, and *Into the Wind,* a book about an international sailing race.

Robert Behre, 45, began his newspaper career with the *Greenville (S.C.) Piedmont* and has worked as a reporter, columnist and editor for *The Post and Courier* for almost 18 years. He has won awards from the

South Carolina Press Association, the South Carolina chapter of the American Institute of Architects and the Historic Charleston Foundation.

Nita Birmingham, 50, is a police reporter, primarily covering Dorchester and Berkeley counties. She joined the *Post and Courier* staff in 2004. She received her bachelor's degree in journalism from the University of Georgia in 1980 and has worked for daily newspapers in Louisiana, Florida and Georgia.

Edward C. Fennell, 57, is a Charleston native and graduate of the University of South Carolina. He came to work for the former *News and Courier* in 1975 and has been with the company for 33 years. He currently covers news in Summerville.

Prentiss Findlay, 53, has been a reporter with *The Post and Courier* for the past 22 years, currently covering the city of Mount Pleasant, and previously was the paper's television reporter and critic.

Noah Haglund, 32, covers crime and breaking news for *The Post and Courier.* Originally from the Seattle area, he worked at *The Island Packet* in Beaufort County before moving to Charleston in 2005.

Stephanie Harvin, 53, is the paper's region editor. She is a 30-year veteran of the newspaper, working as a photographer, reporter and editor, covering beats including sports, features, education and government.

Jessica Miller Johnson, 33, is a Lowcountry news reporter. She previously worked for *The Messenger* in Fort Dodge, Iowa, and *The Courier* in Waterloo, Iowa. She won awards for a two-day series called "Innocence Lost" about the unsolved murder of a young girl, including first place for investigative reporting in the Iowa Associated Press Managing Editors contest.

Andrew Lyons, 33, is the metro editor. He has worked at the newspaper for two and a half years, and is currently in charge of the paper's downtown newsroom. He spent most of his career as a reporter and bureau chief at *The Daytona Beach News-Journal* and has received numerous state honors for feature writing in Florida.

Ron Menchaca, 35, is a special projects reporter who has worked at the paper for 10 years on such beats as county government, higher education and the Charleston waterfront. His awards include two National Headliner Awards and recognition from the National Education Writers Association and Associated Press Managing Editors.

Doug Pardue, 60, is now public service editor. Before joining *The Post and Courier* in 2003, he was news projects editor for *USA Today.* His work as a reporter and editor has received a range of recognition that includes five National Headliner Awards, a Robert F. Kennedy Citation, a Gerald

Ford Award for coverage of national defense and two Southern Journalism Awards. He was part of a *Roanoke (Va.) Times* team that was a 1990 Pulitzer Prize finalist for coverage of the yearlong Pittston Coal strike.

Nadine Parks, 46, is night crime reporter for *The Post and Courier.* She served four years as a firefighter in the U.S. Air Force, is a former police dispatcher and has worked in *The Post and Courier* newsroom since 1993.

Bo Petersen, 52, is a general assignment reporter/editor who reports primarily on environmental issues. He has been with *The Post and Courier* for 11 years. Prior experience includes 10 years with *The Gaston Gazette*, Gastonia, N.C., and a year with the *The Sun Journal,* New Bern, N.C.

David Slade, 42, covers Charleston city government and public affairs for *The Post and Courier.* He has worked as a reporter or editor for newspapers and magazines in several states during the past 20 years and has won national and state awards for his coverage of governmental affairs.

Glenn Smith, 43, is a veteran crime and general assignment reporter who has worked for the paper since 1999. A native New Englander, Smith is a University of Connecticut graduate whose previous beats include city and state government, politics and education. Before joining *The Post and Courier,* Smith spent more than a decade working for newspapers in Connecticut.

Katy Stech, 24, began working at *The Post and Courier* in November 2006—eight months before the fatal Sofa Super Store fire. Before that, she worked as an intern at *Newsday* on Long Island, *The Democrat and Chronicle* in Rochester, N.Y., and at her hometown newspaper, the *Duluth (Minn.) News-Tribune.*

Kyle Stock, 30, has covered business for *The Post and Courier* since 2003. Prior to moving to Charleston, Stock reported for Bloomberg News in Brussels and completed a master's program at Northwestern University's Medill School of Journalism.

(**Editor's note:** The titles in the accompanying Q&A reflect the jobs the staffers were filling at the time of the coverage.)

—Bill Mitchell, Director, Poynter Online, The Poynter Institute

Fearless Charleston Firefighters Will Never Be Forgotten

JUNE 20, 2007

By Glenn Smith, Nadine Parks and Noah Haglund

Two-by-two, Charleston firefighters waded through the belly of the burning furniture store. Swirling black smoke choked the air around them and swallowed all light.

Sofas, chairs and bedding blocked their path at every turn. Darkness and confusion enveloped the men. As the blaze turned deadly, calls for help crackled over the fire department's radios. One man prayed. From another: "Tell my wife I love her."

Their tour of duty had come to an end. Nine lives. Gone.

The deaths Monday night at the Sofa Super Store on Savannah Highway marked the nation's worst single loss of firefighters since 9/11, according to the U.S. Fire Administration. In Charleston, which had not lost a firefighter in the line of duty since 1965, the loss was like a punch to the heart.

"Nine brave, heroic, courageous firefighters of the city of Charleston have perished fighting fire in a most courageous and fearless manner, carrying out their duties," Charleston Mayor Joe Riley said. "These people will never be forgotten."

The fallen were Capt. William "Billy" Hutchinson, 48; Capt. Mike Benke, 49; Capt. Louis Mulkey, 34; Engineer Mark Kelsey, 40; Engineer Brad Baity, 37; Assistant Engineer Michael "Frenchie" French, 27; Firefighter James "Earl" Drayton, 56; Firefighter Brandon Thompson, 27; and Firefighter Melvin Champaign, 46.

They were more than men in uniform, they were members of the community they served. One was a devoted family man who loved to take his son fishing. Another was a seasoned veteran, a mentor to his younger colleagues. A third was a part-time barber who gave his firefighting "brothers" haircuts for $2 a head.

"I've just lost nine of my best friends," Charleston Fire Chief Rusty Thomas said, struggling to hold his emotions in check.

No arson is suspected, Riley said, but the State Law Enforcement Division and the federal Bureau of Alcohol, Tobacco, Firearms and Explosives are investigating the fire's cause and origin.

The Post and Courier front page, June 20, 2007.

Charleston fire officials said the blaze started in an outdoor trash bin and quickly engulfed the store and its adjacent warehouse.

The Sofa Super Store didn't have a sprinkler system, which likely would have slowed the blaze, authorities said.

Condolences and messages of support poured in from around the country. The White House released a statement from President Bush mourning the "devastating loss of some of America's bravest."

"Our prayers are with the families and friends of nine firefighters from Charleston, South Carolina, who selflessly gave their own lives to protect their community," Bush said.

"These firefighters were true heroes who demonstrated great skill and courage. Their unwavering commitment to their neighbors and to the city of Charleston is an inspiration to all Americans."

The blaze started about 7 p.m. Monday. As some firefighters attacked the trash-bin fire, 13 more entered the showroom to check for fire inside.

They found none, Charleston Assistant Fire Chief Larry Garvin said.

Then the fire spread to a porch and, suddenly, blew open the back door to the showroom. "We tried to close the door but we couldn't," Garvin said.

Firefighters quickly donned their air masks and started bringing in hose lines to attack the blaze from within. But they didn't stand a chance, Garvin said.

Once inside, the fire rapidly ignited sofa and chair material near the back door. A rolling ball of fire and gas raced toward the front of the building, the combustible furniture fueling its momentum. Flames and smoke belched into the humid Lowcountry night, creating what one witness described as a 30-foot tornado of flames. Hot ash pelted hundreds of onlookers.

Capt. Ralph Linderman of the St. Andrews Fire Department said the blaze was the hottest he could recall in three decades of firefighting. "That fire bent steel like a wet noodle," he said.

Four employees were in the store when the fire started. Two firefighters freed one worker who was trapped in a repair workshop near the building's east side by cutting a hole in the side of the metal building.

Meanwhile, thick, black smoke was filling the showroom, leaving firefighters disoriented as they struggled to find their way through a jumble of sofas, beds and other furniture. "Everything just went bad at one time," Thomas said. "Trying to see with all that furniture in the store and trying to get out, it just didn't happen."

Charleston Fire Capt. Jake Jenkins said the firefighters were spread out in teams when the roof—a steel truss system—collapsed. Other crews fought to get inside the building and rescue the fallen, but the conditions were too bad, he said.

"They tried everything they could to find a door to open, find a window, find some way to get to downed firefighters," said Pete Rogers of the Charleston County Volunteer Fire and Rescue Squad. "They never stopped trying."

In the end, the news was beyond grim. It was enough to shake a city that has endured civil war, hurricanes and countless other tragedies in its storied history.

The charred bodies were scattered about the building in three groups of two firefighters and one group of three, Classen said. He was given the task of making sure they were removed with dignity. Their cause of death has not yet been determined.

"When you pull nine of your best friends out, it's hard," he said. "But you've got to be strong for the rest of them."

Firefighters and police formed two lines and saluted as the bodies, draped in American flags, were carried from the rubble.

"It was real somber out there when they brought the bodies out," said St. Andrews firefighter Tripp Mobley.

Thomas accompanied each of the nine bodies out of the building, and the Rev. Rob Dewey of the Coastal Crisis Chaplaincy prayed over the fallen. Weary, dirty and grieving, firefighters cried, hugged and consoled one another as best they could.

Only three people were injured. Charleston County EMS director Don Lundy said ambulances took two firefighters to Medical University Hospital for minor injuries, one for lacerations and another for heat-related problems. A store employee also was treated for heat-related issues.

Firefighter David Fleming cut his hand while removing metal siding from the building and was taken to Medical University Hospital. He's scheduled for surgery today.

The tragedy drew people from throughout the region. Some came to offer condolences. Others took photographs or simply stared at the store's smoking remains, a twisted tangle of concrete and steel. They felt a need to be there, to show their presence, to show they cared.

One woman handed Mayor Joe Riley a sprig of freshly plucked crape myrtle flowers, telling him that she just had to do something to express her sorrow. A Methodist minister waited nearby, hoping to give the mayor a hug.

"It's just so horrendous, so unreal," Lorraine Tucker of West Ashley said as she snapped a photo of the wreckage. "They were someone's

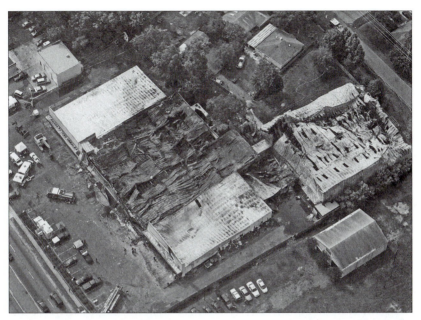

Charred remains mark the Sofa Super Store on Savannah Highway the next morning. Nine Charleston fire-fighters died in the fire the night before. (Photograph courtesy of Brad Nettles/*The Post and Courier*)

father, uncle, husband or brother. It just leaves me with a knot in my stomach."

About 8 a.m., a large wreath of red and yellow flowers was placed on a patch of grass in front of the store. The makeshift memorial grew by the hour as friends and strangers alike left flowers, balloons and signs at the site.

A group of firefighters pounded nine white crosses made from PVC pipe into the earth by the memorial. Someone else added small American flags. Another group hoisted a firefighter atop the sofa store's marquee.

There, he used duct tape to hang a larger version of the stars and stripes, covering block letters announcing a sale that would no longer take place.

Across town, Capt. Gary Taylor sat at a folding table behind the two trucks that carried six of his men to their deaths Monday evening. His fire station, on Ashley Hall Plantation Road, suffered the heaviest loss in the blaze. Taylor struggled to find words to describe his grief amid visits from colleagues, well-wishers and family members who came to empty lockers.

Jacob Forrest, 28, sat nearby on the front bumper of a fire truck. Forrest left his firefighter job with Company 16 a few months ago, thinking he might go back to school. Now he's thinking about returning to the job.

North Charleston firefighters place a flag at one of the nine crosses erected at the scene of the fatal fire. (Photograph courtesy of Grace Beahm/*The Post and Courier*)

He knew his fallen comrades well. After such a loss, the impulse for Forrest is not to recoil from the danger but to embrace it once more, he said. "I haven't had to deal with this before," he said, tears welling in his eyes. "They were amazing guys."

The store was a former Piggly Wiggly grocery store. It opened as Sofa Super Store 16 years ago. The business also has showrooms in North Charleston and Mount Pleasant, but the West Ashley store was the flagship of the operation, with its sole warehouse, president Herb Goldstein said.

Goldstein had no cost estimate on the loss, and he said he will make a decision next week as to how his business will continue to operate. For now, he and his employees will grieve with the rest of the community.

"There are no words to express our sorrow," he said in a written statement. "All of us at Sofa Super Store are devastated and heartbroken by
this tragedy. Our thoughts and prayers go out to the families and loved
ones of the heroic firefighters who lost their lives."

Thomas, chief for the last 20 years, pledged that his 227-person department would soldier on in the face of loss.

"We're going to stand tall now," he said. "Just like 9/11, we will never
forget."

Brad Baity

JUNE 20, 2007

By Tony Bartelme

Brad Baity was an engineer at Station No. 16, a soft-spoken and smart man who sometimes impressed his buddies with his computer skills.

Brad Baity

Baity, 37, had been with the department for nine years, driving Engine 19 for Capt. William "Billy" Hutchinson.

"He was always seeking knowledge, trying to learn new things," said Derek Noffsinger, one of his colleagues at the station.

Sometimes, Baity could be found pecking on his laptop computer, doing virtual tours of faraway countries.

"He would talk about how he had just visited the historic sites in Greece and Rome," Noffsinger said.

Baity wasn't one to bend your ear. Amid the bustle and bravado of a typical fire station, he spoke in a soft voice. "In a day's time, Brad wouldn't say 10 words," Chief Rusty Thomas said fondly. But he was an aggressive firefighter. "It didn't make a difference to Brad Baity. Whatever the task was, he did it."

Like many firefighters, Baity had a second job.

For the last three years, he had worked as a stagehand at the Gaillard Municipal Auditorium, the North Charleston Coliseum and other venues around the area, said Mike Coffey, a member of IATSE Local 333, a union that represents stagehands and technicians.

"Brad was new, but he was always watching and learning," said Coffey, a retired Charleston firefighter himself with more than three decades of service.

Sometimes, he and Baity and another firefighter/stagehand, James "Earl" Drayton, would get together and talk shop. "You get firemen together anywhere, and you're going to start telling stories," Coffey said. "That's the way firemen are."

Drayton also died in Monday's fire.

Baity lived in a quiet neighborhood off the bustle of S.C. Highway 61, where he leaves behind his wife, Heather, and 5-year-old son, Noah.

James "Earl" Allen Drayton

JUNE 20, 2007

By Ron Menchaca

James "Earl" Allen Drayton, 56, was the oldest of the nine firefighters killed Monday.

A 32-year veteran of the Charleston Fire Department, he was known by generations of city firefighters. They called him "old school" around Station No. 19 in West Ashley.

He is survived by his wife Kimberly, five children, three stepchildren and several grand-children.

Kimberly Drayton said she last saw her husband Monday morning as he left for work from their Sangaree home near Summerville. The couple had

James "Earl" Allen Drayton

planned to leave for a cruise to Puerto Rico this weekend. "He was all packed," she said. "He was so excited."

Drayton exuded a quiet confidence. His rhythmic walk and talk earned him the nickname "Cool Earl," said his older brother, Herbert Drayton. "I never really heard him raise his voice."

One of eight children, he was born on Charleston's West Side and his family moved to Amherst Street on the city's East Side when he was a child.

After graduating from C.A. Brown High School, he enlisted in the Marine Corps and served eight years on active duty. He had a reputation for dressing to the nines and meticulously washing his black Chrysler. He was selected several times to drive Mayor Joe Riley in the city's Christmas Parade.

He was on his third retirement with the department, his wife said. "They kept asking him back. He was going to give it two more years."

Drayton also worked as a stagehand. He painted scenes and built sets for countless local performances. He also wore the battle scars of a seasoned firefighter. He was knocked unconscious by an electrical shock while battling a blaze in 1999. His family says he was once trapped in another fire.

Chief Rusty Thomas worked alongside Drayton as the two were coming up through the ranks in the 1970s. Thomas recalled a call that got a rise out of the low-key Drayton. A hot-water heater had caught fire in a house downtown, and as they headed toward the fire, Drayton got excited and blurted, "Rusty, get this going. That's my house."

BEHIND the STORY

Winner's Q&A

An Interview with the Staff of *The Post and Courier*

This edited e-mail interview was conducted by Poynter Online Director Bill Mitchell with staff members of The Post and Courier *of Charleston, S.C. Responses below are from reporters Tony Bartelme, Ron Menchaca and Glenn Smith, and editors Stephanie Harvin, Andrew Lyons and Doug Pardue.*

Reporting and Writing the Main Story

BILL MITCHELL: Glenn, your lead does an extraordinary job of putting the reader inside the fire with the men who died: "Two-by-two, Charleston firefighters waded through the belly of the burning furniture store. Swirling black smoke choked the air around them and swallowed all light." How did you get to that lead? What other approaches did you consider and discard?

GLENN SMITH, reporter: I struggled mightily at first. I just felt the whole weight of this story—the loss, the historical impact, the national spotlight—bearing down on me. We needed to get this right.

I spent a lot of time discussing approaches with Assistant City Editor Andy Lyons and Doug Pardue, the special assignments editor. It helps me to talk it out, and they have always been good sounding boards and sources of advice.

We knew we couldn't go with a straight lead about nine firefighters dying. That had been all over our Web site and national television for hours and hours. It would be extremely old news by the following morning.

The one thing readers hadn't received at this point was a glimpse inside the fire, a sense of how the events unfolded. I have always been a big fan of narrative storytelling. It can be such an effective tool for drawing readers in, helping them understand, giving them a reason to care.

Once we fleshed out the details—many gathered by reporter Nadine Parks' persistent fact-gathering from firefighters—it became clear that we had to take readers into the building. They needed to see the scene that confronted those men, to experience the chaos, the fear they must have felt. As I pored through all the information we had gathered, I just kept seeing that scene in my head.

Tell us about the content and cadence of the next couple of paragraphs: "Sofas, chairs and bedding blocked their path at every turn. Darkness and confusion enveloped the men. As the blaze turned deadly, calls for help crackled over the fire department's radios. One man prayed. From another: 'Tell my wife I love her.'

"Their tour of duty had come to an end. Nine lives. Gone."

GLENN SMITH: Again, I wanted to put readers inside that building, to sense the chaos and fear those men encountered. It must have been unbelievably disorienting and frightening.

That was best done by using a description of the scene from those who were there, as well as snippets from the last radio transmissions of those who died. To convey the action, the sentences had to be short, snappy, quick off the tongue. Bogging things down with lengthy clauses, quotes or attribution would have slowed the action and lost the feel.

Good writing has a rhythm, a certain music to it. A good sentence need not only convey information. It needs to sound a certain way as well—a proper cadence, if you will. That's why I read every sentence aloud to myself as I write. I need to hear how it sounds coming off the tongue.

I was struck by this paragraph: "In the end, the news was beyond grim. It was enough to shake a city that has endured civil war, hurricanes and countless other tragedies in its storied history." How did you arrive at "beyond grim" as the best way to characterize, without directly defining, the nature of what had happened?

GLENN SMITH: Charleston is one of those quintessentially Southern places where history permeates everything. Reminders are everywhere of the Civil War, Hurricane Hugo, the great earthquake of 1886 and a host of other calamities. The city takes great pride in its resiliency, its ability to weather adversity.

Still, this fire seemed to hit people like a punch to the heart. The sense of communal loss and grief was staggering. People here are no strangers to bad news, but this seemed "beyond grim."

Let's back up to your arrival, Tuesday morning, at the scene of the fire still smoldering from the night before. What were your main questions at that point?

GLENN SMITH: How many people were, in fact, dead? How did so many end up inside the building? Why were they there, what were they doing and what events/decisions led up to the final moments before they were lost?

In the initial aftermath, simply getting a correct tally and identifying the lost were paramount. But very early on, we recognized the need to establish a firm timeline of events and an accounting for the decisions and actions that led to the tragedy that ensued.

A firefighter at the scene pointed out the warped and sagging steel truss roof system. He said truss roofs were well-known in the fire service for collapsing under high heat. Did the commanders know that? If so, why were so many men inside when the roof went down? Was that feature noted on the preplanning documents fire officials prepare to document hazards within the buildings in the district?

We also wanted to know the history of the building. When was it last inspected? What sort of problems were identified? Was there a history of violations? Should the building have had sprinklers?

How did you organize the reporting and writing? Did you make an outline?

GLENN SMITH: I had a large pile of notes and faxes on my desk, as well as about 10 or 12 windows open on my computer as I cycled through files, grabbing whatever information I needed. Some reporters filed notes early and often; others sent along large blocks of information later in the day. Good communication was key. I always knew what was coming, so I could leave a space for it in the story or plan in my head where it might fit. I drew information from just about everyone involved. I recall a great sense of teamwork and sharing, reporters just wanting to be of use, to contribute in some way.

We talked a great deal about what we had and how it should be presented, but I don't recall using a written outline. Once I had a lead—a way in—it just seemed to flow from there. As I said, information came by phone, fax and e-mail. But the majority was juggled electronically, cycling between windows and cutting and pasting the information needed for the story. A story like this, with contributions from a multitude of people, tends to come together like a giant puzzle. You scan messages and notes and quickly spot important pieces of information that fill holes, bolster points, assist with transitions.

I try to always have an outline for larger project stories. But the big daily stories sometimes come together best for me when I avoid a rigid format and remain open to the story taking different directions as events unfold.

What sort of responses did you get to the story?

GLENN SMITH: Massive and varied. We received calls and e-mails from all over the country and as far away as Europe. The fire service is a giant brotherhood, and firefighters from every corner of the nation took an intense interest in what had happened here.

Many from the community and the fire service thanked us for the coverage in general and the profiles in particular. Mayor Joe Riley and Chief Rusty Thomas also praised the profiles and the lengths we had gone to in order to put a human face on the men who had died. "You did those nine guys right," Thomas said.

The coverage also drew raw emotions from people who felt the firefighters were sent into harm's way unnecessarily. We were contacted by a host of fire service experts who pointed to flaws in the fire department's command system, tactics and equipment. Those comments gave us direction for how to pursue the story in the days that followed.

Reporting and Writing the Profiles

BILL MITCHELL: With 10 *Post and Courier* reporters at the news conference where details of the fire were provided, how did you decide who would do which profile?

TONY BARTELME, reporter: Our plan before the news conference was to assign one profile to each reporter, and as soon as the news conference ended, we went into a scrum around the two reporters who got the list of the deceased, and then we pretty much grabbed names at random. It was chaotic, but the process only took a few moments.

RON MENCHACA, reporter: The press release listed all of the nine firefighters, their ranks, ages and years of service with the department. The process of assigning the stories went smoothly because it was already late afternoon and we were all anxious to get on the road and start tracking down sources.

As I scanned the list, I noticed that firefighter James "Earl" Drayton was 56 years old and had served in the department for 32 years. That struck me as interesting because it made him the oldest of the nine and a veteran of the department. "I've got Drayton," I called out before hustling back to my car.

Once you had a name, what were your next steps?

TONY BARTELME: Our first stop was the chief. Several of us followed him as he walked to his vehicle after the news conference. Three of us jumped into my car, and we drove to a station near the fire.

No one wanted to talk, and it turned out that Brad Baity, the subject of my profile, was based at another station. After lots of cell phone calls, we found out which one, Station 16. The firefighters there were very good sources of information for several profiles, including mine.

RON MENCHACA: The first thing I did when I got to my car was pull out a Charleston telephone book that I keep in my trunk. Drayton is a common name in Charleston, so I was not surprised when I saw dozens listed in the phone book.

I found a J. Drayton listed at an apartment complex and headed that way. Just as I arrived, a woman answered the telephone at another Drayton residence listed in the phone book. She didn't have a number for Earl but suggested I call his sister, Thelma Mitchell.

I hung up and dialed the sister's number. I knew I had the correct family when the woman who answered sounded as if she were crying. I said I knew it was a terrible time for the family but that the newspaper was trying to talk to the families of all nine firefighters because we wanted to do their lives justice. She gave me her address.

I quickly realized as I pulled up to Mitchell's house that it was the impromptu meeting place for grieving friends and family. I spent about an hour with the family. The interview shifted back and forth between laughter, when someone shared a funny story about Drayton, and sobbing, each time the realization that he was gone set in.

What did you hope to accomplish with the profile?

TONY BARTELME: We hoped to tell a story about the man's life, not what happened in the fire. We would get into that in other stories. I wanted readers to know who died in the fire, to capture his essence as best I could in what was a very small amount of space.

RON MENCHACA: I was concerned that with nine firefighter profiles, our stories might all sound too similar. So I tried to ask questions about what Drayton did besides firefighting that might set him apart from the other guys at his station. I was also curious about why he was still at it, given that he was one of the oldest men in the department and still in a frontline firefighting position when he died.

My first job at the newspaper was writing obits. So I knew that type of story structure well and how it can sometimes seem robotic and impersonal. I tried to highlight those parts of Drayton's life that brought him joy—for example, his car, sharp clothes and plans for an upcoming cruise to Puerto Rico.

How did you organize the reporting and writing? At what point in the day did the focus of your story emerge?

TONY BARTELME: Baity's profile was very difficult in some ways because everyone I talked to said he was so quiet and reserved. What do you do with that? In a sense, a quiet man who keeps to himself provides less ammunition to shape a story than someone who has lots of dramatic twists in his life. Baity was truly a man of few words, and later in the afternoon, after a brief panic attack about what I was going to write, it became clear that this was who he was, and that it would be my focus.

I started writing the story at about 6 p.m. and stopped, thinking I didn't have enough. I had made calls to Baity's family, but someone hung up on me. I decided that I should go make a personal visit, even though I was starting to feel some deadline pressure. Outside the home, I spoke with a friend of the family who was very angry about the media attention. Though I didn't get much meaningful information from that trip, seeing where he lived, in a quiet neighborhood not far from the bustle of a busy suburban strip, gave me a little more confidence in my approach, as well as a nice symbolic reference.

In a story like this, especially one in which you don't have much space, I try to look quickly for universal themes, patterns and symbols—things that can help readers connect at a deeper level.

I thought that concluding with the idea of a quiet man in the midst of a busy and dangerous world had symbolic power, especially in the context of a fatal fire. I think that symbols are important in short stories because they convey very quickly a complex range of experiences and emotions. They can pack a lot of information into a short space.

The same goes with the final sentence. Leaving behind loved ones is a universal experience. Also, in a story that focuses on a man's life, it seemed more natural to put this at the end, instead of letting his death define the story. In retrospect, I might have ended it that way because it's how I ended my reporting that evening—by leaving behind a grieving family in their home.

Ron, you faced one of journalism's most challenging tasks in your profile: interviewing the spouse of someone who has just suffered a violent and

unexpected death. Please tell us how you approached Mrs. Drayton, and what your conversation was like.

RON MENCHACA: I almost did not get to speak with her. I asked Drayton's siblings how I could get in touch with his wife, Kimberly Drayton. Thelma Mitchell agreed to call Kimberly Drayton and see if she was up to talking to me. She declined to meet with me but was gracious enough to answer a few questions over the phone. She said she was still in shock and numb, so I tried to focus on the positive and asked her to tell me something about her husband that made her smile. That's when she mentioned how excited he was about their upcoming vacation and that he'd already packed.

She cried as we spoke. I told her that I was sorry for her loss and that we would do our best to honor her husband and the other firefighters on our pages.

I have had the difficult task many times in my career of interviewing people who have just lost loved ones. But interviewing Drayton's wife and family was by far the hardest because the tragedy that devastated our city was still so raw and personal. Thelma Mitchell gave me a big hug when I left her house.

You wrote that Drayton "exuded a quiet confidence" and reported that his older brother attributed his nickname, "Cool Earl," to "his rhythmic walk and talk." Can you give us a sense of how your conversation with Herbert Drayton happened to yield such detail?

RON MENCHACA: I asked Herbert Drayton to explain what he meant when he said his younger brother was quiet and reserved. I discovered that it wasn't shyness but a quiet confidence: Drayton knew who he was and was comfortable with his place in life. Drayton walked with a strut and talked in an easy cadence. He fussed over his appearance and clothes from an early age and his brothers took to calling him "Cool Earl."

I included some of these details in my story because it seemed to say something about Drayton's chosen profession. Part of his coolness was that nothing rattled him. That seemed like an important attribute for a firefighter, who must remain calm in the face of danger and chaos.

What role did your editor play?

RON MENCHACA: Our editors have had a huge role in guiding our coverage since the fire, particularly on our investigative work. But I did not have any more contact with my editor that day than would be ordinary. He was busy trying to pull the overall fire budget together. I think that's the great thing about our paper—we have a good number of experienced reporters who can work without a lot of handholding. I also believe that having nine reporters writing nine profiles challenged everyone to do their best work.

Planning and Editing the Coverage
BILL MITCHELL: What was the editing process like?

ANDREW LYONS, assistant city editor: All day, I worked and reworked the budget, letting everyone know which reporter was working which story. I just kept e-mailing revised budgets. That's how we kept it all straight. At one point in the afternoon, something like 17 reporters were headed in different directions. And new story lines kept presenting themselves. Doug Pardue, our special assignments editor, and Rick Nelson, our city editor, helped hammer home two points: We needed a "storytelling voice," and we could not repeat stuff. It's a tall order for seven pages of fire coverage. But every editor on the city desk and beyond was looking for repetition.

What obstacles did the reporters encounter in reporting and then in writing?

ANDREW LYONS: Because he'd been working the story since around 6 a.m., Glenn Smith may have had too much time to write. No deadline pressure. Doug Pardue and I offered encouragement all afternoon and into the evening. Finally, the top to the story came to Glenn, and he started it inside the fire. He typed these words: "Two-by-two, Charleston firefighters waded through the belly of the burning furniture store." The rest flowed much easier. He got to the most compelling details as quickly as possible. "One man prayed. From another: 'Tell my wife I love her.'" There are perfect sentences in that story.

How did the trust you established with families and firefighters as a result of your profiles and other coverage help in your subsequent coverage?

ANDREW LYONS: Our efforts to humanize these firefighters set the tone for the months of coverage ahead. Each reporter is permanently assigned to their firefighter's family. Each of the nine reporters would attend their funeral, write occasional stories about the distribution of the various funds and donations, and even check back with them at Christmas time. They're still writing stories about their firefighter's families. But in the days immediately after the fire, everyone from the mayor to the fire chief quickly recalled how we treated their men. We treated them right. This was a national story, but after the profiles ran we had access to key people during the hectic time of planning a large memorial and nine funerals. The access was imperative, because in the coming days, we began asking some very tough questions about what went wrong inside the Sofa Super Store.

After updating your Web site first thing Tuesday morning, how did you use the site throughout the day? Faced with big breaking news in the future, how might you use your Web site differently?

STEPHANIE HARVIN, North Charleston bureau editor: Our server capacity was down for the early portion of the morning because we were doing maintenance on it and the traffic overwhelmed the site. By noon, though, we had moved the site to a server that could handle the capacity. I would say that any newspaper with a major breaking story should check its server capacity.

Underneath the lead story and photo from the paper, which was updated several times, we ran additional headlines with their time stamp visible. It's a "post what you know as you go" philosophy. The stories would have a hard time standing alone, but under a package banner, it works fine. We received a lot of information through the Web site and e-mails about donations and ways to help the firefighters' families. The Web site became a big community bulletin board as we posted whatever information we got, and then culled it back into the newspaper as a community service column of information. The latter generated several million dollars that was eventually donated to the families.

Over time, we have solved a number of issues that became apparent that day: more staff dedicated to the Web; increased capacity to accept photos, video and comments from readers; increased emergency server capacity off-site; and expanded graphics capability. We are also quicker to post our graphics and photo galleries since they proved to be the most popular portion of the coverage.

We learned that many of our readers stayed with us after that day and we elevated the perception of our Web site by responding to the demand for immediate information.

A Critical Tension: Paying Tribute and Pursuing Truth

BILL MITCHELL: How do you balance the tension between paying appropriate respect to the victims of a disaster (and their families) at the same time you raise often unpleasant questions about what went wrong and who made what mistakes?

GLENN SMITH: That is difficult. As the hometown newspaper, it was incumbent upon us to pay proper respect to the loss and its effect on the community. That is why, in the days that followed, we covered each and every funeral in full. Outsiders could parachute in, use some thinly sourced and incendiary information, and then move on their way. We had to show recognition and compassion for the grief, loss and pressure these folks were facing.

As we continued to write about the outpouring of grief and support, we also began to probe at several uncomfortable topics, particularly concerning the way the fire department did its job. A hero mythology quickly develops around large-scale tragedies such as this, and some in the community felt it was highly inappropriate that we pursue any angle that would cast doubt on the actions of the fallen and their comrades.

TONY BARTELME: Timing is key. We knew this story would have an arc—shock, grief, anger and then lots of questions. If you get ahead of this arc, you end up looking like jerks. If you're too slow, you get beat. I think we handled the timing well on this one. Our immediate coverage focused on the men, with a hint of questioning inside. Then, after just a day or two, we started hammering away at the mistakes, while still doing the appropriate tribute stories.

RON MENCHACA: The day's coverage remained a topic of conversation in the newsroom for weeks. Not because we were patting ourselves on the back or second-guessing, but because it taught many of us a lesson about how local newspapers have a special obligation in the wake of such tragedy.

Eventually, we discovered many troubling facts about how the department had long been flirting with disaster. But on the day that we learned the names of the nine, those investigative instincts were largely placed on hold. First, we had to honor our neighbors—men who lived in our community, attended our churches and protected our city.

When I looked at the newspaper the next morning and saw how we had honored the firefighters in such a comprehensive way, telling intimate stories about their lives and families and revealing details about their careers and brotherhood in the Charleston area, I understood why our editors made the decisions they did. I was proud of our newspaper that day.

I think it's in part a practical matter: With so many fatalities, we were stretched thin just covering the profiles. Doug Pardue was the only person I can recall openly asking in the newsroom about the possibility that the tragedy might have been the result of command, training or equipment failures of some type. We knew so little that first day, and much of what we had to go on was our own institutional assumptions: that our fire department was first-rate.

As details were still trickling out, firefighters in our community and around the country were hesitant to say much beyond offering their condolences.

That all began to change the day we published the profiles and other stories. Firefighters had established a command center at a local hotel to begin organizing the massive memorial service. I headed over to the hotel.

One group was smoking cigarettes out on a balcony and I started chatting with them. They seemed sad but also angry. They were upset because they felt the tragedy was avoidable and that nine men had given their lives trying to save couches. We quoted some of their concerns in the next day's coverage. But it would take days and weeks to check out many of their other charges.

Once we had more time to fully investigate what went wrong at the fire—something we continue to do today—I never felt as if it was disrespectful. Quite the opposite: I can think of no more fitting tribute to the firefighters who died than to ask questions that they cannot and to learn why they died so that others might not.

DOUG PARDUE, special assignments editor: Almost from the get-go I suspected that the fire department had messed up by attacking the fire so aggressively from the inside. A couple of years earlier, I had reported and written a series of stories detailing how much of the nation's volunteer fire departments are ill-equipped and ill-trained, especially in some of their damn-the-torpedoes tactics at fires. Some of what I saw in that reporting seemed present in the way Charleston's fire department operated at the Sofa Super Store.

The problem was how to begin putting that in the paper while a deep grief gripped the city and as thousands turned out for memorial services

(From left to right) Front row: Tenisha Waldo, Nadine Parks, Bo Petersen, Jessica Johnson. Middle row: David Slade, Katy Stech, Noah Haglund, Robert Behre, Ron Menchaca, Edward C. Fennell, Prentiss Findlay. Last row : Kyle Stock, Schuyler Kropf, Tony Bartelme, Glenn Smith, Nita Birmingham. (Photograph courtesy of Alan Hawes/The Post and Courier)

and funerals. We gingerly touched on it in one of the sidebars in our June 20 coverage.

We quickly began to realize that the fire department did almost everything wrong. We felt the obligation to detail what happened and let people know how their public safety agencies performed. But we were cautious with how to begin telling that story while fire engines served as hearses taking firefighters to their graves.

While one team of reporters continued covering the funerals and breaking events, we detailed another to chase the story of what went wrong.

During the first week of our coverage, we purposefully underplayed the "what-went-wrong" stories, running them on inside pages. We did this out of regard for community sentiment, respect for the dead firefighters and concern for their families.

We began our coverage of what went wrong on June 21. On Sunday, June 24, six days after the fire, we published our first major look at how the fire department's incident command and firefighting tactics during the fire ran contrary to nationally accepted standards. That story ran on 9A as funerals continued. And we toned it down, stating that there was no way to know if the city's failure to follow nationally recognized standards would have made any difference.

From June 29 on, all of the coverage of what went wrong ran front page. That was the day we published a story revealing that many city businesses don't have fire sprinklers, the best-known way to quickly suppress fires, because the water department charged hook-up fees that can cost $56,000 or more.

Our findings came down particularly heavy on Fire Chief Rusty Thomas, a hometown hero who has been a city firefighter his entire life. The stories revealed that Thomas arrogantly ignored modern firefighting advances and made critical mistakes in training and command. Letters to the editor supporting the chief poured in. Thomas resigned shortly before the one-year anniversary of the fire even though he continued to enjoy the public support of Charleston's powerful mayor, Joseph Riley. Thomas said he thought that by leaving he could help the department heal.

Writer's Workshop

Talking Points

1. Read (or reread) the main story (by Glenn Smith, Nadine Parks and Noah Haglund) in *The Post and Courier's* fire coverage. As you finish reading, make notes of what you learned from the story, how it made you feel and what questions it raised and/or answered. Then go back and trace the elements in the story that prompted each of these responses on your part. How effective was the story in each of these three areas?

2. Two critical tasks in profile writing are clarifying the focus and providing anecdotes that support or challenge it. Read the two profiles by Tony Bartelme and Ron Menchaca and sum up the focus of each in a brief phrase. Then list the anecdotes that relate to the focus.

3. Among the challenges of disaster coverage is the tension between tribute and truth. Journalists have an obligation to pay appropriate respect to the subjects of coverage who have been killed or harmed. They must also try to explain what went wrong. Read what some of *The Post and Courier* staffers say about this tension in the Q&A. What's your view of how best to approach this issue?

Assignment Desk

1. We never know when disaster might strike. But that doesn't make disaster coverage entirely unpredictable. Based on *The Post and Courier's* coverage and the accompanying Q&A, draw up an action plan for disaster coverage by your newsroom. Be sure to address how you'll differentiate coverage you provide on your Web site from what you plan for your next print edition.

2. Develop a system for handling rewrite on a complicated story on deadline. How will you compile reporting sent to you by colleagues? How will you compose the story? What sorts of leads will you consider?

How will you pace yourself against deadline? How will you involve your editors?

3. Develop a system for reporting a short profile on deadline. How will you find your focus? How will you find anecdotes to support your story? How will you know when you've done enough reporting—and that it's time to start writing?

Omaha World-Herald

Finalist: Team Deadline News Reporting

Staff, *Omaha World-Herald*

'It Happened to Us'

DEC. 6, 2007

By Henry J. Cordes

With only 20 shopping days till Christmas, Von Maur customer service workers busily folded bright wrapping paper around the gifts of eager customers.

A nearby elevator door opened. Into the festive scene Wednesday strode Robert A. Hawkins, about to unleash the worst killing spree in Nebraska since the 1958 rampage of Charles Starkweather.

He was toting a Russian semiautomatic rifle.

And suddenly, the light holiday sound of the store's piano was punctuated by the pop-pop-pop of rapid gunfire.

Witnesses said he fired his first shots into the ceiling.

Then he started shooting at people, shot after shot after awful shot.

He went to the spacious atrium that is the high-end store's visual centerpiece, leaned over an escalator railing and, with deadly aim, shot a man in the head.

He shot people in front of the customer service counter.

He shot people behind it.

And in the end, right in front of that counter, Hawkins fired a lethal bullet into his own head.

But before he did, the troubled 19-year-old had killed eight people, wounded five more and shattered the holiday season for an entire city.

"I was up front, and everybody except me was shot," said a shaken Renee Toney, a Von Maur gift wrapper who found herself at the center of the massacre. "Within seconds, they were shot right behind me."

With hands up as ordered by police, shoppers leave the Von Maur store minutes after the nation's latest mass murder. (Photograph courtesy of Kiley Cruse/*Omaha World-Herald*)

All around the store and the adjoining Westroads Mall, hundreds of shoppers and workers fled in terror, ducked into back rooms or hid among racks of clothing, fearing for their lives.

"I thought I would be next," said Roxanne Philip, a Von Maur customer service worker.

She was among the lucky ones.

The deadliest single shooting incident in the state's history killed eight people and the gunman. Police described his victims only as five females and three males.

Authorities declined to release more information on the victims. Two of the five wounded by Hawkins were listed in critical condition at Omaha hospitals Wednesday night.

Hawkins also will go down as the biggest mass murderer in the state since Starkweather killed nine in Nebraska—and 10 in all—during a days-long spree in January 1958.

And Omaha's name will be added to the lengthy list of communities ripped and scarred by a gunman bent on mass murder.

Police were still piecing together Hawkins' movements, but it's clear that he showed up at the Westroads Mall with a purpose.

According to witness and police accounts, Hawkins left a vehicle in a parking lot southwest of Von Maur.

Why he chose Von Maur, arguably Omaha's most elegant department store, with wide aisles and a bright, tasteful décor, remains unclear.

"It appears to be very random, without provocation," said Omaha Police Chief Thomas Warren.

Near the south ground-floor entrance to Von Maur is an elevator that Hawkins apparently rode to the third floor.

Customer Alan Mason, at a checkout counter near the elevators, was among the first to see Hawkins as he left the elevator. Mason said he heard a popping sound and thought it was fuses blowing.

"I didn't think it was shots because you don't think it's shots at the mall," he said.

Then he saw the gunman—and realized it was shots at the mall.

The first 911 call came at 1:42 p.m. At one point there were so many 911 calls that people reported getting busy signals.

The precise sequence of Hawkins' movements was lost in the chaos of fleeing witnesses' glimpses and fleeting accounts.

Von Maur employee Chuck Wright said a co-worker described standing on the second floor near the escalator and looking up toward the commotion. That co-worker said she saw a man with a gun leaning over a third-floor railing. He shot a man standing right next to her, in the head.

There were other random killings on the second and third floors, with the shooter eventually making his way to the customer service department and gift wrapping area behind it.

Mickey Vickroy was wrapping gifts but was out of sight of the service counter when she heard gunshots. Someone yelled, "Gun!" Vickroy and about a dozen customer service employees ran back into a storage area.

Philip, another customer service worker, said the shots were so close it sounded as if they came from right next to her.

Philip said she never saw the shooter. She said she thought her boss had been shot because she heard him moaning.

Toney was among several employees working near the front when the gunman entered the customer service area.

"I turned and left," she said, "and I guess the rest of them, two feet, six feet behind me—none of them made it out."

She said she later was told by a supervisor that the gunman had ordered that the safe be opened. One of the employees moved to do so, but Toney said, "She never made it to the safe. He shot her before she made it."

Police say the entire shooting took only minutes. Chief Warren said all the shooting may have already been over by the time the first officer arrived, six minutes after the initial 1:42 p.m. call.

Officers said the first victim they found was on the second floor, apparently one of the victims Hawkins shot from the floor above.

One person who saw the immediate aftermath described the scene as surreal.

Police and rescue workers found seven people dead, including Hawkins. Two more victims died at a hospital.

Six of the bodies were on the third floor, three near the customer service counter where a telephone receiver dangled off the hook. One apparently was Hawkins. The rifle, with a large ammunition clip, was near his body.

Among the other dead on the third floor was a customer who died sitting in a chair waiting for a gift to be wrapped.

On the second floor, a man was dead in an aisle about 10 to 20 feet straight in front of an escalator.

Shell casings were scattered through the store. One of the victims appeared to have just pulled out his cell phone when he was shot. It lay near his body.

Ultimately, heavily armed police officers swarmed the store and worked their way back to the customer service area, where at 2:12 p.m. they reported finding the gunman down from a self-inflicted wound.

Officers began to evacuate the surviving employees. Their route went past the customer service counter, around a trail of blood.

Vickroy, 74, saw her wounded manager lying on his side. A female co-worker was on her back. Another woman was crumpled. A young man—a boy, to Vickroy's eyes—lay flat on his back, pale and motionless in front of the counter.

"They said not to look, but you couldn't help looking," said Vickroy. "These were people you knew. People you worked with."

BEHIND the STORY

Lessons Learned

By Henry J. Cordes

When I saw one of our police reporters running for the door on Dec. 5, 2007, I couldn't have imagined what was unfolding in Omaha—that a gunman had randomly killed eight people in the city's most elegant department store.

Even before I made it over to the police scanners, managing editor Mike Reilly pointed at me, pegging me to assemble feeds from reporters and write the next day's main story.

I listened to scanner reports of the rising casualty toll and considered my challenge that evening, one of the rare times that our very mid-sized paper had to compete with the national media on a breaking story. It turned out to be one of my most exhilarating and stressful experiences in more than 20 years at the paper, and one that taught me a lot.

Use a rewrite man (or woman).

I never got within seven miles of the mall that day. Obviously, a writer can lose something by not being able to take in the sights and sounds, but he can see the larger picture when he is away from the action. Each of the nearly two dozen reporters at the scene gathered a vital part of the story, but they saw everything through that narrow lens.

Don't be afraid to ask for help.

Beyond the death toll, police provided almost no information that first night. But our reporters did a fantastic job, finding crucial eyewitnesses and obtaining the names of the shooter and several victims.

In fact, I was getting so much information, via e-mails, transcribed blocks of copy and phone calls, that I became overwhelmed. So my daily editor, Mike Holmes, sifted through the notes and highlighted the most important details and interviews. I was able to focus on writing the story.

Be flexible in your approach.

I butted heads with my executive editor, Larry King, about what to include in this story. He wanted it to focus exclusively on the shooter and his movements, saying the main story wasn't the place for descriptions of screaming people running for their lives. I argued that this was a human drama involving many people, including the ones running for their lives.

We decided that I would consider what he wanted and just start writing. As I look at the story now, Larry's approach is what gives the narrative its power. You feel at the beginning like you're following in the footsteps of a killer. Yet I think the survivors' accounts give the story more emotional depth, underscoring the terror this young man had wrought. In the end, both editor and writer were pleased with the result.

Don't run with the media pack—it can be wrong.

Our reporters were getting lots of information, but inevitably amid the chaos, some misinformation, too.

For example, we heard at first on the police scanner that the shooter wore a green army vest. That made it into our early accounts, attributed loosely (probably too loosely) to "police." The army vest was a staple of local and national television coverage throughout the night and next day.

While such attire fit the stereotype of a mass killer, I grew wary of it later that night when a witness who saw the shooter's body reported no such clothing. I dropped the detail about the vest, and I'm glad I did. It turned out that the guy in the army vest was just another shopper at the mall that day, probably running for his own life.

Narrative is tough when the facts are uncertain.

When we take a storytelling approach, we ask our readers to have faith that we have the facts to back everything up—even if we don't attribute the source of each nugget in each sentence. But piecing together a narrative is especially tricky when there is a vacuum of information from official sources.

We made some tough calls that night. For example, we had a pretty solid account from a store worker whose co-worker told him she watched the gunman lean over a railing and shoot a man on a lower floor. But it was secondhand. I questioned whether it was reliable enough to include in my description of the gunman's actions.

Fortunately, we later heard from a law enforcement official who saw a victim, shot in the head, at the same location the co-worker had described. So in my opening narrative I wrote that the gunman had leaned over the railing and shot someone below. I was aware that night that something could surface that contradicted that, but police later confirmed the newspaper's account.

I still wonder, journalistically speaking, if I made the right calls that night. I love the narrative form and agree with those who say it is the future of newspapers. But given the way I sweated every detail that night, I will be satisfied if a big, breaking story doesn't find its way to Omaha for a while.

Henry Cordes has been a state affairs reporter at the Omaha *(Neb.)* World-Herald *since 1985, including six years as the newspaper's statehouse bureau chief. He has won numerous state press association awards and a first-place prize for special projects from the National Association of Agricultural Journalists.*

Other World-Herald *staffers who contributed to the paper's coverage included Steve Jordon, Christopher Burbach, Lynn Safranek, Todd Cooper, Kevin Cole, Joe Ruff, John Ferak, Judith Nygren, Jennifer Palmer, Karyn Spencer, Leia Baez, Nancy Gaarder, Jeffrey Robb, Michaela Saunders, Tom Shaw, Tim Elfrink, Rick Ruggles, Christine Laue, Erin Grace, John Keenan, Elizabeth Ahlin and Robynn Tysver.*

The Washington Post

Finalist: ASNE Team Deadline News Reporting
Winner: Pulitzer Prize for Breaking News Reporting

Staff, *The Washington Post*

Gunman Kills 32 at Virginia Tech in Deadliest Shooting in U.S. History

APRIL 17, 2007

By Ian Shapira and Tom Jackman

BLACKSBURG, Va.—An outburst of gunfire at a Virginia Tech dormitory, followed two hours later by a ruthless string of attacks at a classroom building, killed 32 students, faculty and staff and left about 30 others injured yesterday in the deadliest shooting rampage in the nation's history.

The shooter, whose name was not released last night, wore bluejeans, a blue jacket and a vest holding ammunition, witnesses said. He carried a 9mm semiautomatic and a .22-caliber handgun, both with the serial numbers obliterated, federal law enforcement officials said. Witnesses described the shooter as a young man of Asian descent—a silent killer who was calm and showed no expression as he pursued and shot his victims. He killed himself as police closed in.

He had left two dead at the dormitory and 30 more at a science and engineering building, where he executed people taking and teaching classes after chaining some doors shut behind him. At one point, he shot at a custodian who was helping a victim. Witnesses described scenes of chaos and grief, with students jumping from second-story windows to escape gunfire and others blocking their classroom doors to keep the gunman away.

Even before anyone knew who the gunman was or why he did what he did, the campus community in Southwest Virginia began questioning whether most of the deaths could have been prevented. They wondered why the campus was not shut down after the first shooting.

Some of the wounded are carried from Norris Hall, an academic building where 30 of the slayings occurred. Two other people were killed in a dorm, and about 30 people were injured. (Photograph courtesy of Alan Kim/*Roanoke Times*)

The enormity of the event brought almost immediate expressions of condolences from President Bush, both houses of Congress and across the world.

"I'm really at a loss for words to explain or to understand the carnage that has visited our campus," said Charles W. Steger, president of Virginia Tech, one of the state's largest and most prestigious universities.

The rampage began as much of the campus was just waking up. A man walked into a freshman coed dorm at 7:15 a.m. and fatally shot a young woman and a resident adviser.

Based on witness interviews, police thought it was an isolated domestic case and chose not to take any drastic campus-wide security measures, university officials said. But about 9:45 a.m., a man entered a classroom building and started walking into classrooms and shooting faculty members and students with the two handguns. Virginia Tech Police Chief Wendell Flinchum said investigators were not certain that the same man committed both shootings. But several law enforcement sources said he did.

As police entered Norris Hall, an engineering and science building, shortly before 10 a.m., the man shot and killed himself before officers could confront him. One witness said the gunman was "around 19" and was "very serious but [with a] very calm look on his face."

"He knew exactly what he was doing," said the witness, Trey Perkins, 20, of Yorktown, Va. He said he watched the man enter his classroom and shoot Perkins's professor in the head. "I have no idea why he did what he decided to do. I just can't say how lucky I am to have made it."

The university canceled classes yesterday and today and set up counseling for the grief-stricken campus. Gov. Timothy M. Kaine (D), who had just arrived in Japan on a trade mission, immediately flew back to Virginia. He was expected to attend a vigil today.

"We've been devastated as the death toll has been rising," said Payton Baran, 20, of Bethesda, who is a junior majoring in finance. "I've been calling everyone I know, and everyone I talk to is pretty much in tears. It's really, really depressing."

None of the victims' names was released yesterday by officials, pending notification of their families. University officials said 15 people were injured, but spokesmen at four area hospitals said they treated 29.

Initial reports from the campus raised the specter of "another Columbine," in which two teenagers in Littleton, Colo., killed 13 people inside a high school in 1999 before killing themselves. But soon, the Virginia Tech rampage dwarfed Columbine to become the biggest shooting rampage by an individual in U.S. history.

Students and parents launched a frenzied round of phone calls and text messages yesterday morning, monitoring news reports and waiting for information. And the shootings prompted intense questioning of Steger and Flinchum from a community still reeling from the fatal shootings of a security guard and a sheriff's deputy near campus in August on the first day of classes and the arrest of the suspect on the edge of campus that day.

Although the gunman in the dorm was at large, no warning was issued to the tens of thousands of students and staff at Virginia Tech until 9:26 a.m., more than two hours later.

"We concluded it was domestic in nature," Flinchum said. "We had reason to believe the shooter had left campus and may have left the state." He declined to elaborate. But several law enforcement sources said investigators thought the shooter might have intended to kill a girl and her boyfriend Monday in what one of them described as a "lover's dispute." It was unclear whether the girl killed at the dorm was the intended target, they said.

The sources said police initially focused on the female student's boyfriend, a student at nearby Radford University, as a suspect. Police questioned the boyfriend, later termed "a person of interest," and were questioning him when they learned of the subsequent shootings at Norris Hall. A family friend of the boyfriend's said the boyfriend was stopped by police alongside Route 460 in Blacksburg, handcuffed and interrogated on the side of the road and later released.

Students who lived in the dorm said they received knocks on the door telling them to stay in their rooms but nothing else. Shortly before 9:30 a.m., the university sent out this e-mail: "A shooting incident occurred at

West [Ambler] Johnston [dorm] earlier this morning. Police are on the scene and are investigating.

"The university community is urged to be cautious and are asked to contact Virginia Tech Police if you observe anything suspicious or with information on the case."

Steger said that, even though the gunman was at large, "we had no reason to suspect any other incident was going to occur." He said only a fraction of the university's 28,000 students live on campus, and "it's extremely difficult if not impossible to get the word out spontaneously."

Students on campus and parents were angry. When Blake Harrison, 21, of Leesburg learned of the shootings, he said, he called an administrative help line and was told "to proceed with caution to classes." He said: "I'm beyond upset. I'm enraged."

Yesterday, as officials began to sort out the shootings, tales of the horror began to emerge.

Alec Calhoun, a junior, was in Room 204 in Norris. When the shootings began, people suddenly pulled off screens and pushed out windows. "Then people started jumping," he said. "I didn't just leap. I hung from the ledge and dropped. Anybody who made it out was fine. I fell and I hit a bush to cushion my fall. It knocked the wind out of me. I don't remember running."

About 9:50 a.m., Jamal Albarghouti was walking toward Norris Hall for a meeting with his adviser in civil engineering "to review my thesis. As I was walking, about 300 feet away, I started hearing people shouting, telling me to run or [get] clear."

He started to move away, but he also pulled out his cellphone, which has videorecording capability, and he began filming. His video, which he later shipped to CNN, captures officers running toward the brown three-story building, a couple of flashes from the second floor and 27 gunshots.

The video soon became the defining image of the rampage. "I just didn't think I was in great danger," Albarghouti said later.

In a German class in Room 207, Perkins was seated in the back with about 15 fellow students. The gunman barged in with two guns, shot the professor in the head, then started shooting students, Perkins said.

Panic ensued, he said. "And the shots seemed like it lasted forever." The gunman left Room 207 and tried to return several minutes later, but Perkins and two other students had blocked the door with their feet. He shot through the door.

The last time anyone spoke with Kristina Heeger, she was headed for a 9 a.m. French class in Norris. Within an hour, the sophomore from Vienna had been shot in the back. But she survived.

It was a story that played out across campus, and far beyond, with so many wounded, so many dead. "She's doing better," said [her stepfather], Eric Anderson, last night after seeing her. "She's recovering. We're praying for her right now. She couldn't talk to them yet, or anyone, and they didn't know any details about what happened."

Tucker Armstrong, 19, a freshman from Stephens City, Va., passed by Norris as he headed to a 10 a.m. class. He said in an e-mail that he "noticed several kids hanging and jumping from the second floor windows trying to land in bushes."

Armstrong said he heard repeated bangs. He went to help the people who had leapt from the building, but they yelled at him: " 'Get out of here, run!' At that point I realized they were shots and they just kept going and going."

Police and ambulances poured into the area. Dustin Lynch, 19, a sophomore from Churchville, Md., watched from the nearby Drillfield as unresponsive students were carried out of Norris Hall. "I saw police officers literally carrying kids out," Lynch said. "It basically looked like they were carrying bodies."

Parents arrived at the Inn at Virginia Tech to meet with other grieving families and were distraught at the university's management of the incident. "I think they should have closed the whole thing. It's not worth it. You've got a crazy man on campus. Do something about it," said Hoda Bizri of Princeton, W.Va., who was visiting her daughter Siwar, a graduate student.

Brett Hudner, 23, a communications major from Vienna, was heading toward one of the dining halls and suddenly a scrum of police cars raced by. "The scary thing is I know I'm going to go into classes, and there's going to be empty spaces," Hudner said.

The Bizris, meanwhile, were waiting for news about a friend whom they could not locate. They think she was inside Norris Hall.

Tom Jackman reported from Washington.

'Pop, Pop, Pop': Students Down, Doors Barred, Leaps to Safety

APRIL 17, 2007

By Michael E. Ruane and Jose Antonio Vargas

Yesterday morning. Second floor. Norris Hall. In Room 207, Mr. Bishop's German class is under way. A few doors down, Professor Librescu is posting slides for his engineering students in 204. Outside, the Virginia Tech campus is gray and chilly but pretty normal for a Monday.

"It couldn't have been much more normal," said Richard Mallalieu, one of Liviu Librescu's students.

Suddenly, sometime after 9 a.m., a young man walked into the German class with two handguns and shot instructor Christopher James Bishop in the head.

Then he began firing at the students. Shot after shot, "some 30 shots in all," said Trey Perkins, who was seated in the back of the German class. He shot a girl in the mouth, a boy in the legs.

There were about 15 students, and Perkins said the relentless gunman had a "very serious but very calm look on his face."

"Everyone hit the floor at that moment," said Perkins, 20, of Yorktown, Va., a sophomore studying mechanical engineering.

The gunman left, and Perkins, sounding shaken in a telephone interview yesterday, said "three or four" students appeared to be dead.

In Room 204, the engineering students were watching Librescu's slides on the subject of virtual work when they began to hear shots from what sounded like an adjacent classroom, said Mallalieu, 23, a student from Luray, Va.

"At first I tried to convince myself they weren't gunshots, that if anything, maybe a presentation was going on, to try to convince myself it wasn't," Mallalieu said in a telephone interview from his Blacksburg apartment. "It became evident pretty quick what was going on."

Plus, he said, "there were a few screams." At first, he got down and hid behind a desk as Librescu held the classroom door closed. Then the students went to the windows.

As they pondered whether to jump, the gunshots went on. "A steady pop, pop, pop, pop," Mallalieu said. The gunfire was "more or less continuous."

He said he heard 20 to 30 shots as he and other students noticed there was grass below and decided it was time to jump. "It was scary," he said, "but it wasn't as panicked as you might think it was."

The engineering students pushed open the windows.

On the first floor, custodian Gene W. Cole, 52, was preparing to clean a bathroom when someone reported a shooting in a second-floor lab. Cole took an elevator and got off at 2.

"I walked around the corner, and I saw something in the hallway there," Cole said in a telephone interview. "As I got closer, I saw it was a girl lying on the floor jerking around as if she was trying to get up. There was blood all over her and all over the floor around her."

A man dressed in bluejeans, a dark sweat shirt and a hat stepped out of a classroom and flashed a black handgun.

"He acted like he was angry," Cole said. "I just thought, 'Oh my God, he's fit to kill me.' He didn't say nothing; he just started shooting. He shot at me five times."

Bullets zipped past Cole's head. He ran down some back stairs, saw that several exits had what looked like new chains and locks on them, and escaped through an auditorium. Cole, who has worked at Virginia Tech for 20 years, said the chains and locks had to have been put on the doors shortly before the shooting because they were not there earlier that morning.

Back in Room 207, Perkins, a student named Derek and a female student headed toward the heavy wooden classroom door and held it shut with their feet.

Other students were crying. One vomited. Two minutes later, Perkins said, the gunman came back. But now he couldn't get in. So he started shooting through the door, Perkins said, before leaving again. "Fortunately, we were lying down and weren't in front of the door," he said.

Whispering and trying to compose himself, Perkins, an Eagle Scout, said he told Derek and the female student to keep their feet on the door in case the gunman returned.

Perkins said he went around the room, tending to the wounded students. A student named Garrett was shot in both legs. Perkins wrapped his gray pullover sweater around Garrett's right leg.

Perkins used Garrett's tank top to wrap the other leg. Perkins saw a sweat shirt on a desk and covered the girl with the mouth wound.

"He knew exactly what he was doing," Perkins said of the gunman. "I have no idea why he did what he decided to do. I just can't say how lucky I am to have made it."

In 204, the students had opened the windows and were jumping for their lives.

"It's kind of hard to believe that something like this would happen," Mallalieu said. "You hear things about Columbine....But you never think you'd be involved in that. But at that point I realized it was really happening."

Mallalieu, the son of a chemist, said he climbed out, hung for a moment from the ledge, looked down and let go. "I kind of tried to roll when I landed," he said.

He suffered some scratches. He's not sure everybody got out. Those who did ran for a nearby campus building. As they did, Mallalieu said it sounded as though the gunshots, and the screams, were now coming from 204. He said he heard about 40 shots in all.

There was little conversation as the students fled. "At that point, it was just, get away," he said. "I think everybody kind of had the same feeling about what was going on. We didn't really need to talk about it.

"I don't think it's settled in yet," he said. "I haven't heard how my other classmates who I think were still left behind, you know, what happened to them, be it good or bad."

A man identifying himself as one of Bishop's relatives said the family had no comment. Last night, a woman who answered the phone at Librescu's home and identified herself as his wife said she did not know whether he had survived.

BEHIND the STORY

Lessons Learned

By staff members of *The Washington Post*

The enormity of the tragedy at Virginia Tech required an enormous response. Reporters from just about every part of the paper contributed, from the Virginia bureaus to metro, national, features, sports, foreign and business staffs.

With so many reporters to coordinate, the *Post* combined the tried-and-true with some new ideas.

Each reporter was given a specific assignment, so as not to duplicate efforts. Before we knew the extent of the tragedy, we erred on the side of commission, rather than omission. It would have been easy to pull back the reporters driving to Blacksburg, Va., when we thought this was "just" a domestic shooting at a dormitory.

There were new techniques as well. While reporters in Blacksburg were kept behind police and bureaucratic barricades, those in our Washington and Virginia newsrooms jumped into online social networks where students had gathered to share their fears and stories.

Our work in those initial hours allowed the *Post,* in print and online, to provide anguished families, alumni and the larger "Hokie Nation" with the evolving narrative of what happened and the major themes that would come to dominate public debate.

Here are some reporters' stories of that tragic day.

—*Mike Semel*

The enormity of the event wasn't immediately known. We knew that two people had been killed in a dorm, and that *something* had happened in Norris Hall. But it wasn't until after noon that the Virginia Tech police chief was asked at a press conference how many people were dead in Norris. "At least 20," he said numbly. And he was understating it.

Blacksburg is four hours from Northern Virginia. People were driving down, but we weren't going to have anyone on the ground there for a long time. As the writer of the main story, it was amazing to watch information flow in from dozens of reporters who used every technological tool in existence to find students, professors, politicians, anyone who might have an idea of what was going on.

—*Tom Jackman*

Nothing beats on-the-ground, knock-on-doors reporting. But scouring sites such as YouTube, Facebook and MySpace, where people, especially teenagers and 20-somethings, maintain public diaries, is invaluable when covering a breaking news story. After I saw a brief TV interview with Trey Perkins, who sat in his classroom as the shooter barged in, I found Perkins on Facebook and "friended" him. Perkins was sitting right in front of his computer. He "friended" me, which enabled me to see his whole Facebook profile, including his AOL Instant Messenger (IM) name. I then IM'ed him and landed a 25-minute phone interview. In other words, Facebook reporting counts.

—Jose Antonio Vargas

I figured it was going to be midafternoon to late afternoon by the time our people got to Blacksburg. So we had to start working the phones and whatever else we could think of. I called one of my daughters who has a friend at Tech, but the friend was hunkered down in an off-campus apartment and knew nothing. Next I called a witness I found through a blog. He refused to talk, but he told me about someone else who might.

That guy, it turned out, had jumped from a classroom window just as the killer was forcing his way in. His name was Richard Mallalieu, and he sounded like a gentle young man who felt he had a moral obligation to tell his story. He told me everything he could remember, and I admired him for realizing, as some people do, the sacredness of his narrative. I was shaking when we hung up.

—Michael E. Ruane

Because I had just moved back to Washington after nearly a year covering Virginia Tech football and men's basketball teams, I probably knew more people at the school and in the community than anyone else on staff.

This advantage was offset by a disadvantage: I had to overcome a more personal sense of grief than most other reporters. There was no time to be a mourner; I had to be a journalist. To be most effective, I needed to report as if I were covering a story for inside Metro. This made a lasting impression—journalistic instincts must trump emotions in times of crisis, no matter how difficult that internal conflict may be.

—Adam Kilgore

Less than a year earlier, I had raced to the same campus, where an escaped convict had killed two police officers near the school. He was caught before any students or teachers were hurt, but even then, getting information out of frazzled police and university officials was difficult. Both types of officials, for good reason, are closed-mouthed in these situations. But our job in the press is to keep pushing.

As I called my sources in the state police and the governor's office on April 16, I knew it would be infinitely harder this time. Police and university officials reacted according to their training, trying desperately to keep too much information from getting out. The result was that the media, relying on eyewitnesses and their relatives and friends, reported inaccurate or incomplete information. That was the message I tried to give to my official sources—that their help would minimize inaccurate information. That argument convinced some of them, and they confirmed pieces of the story.

Both sides reached a sort of equilibrium. News organizations reported an increasingly detailed narrative of what became known as the worst mass shooting in the country's history. And officials pieced together what had happened and why. No doubt, officials wished some facts had not been reported that first day. And I know that we in the news business wanted a more complete picture by that first deadline. In the end—as always happens—reporters and officials reached a symbiotic balance.

—*Michael D. Shear*

Before I came to the *Post,* I helped report many large, breaking stories for The Associated Press. I know from such situations that there is a key challenge in the first hours and days: remembering to be deliberate in the midst of chaos. In other words, you need to soak up as much as possible, and make as many contacts as possible, while observations/memories/emotions are still fresh and before people get fatigued and cut you off. Meanwhile, you have to organize the chaos you're seeing, hearing and feeling around a couple of themes, even if the themes are broad.

This helps a reader, someone with no connection to the story, relate to what you're reporting. It also forces discipline as you see so many potential stories at once. You want readers to take away something strong and clear from your story. If you dump a bunch of chaos on them—mixing stories about someone who can't get into his dorm, someone who knew one of the victims and someone questioning why the campus police reacted the way it did, you'll make less of an impact.

In the first hours after I arrived in Blacksburg the first day, I was struck by how the routines that campus life is built upon—course schedules, team practices, academic hierarchy, structure, structure, structure—were blown to bits. People were walking around, aimless. This seemed like an obvious theme on the first day—upended routine.

—*Michelle Boorstein*

Shortly after arriving that day at the Inn at Virginia Tech, the central site for reporters and families to gather for information, I found a group of young girls praying and crying. As one got up to leave, I pulled her aside and, as gingerly as possible, identified myself and asked how she was doing. We began talking about one of her best friends, whom she grew up with in New York.

After we talked for a few minutes about where her friend was during the shootings—in class at Norris Hall—I switched subjects and asked what it was like to go to the same school as her hometown friend. How did she maintain that relationship while she was forging new, possibly more intimate friendships? I wanted to ask probing questions that went beyond the tragedy, and to show her that as a recent college graduate, I could relate to her. Then, after a few more minutes, I moved the conversation back to the shootings and pressed hard on all the wrenching details: What class was your friend in? What was the last thing you said to her? How many times have you called her?

After I wrapped up the interview and called in the feed to the Web site, I promised myself I would stay in touch with her. And I did, for a while. But it's been more than a year since my last conversation with her. I often wonder if she thinks I truly cared or if I was just trying to get a good story. I don't think I want to know the answer.

—*Ian Shapira*

Mike Semel has been Virginia editor of The Washington Post *for about five years, supervising a staff of about 40 editors, reporters and columnists in five bureaus throughout the state. He oversaw the* Post*'s coverage of the Virginia Tech shootings.*

Tom Jackman covered police and courts for The Kansas City Star *for 14 years and has handled the same beats for 10 years at* The Washington Post.

Jose Antonio Vargas, who writes about the marriage of politics and the Internet, is covering the 2008 presidential campaign. He is a 2004 graduate of San Francisco State University.

Michael E. Ruane, a general assignment reporter on The Washington Post*'s metro staff, has covered the Pentagon for Knight Ridder, urban and rural affairs for the* Philadelphia Inquirer, *and the police beat for the* Philadelphia Bulletin.

Adam Kilgore, a native of York, Maine, attended Syracuse University and has been a sportswriter at the Post *for about two years.*

Michael D. Shear is a national political reporter for the Post, *where he has been writing about politics at the local, state and national level for 15 years.*

Michelle Boorstein covered domestic and foreign news for The Associated Press for eight years. In 2002 she joined The Washington Post *where she writes about religion.*

Ian Shapira, who came to the Post *in 2000 after graduating from Princeton, writes about education and youth culture.*

Alec MacGillis, a political reporter for the Post, *was also part of the paper's Virginia Tech team.*

BEHIND the STORY

Online Journalism

Virginia Tech Shooting Coverage

This edited e-mail interview was conducted by Matt Thompson, deputy editor of StarTribune.com, with Meg Smith and Ju-Don Roberts of The Washington Post.

When the Virginia Tech story broke, reporters weren't just posting frequent updates to the Web. They were also reporting through the Web, using sites such as Facebook and Craigslist to quickly locate students connected to the tragedy. Meg Smith, a researcher at the *Post,* describes how she and others culled contacts from the university's online community as the story broke.

Meanwhile, the *Post*'s online editorial and design team faced the challenge of presenting a story that kept getting bigger. This meant making big alterations to the home page on the fly and creating multiple blogs to handle story developments and online reactions, all while the shape of the tragedy was still becoming clear. Ju-Don Roberts, managing editor of washingtonpost.com, discusses that balancing act.

MATT THOMPSON: Social networking Web sites are a relatively new arena for reporters. How much reporting, if any, had to be conducted through Facebook?

 MEG SMITH: As a researcher, my role that day was to find contact information for anyone who might be able to shed light on what happened on campus. During the coverage of the shooting, I was sending phone numbers and names of parents and high school officials from alma maters as quickly as I could find them to over a dozen reporters and editors. We weren't just looking for victims; we were mining the Tech student directory for anyone living in Ambler Johnston Hall [the location of the first shootings] and also chasing down leads that reporters were hearing on campus. At one point, I was looking at sublet ads on Craigslist to find cell phone numbers for anyone living just off-campus whom reporters could talk to during the campus lockdown.

These images from washingtonpost.com show how the online staff handled the developing story, moving from a one-line report low on the home page to the centerpiece at the top, with links to blogs and multimedia. (Images courtesy of washingtonpost.com)

How did you navigate the closed-community aspects of Facebook? For example, did you have to send friend requests to all of your sources, or join any of the groups you wrote about?

MEG SMITH: Julie Tate, one of the researchers at the *Post,* is a Virginia Tech alumna. Though she'd never used Facebook before, she created an account that day using her alumni e-mail address and joined the Virginia Tech network. A student at Tech had created a new Facebook group called "I'm OK at VT" where students could post messages saying they were unharmed. But many of the messages posted in that group were for people who were missing after the shooting.

Many of the plaintive messages were quoted in the story that Jose [Antonio Vargas] wrote on April 18 ["A Chain of Grief with Links on Facebook"]. As soon as I saw them by logging onto Julie's account, I began looking for contact information for the students and teacher who were named and the friends and classmates who had posted the messages.

It would be a day or more before police, the university or the hospitals would confirm the names of any of the victims. This put us in the unusual position of knowing their names too soon. Once I had found contact information for their families and high schools, as well as their campus information and Facebook pages, the editors assigned reporters to verify that they were victims and start working on profiles. Many of the victims listed on Facebook appeared on washingtonpost.com or in *The Washington Post* before the names were released by authorities.

What's the policy at the *Post* for confirming the identity of someone found on Facebook?

MEG SMITH: The *Post* doesn't have an explicit policy yet, though the company is in the middle of creating a policy on quoting from Web sites including Facebook and MySpace. The *Post* has mentioned comments on Facebook or MySpace hundreds of times, mostly in the context of quoting someone who is cooperating with a story, quoting pages that police say belong to criminal suspects or talking about the sites in general. After the Delaware State University shooting that wounded two local students [also in 2007], we paraphrased expressions of concern we found on a victim's MySpace page.

As one of the *Post*'s researchers, it's always been my job to find contact information for sources even when we only have sketchy or incomplete information. So I can usually help track down a person in real life based on what we know from his Facebook profile. If it were important that a specific person made a comment, I could try to find him so reporters could call and confirm it.

There are already rules in place that predate social networking sites but still apply, like the *Post*'s standing policy to get a parent or guardian's permission before quoting someone under 18. I think just about every journalistic standard we have can be applied to the Web with very little difficulty. I don't make policy here, but my opinion is that folks who think the Internet is so different from other kinds of communication that it needs its own rules are wrong. It's still people talking to and about other people, and people shouting from their soapboxes, just like it always has been.

I often verify details sources give to reporters, from finding out who owns a telephone number used to leave a tip, to checking public records to confirm ages, job titles and family relationships. In my work as a researcher, I'm often asking people on Facebook to help me or a reporter get in touch with principal sources, not really conducting interviews per se. So by the time I've found a principal source, the interview usually takes place over the phone or in person, and Facebook was just a way to make a first contact.

Are you still Facebook friends with any Facebook-originated sources?

MEG SMITH: I did not engage students directly by messaging or "friending" them on this story, though I've since used that in other stories.

But I always keep people on my friends list after a story runs. Not only is it good to keep channels open for follow-ups when trials begin and anniversaries come around, I also think it's every bit as valid a connection as any other reason people "friend" each other on social networking sites. I don't want people I talked to once to think I don't want to hear from them in the future. Also, crime victims and their families here in the Washington, D.C., area are often located in the center of a bigger storm— they may end up being witnesses to future crimes, or just able to shed light on their neighborhood if something else happens there. I can't think of a reason to "un-friend" anybody, though I can understand why a grieving friend or family member might "un-friend" me somewhere down the line.

Is your presence on Facebook more personal or professional? If both, how do you balance the two?

MEG SMITH: My presence on Facebook and MySpace was meant to be solely professional—I use my full name on both and make my contact information and *Washington Post* affiliation clearly visible to all. Unfortunately, my friends all found me on there, so some of the comments are from people who know me personally. I'm glad they're there, however, because I think if my pages looked too sterile, potential sources might shy away from me when I come calling. But I don't take it to an extreme—I try to keep my pages friendly and colorful but not overly personal. After all, I'm friends with [*Washington Post* Company chairman] Don Graham!

Washingtonpost.com was itself host to a community of Web surfers reacting to the tragedy. What dimension does that community add to the coverage?

MEG SMITH: On local stories, it's more like a telephone than a Web site— we really do read those comments at the bottom of stories, and we notice who's linking to the stories on their blogs. One of the reasons I get involved in stories is to take the clues people leave about themselves online and try to find the real people behind those avatars, so reporters can interview them further if they have firsthand knowledge. Sadly, I have to do it the hard way and follow their online breadcrumbs; I can't just call up the Web site and ask who owns an account or blog. Come to think of it, I wouldn't do it even if I could—it isn't very sporting.

While Smith and other *Post* journalists were working to advance the story, online editors were changing the Web site to accommodate developments. What special templates or new home page presentations did the story demand?

 JU-DON ROBERTS: Our page is usually configured [through the site's content management system] to have a lead story, presented with or without visual elements. With a story as multifaceted and as fast-moving as Virginia Tech, we had to use a special layout to accommodate all of the coverage we needed to present, as well as to convey the gravity of the situation. That layout was all in HTML code and had to be built while we were on deadline.

Within minutes of reports of a gunman on the Virginia Tech campus, the print and online staffs began pulling together our coverage plan. Within the first few hours, we not only had an article explaining the extent of the carnage on the campus, but also a locator map, video of the news conferences, audio from faculty and students, images from the scene, a live discussion with the editor of the student newspaper and reaction from [washingtonpost.com] readers.

Given that the story grew from what was thought at first to be a domestic shooting, at what stage did you decide it merited the special home page treatment?

JU-DON ROBERTS: If you remember the early stages of the coverage, there were a lot of mixed reports about whether a gunman was on the loose, whether anyone was injured or whether anyone was killed. Initially, we created a special "breaking news" section that carried the headline "Gunman Reported on Virginia Tech Campus." Once we confirmed at least one person had been killed, we went to a headline and blurb treatment: headline, "Shooting Reported at Va. Tech"; blurb, "At least one person is dead and more are wounded in attack that leaves university on lockdown."

By the time we had that confirmed, our home page editor was preparing to move the story to the lead of the site. Shortly after the headline and blurb went up, we moved to the banner headline treatment that read "Va. Tech: At Least 20 Killed in Campus Shootings." We continued to build out that layout (same layout, but it got deeper as the content grew) as we added more elements, including the multimedia elements, to the package.

By the second day, we had full victim profiles with tributes from readers, a latest developments blog, a Web reaction blog, a then-exclusive video with a witness and other video, an interactive timeline, galleries, information on local vigils and live discussions with officials, students and experts.

How did you decide blogs were the way to go for covering the latest developments and Web reaction?

JU-DON ROBERTS: When you have a story this big with a lot of uncertainty in the beginning, it cries out for a way to do quick updates that might not immediately impact the lead story. The blog was an obvious way to do that. Initially, we didn't roll out the blog because the lead story was changing pretty quickly, but once you have a really solid story, the blog becomes a necessary appendage to allow for incremental updates. It wasn't the first time we've used a blog/dispatches mode as a device to give quick updates. In fact, we've used the technique for years—even before blogging software was available to us.

What was involved in creating a special home page layout while the story was breaking?

JU-DON ROBERTS: Our home page is configured to allow for an "include" [a spot on the page where the contents of another file can be inserted] at the top of it. In that include, we can drop in HTML code, images, etc. We had our designer and developer work together to give us the code to change the look of the page while we focused on the developing story.

Did this prompt you to make any more preparations for future breaking news stories?

JU-DON ROBERTS: We've talked a lot about creating some templates for breaking news layouts, but our tool doesn't allow us to just flip a switch and roll out a new layout. However, we do have in our toolkit some layouts that were built for projects, layouts that are very similar to the ones we would use for breaking news and that we can quickly dust off and use in breaking news situations.

When and how do you decide that a story rises to the level of requiring a new home page structure?

JU-DON ROBERTS: Deciding to move your home page to a new layout is a judgment call every time. If you would have asked me before Virginia Tech happened whether we would run a banner if 32 people were gunned down on a college campus, I would have said, "Absolutely." It wouldn't have mattered that the school is in our backyard—as Virginia Tech is— and draws many of its students from our region. But as I've outlined, we didn't know what the real story was initially, so moving to a special layout is a process of decision-making based on the facts you have at your disposal. On the Web, those facts impact your decisions minute by minute, so your plans can change numerous times in a short amount of time. I would advise editors to trust their instincts. They should also consider their own investment of resources to cover the news event. If they are expending a lot of resources, then they should invest in creating a layout that presents the content well.

What else did you learn from this story that you might apply to future breaking news situations?

JU-DON ROBERTS: Virginia Tech came right on the heels of our newsrooms changing the way we deal with our 24-hour coverage. Prior to Virginia Tech, we had a centralized continuous news desk at the newspaper that worked closely with the Web site's news desk to plan coverage and move copy. We had recently moved to a more decentralized approach— with each desk at the newspaper having its own continuous news desk editor focused on daily Web duties.

Virginia Tech was the first big news event after that change. We encountered some communication challenges in that so many people were involved in the coverage that it was difficult to harness all of those conversations. However, we quickly adapted, pulling together several check-in meetings with our senior team and sending one of our editors over to the paper to help coordinate from there. We sent the editor over several more times during the week and found it to be very helpful. We all agreed that the next time, it will be one of the first things we do.

The Boston Globe

■ Finalist: Individual Deadline News Reporting

Dan Shaughnessy

On Top of the World Again

OCT. 29, 2007

DENVER—If you go to a high school graduation in New England in the year 2026, you will hear a lot of Jacobys, Dustins, Jonathans and Hidekis when they call the roll. And it will remind you of a special time when it seemed that the beloved local baseball team simply could not lose.

Five thousand feet above sea level and 1,800 miles from Fenway Park, the Boston Red Sox last night won their second World Series in four seasons, beating the Colorado Rockies, 4–3, to complete a four-game sweep of the 103d Fall Classic. Frustrated for the final eight decades of the 20th century, the Sox have emerged as hardball monsters of the new millennium.

As they did in 2004, Terry Francona's men shredded their National League rivals like so many cardboard cutouts, beating the Rockies by an aggregate score of 29-10 over four games. Once famous for autumnal folds, the Sox have won eight consecutive World Series games and finished the 2007 playoffs with seven straight wins.

In the last two weeks, Sox fans who worship Curt Schilling, David Ortiz and the other curse-breaking veterans of 2004 discovered a new generation of October warriors; young men developed by the Theo Epstein administration ... Dustin Pedroia, Jacoby Ellsbury, Jonathan Papelbon and Jon Lester.

It was Lester, one year removed from chemotherapy treatments for lymphoma, who took the ball in the clincher and pitched $5\,2/3$ innings of shutout ball to earn the victory. Mike Lowell, who hit a home run and a double last night, was named World Series MVP.

Papelbon struck out Seth Smith on a 94-mile-per-hour fastball for the final out. The game ended at 12:05 this morning. Catcher Jason Varitek put the baseball in his back pocket.

Bobby Kielty's home run in the eighth inning proved to be the difference.

"It feels like a dream," said Sox chairman Tom Werner.

"Don't wake me up," added owner John W. Henry.

The national pastime's (past bedtime, actually) finale was played three years and one day after the champagne bath that cleansed 86 years of a region's pain in 2004. The home plate umpire was Chuck Meriwether, who also worked the dish in Game 4 in St. Louis, and the Sox shot out to a 1–0 lead in the first inning, just as they did in '04.

Ellsbury, the rookie of Navajo descent who started the season in Double A, hit the second pitch of the night into the left-field corner for a double and came around to score on a single by Big Papi. New generation meets old. Same result.

The Sox tacked on a second run in the fifth when Mike Lowell doubled and scored on a single by Jason Varitek. Lowell homered leading off the seventh to chase Rockies starter Aaron Cook, who hadn't pitched since Aug. 10.

The 23-year-old Lester hadn't started a game in the majors in more than a month. He finished the season in the minor leagues and was not included on the Sox 25-man roster for the Division Series against the Angels. Then he went out and won the clinching game of the World Series exactly one year after his chemo treatments. Jake Gyllenhaal is already lined up to play the lead in *The Jon Lester Story,* a major motion picture coming soon to theaters near you.

Lester gave up three hits and three walks. Manny Delcarmen finished the sixth, but gave up a homer to Brad Hawpe to start the seventh. When Delcarmen put another man on base, 41-year-old Mike Timlin—another holdover from '04—came on and fanned two of the Rockies best hitters.

There was stardust sprinkled all over the Sox dugout. Pinch hitting in the eighth, Kielty homered on the first pitch thrown by Brian Fuentes. It was Kielty's only appearance in the World Series.

In the eighth, a fatigued Hideki Okajima surrendered a two-run homer to Garrett Atkins and Papelbon was summoned for the five-out save. Papelbon pitched $10^2/_3$ postseason innings without giving up a run.

Francona, Boston's oft-maligned manager, is 8-0 lifetime as a World Series skipper. And his boss, Epstein—who walked away from the job for a few months in 2005—has a second championship ring.

"Our goal is to get into the postseason as often as possible and win multiple World Series," said Epstein. "We used to say, 'Well anyone can win one.' A lot of people worked hard to make this happen."

And so on the day the Patriots officially moved halfway to perfection while the Boston College footballers enjoyed another 24 hours as the No. 2 team in the nation, the Red Sox won their seventh World Series in franchise history. How do New England parents explain to children there was a time when local sports fans endured failure and collapse and actually *waited* for a rare championship season to unfold?

In October of 2007, the streets of Boston are paved with gold and this week those streets will be packed with the legions of Red Sox Nation, saluting the World Champion Boston Red Sox. Again.

BEHIND the STORY

Lessons Learned

By Dan Shaughnessy

I'm sometimes asked, "How long did it take you to write that story?" My answer depends on how old I happened to be when the article was written.

It took 54 years to write the story of the Red Sox clinching the World Series in Denver on Oct. 28, 2007. Everything I'd lived and learned went into the preparation and writing of that game account.

For more than a decade I've had the honor and responsibility of writing Page One articles for *The Globe* when Boston teams are involved in championship events (and there have been many of them lately). Most of the games are late at night, and routinely we are still cobbling things together, sometimes completely changing the story, as presses and trucks await the final outcome.

Preparation is crucial. Why wait? Only two things can happen at a ballgame—the local team is either going to win or lose. Given how little time I have at the end of these games, I made a short list beforehand of talking points, one-liners and phrases that might fit in the event of a Sox victory or defeat.

Writing for Page One, I am ever mindful that I am not addressing the usual sports crowd. It's important to avoid jargon and inside sports terminology. This means no references to the infield fly rule or Cover-2 defense—standard stuff when writing for sports fans. In this report, I want a non-fan to be able to understand why this game is important and lasting to our region. The simple style creates confusion for hard-core Sox fans who read online and wonder why I'm being so elementary.

Throughout the story, game information and play-by-play is minimized. Readers would already know the Sox won the World Series, and most would have seen numerous television replays of the game's highlights.

My job is to capture the feeling of being there, and to give voice to the historical significance of the event. This is why it took 54 years to write. I had the perspective of growing up in Massachusetts as a Red Sox fan and witnessing decades of the franchise's triumphs and travails.

There's a delicate news balance in the assignment. It's necessary to record relevant details up high (score, dates, top performers) without getting bogged down in a generic news report that would suck all the drama from an event that is entertaining and (in New England, at least) eternal.

For the lead I went with the idea of people naming their children after the ballplayers. I had heard of a couple expecting a baby who planned to name him Hideki, which gave me the idea for a bunch of future Jacobys and Dustins—unusual names that demonstrate the passion of Boston's baseball fans and underscore this night as one fans will always remember.

It's unusual to go six full paragraphs before the first quote, but I believe quotes are overrated in these accounts unless someone says something truly extraordinary. And that rarely happens in sports anymore.

The story sags in the middle as events are highlighted and people are quoted, but I think it bookends nicely in the last two paragraphs.

You look at a story like this and there are always things you'd change. I'll try to do better next time the Red Sox win the World Series.

Of course, someone at *The Boston Globe* said that to himself after the 1918 World Series, but there wasn't another opportunity for 86 years.

Sometimes you only get one shot. Be ready.

Dan Shaughnessy covered the Celtics and the Red Sox for The Boston Globe *before becoming a sports columnist in 1989. He has been named Massachusetts Sportswriter of the Year seven times, and seven times has been voted one of America's top 10 sports columnists by Associated Press Sports Editors. He has written 11 books, including* The Curse of the Bambino *and* Senior Year: A Father, A Son, and High School Baseball.

Chicago Tribune

Finalist: Individual Deadline News Reporting
Jeff Coen

Outfit Insider Recounts His First Hit

JULY 18, 2007

Nicholas Calabrese paused a moment in the silent courtroom, his voice dropping off as he spoke Tuesday of the first time he took part in a murder for the Chicago Outfit.

"We gotta put somebody in a hole," Calabrese said his brother, Frank Sr., told him without elaboration in the summer of 1970. At first, Calabrese said, he thought it was a test of his courage. The brothers then proceeded to dig the hole at a construction site near old Comiskey Park.

But the real test came days later, Calabrese said, when he helped hold down a man's arms while his brother strangled him with a rope—and then slit his throat just to make sure he was dead. Nicholas Calabrese, then in his late 20s, didn't even know the victim's name, he testified.

"He was put in the hole, and we started shoveling the dirt in," said Calabrese, again pausing to keep his composure. "During this time I wet my pants I was so scared."

His brother didn't catch on, Nicholas Calabrese said, because "I had a lot of dust and dirt on my pants so you couldn't really tell."

Sitting nearby on Calabrese's first full day on the witness stand in the landmark Family Secrets trial in the Dirksen U.S. Courthouse was Frank Calabrese Sr., one of five defendants, who was resting his chin in his hand and smirking.

Nicholas Calabrese's testimony Tuesday was a flurry of mob imagery—multiple murders, bombings, scraps of paper with scribbled notes about "street taxes," a 300-pound enforcer nicknamed "Gumba" and buried Outfit cash. He spoke of sending warnings with dead chickens and puppy heads, and mice strung up with "little nooses" and left on a windshield.

And he used nickname after nickname. There was "Mugsy," "young Mugsy," Johnny "Bananas" and Johnny "Apes," not to be confused with Angelo "the Monkey."

And there was Michael "Bones" Albergo, a collector of high-interest "juice" loans. Nicholas Calabrese said Albergo had once warned that if he was going to jail, he wasn't going alone.

Calabrese said he only learned it was "Bones" in the hole near the White Sox ballpark years later when he saw Albergo's photo in a pamphlet put out by the watchdog Chicago Crime Commission.

Nicholas Calabrese, the government's star witness, is expected to blame his brother, a reputed leader of the mob's 26th Street crew, for more than a dozen Outfit killings in the 1970s and '80s. He began with the slaying of Albergo, whose remains authorities searched for unsuccessfully after Calabrese began cooperating in 2002.

Lurid Details

While testifying in sometimes lurid details about the gangland slayings, Calabrese kept his composure, occasionally gesturing with his hands to make a point. He traded in the sweatsuit he wore on Monday for a pale collared shirt, worn untucked, and blue pants.

He sometimes leaned toward a computer screen on the witness stand to look at a betting slip or identify a photograph, a reflection of the image visible in his eyeglasses.

After describing Albergo's death, Calabrese recounted four more murders in which he said he took part. The next was the 1976 homicide of 27-year-old Paul Haggerty, a convict who was living in a halfway house and whom Outfit bosses wanted to question about his dealings with a suburban jewelry store.

Calabrese said he had arrived at his brother's Elmwood Park home and gotten another cryptic greeting. "He said, 'Don't make any plans, we're gonna be busy,'" Nicholas Calabrese said, continuing to refuse to look in his brother's direction after quickly identifying him in court earlier Tuesday.

For weeks, Calabrese said, he had followed Haggerty with a team that included hit man Frank "Gumba" Saladino and mob associate Ronnie Jarrett, nicknamed "Menz," the Italian word for half, because he was half Irish and half Italian.

Looking for Patterns

The men watched Haggerty's movements for patterns, Calabrese said, following him to the bus and work. Eventually, they snatched him and drove him to Jarrett's mother-in-law's garage, he said.

After Haggerty was questioned, Calabrese said, he was left alone with him for a time, his hands cuffed and his eyes and mouth taped. He said he gave Haggerty some water and helped him use the bathroom, but the rest of the men soon returned with a stolen car to finish the job.

"I held him and Ronnie held him and my brother strangled him with a rope," he said.

Calabrese also testified about the murder of burglar John Mendell, who was killed in 1978 as an example for burglarizing mob boss Tony Accardo's home. Mendell was lured to the same garage where Haggerty was killed and then he was jumped, Nicholas Calabrese said. His brother strangled Mendell with a rope, but this time there was a twist, he said.

"My brother handed me the knife, and he said 'You do it,'" Calabrese said.

Asked by a prosecutor whether he did as instructed, Calabrese answered, "Yeah, yes I did." Next, Calabrese testified about the murders of thief Vincent Moretti, who was also killed in the wake of the Accardo burglary, and Donald Renno, who made the mistake of being with Moretti at the time.

Calabrese said he helped his brother kill Moretti at a Cicero restaurant using a rope, pulling one end as he braced a foot against the victim's head. He said the brothers referred to the slayings in code as "Strangers in the Night," the song that was playing on the restaurant's jukebox as the slaying took place.

Though he wasn't an eyewitness, Nicholas Calabrese said, his brother told him of how in 1980 he drove a car that blocked one driven by federal informant William Dauber and his wife, Charlotte, enabling mobsters to fatally shoot the couple from a passing van in Will County.

Earlier Tuesday, Calabrese told jurors about a variety of work he carried out for his brother beginning in 1970, collecting "street taxes" and juice loans and running gambling operations. He also dutifully followed directions when it came to extorting businessmen, he said, using dead animals as threats until he had to scare one into paying by blowing out the back window of his car with a shotgun.

Misplaced Money

Calabrese said his brother had hundreds of thousands of dollars to lend on the street, a claim that caused Frank Sr. to rock back in his chair and chuckle with his hand in front of his mouth. Once, Nicholas Calabrese said, his brother misplaced more than $400,000 by losing track of a safety-deposit box. Another time, he said, the brothers buried $250,000 in cash in a steel box in Wisconsin. But on digging it up later, the money was wet, mildewed and smelly. "We tried to use cologne," Calabrese testified. "It made the smell worse."

Calabrese said cash collections had to be split, with half going to their boss, Angelo LaPietra.

Calabrese said he sometimes drove the payment to LaPietra's Bridgeport garage, stuffing the envelope into a barbecue mitt that was hanging from a nail. He flipped the mitt over and pointed its thumb in the opposite direction to alert LaPietra to the hidden cash, he said.

Calabrese said that in the 1980s he and his brother bombed several businesses, including the Drury Lane Theatre in Oakbrook Terrace; Marina Cartage, which is owned by Michael Tadin, a friend of Mayor Richard Daley; and Tom's Steakhouse in Melrose Park.

Calabrese said he never learned the motives for the bombings, but prosecutors have said that the Outfit sometimes resorted to violence to extort street taxes from even legitimate businesses.

Theater Bombed

An explosive was set off against the wall of the Oakbrook Terrace theater during off-hours. "We talked about how loud it was," Calabrese said.

Calabrese said he also threw a dynamite-packed device onto the roof of the steakhouse. It landed near an air-conditioning unit and exploded, he said.

"I lit the fuse in the bag," he said. "I got out of the car and jumped up on a Dumpster."

Calabrese said he sometimes brought along "Gumba" Saladino, who was 6 feet tall and weighed 300 pounds, to collect late payments on juice loans.

"I told him, 'You stand behind me and don't say nothing, just look at the guy,'" Calabrese testified. "'Give him one of those looks.'"

Calabrese said he warned the debtors that the 5-percent-a-week loans weren't going away and that "next time, I'm not gonna come—he's gonna come." He said he then would point toward the imposing Saladino.

BEHIND the STORY

Lessons Learned

By Jeff Coen

It was a case and a trial that had it all: 18 gangland murders, leaders of Chicago's mob underworld, a decades-long conspiracy, a collection of brash and funny defense lawyers and some of the city's toughest prosecutors. An embarrassment of riches, even for a town that's seen plenty of wiseguys dragged in front of a jury.

It promised to be a sprawling proceeding in federal court that would go on for months and have multiple storylines, including a hit man, Nicholas Calabrese, who would testify against his brother. The trial would receive plenty of nightly TV news coverage, and many of Chicago's news organizations (including the *Chicago Tribune*) would file online reports to keep readers updated throughout the day.

With those factors in play, we set out to make the print stories a different experience. A couple of weeks before the trial, editor Peter Kendall suggested that we make the newspaper stories into daily destinations by bringing the characters to life and telling a story about a trial. Rather than merely repeating testimony and tapping out the news of the day in classic form, I would pull out the vivid details and set scenes. Think summer serial or a beach novel.

I covered the trial solo, which meant I had to write quick dispatches during the day for our Web site and handle the longer newspaper stories each evening after the proceedings. It made for an awfully busy few months, but they were full of lessons.

Get prepared.

Especially if you are dropped into a story, as I was in this case, you have to get ready. I hadn't covered the case when the charges were issued in 2002, so I reviewed most of the case record, read old news stories and did preliminary interviews with lawyers, retired agents and experts. It's basic. But you can't write about the characters if you don't know them. Being familiar with the facts ahead of time also freed me from having to learn them during the trial.

Think in three dimensions.

That's what I call it, anyway. What it means is to activate all of your antennae. We do that on feature stories or at the scene of breaking news, but inside the courtroom a reporter can be tempted to sit and wait for something to happen.

Instead of a flat world in which I simply took notes on what the witness was saying, everything in the courtroom was fair game. Essentially we tried to turn the color volume all the way up. I reported who was wearing what, who was looking at whom, the fact that jurors were using blue pens and passing peppermints to each other, the expressions on the defendants' faces—anything that would make readers feel as if they were there while everything unfolded.

I did the same with the testimony itself. I tried to pull the reader into the situations that were being described by picking up on the little details that made them real. I started thinking of witnesses almost like sources whose information enabled me to retell detailed anecdotes within the news stories. I couldn't ask the questions, of course, but I still got enough detail to employ good storytelling techniques.

Relax and tell the story.

There were a number of days that we abandoned the traditional news lead, dropping the reader into a scene in the courtroom or within a witness' testimony. We weren't as concerned with every nugget of news as we were with making the stories interesting and fun to read, while still reporting new information.

The anecdote at the end of this story, in which Nicholas Calabrese described how he brought an imposing man with him to collect on loans, was a good example. It might have been overlooked on a day when Calabrese, the star witness, started talking about multiple murders. Instead we got a bit of insight into how these Outfit characters operated.

This won't work every time.

The approach was successful because of the material we had to work with. It wouldn't come together as well on other cases. Trial coverage can be looked at strategically, just as newspapers make decisions on how to cover other stories.

For example, the next major trial the *Tribune* covered was a political one, in which the most important thing each day was which politician was named in connection with which corrupt scheme. A reporter still can set scenes in such trials, but that becomes secondary when you have major news coming out of the testimony.

That said, we still can make court stories more compelling and interesting by paying closer attention to the details and moments that are often
overlooked. Readers won't feel like they're in the courtroom unless we
take them there.

*Jeff Coen covers federal courts and law enforcement for the Chicago
Tribune, where he has worked for 10 years. His courthouse work has
led him to write about the kinds of topics that unfortunately shape
Chicago's national reputation: corrupt politicians, crooked cops,
mobsters and white-collar cheats. In 2005 he won local awards for his
coverage of the murders of two members of U.S. District Judge Joan
Lefkow's family.*

PART 2

Column Writing

Kevin Cullen

Kevin Cullen writes a twice-weekly metro column for *The Boston Globe*. His father and grandfather were Irish-American firefighters, working in secure civil service jobs that his Depression-era mother expected Cullen to pursue.

Like many reporters, Cullen says his first dream was to write the great American novel, but he soon realized he'd need a day job. A voracious newspaper reader since boyhood, he considered a job in journalism. But the idea of a newspaper career didn't take shape until his freshman year at the University of Massachusetts, when he took an intro to journalism course with Howard Ziff.

Ziff had been a Chicago newspaperman, and regaled his classes with "Damon Runyonesque tales of shady places where your mother told you never to go, where you got to meet cops, criminals, pimps, wiseguys, wiseguy lawyers," Cullen said. That sounded like fun.

Cullen wrote for the student newspaper and began his career at the *Holyoke Transcript-Telegram* in Massachusetts "for the princely sum of $200 a week." In Holyoke, the urge to write fiction wore off. "The real world I encountered, in tenements, in bars, in the back rooms of police stations, seemed far more interesting than anything I could dream up," he said.

Cullen's next stop was a tryout for the *Boston Herald*, which quickly became a full-time job, mostly covering cops. Cullen says he had impressed the managing editor because, during his tryout, he interviewed a Haitian woman whose son was shot dead, by accident, by his cousin. The cousin was charged with murder. *The Boston Globe* relied on the police account. After Cullen's story ran, the charges were reduced. He spent two years at the *Herald* before the *Globe* recruited him in 1985 to work as a reporter.

Cullen began at the *Globe* covering police and the legal beat, and then won a plum assignment to the Spotlight team, the paper's investigative unit. That assignment taught him the importance of patience and teamwork.

Between assignments, he convinced his editors to send him occasionally to Northern Ireland to cover the conflict there. He argued that since up to half of the *Globe*'s readers were of Irish descent, it was a foreign *and* a local story. In 1997, covering the peace process in Ireland became his full-time assignment. He later moved to London to cover Tony Blair and reported on hostilities in the former Yugoslavia.

After four years abroad, he returned to Boston and joined the paper's Pulitzer Prize-winning investigation of sexual abuse in the Catholic Church. He won a Nieman fellowship in 2003. Upon his return to the *Globe,* he wrote long narrative projects.

In 2007, he was a finalist in the nondeadline writing category of the ASNE awards for his series that followed the rehabilitation and repatriation of a 12-year-old Iraqi boy, paralyzed and orphaned when a U.S. Army patrol mistook the family for suicide bombers and opened fire on their car.

"My kids used to visit him at Massachusetts General Hospital, because he had no one with him the last few months," Cullen said. "We'd take him out of the hospital on day trips and to a Celtics game and stuff like that. He actually spent Christmas with my nutty family, which includes a Muslim brother-in-law, Armenians and the dysfunctional Irish. He loved it."

—Christopher Scanlan, Senior Faculty in Reporting,
Writing and Editing, The Poynter Institute

Editor's note: The boy, Rakan Hassan, went home after his treatment. In June 2008, a bomb exploded at his home in Mosul, Iraq, killing him. Insurgents may have targeted the family, a relative told Cullen, for cooperating with the Iraq government or accepting help from Americans. "But the truth is, we don't know why," Cullen wrote in August after confirming Rakan's death. "We only know Rakan is dead."

The Batten Medal honors reporter, editor and newspaper executive James K. Batten and is intended to celebrate the journalistic values for which he stood: compassion, courage, humanity and a deep concern for the underdog.

Lost in Translation

SEPT. 20, 2007

By Kevin Cullen

Ngan Nguyen wasn't big on the communists, so in 1982, when they weren't looking, she fled Vietnam.

She was determined to get to America to work and send money back to her five siblings and many nieces and nephews.

Hers has been a meager existence on the fringes of the Vietnamese community here, working as a nanny, a house cleaner, often living with the families she worked for. She never married, never took a vacation, never owned a home, because she sent most of the money she earned back to Vietnam.

And for the last few years, she has been homeless. She has been trying to get an apartment through the Boston Housing Authority, and this is where it gets interesting.

Four months ago, the BHA offered her a one-bedroom apartment in East Boston. At least that was what was offered in the BHA letter she showed me. But there was confusion, not surprisingly, because Nguyen does not speak English. Somebody showed Nguyen a studio apartment, and when Nguyen later delivered a paper bag with $500 in cash and $200 in gift certificates to a housing office, the BHA decided this constituted an attempted bribe.

Let me repeat: The BHA believes a 68-year-old homeless woman tried to bribe them so she could get a bigger apartment.

Nguyen's friends—including Kim Pham, a fashion designer who has been letting Nguyen sleep in the fitting booth at her Chinatown shop—said Nguyen was offering a gift, not a bribe. They said it was all a cultural misunderstanding. They said the paper bag contained most of the money she had.

Lydia Agro, a spokeswoman for the BHA, said the case is under investigation by federal authorities. Agro said it was more than just the alleged bribe. "She told us she had no income," Agro said.

According to Nguyen's friends, she has no steady income, but picks up odd jobs where she can.

While no one will say this publicly, there are people at the BHA who think Nguyen is a con artist, that she has bags of money stashed somewhere and that she was not guileless when, on more than one occasion, she left behind for housing officials what former state representative Vinnie Piro once described to an FBI agent as "a little walking-around money."

But people who know Nguyen—not people who have met a confused old woman on the other side of a counter, but people who have known her for many years—scoff at that. They say she has been living hand-to-mouth for years.

Tom Daley, a friend, said Nguyen has been in and out of shelters, which terrify her. "She's no con artist," he said. "She's a little old lady who doesn't understand how this society works."

Donna Agnew, who runs an art gallery in the North End, said that whenever she arranged for Nguyen to clean friends' houses, Nguyen left gifts behind.

"Giving a gift to someone who gives you something is part of this woman's culture," said Agnew. "The idea that she was trying to bribe someone is ridiculous. The communists put her in a re-education camp. She escapes, makes a life here, and this is how it's going to end?"

The idea that Nguyen was offering a bribe for a bigger apartment looks even more dubious when you consider she gave up a subsidized apartment in Dorchester in 2001 because it was too big.

"She said she knew there were people with kids who needed the space, so she gave it back," said Tin Tran, Pham's son, who translated for Nguyen as we sat in a Buddhist temple in East Boston. "She lives very simply."

No doubt this federal probe, already four months in the making, will be one of the most intensive, thorough investigations in the history of the world.

But here's the bottom line: An elderly woman with bad legs and respiratory problems has been sleeping on floors while the BHA lives up to the well-deserved stereotype of an uncaring, soulless bureaucracy. Marvelous.

When Dreams Are a Lifeboat

SEPT. 27, 2007

By Kevin Cullen

They are dressed in identical school uniforms: white blouse, blue skirt, white knee socks.

Penny Labadie, 6, is the quiet, thoughtful one; her sister, 5-year-old Abby, is the sassy one.

"Would you like to hear me sing?" Abby asks, her arms folded.

A tiny voice, she launches into a football cheer.

"Firecracker, firecracker, boom boom boom. The boys have the muscles, the girls have the brains."

Penny giggles in between bites of the ready-made macaroni and cheese that her father heated up in the microwave that sits atop a small refrigerator.

The girls are sitting on a bed in a Cambridge motel that is sandwiched between a bowling alley and a long-defunct nightclub. Since Friday, when their family was evicted from their Roxbury Crossing townhouse, this has been home.

Penny and Abby Labadie are blissfully unaware of just how adrift their family is. The motel stay, which has complicated their commute to the Renaissance School in Back Bay, has been sold to them by their parents as a great adventure. The girls seem to buy it, and ask to invite friends over. But they know something is wrong, because their mother, Bedellia Labadie, occasionally weeps. The girls take turns walking over and wrapping themselves around their mom.

Trying to make sense out of why the Labadies are homeless is no easy task. At one level, their eviction, ordered by Judge Marylou Muirhead in Boston Housing Court, was all done by the book. But on closer inspection, you get the sense the books were cooked, that there was no way their rent dispute with Cornerstone Corp., the company that owns 51 percent of the 346-unit Roxse Homes development where they lived the last four years, was going to end in compromise.

Bedellia and her husband, John, believe they are being punished not for late payment of rent, but for being among the tenants who have backed a legal effort to get rid of Cornerstone and its property manager, Linda Evans.

Evans didn't call me back. Bob Russo, Cornerstone's lawyer, was unapologetic for getting the Labadies evicted and denied it was retaliatory.

"We bent over backwards to help this family," he said. "They failed to cooperate. These people flaunted the system. People like the Labadies look at you and smirk. They do a disservice to their family."

Russo said he wasn't on speaking terms with the Labadies' lawyer, David Fried, whom Russo had disqualified from the case on the grounds that Fried's representing the tenants' council in a separate legal matter amounted to a conflict of interest.

"Had he called me up, hey, maybe this could have been worked out," Russo said.

Fried said the Labadies' eviction is part of a pattern of arbitrary and vindictive actions carried out by Cornerstone and pointed out that it comes just weeks before tenants will vote on whether to continue the case against Cornerstone. He says that, if anything, the Labadies paid more rent than they owed, as Cornerstone manipulated the payment schedule to put the Labadies in arrears.

In the end, the amount in dispute was $89, which, by coincidence, is the day-rate posted on the sign outside the motel.

Somewhere along the way, while the adults were squabbling, everybody seemed to forget that the people with the most to lose in this whole sorry saga were those with the least say: Penny and Abby.

The Labadies, who also have a 17-year-old son living with them, have not told their daughters that the motel voucher runs out tomorrow. They have been trying to find a place to live, but don't have enough for a deposit.

Penny turns 7 on Saturday.

"I want to be a designer," Penny says, looking to the ceiling of the motel room as if it were the future.

Abby wants to be a teacher.

"But I'll still sing," she insists.

Two little girls, sitting in a motel in Cambridge, where everything has been taken from them but their dreams.

Clear Signs of Greed

OCT. 18, 2007

By Kevin Cullen

For 34 years, Bill Trowbridge was a sign hanger, one of those guys who puts up billboards.

He started working when he was 17. The company changed names and ownership over the years, from Donnelly, to Ackerley, to AK Media, but it prospered, and Trowbridge and the other guys who wallpapered billboards all over Eastern Massachusetts made a decent living.

Five years ago, the media conglomerate Clear Channel bought the company and tried to make a profitable business more profitable. They offered buyouts that cut the 48 employees in Local 391 of the sign workers in half. But that wasn't enough.

Last March, Clear Channel told the remaining workers that they were unilaterally changing their hours, wages and benefits. Men who were making $24 an hour, working a 40-hour week, were told they would be paid $15 per sign and would have to hustle to do as many signs as they could, safety be damned, with work hours set arbitrarily by management.

"They brought us in on a Friday and gave us 10 pizzas and some soda and said this was how it was going to be," Trowbridge said, sitting in a Dunkin' Donuts near his Norwell home. "We figured it was a 30 percent pay cut, right off the bat. But it was more than that. Every guy in our local has a family; every guy has kids."

Basically, the company said this: We don't care if a regular schedule and paycheck allowed you to have a family life, because now you belong to us.

For Trowbridge, the change in working hours was a particular hardship, because his wife, Robin, was battling cancer. He had to do a lot for their 12-year-old son and 10-year-old daughter.

On March 19, Trowbridge and 23 others went on strike. Clear Channel brought in replacement workers from across the country. Guys from Texas, Florida and Georgia came in and took jobs that had been in Massachusetts families for generations. The strikebreakers were paid off in the dark. One said he was making $9 an hour, which apparently is big money back in Texas.

Just before Memorial Day, Clear Channel notified the strikers that even if the strike was settled, they could not have their jobs back. The timing was a nice touch, given that many of the sign hangers are veterans.

It got nasty on the picket lines. Trowbridge got arrested, accused of throwing a bottle at a strikebreaker in Fall River. Trowbridge says he didn't do it. He faces trial next month.

In August, 13 months after she was diagnosed and four months after her husband went on strike, Robin Trowbridge died. She was 42 years old.

"Going out on strike was a blessing in disguise," Bill Trowbridge said. "I was able to be home with my wife. I've been able to help the kids make the transition back to school and all that."

He stared at the cup of coffee in his hands.

"And you know what? The way they treated us, I'm glad to be out of there. If they said tomorrow, 'Strike's over, come back,' I don't think I would. I don't want to work for people who treat families like that. This was a successful company, and they gutted it. For what? So the stockholders could make more money? This is all about greed."

The Mays family, the moneybags behind Clear Channel, like to portray themselves as part of the family-values crowd. But if you value your family, you can't work for their billboard company.

Bill Trowbridge was making about $50,000 a year. Mark Mays, the Texas-based Clear Channel president who heads the billboard division of the company founded by his father, was paid more than $5 million last year.

The unemployment checks run out next week, and at this point Trowbridge doesn't know what he'll do to support his kids.

But he does not regret, for a moment, going out.

"I've got to look in the mirror every day," Bill Trowbridge said.

A Family Seeks Answers

OCT. 29, 2007

By Kevin Cullen

It was just after noon, Oct. 15, 1994, and Darrell Robinson had just dropped off his girlfriend's jacket at the dry cleaners when they surrounded him on a Roxbury sidewalk.

They shot him so many times he was probably dead before he hit the ground.

He was 26, and when the cops arrived his eyes were still open.

Robinson's sister, Annie Powell-Konyeaso, and his mother, Emma Ross, were in a car on Dudley Street and were trying to drive down East Cottage Street but got turned back by a police cordon.

Had they been able to, they would have driven right by Darrell's body. As it was, they didn't find out until later that evening that Darrell had been killed.

In the 13 years that have lapsed since a detective told them Darrell had been shot to death, his family has not heard a word from anyone in any position of authority.

Not a visit, not a phone call, not a letter.

Nothing.

Not only does Darrell Robinson's killing remain unsolved, his family has received no information about the circumstances surrounding it.

"It hurts. It still hurts," Annie was saying, sitting on the sofa in her Roslindale home while her 13-year-old daughter, Ashley, sat at the dining room table, studying for a test.

According to testimony in an unrelated federal case two years ago, Darrell Robinson fell afoul of a group of Cape Verdean gangbangers led by a guy named Gus Lopes.

After he got caught with guns, Gus Lopes became a government witness and testified that his brother Nardo Lopes and three others—Danny Ortiz, Adielo DaRosa and Joe Rosa—formed the assassination team that cornered Darrell Robinson on that sidewalk 13 years ago. Gus Lopes testified that he got rid of the weapon used in the killing.

Despite that admission, no one has been charged with Darrell Robinson's killing. His family read about Gus Lopes's testimony in the *Globe* three months ago and, reluctantly, came forward to ask why nothing has happened.

Robinson's family says it didn't know he had anything to do with the young men who are alleged to have killed him. They say Darrell was smart—he got into Boston Latin School and attended Fisher College—but got hooked on drugs, messing up what looked like a bright future.

He went through rehab and got cleaned up, got a job at a day-care center not far from the spot where he was killed.

He had two kids, a boy and a girl. His daughter, Tiesha, is 20, just got out of college and wants to open a day-care center.

"As I get older, I think about my dad more," Tiesha said, sitting across from her Aunt Annie.

"I think, what would it have been like to have my daddy. Most of all, I want to know what happened to him, and why."

Robinson's family is a big clan, and every two years they gather for a reunion, some 200 of them. They had it at the Sheraton in Back Bay a couple of months ago. "It's a joyous occasion," Odell Robinson, Darrell's 50-year-old brother, said.

"But you know something? At every reunion, what happened to Darrell comes up, and we all sit there looking at each other and no one knows what to say."

Emma Ross went to her grave last year, consumed by uncertainty.

As she lay on her death bed, she turned to her daughter and asked, "Did they ever catch the ones who killed my baby, my Darrell?"

"No, mama," Annie replied. "They never did."

Annie Powell-Konyeaso knows the police and prosecutors and everybody else who is supposed to speak for the dead are busy.

But she wonders if, to some, her brother just wasn't important enough, just another young African-American man, dead on the street, forgotten.

"Darrell was loved," Annie said, nodding.

"He mattered. He was my brother."

A Lesson in Courage

DEC. 13, 2007

By Kevin Cullen

Marvin Garcia was sitting in a big chair on the ninth floor of Beth Israel Deaconess Medical Center, watching the drugs that keep him alive seep from a bag, through an IV line, into his arm.

"I can't feel my fingers," he said. "My whole hand is numb."

That's better than the pain that follows, surely as night follows day, a pain so heavy that his bones ache. Then there's the nausea that washes over him, relentlessly, like waves pounding the beach in a storm.

Marvin Garcia is dying. He cannot beat the cancer that has invaded his body. He can only fight it, and he's giving it hell. He is 37 years old, he has a son and he wants to live.

His goals, what made him get out of bed every morning, have changed so much since he came here from his native Guatemala on Pearl Harbor Day, Dec. 7, 1993. He got a job at the Marriott Long Wharf, working his way up to catering supervisor. He got married, had a kid, had a dream. But in the spring of 2006, he felt a sharp pain in his stomach. Doctors found a tumor. They also found a rare sarcoma that no one has ever beaten.

The cancer threw him for a loop. He couldn't work. His marriage collapsed. He rented a small, single room in a house on Harvard Street in Dorchester, venturing out for his treatment or to visit his son.

A couple of weeks ago, in the middle of his ninth cycle of chemotherapy, his landlady told him he had to leave his rented room.

"She needs the room back, for her sister," he said. "Her sister's really sick, she's in the hospital, but she's getting out soon and they need the room for her."

He bears his landlady no ill will.

"That's family. You've got to take care of family first," Marvin Garcia said. "I understand."

He has no relatives here. His mother came up from Guatemala to tend to him after his surgery last year. She slept on a cot, in the hospital, for 19 days. But she had to return home.

He could leave his adopted country for his homeland. He would have the succor of family, but not the medical treatment that is keeping him alive, nor the visits with his son that keep him holding on.

The people who have been taking care of Marvin Garcia have been scrambling to find him a place to live. In doing so, they learned something that stunned them: When it comes to finding emergency housing, there is no preference given the terminally ill.

"Marvin's one of those cases that falls through the cracks," said Laura Brigham, his social worker at the hospital. "He's a single male, no minors with him. He's way down the list."

Garcia's physician, Dr. Gregg Fine, says his health will be severely compromised if he is forced into a homeless shelter.

"You can't give someone chemo and send them to a shelter. It just doesn't work that way," said Fine.

As a legal resident, Marvin Garcia possessed an American dream that was limitless. He could do anything. Now he wants only a place where he can rest, where, down the road, his mother can come back to care for him.

It would be easier to give up. No one would blame him. But he would blame himself if he doesn't live every single possible day.

"My boy," he said, smiling weakly. "I can't give up. I have to keep going for my boy, my son. I want to be here for him as long as I can. I can still teach him things."

Eduardo Armani Garcia is 4 years old. His father is determined to teach him one last, great lesson: how to live, and how to die, with something called dignity.

BEHIND the STORY

An Interview with Kevin Cullen

This edited e-mail interview was conducted by Poynter Institute senior faculty member Christopher Scanlan with Kevin Cullen, winner of ASNE's Batten Medal.

CHRISTOPHER SCANLAN: Many reporters dream of getting a column someday. How did you get this gig at the *Globe?*

KEVIN CULLEN: I am the beneficiary of the downsizing that is killing American newspapers. Eileen McNamara, my old pal and hero, who won a Pulitzer for her column writing, decided to take a buyout. Meanwhile, Brian McGrory, who had been writing a metro column for eight years, and had managed to turn out a handful of successful novels on the side, proved to all of us that he has lost his mind by agreeing to give up his column and become Metro editor. So with a couple of columns suddenly open, some others and I applied for one of them. Like most everything in this business, it was a combination of luck and being in the right place at the right time.

How would you describe the mission of your column?

I'm probably old-fashioned in this regard, but I think of a column as being especially a place where ordinary people get into the paper more than they would in other sections. If you have to reduce it to a soundbite, it's the old "afflict-the-comfortable-and-comfort-the-afflicted." Our culture is now so celebrity-obsessed. I'm obsessed with the anti-celebrity, the ordinary guy. So if it's an individual up against the government or bureaucracy, I'm interested. If it's a working stiff, or some poor bastard who's just trying to survive, I'm naturally sympathetic. But most of all, I'm looking for a good story, one that has something roughly resembling a beginning, a middle and an end.

Your columns show great variety. Where do you get your column ideas and how do you decide which ones make the cut?

The variety part is conscious. You could probably do a sob story every other column, but that would dilute the impact of them after a while. Same with politics. I don't want to write about politics too often, especially because we have op-ed columnists who get paid to do that. The first few months, the columns were generally all my ideas, but after a while I started getting suggestions from readers and ordinary people, so now it's a nice mix.

What role do editors play in your work?

The best editors I've had throughout my career have trusted my instincts on stories and have warned me when they see me going back to the same well too often. That's how it is now. I think I wrote two or three columns in a row about cops and criminals and wiseguys and McGrory told me, "All right. I know you know cops and robbers. Now do something else." So I did. The best relationships between writers and editors I've seen are based on trust and mutual respect. You don't have to love each other.

What's the easiest part of being a columnist?

The actual writing. It doesn't take long. And the freedom. I literally can write about anything, within reason and as long as there's a local angle.

What's the hardest part?

Getting the damn thing under 700 words. The last column I wrote is a classic example. It was about the family of an innocent man who was murdered by a gangster who was protected by the FBI. I know the family. They are salt of the earth. And watching the Justice Department lawyers nickel-and-dime them and suggest that they are racists or somehow deserving of the fate that befell their husband and father, I was very pissed off. I spent a couple of days in the federal courthouse, listening to testimony. I wrote the column in about 15 minutes, but spent more than an hour trying to cut it down to fit. I probably spent 20 minutes losing the last 20 words. But that's the nature of the beast.

Your columns often produce dramatic results—subjects get new jobs, houses; a bereaved family learns how their loved one died, 13 years after he was murdered. What is it about your columns that generate such positive responses?

I think everybody who writes for a newspaper wants to get a reaction. I also think that a metro column, or any column, remains a powerful vehicle for good. If you write about people who are down on their luck, or are fighting a faceless bureaucracy, there is always a percentage of people who will be moved by that and want to do something to help. In some cases, I consciously write something with the hope that good people will step forward to help. But I'm also usually very conscious of not overtly asking for donations or a job or housing or whatever. First of all, I think that reads a little tacky. Secondly, readers aren't stupid. So far, and I'm relatively new at this, good people have come forward and offered money or some other kind of help for the sad cases I've written about.

Not long ago, I wrote about an Iraqi who worked as a translator for U.S. forces in Iraq and has been screwed over by the U.S. government. I spent the next few weeks responding to literally hundreds of offers of money for the poor bastard, who had to leave his wife and kids behind in Iraq because the government doesn't pay for the resettlement of Iraqis who helped U.S. forces and now find themselves being murdered in huge numbers. It was nice to help this guy, but frankly my column suffered for a couple of weeks because I spent more time shepherding donations and offers of jobs and stuff like that than I did writing my column. Still, there was a happy ending. Armed with the money of strangers, the guy went to Jordan and spirited his wife and two kids out of Iraq. I just had tea with them in their apartment outside Boston, where my theory about the similarity of Muslim mothers and Jewish mothers was reaffirmed: The guy's wife kept trying to feed me and wouldn't take no for an answer.

Why do you take up the causes of the poor, the homeless, the screwed-over and the marginalized, be they white, brown or black?

Because they're good, compelling stories. If I said anything else, I'd be suggesting I'm a social worker, and I'm not. Believe me, I want to help people who get screwed over, but if it's not a good story, I'm probably not going to do it. I'd like to think that most of us who got into newspapers many years ago, and even the younger kids who do so today, do so at least in part for idealistic reasons. We want to speak truth to power and all that jive. And I think sticking up for the marginalized is one of the most important things we can do in our business, because if we don't, who will? I figure if I do a column once in a while about some poor person who is struggling, or has been put upon by forces beyond their control, I'm doing what the nuns at Cheverus Centennial School drilled into me, that we should care about the less fortunate around us.

What are the challenges of writing columns that reflect the multicultural realities of a 21st-century Boston?

The biggest challenge is not settling for the easy one all the time. I could write a column every week about the Irish, because I am of them. It's harder to get out into the newer immigrant community, especially if there are language issues. But there are ways to do it. And, when it comes to new immigrant groups, especially, I think I'm sympathetic because I know my own family history. My family didn't have it easy when they first got here. But I also recognize the difficulty of assimilating when, unlike the Irish, you're not white and aren't a native English speaker. I think most immigrants who come to the United States are doing so for the same reasons my grandfather left a godforsaken part of Connemara: to work, to better their lives and the lives of their children. When I write about a Vietnamese lady made homeless by a stupid government agency, I figure I could have written the same thing 100 years ago about some guy from my grandmother's village. These stories are universal, even if my cultural ignorance about some groups makes it harder to get them. A doctor at Beth Israel Hospital told me about a guy from Guatemala who was dying of cancer and was being evicted from his apartment. That's a universal story, and it wouldn't matter if he was from Dublin or Dubai. But if the doctor doesn't give me a call, I don't get that story. You're only as good as your sources.

You end your columns in a variety of ways: quotes, irony in a single word ("Marvelous."), ending with a scene and your voice: "Two little girls, sitting in a motel in Cambridge, where everything has been taken from them but their dreams." How do you decide where and how to end?

For as long as I can remember, whenever I'm reporting, I sort of know when I get a line, a quote or a scene that will become a kicker. I did it when I was a reporter, and I do it now that I'm a columnist, which is really just a term to describe a reporter who's either old or lucky enough to use opinion to infuse their reporting with something more personal. I think the reporting process always leads you to a lead and a kicker. The rest is filling in the middle.

In the case you describe in your question, that image of Penny and Abby, the two little girls who were homeless, that was the last image I had of them as the motel room door closed. So when I was driving away from the motel, on the way back to the paper to write it, it was just a line that came into my head. Everything had been taken from them except the dreams they still had, despite all that was going on around them, out of their control.

Unforgettable details haunt your work. Of a murder victim, you wrote: "He was 26, and when the cops arrived his eyes were still open." How do you report them and when do you use them?

That particular detail came from a friend of the family who was in the area when the shooting took place, and who watched from pretty close by as cops and the EMTs arrived. He got close enough to see that Darrell Robinson's eyes were still open as he lay there dead on the ground. I felt comfortable using that detail because the family described the witness as reliable. I talked to one of the EMTs who responded to that call because I've known him for more than 20 years. He said he couldn't remember whether Robinson's eyes were open, but that it wasn't unusual to find a corpse with open eyes, especially a gunshot victim.

Your columns often read like short stories; they focus on characters, rely heavily on dialogue and are driven by complications that lead to a frequently tragic resolution. How conscious are you of this narrative form as you report, plan, write and revise?

I've always approached newspaper stories, whatever their length, as short stories, or maybe even a poem. You just don't have a lot of space, so every word counts. Dialogue can establish how somebody speaks, which can tell you a lot about them. When I got the column, Jimmy Breslin called me and gave me the business. He just started yelling at me, saying, "Don't stop working." I protested, asking him who said I'd stop working, and Breslin goes, "No one did. I'm telling you, don't stop working. Just because you have a column, that doesn't mean you can sit on your ass. Nobody cares what you think. People care what you know." Jimmy's crazy, but as usual he's right. He told me that I could never put too much dialogue in a column, especially if it's stuff said in court, or in a barroom, or something that reveals boneheaded politicians or people who think they're important. Breslin's the best. He's nuts.

Don Murray, the late writing coach and *Globe* columnist, identified six steps of the writing process: Idea, Focus, Report, Organize, Draft and Revise. Which of these occupy most of your attention, and why?

I'd say the "report" part. My experience is that if you do the reporting, and you have enough good detail and quotes, everything else takes care of itself. It ain't rocket science.

What advice would you give columnists out there who want to do better work?

Be yourself, find a voice, and as Breslin says, don't stop working. Frank McCourt told me it took him years to figure out how to write *Angela's Ashes.* He and his brother, Malachy, had more or less performed the book as vaudeville over the years, but he wanted to write it in book form, and he couldn't quite figure out how to do it until one day when he was babysitting his grandchild and noticed the child's short, staccato sentence structure. There was a rhythm to the speech that was compelling and authentic. Frank had found his voice, and one of the best-selling books in history was born. I think I'm still in the process of doing so, finding an authentic voice, because I'm new to the game.

What advice would you give an aspiring columnist?

Keep the day job. All you can do is establish yourself as a good reporter, and then get lucky. Good reporters who can write with voice are really just columnists who haven't yet been officially allowed to use overt opinion.

I'm sorry to bring up a painful subject, but in the 1990s, the *Globe* was home to two popular columnists—Mike Barnicle and Patricia Smith— who were forced to resign after accusations of fabrication and plagiarism. How do their fates affect you and your editors?

I guess not just their fates but all of the high-profile cases of plagiarism and fabrication mean that there is more scrutiny paid to what we do. It's just the way it is. For example, you mentioned the dead guy with the open eyes. When he was editing the story, Brian McGrory asked me how I knew that, and I told him. Ten years ago, I doubt an editor would have asked a metro columnist how he knew what he knew.

What ethical challenges do you face as a columnist?

The biggest ethical challenge is probably being fair, because by definition, as a columnist, you're supposed to take a side. I did a column recently that indirectly whacked Boston's Roman Catholic archbishop, Cardinal Seán O'Malley. I wrote about a woman who is among those who are occupying a church that O'Malley ordered closed to save money. I didn't engage in any straight opinion, but I think from reading it you would get the idea that I'm on the side of the parishioners who want to keep their church open, not the hierarchy that needs to pay off lawsuits because their bishops looked the other way while priests were raping kids.

The archdiocese spokesman sent me an e-mail saying the archdiocese didn't know about the story and thought I had an obligation to at least give them a chance to respond. I don't agree. I think what I wrote was well within the bounds of commentary, and that none of the assertions made in it required me to run it by them so they could, as the spokesman put it, decide whether they would respond or not. But, I've got to admit, having been a reporter for so long, I felt pangs of guilt at first. My pal and fellow *Globe* columnist Adrian Walker told me that becoming a columnist doesn't mean you have to learn new things as much as you have to unlearn old things, such as having the instinctive inclination to be open-minded and fair and give each side the same amount of space, etc. Of course, a columnist needs to be fair and all. But it's a challenge when you want to be opinionated, because almost by definition you are going to praise someone and bury someone else.

In "When Dreams Are a Lifeboat," you include comments from your subject's adversaries. In "Clear Signs of Greed," you make some pretty strong accusations about Clear Channel Communications's treatment of their sign hangers, apparently based on one source—the victim. What are your guidelines for attribution?

Every column is different on the attribution aspect, but I very often don't want to do traditional attribution because it can bog down, or bore down, the narrative flow. I often find myself editing "he said" or "she said" out of my copy on the final read-through. In the sign hanger case, I actually had multiple sources for some of the accusations against Clear Channel, but maybe I didn't do a good enough job to make that clear. I felt pretty comfortable airing those accusations against Clear Channel. It wasn't just that one guy's word on it. Brian McGrory and Mike Larkin will often ask me how I know something, even if there's no traditional attribution in the piece.

You're the winner of the Batten Medal, awarded in memory of the late Jim Batten, a former reporter who became CEO of Knight Ridder and died of cancer in 1995. How do you feel about that connection?

I met Jim Batten once, briefly, at a journalism gig. We talked a short time, and I told him I was trying like hell to get posted full-time overseas, but that I didn't want to wear brown wing tips and try to get an interview with a prime minister. I said there were always better stories in barrooms and courtrooms. He seemed to like that. He said people like to read about people. Sounds simple, maybe corny, but it's true. When I met him, he was one of the suits. But I could tell he was one of us, because his eyes lit up when the war stories started flowing. Sort of like that feeling I had when I was a freshman at the University of Massachusetts, and Howard Ziff started talking about covering murders in Chicago. It's always the story and the chase.

"listening posts," such as temples, mosques and other religious institutions, and ethnic restaurants where a reporter can soak in the
authentic sounds of a community. Seek out cultural guides who can
serve as a trusted intermediary between reporters and undercovered
communities. Make a goal to generate ideas for a dozen untold stories, and then tell them.

3. Before you turn in any story, go through it and ask the question
   Cullen's editor asked him: "How do you know that?" If you can't
   answer that with a document, a verifiable answer from a reliable
   source or digging for it with additional reporting, leave it out.

4. Columnists enjoy freedoms—the ability to inject their opinions, for
   instance. But they pay for that with a set length—in Cullen's case, 700
   words and under. Enroll at News University, Poynter's distance learning program (www.newsu.org), and sign up for the free course, "Get
   Me Rewrite: The Craft of Revision."

Winner: Column Writing

Leonard Pitts Jr.

Leonard Pitts Jr. talks to God and God talks back.

That's a big-time claim, even for a Pulitzer Prize winner. But at the core of Pitts' powerful commentary is a mix of style, voice, topic and tone that helps him drive a point home with everything from a whimsical conversation with the Almighty to a scathing letter to a bigot.

Pitts has been doing that sort of thing since 1976, first as a freelancer specializing in pop music, now as an award-winning syndicated columnist for *The Miami Herald*. In between, he has written for the likes of *Essence, Billboard, Reader's Digest* and *Casey's Top 40* with Casey Kasem. His 1999 book, *Becoming Dad: Black Men and the Journey to Fatherhood,* was a bestseller.

He won his first ASNE commentary prize in 2001 and was a finalist in 2002, largely on the strength of a post-Sept. 11 column that circulated around the globe and inspired more than 30,000 reader responses. The column, "We'll Go Forward from This Moment," ended with this warning to the terrorists:

"It occurs to me that maybe you just wanted us to know the depths of your hatred. If that's the case, consider the message received. And take this message in exchange: You don't know my people. You don't know what we're about. You don't know what you just started. But you're about to learn."

The Miami Herald

Pitts won a Pulitzer Prize three years later.

Pitts, who was raised in Southern California, lives with his wife in Bowie, Md. They have five children. His name is etched on award lists throughout journalism and beyond: The American Association of Sunday and Feature Editors; the Gay & Lesbian Alliance Against Defamation; the National Association of Black Journalists; the Simon Wiesenthal Center; the Society of Professional Journalists; the National Headliner Awards; the National Society of Newspaper Columnists.

Pitts now devotes some of his columns to "What Works," a series of stories highlighting efforts, he says, to "change the culture of dysfunction that entraps too many African-American kids."

His 2008 winning columns show a breadth of style Pitts says is meant to "keep myself challenged." They show a range of subjects calculated to hold not just the reader's interest, Pitts says, but his own as well. He writes about Mother Teresa's crisis of faith; about life in a FEMA trailer and the ongoing tragedy of Hurricane Katrina; about being the son of a soldier on Memorial Day. Into those stories he injects all the humor, sarcasm, anger and love that define the lives of ordinary people. And, when necessary, he summons the Divine.

—Keith Woods, Dean of Faculty, The Poynter Institute

'Murder Is the Greatest Injustice of All'

DEC. 2, 2007

By Leonard Pitts Jr.

And once again, this is how we die.

Fallen, crumpled, bleeding from a bullet's hole. Woman and child left to wail, left to mourn. Left.

It was, of course, not a "we" who died that way last week in Miami, but a "he," NFL star Sean Taylor, 24, shot in his home by a burglar. But maybe we can be forgiven, we African-American people in general, we African-American men in particular, for placing a "we" where others would a "he," for seeing in the fate of this singular individual all the brothers and sisters we have wept and mourned and given back to the soil. Maybe we can be forgiven for feeling the only difference is that the world knows his name and did not know theirs.

And this is how we die. We die in profligate numbers. Just under 15,000 Americans were murdered in 2006. Roughly half of them—7,421—were black. African Americans are 12 percent of the nation's population.

And this is how we die. We die young. Of the 7,421 African-American murder victims of 2006, more than 40 percent—3,028—were Taylor's age or less.

And this is how we die. We kill one another. Of the 3,303 African-American murder victims whose assailants are known to authorities, 92 percent were killed by other blacks.

It's easy to make too much of that last statistic. After all, murder, like other violent crime, tends to be a segregated thing. About 82 percent of white murder victims owe their demise to another white person, yet one never hears lamentations about the scourge of "white on white" crime. Violent crime is, more than anything, a matter of proximity and opportunity.

Still, with all that said, that difference of 10 percentage points of likelihood whispers a soft suggestion that sometimes we don't much value us, that some of us have learned to see our lives the way the nation historically has: as cheap and lacking in worth. Note that even before three people were detained Friday, it was being taken for granted by some Internet posters and at least one African-American columnist that Taylor's assailant would prove to be black. That is a dangerous, and potentially embarrassing, assumption. But at the same time, no one will exactly be shocked if police end up parading disheveled black kids past television cameras.

Because this is how we die.

We die shot in the head and shot in the gut and shot in the back and shot in the chest and shot in the thigh. We die on asphalt and on concrete, and lying in bed and slumped against refrigerators and prostrate on gurneys in the back of ambulances hurtling down city streets and quietly inside, too, in the soul a little, at the carnage our communities have become.

We die and it goes unremarked, die so much it's hardly news anymore. A child dies from random bullets or a famous man dies at a burglar's hand and the media are all over it, yeah. But 12 percent of the nation is 50 percent of the murder victims, and it's mainly business as usual. No government task force convenes to tell us why this is. No rallying cries ring from podiums and pulpits. Crowds do not march as they did in Jena, demanding justice.

But one could argue that murder is the greatest injustice of all. And life the most fundamental of civil rights.

We ought not—*I* ought not—deny Sean Taylor his singularity, his personhood, in the rush to make him a symbol. So let us say here for the record: No, this is not 7,421 murders. This is one. One heartbeat stilled. One child fatherless. One family shattered. One.

I understand all that. Still, maybe we can be forgiven for feeling that, in the broadest outlines, we've seen this story before. Because this is how we die. And yes, Sean Taylor is one man.

But he's also one more.

Great pickel.
How long to
find it,
the theme
are perfectly.

Memorial to a Father Who Served Proudly

MAY 28, 2007

By Leonard Pitts Jr.

I never listened to the stories he told.

Either *Speed Racer* was on or the new *Fantastic Four* was out or the Spinners were on the radio. Whatever. I never listened.

Things were not good between us. He had a drinking problem, which meant he had a hitting problem. I tried to stay out of his way.

But sometimes, when things were quiet and his mood contemplative, my father just wanted to talk, to tell me who he'd been and what he'd seen in the years before I came along, the years of worldwide war.

What did I care? *Speed Racer* was on. What did those days, those olden days, mean to me, child of the era of perpetual new?

I never listened.

"This was taken in Belgium," he would say, pointing to some black-and-white picture of him as a 20-something soldier, his uniform crisp, his salute crisper. "Um hmm," I would say, giving a cursory glance before moving back to more important things.

I never listened.

Records Destroyed

Years later, I would wish I had. Years later, when the military told me the records of his service were lost, burned in a fire, I'd wish I had paid attention. If I had, I might know more than the fact that at some point, he was in Belgium.

I do know that he was a driver on the Red Ball Express. I learned this because he told my cousin Nate, who told me. Nate was older than I. He had been in Vietnam. So he listened.

The Red Ball Express was 6,000 truck drivers, many of them African American, who ferried supplies to the Allies as they advanced through occupied France. And I realize now that this is what he was referring to when he used to boast that he could drive anything on wheels. "Can you drive a tank?" one of us would ask. And he would say yes, he could drive a tank.

"Can you drive an airplane?" I would ask.

He would point out that an airplane is not a ground vehicle. "But it has wheels," I would say, because I could be a pill when I wanted to, even at 10 years of age.

He died two days after Christmas in 1975. Cigarettes, throat cancer. At the funeral, two soldiers took the American flag that draped his casket, folded it into a tight, triangular wedge, and presented it to my mother. When she died, it passed down to me.

Flag Unfolded

For years, I kept his flag on a shelf in my closet with her Bible. A few years back, the kids got into the closet and I found the flag unfolded, just lying there. I was furious. Tried to explain to them what this flag was. But you know how it is with kids. They don't listen.

I took the flag to a military recruiting station where two young soldiers refolded it for me. It sits in a frame on the mantel now.

Somewhere in Northern California, there is, or was, a man whose name is the same as mine. He was a teacher and apparently a very good one, because not a month goes by that one of his former students doesn't send me a note praising him and wondering if he was my father.

Memorial Day, this day we set aside to remember and honor the sacrifices of men and women in uniform, seems an apt day to clear up the confusion. That teacher sounds like a wonderful man, but he wasn't my father.

My father was Cpl. Leonard G. Pitts, United States Army and, later, United States Marines. He was not a perfect man, but he could drive anything with wheels.

He was a soldier.

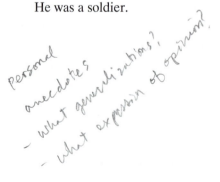

After the Flood, the Big Easy
Is Still a Target

APRIL 9, 2007

By Leonard Pitts Jr.

Your home is a FEMA trailer.

There was a time when your home was a home like anybody else's, but that was before Hurricane Katrina drowned everything. Now your home is a trailer, where late at night you fix yourself a drink and talk to the dog about how it hurts to see your city in ruins, how frustrating it is trying to navigate a rebuilding process the local newspaper calls "nightmarish."

So one day, you are invited to appear on a panel in late March before a convention of newspaper editors in Washington. You were one of the most memorable voices in Spike Lee's HBO documentary, *When The Levees Broke,* and you and other survivors have come to exhort the editors to stay with the story, follow the rebuilding of a major American city at least as closely as they do Anna Nicole Smith, Britney Spears and other important newsmakers.

Afterward, this guy comes up, identifies himself as a columnist with *The Miami Herald.* You give him your card. It identifies you as Gralen B. Banks, managing director of a New Orleans consulting firm.

Internet Screeds

The columnist wants your response to something that's been circulating on the Internet. It was supposedly written by an emergency manager in Colorado, though different versions carry different points of origin.

The e-mail describes how the area has just recovered from a blizzard of "Biblical proportions"—44 inches of snow, winds up to 90 miles an hour, utility poles down, roads closed, communities cut off.

And yet, says the e-mail writer, "George Bush did not come. FEMA did nothing. No one blamed the government.... Jesse Jackson or Al Sharpton did not visit.... Nobody demanded $2,000 debit cards. No one asked for a FEMA trailer. No one looted. We did not wait for some affirmative action government to get us out of a mess created by being immobilized by a welfare program that trades votes for 'sittin at home' checks."

What's your response? Your response is to smile. A tolerant smile. A Lord-give-me-strength smile. You point out patiently, calmly, that no snowstorm compares to Hurricane Katrina. "When the snow melted," you say, "your city was still there, so you're comparing apples to transmissions."

Keep Your Cool

But it is hard to stay patient and calm. It just gets to you, how niggardly, stupid and flat-out cold some of your own countrymen can be. Why, you ask, do they play this game of Whose Disaster Was Bigger? "What's the f—— point of that? We have a disaster and we expect help. Are we arrogant, are we wrong for expecting it? Why are you pissed off with us? What did we do other than ask for what anybody else would quite naturally ask for and in all likelihood get quicker than we did?"

People were not this nasty toward Miami after Hurricane Andrew. So what is it about you?

"New Orleans," you say, "has always been known as the place where anybody can come. You're an accountant in real life and you want to be Marilyn Monroe? Do your thing. We ain't gon' say nothin'. But what did we do to you that would make you turn on us, that would make you say something like, 'We had 10 feet of snow, f—— 'em.' What were we, other than citizens in a position where something happened to us same way something could happen to you?"

You cannot take it in. It does not compute.

You are the son of a funky little river town once known as the place the world went to hear jazz and taste beignets and walk where Satchmo walked. But all that is part of another world now, another world 19 months gone and so five minutes ago.

Now you live in this new world of government forms and empty places and fools who think a snowstorm compares to the loss of everything you've ever known. So you smile ("Lord, give me strength") and you try to be patient and you try to explain it to them.

At night you go home. And home is a FEMA trailer.

I Know He's Out There—Somewhere

SEPT. 2, 2007

By Leonard Pitts Jr.

I was sitting on the deck in a chaise lounge. God was floating on His back in the pool.

I pointed to the night sky, a white disk of moon rising magisterially into an infinity of black. "Nice work," I said. God didn't answer.

"And hey, thanks for the weather today," I said. "75 degrees, low humidity, a nice breeze. Well done."

Still no answer. He gets in these quiet moods sometimes.

"Now I know how Mother Teresa felt," I groused, laughing to show Him I was just kidding. Might as well have been laughing at the moon.

I picked up the copy of *Time* magazine from where it had fallen during my nap, held it up so He could see the Mother's portrait on the cover. "You should read this," I said. "It's fascinating."

The article was about a new book, *Mother Teresa: Come Be My Light,* based on 66 years of her correspondence. The letters reveal a startling fact: For the last 50 years of her life, this iconic, holy woman felt spiritually abandoned, cut off from God. She felt no Presence. She felt alone.

"…[T]he silence and emptiness is so great," she wrote in 1979, "that I look and do not see,— Listen and do not hear…."

"…I am told that God loves me," she wrote in an undated letter, "—and yet the reality of darkness & coldness & emptiness is so great that nothing touches my soul."

"You know," I said, "you could have given her a sign. Would that have killed you?"

Nothing.

"Answer me when I'm talking to you!" I was mortified to hear myself yelling at Him, but I couldn't make myself stop. "Do you have any idea how much easier you make it for atheists when you act like this? It makes their argument so much simpler. If a woman who had given her very life over to this 'God' couldn't get a word out of Him for years, isn't the logical conclusion that He does not exist? Is that really what you want people to think?" God drifted in the pool, silent.

"Is this a faith thing?" I asked. "Is that it? Even though she had doubt, she continued to minister to people in one of the poorest places on Earth. Is that your point? Have faith?"

The sound of a breeze playing among the trees drew me around sharply. "Was that You?" I said.

Silence. I said, "You know you're making me crazy here, right? I feel like the conflicted priest from that TV show, *Nothing Sacred*. There was this one episode where he gave a homily and asked, 'Which man is crazy, the one who hears thunder and thinks it's the voice of God, or the one who hears the voice of God and thinks it's only thunder?'"

I sighed my frustration. For a moment, the only sound was the water lapping in the pool. Then I said softly, "You know, sometimes, I think atheists have a point. When you see nothing, when you feel nothing, isn't it logical to conclude it's because there is nothing?" I couldn't bear to look at Him as I said this.

"I think the only reason I don't go with them," I whispered, "is because of all those other times when you do see… something. When you feel connected to something so vast it defies comprehension. It fills you. It settles you. It gives you peace. And you say to yourself, 'Lord, where did that come from? It couldn't be my imagination, because I couldn't imagine anything so… perfect.'"

Still He was silent.

I looked up.

"You know, this mysterious ways thing gets a little…"

I froze. God wasn't there. God was gone. Sitting alone under the blind white cataract of the moon, I shivered. Then I saw Him. He had climbed out of the pool and was drying himself with a towel. He had been there all along.

"Thank God," I breathed.

"I used to like that show," He said thoughtfully.

"Huh? What show?"

"That *Nothing Sacred*. That was a good show. I hated when they canceled it."

God finished drying Himself and went into the house. It started to rain.

Multiply Sense of Betrayal by 388 Years

SEPT. 26, 2007

By Leonard Pitts Jr.

Please indulge me as I answer an e-mail I received last week in response
to a recent column decrying unequal justice as represented by the controversy in Jena, La. A fellow named John wrote:

> Your columns usually merit reading. But this time, You sound like
> the typical Black guy crying "victim." Leonard, you list instances of
> Black injustice and I'm sure there are many. However have you for-
> got about O.J.? He got away with murder Leonard. He killed his
> white wife!... Or how about Sharpton and the Brawley case?... Or
> the Duke case.... I could go on and on. You want more respect for
> you and your race? Stop sounding like a nigger and start sounding
> and acting like a Black man. You'll get respect and justice. Try being
> a Black man all the time, not just when it fits your agenda.

John, thank you for writing. Here are a few words in response.

That column you disliked argued that Jena, where six black kids were
initially charged with attempted murder after they gave a white kid a black
eye and knocked him out, is part of a long pattern of the justice system
being used to keep African Americans in line. Indeed, black students at
Jena High report that even before the fight, the DA warned them in an
assembly that he could make their lives go away "with the stroke of a pen."

The students say he was looking directly at them when he said it. The
DA has denied this, but I find the denial less than credible given the
unfathomable charges he sought to file against the black kids while a white
kid who attacked a black one got off with a comparative slap on the wrist.

Anyway, you were one of a number of readers who wrote to remind me
of Simpson. If the point of your reference to him, Tawana Brawley and the
Duke lacrosse case was that the justice system has repeatedly and historically mistreated whites, too, on the basis of race, I'm sorry, but that's
absurd. Not that those cases were not travesties. They were. And if those
travesties leave you outraged, well, I share that feeling.

But, here's what I want you to do. Take that sense of outrage, that sense
of betrayal, of having been cheated by a system you once thought you could
trust, and multiply it. Multiply it by Valdosta and Waco and Birmingham

and Fort Lauderdale and Money and Marion and Omaha and thousands of other cities and towns where black men and women were lynched, burned, bombed, shot, with impunity. Multiply it by the thousands of cops and courts that refused to arrest or punish even when they held photographs of the perpetrators taken in the act. Multiply it by a million lesser outrages. Multiply it by L.A. cops planting evidence. Multiply it by the black drug defendant who is 48 times more likely to go to jail than the white one who commits the same crime and has the same record. Multiply it by Abner Louima and Amadou Diallo. Multiply it by 388 years.

And then come talk to me about O. J. Simpson.

You may call all that "playing victim." I call it providing context. Jena did not happen in a vacuum. It did not spring from nowhere. So this false equivalence, this pretense that the justice system as experienced by white people and black ones is in any way similar, is ignorant and obnoxious.

Much like your turning to a racial slur to describe how you think I "sound." I found that word interesting coming near the end of an e-mail whose tone, while critical, had, until that point, been reasonable. I suppose you just couldn't help yourself.

It says something about the intransigence, self-justification and retarded self-awareness of American racism that a man who uses the language you do would, in the same breath, offer advice to black folks seeking "respect and justice." Appreciate the effort, John, but I'm afraid you can't solve the problem.

See, you are the problem.

BEHIND the STORY

Winner's Q&A

An Interview with Leonard Pitts Jr.

This edited e-mail interview was conducted by Poynter Institute Dean of Faculty Keith Woods with Leonard Pitts Jr., winner of the ASNE Distinguished Writing Award for Commentary/Column Writing.

KEITH WOODS: Do you have a system for finding column ideas?

LEONARD PITTS JR.: Yes. It's called: Anything and Everything. Read the paper, surf the Net, listen to news radio, watch cable news, talk to people. Column ideas hide pretty much everywhere and as a columnist, you go through them at a prodigious pace, so I'm always on the hunt.

Some writers plunge right into a piece. Some need to know the ending before they begin. Some need to perfect the first sentence before they continue. What's your writing routine?

I need to have spent some time living with the topic. Almost always, what I write about will be something I've had a chance to sleep on. Ideally (though not usually) it's something I've been chewing over for a couple of days. I love to know the ending before I get there, as it makes the work much easier. Doesn't always happen that way, though. Sometimes I don't have it till halfway through, sometimes I get there and have nothing, which necessitates a walk around the room and a plea to the ceiling. I'll almost always have the lead when I sit down to write, though; that's what living with the topic is for. And I usually polish and edit as I write and then repeat the process a few times after I've got a basic draft down.

Your winning stories cover a range of emotions, from deep sadness to nostalgia to rage to humor. How do you get yourself into each of those frames of mind before you write?

The topic usually dictates that. Some topics are best illuminated through humor or sarcasm, some seem as if other approaches might work better. It depends on what I'm trying to accomplish as I write. But getting into whatever frame of mind the column springs from is not generally a problem. Having spent at least a day mulling over a given topic and figuring out what approach to take, I'm usually "there" when I sit down to write.

You end the column "Multiply Sense of Betrayal by 388 Years" with a five-word sentence—"See, you are the problem." You seem to favor the short, punchy ending. How do you land on those endings?

I like the endings to have a sense of finality. To my ear, at least, that's most easily achieved with concise wording. If you look, you'll find that my leads, for the most part, tend toward concision as well.

You take several approaches to your columns—a conversation with God; a direct response to an e-mail; the voice of a Katrina victim. What do you try to accomplish by mixing voices this way?

I want to keep myself challenged. If you write the same column in the same way week after week, I think it gets old fast. If you change up your approach constantly, you maintain your own interest and, theoretically, the reader's interest as well.

In the "I Know He's Out There—Somewhere" column, you use God's silence as a tool, connecting it both to the Mother Teresa book and to your conversation with Him. Describe how that idea came to be.

I think that's the fourth "God-and-I" column I've done, and in the other three, He is chatty to a fault. But this one dealt with Mother Teresa's impression of Him as being silent toward her, leaving her alone in the world, which is a feeling I think all believers can relate to at some point along the way. So I didn't want to take the easy way out and have God speak some Hallmark card wisdom that "explained" everything. I thought it was important to deal with the inscrutability of God straight on, which is something people of faith often fail to do. Everybody always seems to have a facile explanation for the things God does or doesn't do, but I've always felt that if God is what believers claim Him to be—sovereign author of all creation—then most of what He does will be, by definition, far beyond human comprehension and may even seem to us callous or uncaring. Sometimes, you can't figure God out, and that's the whole point. Hence, the column's presentation of a God who is present, but frustratingly silent. And yet, when He is, or seems to be, gone (not just silent, but gone), the world turns into a colder, more frightening place.

In "Multiply Sense of Betrayal" you write to a man named John who uses a racial slur in his e-mail to you. What struggles do you have about using racial slurs—spelled out—in your columns?

I was once more liberal in their use, but that's changed. In the column in question, though, I thought it important that the reader be as blindsided by the clueless arrogance of John's racism as I was. In my experience, racism is often clueless and arrogant and I thought this was a way of driving that home. And using an "N" with dashes or "expletive deleted" in brackets wouldn't have had nearly as powerful an effect.

How did readers react to that one?

Many were, as I'd wanted them to be, stunned by John's blithe stupidity.

Given all the new ways to reach readers online, have you tried doing your columns in any other formats—podcasts, a blog, vodcasts, etc.?

No. (I have no idea what a vodcast even is! Video, I'm guessing?) As far as writing is concerned (as far as a lot of things are concerned, now that I think of it) I'm pretty unrepentantly old school. My métier (pardon the pretentious SAT word, but I couldn't think of anything better!) is the written word. So I've had little interest in doing electronic columns. And blogs, even those written by writers whose talent I respect, always seem to me rather dashed-off and half-finished, which I suppose is the point of that medium. But me, I'm too much a noodler and a polisher to see something of mine go public in that state. It would be like walking outside with your teeth unbrushed or your fly unzipped.

How difficult is it for you, given the attention you give to rhythm and flow in your writing, to work with editors? What helps? What hurts?

It's not difficult at all, assuming they have a similar respect for rhythm and flow. I've been lucky in that regard.

When you're writing, do you read your work aloud?

I sometimes catch myself mumbling lines and words (I just caught myself mumbling the word "mumbling!") but I don't do a full-fledged, beginning-to-end reading, no.

How long does it take on average to write a column?

About five hours.

Your entry contains columns about some really tough things—racism, murder, the mayhem of Katrina. Do you have internal tools to ensure that the writing doesn't grow formulaic, that it stays sharp and bold?

I just listen to my gut. I've always believed that if the writing pleases me, then it will impress other readers. And I try to avoid running any given technique into the ground.

You've taught writers and you're asked to speak on the subject often. What's the first thing you most often tell writers about the craft?

I tell them I can't teach them to write, but I can teach them to teach themselves. Lesson one is that complacency is a four-letter word.

Writer's Workshop

Talking Points

1. Good writing sometimes is as much about what isn't said as what is. In "Memorial to a Father Who Served Proudly," Pitts refers to his father's drinking problem, saying his dad also had "a hitting problem." How did you complete the idea of abuse introduced by that sentence? What about this sentence—"Crowds do not march as they did in Jena, demanding justice." What's the rest of that thought in "Murder Is the Greatest Injustice of All"? What is the effect of the writer's leaving some of the thought to be completed by the reader?

2. A substantial portion of Pitts' argument in "Murder Is the Greatest Injustice of All" is grounded in statistics that the writer does not attribute. What did you assume to be the source of that data? How necessary, if at all, do you think it is that a columnist attributes that kind of information?

3. In his interview, Pitts says he's "unrepentantly old school" and eschews the trappings of Internet communications. What do you think of his position? Can you suggest ways that Pitts might use online formats, such as blogs, with the same sort of power that he achieves in print?

Assignment Desk

1. Leonard Pitts mixes up the voices he uses as much as he varies the topics for his columns. Try using different voices with a series of columns: a letter to an acquaintance like "Multiply Sense of Betrayal"; a second-person piece similar to "After the Flood"; a conversation with a recurring character like "I Know He's Out There—Somewhere."

2. Highlight the ways Pitts employs short, crisp sentences to begin and end his columns. Short sentences, he says in the interview, "have a sense of finality" to them. Experiment in a column by varying sentence

length, particularly in the lead and kicker, to guide the effect you're trying to achieve.

3. There is purposeful ambiguity in two of these columns—"Memorial to a Father" and "I Know He's Out There." One story could be about fatherhood or patriotism. The other could be about doubting or affirming faith. Try to identify the subtle techniques Pitts uses in each of these columns to get his points across.

THE PLAIN DEALER

Finalist: Column Writing

Connie Schultz

A Boy and His Dog, a Story of True Love

APRIL 24, 2007

All he wanted was a plain brown dog.

No froufrou pooch or designer breed for Chris Kuzma. Those fancy dogs always can find a home. This boy wanted to pour his love into the kind of dog other people ignored.

For most of his life, it had been just Chris, his mom, Karen, and his sister, Nikki. They didn't have much money, but they were the kind of family that closed ranks and made it work.

He was an A student who never asked for anything. When he asked for the plain brown dog, his mother listened.

He promised to save every penny to buy a dog bowl, a leash and a collar. He'd train her, too, and always take time to play with her.

"Wait till I can buy a house," his mother always said. "We can't rent and have a dog."

In 1993, her own dream came true. Karen bought a house in Lakewood, and, right away, 12-year-old Chris was yapping at her heels.

"You want a plain brown dog?" she said, grinning. "Then let's go find one."

She took her boy to the Animal Protective League, where lost and abandoned orphans press wet noses through wire-cage doors and plead for an end to their loneliness.

Chris knew as soon as he laid eyes on her that she was the one.

Her name was Cricket, and she had clearly descended from a long line of philanderers that included a boxer, a terrier and a beagle. She was chestnut brown, with little white patches on her chest and paws. Chris leaned down and scooped her up.

"She's bowlegged," Karen said.

"She's perfect," Chris said between puppy-breath kisses.

They were nose-to-nose from that moment on.

Every day, Cricket and Chris rolled and tumbled in the grass like they hadn't seen each other in weeks. Karen had never seen a kid who loved animals more. Once, Chris found a sick kitten on the street that had to be put down. Chris burst into tears at the news.

He peppered Karen with questions:

"Did the kitten understand?"

"Did the kitten know how much we cared about him?"

"Did he know it wasn't supposed to end this way?"

Some words you can't forget no matter how long you live.

About a year and a half after Cricket had met the love of her life, Chris set out without her on his new mountain bike to hang out with friends before dinner. He never came home.

When police told Karen over the phone that Chris had been hit by a train, she fell to her kitchen floor and screamed for Jesus. She found her boy at the hospital, hooked up to life support, his body still perfect but his head injuries beyond any version of hope. He died three days later, on Aug. 12, 1995.

Karen donated his organs. It helps to know a young mother got Chris' heart.

"A part of Chris lives on," Karen says. "In that heart, you know?"

Another part of Chris lived on in Cricket. She became Karen's protector, walking miles and miles with the grieving mother, sometimes long after midnight. She followed Karen around the house, too, keeping an eye out.

For the 12 years that Cricket was around, a part of Chris was, too.

About six weeks ago, Karen knew before the vet told her that something was wrong. Cricket didn't want to eat, and instead of prowling the house, she just lay in her favorite chair by the window all day long. X-rays confirmed what Karen knew but couldn't bear to say: Cricket was dying.

Karen lay down with her for the final injection that would end Cricket's suffering. Her own pain, she says, was physical, it hurt so much. Another piece of her son was gone.

On Chris' birthday, April 13, Karen placed an "In Memoriam" ad with a photo of Chris and Cricket in the classified section of this paper. She wanted everyone to know there was once a boy named Chris who loved a plain brown dog named Cricket.

Maybe they're together, she says, but she's not sure.

One thing she does know: It wasn't supposed to end this way.

How Many Will Die Before the Dust Settles?

DEC. 4, 2007

By Connie Schultz

It happens in large families all the time: Parents organize kids by age and ability and divvy up the chores.

Kati Maloney was the second-oldest daughter of eight, and her job was the laundry. Week after week, she gathered and sorted the clothes in the family's basement on Cleveland's West Side.

Her father's work clothes took extra effort. She'd grab one shirt at a time, turn her head and shake. With every snap, dust particles from asbestos filled the air.

Week after week, Kati breathed in the dust.

Four decades later, Kati couldn't breathe anymore.

Kathleen Maloney LoPresti died at 55 from mesothelioma, the same asbestos-related disease that killed her father and her uncle. Unlike her dad, she never worked directly with the deadly "magic mineral." But she took good enough care of him for it to kill her anyway.

The question looms: How many more Kati's are there?

"We know the secondary victims of asbestos are out there," said Dr. Pasi Janne, a thoracic oncologist at Dana-Farber Cancer Institute in Boston and one of Kati's doctors. "We don't know how many there are, and we don't know yet if they're mostly women."

It may be getting easier to connect the dots from what we do know.

So far, mostly white, male laborers get mesothelioma, Janne said. They were the guys who got the better-paying, often union, jobs that exposed them to asbestos, which also increased their chances of lung cancer.

It was mostly women—their mothers, wives and daughters—who washed their clothes.

It takes anywhere from 10 to 50 years after exposure for the first symptoms of the deadly disease to show up. By then, the news is so bad, so certain, that the only question remaining is, "How long?"

The list of workers exposed to asbestos could fill this column, and includes pipefitters, carpenters, brake mechanics, painters, electricians, welders, engineers, longshoremen, roofers, plumbers and just about any kind of plant worker you could name. Asbestos is still found today in thousands of products, including ceiling and floor tiles, chalkboards, plaster, carpeting, fireproofing materials and all sorts of insulation.

Kati was initially misdiagnosed, but in her heart, she knew, and she found the doctors to prove it. Her husband, Michael LoPresti, said she settled several lawsuits against the companies that exposed her father, and then her, to asbestos. That money helped fuel both her treatment and her charity, Kati's Hope Foundation for Mesothelioma (www.katishope.com).

But one of the conditions of settlement was Kati's silence, a legal machination designed to mask any acknowledgement of blame and keep other deserving plaintiffs in the dark. So I can't tell you who they are. Yet another longstanding tradition of companies that exposed their workers to the risks of asbestos long after they knew it could kill them.

There's much we don't know yet about mesothelioma. We don't know why some people get it, and others don't. We don't know if one, big-time exposure is worse than chronic, low-dose exposure. And we don't know how many more women will get it.

What we do know is that, right now, it is a death sentence.

Time will tell how many more women like Kati are out there. One of the reasons her story haunts me is the memory of my own mother, a non-smoker who died at 62 of a lung disease doctors insisted had no known cause.

My father worked at an electric plant, where he was regularly exposed to asbestos. He always worried about money and insisted that none of his daughters be allowed near the washer because he was certain we would waste water with half-empty loads.

And so, week after week, my mother stood on the back porch and shook out his work clothes, which she washed separately.

I remember the snap of the shirts in the wind.

I remember the dust flitting around her like sparkles.

And I remember her sometimes saying, to no one in particular, "Would it kill you to do the laundry?"

BEHIND the STORY

Lessons Learned

By Connie Schultz

Longtime journalists should never let themselves start thinking they've seen it all.

That's the sort of attitude that turns us into energy-sapping bores in the newsroom. It also makes us blind to the perfect story sitting right in front of us. This is especially true for columnists. Columnists like me, for example.

what makes different

I'm not proud of this, but I had nothing to do with the initial discovery of the "In Memoriam" ad that led to the column about a boy and his dog. The ad ran in our newspaper, but I had skipped over the death notices that morning and plowed through the rest of the paper.

Fortunately, the *Plain Dealer* employee who took the order for the classified ad couldn't get that boy and his dog out of his head. He handed a copy of the ad to then-managing editor Tom O'Hara, who gave it to my editor, Stuart Warner, who walked over to my desk and said, "I have something that might interest you."

Immediately, I saw the picture of a boy and his dog.

I read the notice once.

Took a deep breath.

Read it again.

"I've got to find this mother," I said.

Stuart nodded. "Yeah," he said. "You do."

The column about a woman named Kati came about because a boy and his dog had changed my lazy ways. Now I always read the death notices and obituaries. I remember the moment I stopped breathing—I had just read "laundry" and "asbestos" in the same sentence—and decided that I had to make the call most journalists hate: I had to talk to her grieving husband.

Lesson No. 1: Narrative trumps melodrama every time. The more dramatic the story, the more we need the discipline of narrative to avoid turning out soap-opera prose. We're not writing for the Lifetime channel, but we can tell true stories that soften hearts in all the hard places.

Narrative helps us avoid that awful habit of telling readers how they should feel. Pull them through a story they can't resist, and they'll feel plenty all on their own. In both of these cases, the survivors provided me with crucial chronology and context that enabled me to write a strong beginning, a middle and an end that just might leave the reader sucking in air.

Lesson No. 2: Age is an advantage. The older we get, the more we realize just how much we don't know. We learn to talk less and listen more, and the experiences behind us help us understand the pain unfolding before us. Twenty years ago, I would have surrendered to sappy writing about that boy. Fear of my own family's exposure to asbestos would have forced me to turn away from Kati's story. But I'm at the age where you realize that life sneaks up on all of us, and we never lose interest in how others negotiate the cliffs and gullies.

My column about Kati, in particular, was driven by more than a journalist's curiosity. That's why I did a double-take when I noticed her obituary. In 1999, at the age of 62, my mother died from a lung disease that doctors said had no known cause. Now it appears that she died from exposure to the asbestos dust that clung to the clothes of my father, who worked at a power plant. Like Kati, my mother did the laundry.

Finally, **Lesson No. 3: Never, ever write for other journalists.** Nothing will kill our creativity and our courage faster when we sit down to write than telling ourselves that what matters most is what our colleagues think. Newsrooms are full of hard-core cynics who are always afraid of being duped. That's good for unearthing corruption and holding government officials accountable. It makes for great stories about how smart we are during rounds of chest-thumping over beers.

Not so great, though, is when we let the fear of groans and eye rolls in the newsroom freeze our fingers at the keyboard. If I cared only about the begrudging approval of my fellow journalists, I never would have written about Chris Kuzma and his best pal, Cricket.

And that would have been a shame, because I would have missed out on all those tender messages from crusty colleagues who said the story made them cry.

Not to worry, guys. Your secret is safe with me.

Connie Schultz is a nationally syndicated columnist for The (Cleveland) Plain Dealer. *In awarding her the 2005 Pulitzer Prize for commentary, judges praised her "pungent columns that provided a voice for the underdog and the underprivileged." She won the James Batten Medal in 2004, and she was named a 2003 Pulitzer finalist for feature writing for a series about a man who was wrongly imprisoned for 13 years for rape.*

The Oregonian

Finalist: Column Writing

David Sarasohn

Lincoln Hall's Leaky Roof Is Metaphor for Higher Ed

APRIL 8, 2007

In a few rare college courses, there's a single moment that grabs your attention and stays with you long after you've closed your books.

For Patrick Beisell, in a class at Portland State on the American novel, it was when the ceiling started leaking.

No literature class anywhere offered a better sense of symbolism.

Beisell's class was in Lincoln Hall, built in 1911, a building that already had structural problems when Vanport College, the ancestor of PSU, inherited it from Portland Public Schools in 1949. Now, it's a relic in need of $36 million in deferred maintenance and seismic upgrades, where 40-year-old acoustic tiles fall off the ceiling, the electrical system is near collapse and, since a 2001 pump failure, a jerry-built array of pipes and wooden slabs holds up the sidewalk.

But Lincoln Hall also contains 12 percent of the instructional area of the highest-enrollment university in Oregon, with classes running from 6 in the morning until 10:30 at night, and it's the home of the PSU arts programs—including a large auditorium that is, in the words of PSU facilities manager Robyn Pierce, "in a seismic event, not a place where you want a large crowd gathering."

You could say that Lincoln Hall is the Walter Reed Army Medical Center Building 18 of the Oregon University System.

Except in real estate terms, you might call the entire system a fixer-upper.

After 30 years of diligent legislative neglect, the state is about $650 million behind in higher education maintenance. To make a dent, Gov. Ted

Kulongoski asked the Legislature for $325 million in capital construction bonds. The Ways and Means co-chairs' budget cut that to $50 million—which, after general maintenance, won't be enough to deal even with Lincoln Hall.

Let alone all the other overburdened, undermaintained buildings at PSU—or on the system's other six campuses.

And the buildings aren't even the system's main problem. The buildings are also—as someone might have said when the rain let up in Patrick Beisell's American Novel class—a metaphor.

For the past 15 years, Oregon cut its higher education spending faster than any other state. Now, the co-chairs also cut $35 million from the governor's proposed Oregon University System operating budget.

Meanwhile, even under the governor's proposed budget, Portland State needs to cut about $5 million for next year. The university is hoping that a lot of full professors retire.

We tunneled down to this structurally unsound bargain basement by steady disinvesting in our higher education system, until Oregon now spends $2,400 less per student than the national average. During that time, we have also had the fifth-largest tuition increase in the country, until Oregon universities now get only 85 percent of the national average in revenue but collect 120 percent of the national average in tuition. Just since 1999–2001, the state's funding of the system has fallen from the largest share, around 50 percent, to about 35 percent, while the student share is now approaching 60 percent.

This is why Patrick Beisell, about midway through his college career, is already $11,000 in debt so he can study in classrooms where the ceiling leaks.

The co-chairs' budget does fund the governor's affordability effort. But as Kulongoski told the Portland City Club on Friday afternoon, "Affordability is an empty promise without first-rate faculty, state-of-the-art research facilities, modern buildings and adequate maintenance."

Meaning, around here, affordability is close to becoming an empty promise.

In universities, different shortfalls flow into each other. A place where the buildings are decrepit has trouble attracting top faculty, and a place obliged to hope that full professors retire—or maybe get recruited by other universities, which would also save money—has trouble attracting private support.

"These things run on parallel lines," says Robert Daasch, who as professor of electrical and computer engineering at Portland State, and director of the Integrated Circuits Design and Test Laboratory, has a pretty good claim on lab and research space—and yet a shortage of it.

"We are losing ground in terms of competing for the best high school students, we're losing ground in competing for the best faculty, and we're losing infrastructure.

"The dominant thought process is how to build the compromises, not how to exploit the opportunities."

And yet, a higher education system—and a state's economic future—has to be all about exploiting the opportunities.

And Lincoln Hall isn't the only thing leaking.

BEHIND the STORY

Lessons Learned

By David Sarasohn

In the middle of another meeting with Oregon college students complaining that the state university system was an academic afterthought, one of them mentioned that the roof had started to leak while he was sitting in a recent class.

It seemed a perfect metaphor, except that good metaphors don't leak.

I had just written my eighty-seventh column, by rough count, trying to get the Oregon Legislature to notice what was happening—or rather not happening—with Oregon universities. And, for the eighty-seventh time, by exact count, it seemed that the Oregon Legislature had other things on its mind.

This was getting boring, at least for me, not to mention the legislators.

So I suggested to my editor that we do something different: I would write about the condition of higher education in the state every Sunday during the legislative session, until the Legislature set a budget. The plan included an unspoken assumption—and soon, a spoken warning from someone in *The Oregonian*'s management—that in going back to the well so often, this better not get boring.

It would have been hard to miss with the dripping classroom metaphor, especially considering that the student's class was The American Novel. And as I set off to conduct my own course, for about the length of an academic quarter, several guiding principles emerged:

If the people you're talking to don't hear you the first time, say it again, louder. Eventually they will notice you, although they may not do what you want. Still, if you keep going to the same place, you have to get there in different ways.

It's always about the people. The story about Lincoln Hall wasn't really about the building, it was about the student watching his classroom leak—so he kept showing up in the piece. When I started to think about Oregon kids who wouldn't even consider the system, I found Tony Tran, an impressive kid who was on track to becoming a doctor somewhere—probably in the state where he went to college, which wasn't going to be Oregon. Many people liked the column, mostly because they liked Tony Tran.

As my wife has told me too many times, reciting numbers—even numbers as dramatic as the Oregon system's—won't change anything.

Surround your subject, and your audience. I hit the issue each Sunday from a different angle—from buildings, to students, to businessmen concerned about the system's shortfall of qualified graduates, to university systems in other states and countries that far surpassed Oregon's. Since there are Oregonians, and legislators, who regard the University of Oregon with distaste and Portland State University as poisonous, I made sure to collect quotes and examples—and especially people—from all the campuses.

Readers, and even legislators, started to notice the columns. They became something locals expected every Sunday, like rain. And pretty soon, people began to contact me with more examples and themes.

I wrote about higher education for more than 10 Sundays in a row, and the universities had an unusually good year at the Legislature. I can't really claim credit, but a lot of people in the university system were appreciative.

So was I. The experience ended with another lesson, maybe the most reassuring one for a newspaper columnist in these times: If you commit to your subjects, they'll commit to you.

David Sarasohn received his Ph.D. in history from UCLA in 1976 and taught at Reed College in Portland, Ore., for three years. He moved to The Oregonian *in 1983 to handle the paper's opinion section and has been writing editorials and columns ever since. In 2002 he received a fellowship to write about the bicentennial of the Lewis and Clark expedition and the future of the West. That project turned into the book* Waiting for Lewis and Clark.

PIONEER PRESS

Finalist: Batten Medal

Rubén Rosario

She Was Ready to Say, 'I Do.' County Replied, 'You Can't.'

SEPT. 9, 2007

Say hello to Bethny Libsock. She is 36 years old, lives alone, works and has a virtually spotless driving record.

Like most of us, she has the right to vote, drink and freely associate with whomever. But when Libsock, who has a mild mental disability, informed her social worker and a service provider that she had fallen in love and planned to marry, Sherburne County officials assumed the role of the strongly disapproving parent.

It moved in court to block the marriage as well as have a judge review the fitness of Libsock's legal guardian, who is her mother and a former county foster parent. It also raised the possibility that both the mother and groom-to-be could face criminal charges if the marriage took place.

The county's decision to meddle into this affair of the heart touched off an intriguing, nearly yearlong court battle that pitted the civil and human rights of a mentally disabled person against the government's stated interest in protecting a vulnerable adult—one with the estimated mental capabilities of a 12-year-old—from perceived or potential harm.

In the end, does Bethny Libsock have the inherent right to marry, regardless of her disability or whether the suitor turns out to be Mr. Right or a creep? And does the government have any authority to stop it from taking place? Alas, the case's somewhat anti-climactic ending never really provided answers.

Bethny Libsock dotes on her cat, Sam, in her Monticello, Minn., apartment while talking with her mother, Betty Libsock. Bethny Libsock, 36, has worked for eight years at Cub Foods, maintains a circle of friends and has an active life that includes church and sports. (Photograph courtesy of Jean Pieri/*Pioneer Press*)

"The truth of the matter is that in this area, there aren't a lot of black or white answers," said Barnett Rosenfield, a lawyer for the Minnesota Disability Law Center.

Still, the county, which has provided and funded limited services for Libsock for nearly 18 years, has taken a lambasting from people ranging from Libsock's parents and circle of friends to a state watchdog group that monitored the case.

"When a person with a disability asks government for help with an aspect of their life, they do not expect government to take over all aspects of their life," said Roberta Opheim, the state's ombudsman for mental health and developmental disabilities. "When parties disagree and government brings all of its resources to bear against the individual, it risks becoming the abuser.

"Having the government tell a person with a developmental disability that they can only date or marry another developmentally disabled person appears to me to be abusive."

Sherburne County Attorney Kathleen Heaney strongly disagrees and defends her office's decision.

"The issue that we were faced with was not whether a person should marry, but the statutory issue of whether an individual had the capacity to marry," Heaney wrote in a prepared statement. "(Bethny) had been appointed a guardian/conservator because she 'lacked sufficient understanding or capacity to make or communicate responsible personal decisions.' The professionals brought this issue forward. After an analysis based upon the facts and the law, my duty is to inform the court."

Lawyers on both sides agree on one thing: They've never seen a case quite like it before.

The Relationship

This detoured march to court instead of the altar began last summer after Libsock's social worker of six years, Pat Kuehn, got wind of Libsock's relationship with a 55-year-old, thrice-divorced former Green Beret she met while visiting her parents in 2005 at their retirement home in Arizona. At the time, Bethny Libsock received about five hours daily of supported living services. Judged to have an IQ of 67, Libsock has difficulty reading and handling finances.

"Beth had had friends before, but she really took to him, and he was gracious, gentle and very kind with her," said Betty Libsock, Bethny's mother. "I had never seen Beth so happy, with such joy."

The relationship continued by phone after Bethny Libsock returned to Minnesota. Her parents had several "deep" conversations with the man about his intent toward their daughter.

"Like most parents you have doubts, and this was not the man that I would have chosen because he was 20 years older and divorced," said Betty Libsock, who also operated a treatment group home and a crisis nursery. "But I told her to follow her heart and not rush into anything. She said that she won't marry unless he's a Christian and puts the Lord first."

The Official Objections

Where the Libsocks saw love and happiness, Kuehn and others saw red flags.

Kuehn, who now works for Ramsey County's human services division, expressed concerns about the man's past marriages and his age, and that he was a normal, functioning male, according to court documents. She shared those concerns with Dr. Jean Rafferty, Bethny Libsock's therapist, and Tracy Harris, an assistant Sherburne County prosecutor.

A meeting was held Aug. 15, 2006, at Rafferty's office in Monticello, where Libsock has lived for several years.

"We walk in there and the first thing they tell us is that the relationship has to be terminated immediately—no 'hello,' no 'how are you,'" recalled Bethny's father, Bob Libsock. "We were stunned."

Rafferty, according to court papers, told the Libsocks that "she has worked with sexual offenders in the past and reviewed with them the possibility that (Bethny's fiance) may be 'grooming' them and Beth, using religion as a tool."

During the meeting, Kuehn handed Betty Libsock two sheets of paper. One of them contained the statute on criminal neglect involving "a caregiver or operator who intentionally neglects a vulnerable adult or knowingly permits conditions to exist that result in the abuse or neglect of a vulnerable adult."

The other centered on third-degree criminal sexual conduct involving an offender who knowingly has sexual intercourse with someone who is "mentally impaired, mentally incapacitated, or physically helpless."

"It was like she hit me with a 2-by-4," said Betty Libsock. The court battle began in earnest after the Libsocks refused to voluntarily halt the marriage plans.

"All are concerned for Beth's safety and risk of harm," Kuehn wrote in a letter to the court suggesting it stop the "romantic relationship" and perhaps replace Betty Libsock as her daughter's guardian.

The Court Debate

In court, the county argued that Betty Libsock was at risk of harm and basically lacked the mental capacity to enter into marriage. It produced, among other documents, a 1997 evaluation concluding that Libsock functioned "at the level of a 5-year-old in the area of communication, at the level of a 14-year-old in the area of daily living skills, and at the level of a 10-year-old in the area of socialization."

Lawyers for Libsock and her parents presented a radically different picture. It was the profile of a middle-aged woman who has been living independently for more than a decade, has worked eight consecutive years at the Cub Foods store in Monticello, maintains a circle of friends and enjoys an active life that includes church, sports and taking an elderly neighbor grocery shopping.

She and her fiance also underwent pastoral and marriage counseling several times before and after the court proceedings began. A therapist found that Libsock, contrary to county assertions, "has a basic understanding of marriage and sexuality and... functions above her cognitive ability level in many areas in her life."

The Minnesota Disability Law Center also chimed in.

"In this case, it appears as though the guardian has been particularly conscientious in balancing the need to protect Ms. Libsock from any reasonable threat of harm with the concomitant need to assure Ms. Libsock's basic right to make choices of her own free will—including the choice of whom to date," the group wrote to Sherburne County District Judge Robert Varco.

Perhaps the surprise here was that the social workers and county officials never called, questioned, investigated or apparently conducted a criminal background check on Libsock's fiance. Her parents said they did on their own and found nothing.

The case took a significant turn earlier this year when the Libsocks pulled the plug on county services for their daughter. The county argued it still had standing, but Varco ruled otherwise in late June after sitting down with Bethny and others to make sure the termination of services would not adversely harm her.

"He found her to be coherent and quite articulate in her wishes," recalled her lawyer, Thomas Richards. "She presented herself very well."

The Right to Decide

The county was out of the picture, but in the end, they indirectly got their wish.

Libsock's engagement fizzled by mutual agreement shortly before the case was dismissed. Libsock and her parents believe the legal wrangling played a role in the eventual break-up.

Libsock says she plans to personally return the engagement ring to her former fiance when she visits her parents in Arizona during the coming holiday season.

"He was very kind," Libsock told me last week. "He left a message on my machine saying that he was sorry that it all happened."

Her parents, meanwhile, spent more than $10,000 on legal fees and also were forced to remain in Minnesota for eight months because of the court proceedings.

"Our daughter has been a great joy to us in our lives and we are very proud of her high moral living standards and her accomplishments," Betty Libsock wrote to the judge. "We refuse to allow the negativity of this court action to diminish Beth's achievements or future happiness."

The wedding was supposed to take place Sept. 1. Because of it, Libsock gave up her position as an alternate member of a national Special Olympics basketball team that recently traveled to China.

I'm no expert on these matters, but it seems to me that, given that nearly half of all marriages end in divorce, perhaps there's an argument to be made that many of us also lack the mental capacity to truly understand commitment.

Libsock's Special Olympics coach, Darlene Nichols, perhaps best summed up the bottom line in this case.

"It is my opinion that, whenever possible, it is best to leave decisions related to the well-being of an individual up to the family rather than to a government agency," Nichols wrote in a letter to the judge. "Beth deserves all the happiness she can possibly have. If that includes falling in love and being loved, who has the right to decide that for her?"

BEHIND the STORY

Lessons Learned

By Rubén Rosario

"Someone recommended that I call you," Betty Libsock said over the phone. "It's about the county and what happened to my daughter."

Oh, no. Another "county done me wrong" call. I wasn't in the mood. It was getting late in the week and another column was due.

The last thing I needed was another fruitless series of phone calls to county social service workers, whom I already knew are barred by state law from speaking publicly about a case—particularly one involving a mildly disabled woman receiving county services. I rued sifting through incomplete public documents knowing that many others would be confidential and inaccessible. All this hassle and work to learn, as I had in other frustrating and futile quests for the truth, that there are at least two sides to most stories of conflict.

I was half-listening when Libsock found my "outrage" button. "The county went to court to block my 36-year-old daughter, Bethny, from getting married, and threatened to file criminal charges against us."

Are you kidding me? Is this true? It turned out that it was.

Lesson: Don't get jaded. You think you've heard it all after 30 years in journalism. Then Bethny Libsock walks into your life, offering you the privilege of telling her moving story while biting government's ankles and touching on that most universal of human matters: affairs of the heart. That's a titillating trifecta in my profession.

I forget what column I ended up banging out that week. Betty Libsock sent me a batch of papers concerning her daughter and documents from the yearlong court battle. The papers not only contained write-ups favorable to Bethny, but also unfavorable psychological evaluations, daily case management reports and detailed accounts from the county as to why it moved to block Bethny's wedding to a thrice-divorced man significantly older than her. That surprised me and showed that Betty was not just an angry mom seeking revenge. She wanted me to hear both sides.

Writer's Workshop

Talking Points

1. Vivid details are a hallmark of Kevin Cullen's columns. Look for three to five such details in each column. What is it about significant and relevant details that can have such a strong impact on readers?

2. Cullen says the biggest ethical challenge he faces as a former reporter is "probably being fair, because by definition, as a columnist, you're supposed to take a side." Whose side does he usually take? Find some examples in his columns where he is clearly taking a side. How does Cullen's approach differ from a reporter's responsibility to be fair?

3. In recent years, *The Boston Globe* was one of several newspapers that removed popular columnists accused of fabrication and plagiarism. One result, Cullen says, is that there "is more scrutiny paid to what we do." He cites a detail from one column that describes a homicide victim lying on the street with his eyes open. His editor asked him how he knew that occurred. "Ten years ago," Cullen says, "I doubt an editor would have asked a metro columnist how he knew what he knew." Who benefits from such a change? Are there any downsides?

Assignment Desk

1. Cullen opens several columns with a quick sketch of the main character. It's a conscious choice, he says, to establish the person as an individual worth caring about. Study how his reporting and writing achieves this. Observe someone, choose an attribute that sets him or her apart and write a lead modeled on this feature of Cullen's work.

2. Cullen acknowledges that it would be easy to write a column every week about the Irish "because I am of them." Despite language differences, he clearly makes an effort to write about America's newest immigrants, including Vietnamese and Guatemalans, and other groups whose lives are rarely reflected in today's news. Explore the diversity within your community or beat to find untold stories. Visit

I had more than enough material for a quick-turn column on how the county shafted Bethny. But her plight deserved more than that. It demanded calls, reviews of more documents and face-to-face interviews.

Lesson: Let the facts get in the way of a good column. I'm not crazy about columns driven mostly by opinion or pontification. I admire a very short list of people who do it well. But it's not my style. My former newsroom colleagues and inspirations—Jimmy Breslin and Pete Hamill—corrupted me early in my career about the great value and impact of reported columns.

Lesson: Give it to me straight, no chaser. Some columns—like Bethny Libsock's story of how her wedding plans were derailed by the same county that praised her for her success at independent living—are best served straight. Quips, snipes and hyperbole were put on the shelf this time. They would not properly do justice to Bethny's story and the larger issue it illustrated: the balance between a disabled person's civil and human rights and government's responsibility to protect a vulnerable adult from harm.

More than 100 readers called or e-mailed me about the piece. Many more engaged in a highly charged and scintillating debate over who was right. In the end, most concurred with the sentiments expressed by Bethny's Special Olympics coach: "It is my opinion that, whenever possible, it is best to leave decisions related to the well-being of an individual up to the family rather than to a government agency. Beth deserves all the happiness she can possibly have. If that includes falling in love and being loved, who has the right to decide that for her?"

Took the words right out of my mouth.

Born in San Juan, Puerto Rico, and raised in New York City, Rubén Rosario is a veteran journalist. In 11 years with the Daily News, *he covered some of New York City's most notorious crime stories. In 1986, he wrote* Journey into the Den of Lost Souls, *which documented the city's devastation from crack cocaine. After five years as an editor at the St. Paul, Minn.,* Pioneer Press, *he launched his award-winning column.*

BEHIND the STORY

Sources Say

An Interview with Betty Libsock

This edited phone interview was conducted by Mallary Jean Tenore, Naughton Fellow at The Poynter Institute, with Betty Libsock.

MALLARY JEAN TENORE: What surprised you about being part of the story?

BETTY LIBSOCK: [Rubén] heard and understood our story. It was shocking and painful to come to the realization that local government officials can be so powerful and so untouchable. We got used to people not really hearing our story. We went to the governor and appealed to him. We wrote letters and sent packets to senators. We spent hours on the phone just trying to tell our story and trying to get some help. The people we talked to were tolerant and they listened, but nobody did anything.

I kept thinking, "But we live in America." Beth, in the middle of all this, would say, "Mom, I haven't done anything wrong."

My husband and I lived in a Minneapolis suburb, so we didn't have much to do with the [*Pioneer Press*], but a [government] ombudsman we were working with told me to call Rubén. I called him and could tell what a kind, gentle person he was. Originally, we were expecting a reporter to just come and write down what we had to say and then leave. But Rubén listened. He looked in our eyes and had a heart for what we were saying and all we had gone through. He wanted to help us.

What have you learned from this experience?

[I learned that] the newspaper was our only hope for getting our story exposed. Rubén encouraged us. He gave us hope that somebody in this world would hear our story.

We read Rubén's article to Beth and she smiled and said, "Wow, that story and those pictures are great." We bought extra papers, and Beth took them around to all of her friends. She took them to work and put [the article] on the bulletin board.

Rubén's kindness was so good for us. It helped heal us. We'd been so battered. I can't tell you the pain and the cruelty and the harshness of attorneys and county commissioners who wouldn't understand. Then along came Rubén, and it was just healing to know that he "got it." He gave us guidance. He sat down with Beth and gave her his number. She took it and was very happy.

What would you like to say to other journalists who cover similar fields or situations?

Hear the heart of those you cover. Hear what the issues are and try to get to the bottom of them. Journalism is our only hope that stories will be told and that there can be some exposure as to how the state government is handling issues concerning vulnerable people.

In our case we were strong enough to say to government officials, "No, you're not going to run over us like a freight train. You're not going to take over and make life decisions for Beth." But there were many times when we were so weary, that it's an awful thing to even remember. It would be my prayer that there would be more people who would just care and listen. So often the news is so slanted and cold. Rubén looked at all sides of the story. He talked to the county attorneys. He gave his opinion in the article, and yet it was fair and balanced and honest.

Investigative
Journalism

Winner: ASNE Local Accountability Reporting
Winner: Pulitzer Prize for Public Service

Anne Hull and Dana Priest

Dana Priest

It started innocently enough: a tip from an acquaintance's friend. But that one small tip led *Washington Post* reporters Dana Priest and Anne Hull to spend four months interviewing soldiers and their loved ones at Walter Reed Army Medical Center.

What they dis-covered became a national scandal: the poor treatment of wounded soldiers and harsh living con-ditions at a facility that was once per-ceived as the crown jewel of military medicine.

Anne Hull

More than five years "of sustained combat have transformed the venerable 113-acre institution into something else entirely—a holding ground for physically and psychologically damaged outpa-tients," Priest and Hull wrote in the story that launched the series.

"Almost 700 of them—the majority soldiers, with some Marines—have been released from hospital beds but still need treatment or are awaiting bureaucratic decisions before being discharged or returned to active duty.

"They suffer from brain injuries, severed arms and legs, organ and back damage, and various degrees of post-traumatic stress.... The average stay is 10 months, but some have been stuck there for as long as two years."

Priest and Hull's reporting caused a firestorm. A day after the first set of stories ran, the Army began cleaning up the substandard housing. "Within weeks, the commander of Walter Reed, the secretary of the Army and the surgeon general of the Army were all removed from their jobs. A high-level commission to look into the care of veterans was appointed," Philip Bennett, *The Washington Post*'s managing editor, wrote in his nominating letter to the ASNE Awards judges.

Hull and Priest were swamped with e-mails and voicemails from soldiers across the country, which led to an examination of veterans' care elsewhere.

For their investigative reports on Walter Reed and beyond, the reporters won the ASNE Distinguished Writing Award for Local Accountability Reporting and the Pulitzer Prize for Public Service.

Neither is a stranger to such recognition.

Hull, an enterprise reporter on the *Post*'s national staff, has been a Pulitzer finalist several times and is a repeat winner of the ASNE Awards. She has taught at Princeton University, Stanford University, Brown University and the University of California at Berkeley. Prior to joining the *Post* in 2000, she worked for 15 years at the *St. Petersburg Times*. She is a member of The Poynter Institute's board of trustees.

Priest, an investigative reporter at the *Post,* received several awards for her reporting on CIA secret prisons and counterterrorism operations overseas, including the Pulitzer Prize for Beat Reporting and the George Polk Award for National Reporting. Priest was the *Post*'s Pentagon correspondent for several years and covered the Panama invasion, reported from Iraq, covered the Kosovo war and has also reported from Asia, Africa and South America. Her 2003 book, *The Mission: Waging War and Keeping Peace With America's Military*, was a Pulitzer finalist.

The Walter Reed series is a strong blend of investigative reporting and narrative writing. That's no surprise, as Priest, the investigative reporter, and Hull, the narrative writer, learned much from each other.

Hull told Poynter's Al Tompkins: "One thing I learned from [Priest] is the value in casting something in black and white. Often I'm carried away by the gray. Instantly, Dana can figure out the mission statement or promise—'only the best of care for our nation's wounded'—and juxtapose it with the brokenness of something.... She is an accountability reporter and relentless about her obligation as a journalist."

And about Hull, Priest said: "I wanted to pin down as many moving parts as possible, as quickly as possible, and she wanted to do the opposite—to let a thousand flowers bloom, slowly, at their own, slow-as-molasses, natural pace. What she draws from this is a rare intimacy, and because she is such a great writer, she can then put that on the page for all to feel."

Together, Hull and Priest realized the power that journalists have to create change.

"The Walter Reed stuff landed with a ferocious wallop," Hull said. "Washington—Congress, the Pentagon, the White House—all reacted in dramatic fashion. It was a reminder to everyone in the *Post* newsroom that journalism is still this mighty tool for good."

—Thomas Huang, co-editor of *Best Newspaper Writing*

The Other Walter Reed, Part 1: Soldiers Face Neglect, Frustration at Army's Top Medical Facility

FEB. 18, 2007

By Dana Priest and Anne Hull

Behind the door of Army Spec. Jeremy Duncan's room, part of the wall is torn and hangs in the air, weighted down with black mold. When the wounded combat engineer stands in his shower and looks up, he can see the bathtub on the floor above through a rotted hole. The entire building, constructed between the world wars, often smells like greasy carry-out. Signs of neglect are everywhere: mouse droppings, belly-up cockroaches, stained carpets, cheap mattresses.

This is the world of Building 18, not the kind of place where Duncan expected to recover when he was evacuated to Walter Reed Army Medical Center from Iraq last February with a broken neck and a shredded left ear, nearly dead from blood loss. But the old lodge, just outside the gates of the hospital and five miles up the road from the White House, has housed hundreds of maimed soldiers recuperating from injuries suffered in the wars in Iraq and Afghanistan.

The common perception of Walter Reed is of a surgical hospital that shines as the crown jewel of military medicine. But 5 1/2 years of sustained combat have transformed the venerable 113-acre institution into something else entirely—a holding ground for physically and psychologically damaged outpatients. Almost 700 of them—the majority soldiers, with some Marines—have been released from hospital beds but still need treatment or are awaiting bureaucratic decisions before being discharged or returned to active duty.

They suffer from brain injuries, severed arms and legs, organ and back damage, and various degrees of post-traumatic stress. Their legions have grown so exponentially—they outnumber hospital patients at Walter Reed 17 to 1—that they take up every available bed on post and spill into dozens of nearby hotels and apartments leased by the Army. The average stay is 10 months, but some have been stuck there for as long as two years.

Not all of the quarters are as bleak as Duncan's, but the despair of Building 18 symbolizes a larger problem in Walter Reed's treatment of the

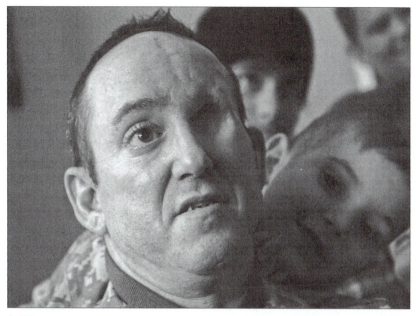

Staff Sgt. John Daniel Shannon has spent more than two years as a patient at Walter Reed Army Medical Center. The former sniper's skull was shattered in a gun battle in Iraq, and he has post-traumatic stress disorder. With him is his 6-year-old son, Drake. (Photograph courtesy of Michel du Cille/*The Washington Post*)

wounded, according to dozens of soldiers, family members, veterans aid groups, and current and former Walter Reed staff members interviewed by two *Washington Post* reporters, who spent more than four months visiting the outpatient world without the knowledge or permission of Walter Reed officials. Many agreed to be quoted by name; others said they feared Army retribution if they complained publicly.

While the hospital is a place of scrubbed-down order and daily miracles, with medical advances saving more soldiers than ever, the outpatients in the Other Walter Reed encounter a messy bureaucratic battlefield nearly as chaotic as the real battlefields they faced overseas.

On the worst days, soldiers say they feel like they are living a chapter of *Catch-22*. The wounded manage other wounded. Soldiers dealing with psychological disorders of their own have been put in charge of others at risk of suicide.

Disengaged clerks, unqualified platoon sergeants and overworked case managers fumble with simple needs: feeding soldiers' families who are close to poverty, replacing a uniform ripped off by medics in the desert sand or helping a brain-damaged soldier remember his next appointment.

"We've done our duty. We fought the war. We came home wounded. Fine. But whoever the people are back here who are supposed to give us the easy transition should be doing it," said Marine Sgt. Ryan Groves, 26, an amputee who lived at Walter Reed for 16 months. "We don't know what to do. The people who are supposed to know don't have the answers. It's a nonstop process of stalling."

Soldiers, family members, volunteers and caregivers who have tried to fix the system say each mishap seems trivial by itself, but the cumulative effect wears down the spirits of the wounded and can stall their recovery.

"It creates resentment and disenfranchisement," said Joe Wilson, a clinical social worker at Walter Reed. "These soldiers will withdraw and stay in their rooms. They will actively avoid the very treatment and services that are meant to be helpful."

Danny Soto, a national service officer for Disabled American Veterans who helps dozens of wounded service members each week at Walter Reed, said soldiers "get awesome medical care and their lives are being saved," but, "Then they get into the administrative part of it and they are like, 'You saved me for what?' The soldiers feel like they are not getting proper respect. This leads to anger."

This world is invisible to outsiders. Walter Reed occasionally showcases the heroism of these wounded soldiers and emphasizes that all is well under the circumstances. President Bush, former defense secretary Donald H. Rumsfeld and members of Congress have promised the best care during their regular visits to the hospital's spit-polished amputee unit, Ward 57.

"We owe them all we can give them," Bush said during his last visit, a few days before Christmas. "Not only for when they're in harm's way, but when they come home to help them adjust if they have wounds, or help them adjust after their time in service."

Along with the government promises, the American public, determined not to repeat the divisive Vietnam experience, has embraced the soldiers even as the war grows more controversial at home. Walter Reed is awash in the generosity of volunteers, businesses and celebrities who donate money, plane tickets, telephone cards and steak dinners.

Yet at a deeper level, the soldiers say they feel alone and frustrated. Seventy-five percent of the troops polled by Walter Reed last March said their experience was "stressful." Suicide attempts and unintentional overdoses from prescription drugs and alcohol, which is sold on post, are part of the narrative here.

Vera Heron spent 15 frustrating months living on post to help care for her son. "It just absolutely took forever to get anything done," Heron said.

"They do the paperwork, they lose the paperwork. Then they have to redo the paperwork. You are talking about guys and girls whose lives are disrupted for the rest of their lives, and they don't put any priority on it."

Family members who speak only Spanish have had to rely on Salvadoran housekeepers, a Cuban bus driver, the Panamanian bartender and a Mexican floor cleaner for help. Walter Reed maintains a list of bilingual staffers, but they are rarely called on, according to soldiers and families and Walter Reed staff members.

Evis Morales' severely wounded son was transferred to the National Naval Medical Center in Bethesda for surgery shortly after she arrived at Walter Reed. She had checked into her government-paid room on post, but she slept in the lobby of the Bethesda hospital for two weeks because no one told her there is a free shuttle between the two facilities. "They just let me off the bus and said 'Bye-bye,'" recalled Morales, a Puerto Rico resident.

Morales found help after she ran out of money, when she called a hotline number and a Spanish-speaking operator happened to answer.

"If they can have Spanish-speaking recruits to convince my son to go into the Army, why can't they have Spanish-speaking translators when he's injured?" Morales asked. "It's so confusing, so disorienting."

Soldiers, wives, mothers, social workers and the heads of volunteer organizations have complained repeatedly to the military command about what one called "The Handbook No One Gets" that would explain life as an outpatient. Most soldiers polled in the March survey said they got their information from friends. Only 12 percent said any Army literature had been helpful.

"They've been behind from Day One," said Rep. Thomas M. Davis III (R-Va.), who headed the House Government Reform Committee, which investigated problems at Walter Reed and other Army facilities. "Even the stuff they've fixed has only been patched."

Among the public, Davis said, "there's vast appreciation for soldiers, but there's a lack of focus on what happens to them" when they return. "It's awful."

Maj. Gen. George W. Weightman, commander at Walter Reed, said in an interview last week that a major reason outpatients stay so long, a change from the days when injured soldiers were discharged as quickly as possible, is that the Army wants to be able to hang on to as many soldiers as it can, "because this is the first time this country has fought a war for so long with an all-volunteer force since the Revolution."

Acknowledging the problems with outpatient care, Weightman said Walter Reed has taken steps over the past year to improve conditions for the outpatient army, which at its peak in summer 2005 numbered nearly 900, not to mention the hundreds of family members who come to care for them. One platoon sergeant used to be in charge of 125 patients; now each one manages 30. Platoon sergeants with psychological problems are more carefully screened. And officials have increased the numbers of case managers and patient advocates to help with the complex disability benefit process, which Weightman called "one of the biggest sources of delay."

And to help steer the wounded and their families through the complicated bureaucracy, Weightman said, Walter Reed has recently begun holding twice-weekly informational meetings. "We felt we were pushing information out before, but the reality is, it was overwhelming," he said. "Is it fail-proof? No. But we've put more resources on it."

He said a 21,500-troop increase in Iraq has Walter Reed bracing for "potentially a lot more" casualties.

Bureaucratic Battles

The best-known of the Army's medical centers, Walter Reed opened in 1909 with 10 patients. It has treated the wounded from every war since, and nearly one of every four service members injured in Iraq and Afghanistan.

The outpatients are assigned to one of five buildings attached to the post, including Building 18, just across from the front gates on Georgia Avenue. To accommodate the overflow, some are sent to nearby hotels and apartments. Living conditions range from the disrepair of Building 18 to the relative elegance of Mologne House, a hotel that opened on the post in 1998, when the typical guest was a visiting family member or a retiree on vacation.

The Pentagon has announced plans to close Walter Reed by 2011, but that hasn't stopped the flow of casualties. Three times a week, school buses painted white and fitted with stretchers and blackened windows stream down Georgia Avenue. Sirens blaring, they deliver soldiers groggy from a pain-relief cocktail at the end of their long trip from Iraq via Landstuhl Regional Medical Center in Germany and Andrews Air Force Base.

Staff Sgt. John Daniel Shannon, 43, came in on one of those buses in November 2004 and spent several weeks on the fifth floor of Walter Reed's hospital. His eye and skull were shattered by an AK-47 round. His odyssey in the Other Walter Reed has lasted more than two years, but it began when someone handed him a map of the grounds and told him to find his room across post.

A reconnaissance and land-navigation expert, Shannon was so disoriented that he couldn't even find north. Holding the map, he stumbled around outside the hospital, sliding against walls and trying to keep himself upright, he said. He asked anyone he found for directions.

Shannon had led the 2nd Infantry Division's Ghost Recon Platoon until he was felled in a gun battle in Ramadi. He liked the solitary work of a sniper; "Lone Wolf" was his call name. But he did not expect to be left alone by the Army after such serious surgery and a diagnosis of post-traumatic stress disorder. He had appointments during his first two weeks as an outpatient, then nothing.

"I thought, 'Shouldn't they contact me?'" he said. "I didn't understand the paperwork. I'd start calling phone numbers, asking if I had appointments. I finally ran across someone who said: 'I'm your case manager. Where have you been?'

"Well, I've been here! Jeez Louise, people, I'm your hospital patient!"

Like Shannon, many soldiers with impaired memory from brain injuries sat for weeks with no appointments and no help from the staff to arrange them. Many disappeared even longer. Some simply left for home.

One outpatient, a 57-year-old staff sergeant who had a heart attack in Afghanistan, was given 200 rooms to supervise at the end of 2005. He quickly discovered that some outpatients had left the post months earlier and would check in by phone. "We called them 'call-in patients,'" said Staff Sgt. Mike McCauley, whose dormant PTSD from Vietnam was triggered by what he saw on the job: so many young and wounded, and three bodies being carried from the hospital.

Life beyond the hospital bed is a frustrating mountain of paperwork. The typical soldier is required to file 22 documents with eight different commands—most of them off-post—to enter and exit the medical processing world, according to government investigators. Sixteen different information systems are used to process the forms, but few of them can communicate with one another. The Army's three personnel databases cannot read each other's files and can't interact with the separate pay system or the medical recordkeeping databases.

The disappearance of necessary forms and records is the most common reason soldiers languish at Walter Reed longer than they should, according to soldiers, family members and staffers. Sometimes the Army has no record that a soldier even served in Iraq. A combat medic who did three tours had to bring in letters and photos of herself in Iraq to show that she had been there, after a clerk couldn't find a record of her service.

Shannon, who wears an eye patch and a visible skull implant, said he had to prove he had served in Iraq when he tried to get a free uniform to replace the bloody one left behind on a medic's stretcher. When he finally tracked down the supply clerk, he discovered the problem: His name was mistakenly left off the "GWOT list"—the list of "Global War on Terrorism" patients with priority funding from the Defense Department.

He brought his Purple Heart to the clerk to prove he was in Iraq.

Lost paperwork for new uniforms has forced some soldiers to attend their own Purple Heart ceremonies and the official birthday party for the Army in gym clothes, only to be chewed out by superiors.

The Army has tried to re-create the organization of a typical military unit at Walter Reed. Soldiers are assigned to one of two companies while they are outpatients—the Medical Holding Company (Medhold) for active-duty soldiers and the Medical Holdover Company for Reserve and National Guard soldiers. The companies are broken into platoons that are led by platoon sergeants, the Army equivalent of a parent.

Under normal circumstances, good sergeants know everything about the soldiers under their charge: vices and talents, moods and bad habits, even family stresses.

At Walter Reed, however, outpatients have been drafted to serve as platoon sergeants and have struggled with their responsibilities. Sgt. David Thomas, a 42-year-old amputee with the Tennessee National Guard, said his platoon sergeant couldn't remember his name. "We wondered if he had mental problems," Thomas said. "Sometimes I'd wear my leg, other times I'd take my wheelchair. He would think I was a different person. We thought, 'My God, has this man lost it?'"

Civilian care coordinators and case managers are supposed to track injured soldiers and help them with appointments, but government investigators and soldiers complain that they are poorly trained and often do not understand the system.

One amputee, a senior enlisted man who asked not to be identified because he is back on active duty, said he received orders to report to a base in Germany as he sat drooling in his wheelchair in a haze of medication. "I went to Medhold many times in my wheelchair to fix it, but no one there could help me," he said.

Finally, his wife met an aide to then-Deputy Defense Secretary Paul D. Wolfowitz, who got the erroneous paperwork corrected with one phone call. When the aide called with the news, he told the soldier, "They don't even know you exist."

"They didn't know who I was or where I was," the soldier said. "And I was in contact with my platoon sergeant every day."

The lack of accountability weighed on Shannon. He hated the isolation of the younger troops. The Army's failure to account for them each day wore on him. When a 19-year-old soldier down the hall died, Shannon knew he had to take action.

The soldier, Cpl. Jeremy Harper, returned from Iraq with PTSD after seeing three buddies die. He kept his room dark, refused his combat medals and always seemed heavily medicated, said people who knew him. According to his mother, Harper was drunkenly wandering the lobby of the Mologne House on New Year's Eve 2004, looking for a ride home to West Virginia. The next morning he was found dead in his room. An autopsy showed alcohol poisoning, she said.

"I can't understand how they could have let kids under the age of 21 have liquor," said Victoria Harper, crying. "He was supposed to be right there at Walter Reed hospital.... I feel that they didn't take care of him or watch him as close as they should have."

The Army posthumously awarded Harper a Bronze Star for his actions in Iraq.

Shannon viewed Harper's death as symptomatic of a larger tragedy—the Army had broken its covenant with its troops. "Somebody didn't take care of him," he would later say. "It makes me want to cry."

Shannon and another soldier decided to keep tabs on the brain injury ward. "I'm a staff sergeant in the U.S. Army, and I take care of people," he said. The two soldiers walked the ward every day with a list of names. If a name dropped off the large white board at the nurses' station, Shannon would hound the nurses to check their files and figure out where the soldier had gone.

Sometimes the patients had been transferred to another hospital. If they had been released to one of the residences on post, Shannon and his buddy would pester the front desk managers to make sure the new charges were indeed there. "But two out of 10, when I asked where they were, they'd just say, 'They're gone,'" Shannon said.

Even after Weightman and his commanders instituted new measures to keep better track of soldiers, two young men left post one night in November and died in a high-speed car crash in Virginia. The driver was supposed to be restricted to Walter Reed because he had tested positive for illegal drugs, Weightman said.

Part of the tension at Walter Reed comes from a setting that is both military and medical. Marine Sgt. Ryan Groves, the squad leader who lost one

In his room in Walter Reed's Building 18, Spec. Jeremy Duncan lives with black mold, damaged walls and a hole in the ceiling of his shower. But he says he would rather live there than share a different room with a stranger. (Photograph courtesy of Michel du Cille/*The Washington Post*)

leg and the use of his other in a grenade attack, said his recovery was made more difficult by a Marine liaison officer who had never seen combat but dogged him about having his mother in his room on post. The rules allowed her to be there, but the officer said she was taking up valuable bed space.

"When you join the Marine Corps, they tell you, you can forget about your mama. 'You have no mama. We are your mama,'" Groves said. "That training works in combat. It doesn't work when you are wounded."

Frustration at Every Turn

The frustrations of an outpatient's day begin before dawn. On a dark, rain-soaked morning this winter, Sgt. Archie Benware, 53, hobbled over to his National Guard platoon office at Walter Reed. Benware had done two tours in Iraq. His head had been crushed between two 2,100-pound concrete barriers in Ramadi, and now it was dented like a tin can. His legs were stiff from knee surgery. But here he was, trying to take care of business.

At the platoon office, he scanned the white board on the wall. Six soldiers were listed as AWOL. The platoon sergeant was nowhere to be found, leaving several soldiers stranded with their requests.

Benware walked around the corner to arrange a dental appointment—his teeth were knocked out in the accident. He was told by a case manager that another case worker, not his doctor, would have to approve the procedure.

"Goddamn it, that's unbelievable!" snapped his wife, Barb, who accompanied him because he can no longer remember all of his appointments.

Not as unbelievable as the time he received a manila envelope containing the gynecological report of a young female soldier.

Next came 7 a.m. formation, one way Walter Reed tries to keep track of hundreds of wounded. Formation is also held to maintain some discipline. Soldiers limp to the old Red Cross building in rain, ice and snow. Army regulations say they can't use umbrellas, even here. A triple amputee has mastered the art of putting on his uniform by himself and rolling in just in time. Others are so gorked out on pills that they seem on the verge of nodding off.

"Fall in!" a platoon sergeant shouted at Friday formation. The noisy room of soldiers turned silent.

An Army chaplain opened with a verse from the Bible. "Why are we here?" she asked. She talked about heroes and service to country. "We were injured in many ways."

Someone announced free tickets to hockey games, a Ravens game, a movie screening, a dinner at McCormick and Schmick's, all compliments of local businesses.

Every formation includes a safety briefing. Usually it is a warning about mixing alcohol with meds, or driving too fast, or domestic abuse. "Do not beat your spouse or children. Do not let your spouse or children beat you," a sergeant said, to laughter. This morning's briefing included a warning about black ice, a particular menace to the amputees.

Dress warm, the sergeant said. "I see some guys rolling around in their wheelchairs in 30 degrees in T-shirts."

Soldiers hate formation for its petty condescension. They gutted out a year in the desert, and now they are being treated like children.

"I'm trying to think outside the box here, maybe moving formation to Wagner Gym," the commander said, addressing concerns that formation was too far from soldiers' quarters in the cold weather. "But guess what? Those are nice wood floors. They have to be covered by a tarp. There's a tarp that's got to be rolled out over the wooden floors. Then it has to be cleaned, with 400 soldiers stepping all over it. Then it's got to be rolled up."

"Now, who thinks Wagner Gym is a good idea?"

Explaining this strange world to family members is not easy. At an orientation for new arrivals, a staff sergeant walked them through the idiosyncrasies of Army financing. He said one relative could receive a 15-day advance on the $64 per diem either in cash or as an electronic transfer: "I highly recommend that you take the cash," he said. "There's no guarantee the transfer will get to your bank." The audience yawned.

Actually, he went on, relatives can collect only 80 percent of this advance, which comes to $51.20 a day. "The cashier has no change, so we drop to $50. We give you the rest"—the $1.20 a day—"when you leave."

The crowd was anxious, exhausted. A child crawled on the floor. The sergeant plowed on. "You need to figure out how long your loved one is going to be an inpatient," he said, something even the doctors can't accurately predict from day to day. "Because if you sign up for the lodging advance," which is $150 a day, "and they get out the next day, you owe the government the advance back of $150 a day."

A case manager took the floor to remind everyone that soldiers are required to be in uniform most of the time, though some of the wounded are amputees or their legs are pinned together by bulky braces. "We have break-away clothing with Velcro!" she announced with a smile. "Welcome to Walter Reed!"

A Bleak Life in Building 18

"Building 18! There is a rodent infestation issue!" bellowed the commander to his troops one morning at formation. "It doesn't help when you live like a rodent! I can't believe people live like that! I was appalled by some of your rooms!"

Life in Building 18 is the bleakest homecoming for men and women whose government promised them good care in return for their sacrifices.

One case manager was so disgusted, she bought roach bombs for the rooms. Mouse traps are handed out. It doesn't help that soldiers there subsist on carry-out food because the hospital cafeteria is such a hike on cold nights. They make do with microwaves and hot plates.

Army officials say they "started an aggressive campaign to deal with the mice infestation" last October and that the problem is now at a "manageable level." They also say they will "review all outstanding work orders" in the next 30 days.

Soldiers discharged from the psychiatric ward are often assigned to Building 18. Buses and ambulances blare all night. While injured soldiers pull guard duty in the foyer, a broken garage door allows unmonitored entry from the rear. Struggling with schizophrenia, PTSD, paranoid delusional disorder and traumatic brain injury, soldiers feel especially vulnerable in that setting, just outside the post gates, on a street where drug dealers work the corner at night.

"I've been close to mortars. I've held my own pretty good," said Spec. George Romero, 25, who came back from Iraq with a psychological disorder. "But here…I think it has affected my ability to get over it…dealing with potential threats every day."

After Spec. Jeremy Duncan, 30, got out of the hospital and was assigned to Building 18, he had to navigate across the traffic of Georgia Avenue for appointments. Even after knee surgery, he had to limp back and forth on crutches and in pain. Over time, black mold invaded his room.

But Duncan would rather suffer with the mold than move to another room and share his convalescence in tight quarters with a wounded stranger. "I have mold on the walls, a hole in the shower ceiling, but…I don't want someone waking me up coming in."

Wilson, the clinical social worker at Walter Reed, was part of a staff team that recognized Building 18's toll on the wounded. He mapped out a plan and, in September, was given a $30,000 grant from the Commander's Initiative Account for improvements. He ordered some equipment, including a pool table and air hockey table, which have not yet arrived. A Psychiatry Department functionary held up the rest of the money because she feared that buying a lot of recreational equipment close to Christmas would trigger an audit, Wilson said.

In January, Wilson was told that the funds were no longer available and that he would have to submit a new request. "It's absurd," he said. "Seven months of work down the drain. I have nothing to show for this project. It's a great example of what we're up against."

A pool table and two flat-screen TVs were eventually donated from elsewhere.

But Wilson had had enough. Three weeks ago he turned in his resignation. "It's too difficult to get anything done with this broken-down bureaucracy," he said.

At town hall meetings, the soldiers of Building 18 keep pushing commanders to improve conditions. But some things have gotten worse. In December, a contracting dispute held up building repairs.

"I hate it," said Romero, who stays in his room all day. "There are cockroaches. The elevator doesn't work. The garage door doesn't work. Sometimes there's no heat, no water…. I told my platoon sergeant I want to leave. I told the town hall meeting. I talked to the doctors and medical staff. They just said you kind of got to get used to the outside world…. My platoon sergeant said, 'Suck it up!'"

The Other Walter Reed, Part 2: The Hotel Aftermath

FEB. 19, 2007

By Anne Hull and Dana Priest

The guests of Mologne House have been blown up, shot, crushed and shaken, and now their convalescence takes place among the chandeliers and wingback chairs of the 200-room hotel on the grounds of Walter Reed Army Medical Center.

Oil paintings hang in the lobby of this strange outpost in the war on terrorism, where combat's urgency has been replaced by a trickling fountain in the garden courtyard. The maimed and the newly legless sit in wheelchairs next to a pond, watching goldfish turn lazily through the water.

But the wounded of Mologne House are still soldiers—Hooah!—so their lives are ruled by platoon sergeants. Each morning they must rise at dawn for formation, though many are half-snowed on pain meds and sleeping pills.

In Room 323 the alarm goes off at 5 a.m., but Cpl. Dell McLeod slumbers on. His wife, Annette, gets up and fixes him a bowl of instant oatmeal before going over to the massive figure curled in the bed. An Army counselor taught her that a soldier back from war can wake up swinging, so she approaches from behind.

"Dell," Annette says, tapping her husband. "Dell, get in the shower."

"Dell!" she shouts.

Finally, the yawning hulk sits up in bed. "Okay, baby," he says. An American flag T-shirt is stretched over his chest. He reaches for his dog tags, still the devoted soldier of 19 years, though his life as a warrior has become a paradox. One day he's led on stage at a Toby Keith concert with dozens of other wounded Operation Iraqi Freedom troops from Mologne House, and the next he's sitting in a cluttered cubbyhole at Walter Reed, fighting the Army for every penny of his disability.

McLeod, 41, has lived at Mologne House for a year while the Army figures out what to do with him. He worked in textile and steel mills in rural South Carolina before deploying. Now he takes 23 pills a day, prescribed by various doctors at Walter Reed. Crowds frighten him. He is too anxious to drive. When panic strikes, a soldier friend named Oscar takes him to Baskin-Robbins for vanilla ice cream.

Cpl. Dell McLeod injured his head and spine in an accident on the Iraqi border and was sent to Walter Reed Army Medical Center for treatment. He and his wife, Annette, lived in Mologne House for more than a year, waiting for an Army decision about his future. (Photograph courtesy of Michel du Cille/*The Washington Post*)

"They find ways to soothe each other," Annette says.

Mostly what the soldiers do together is wait: for appointments, evaluations, signatures and lost paperwork to be found. It's like another wife told Annette McLeod: "If Iraq don't kill you, Walter Reed will."

After Iraq, a New Struggle

The conflict in Iraq has hatched a virtual town of desperation and dysfunction, clinging to the pilings of Walter Reed. The wounded are socked away for months and years in random buildings and barracks in and around this military post.

The luckiest stay at Mologne House, a four-story hotel on a grassy slope behind the hospital. Mologne House opened 10 years ago as a short-term lodging facility for military personnel, retirees and their family members. Then came Sept. 11 and five years of sustained warfare. Now, the silver walkers of retired generals convalescing from hip surgery have been replaced by prosthetics propped against Xbox games and Jessica Simpson posters smiling down on brain-rattled grunts.

Two *Washington Post* reporters spent hundreds of hours in Mologne House documenting the intimate struggles of the wounded who live there. The reporting was done without the knowledge or permission of Walter

Reed officials, but all those directly quoted in this article agreed to be interviewed.

The hotel is built in the Georgian revival style, and inside it offers the usual amenities: daily maid service, front-desk clerks in formal vests and a bar off the lobby that opens every afternoon.

But at this bar, the soldier who orders a vodka tonic one night says to the bartender, "If I had two hands, I'd order two." The customers sitting around the tables are missing limbs, their ears are melted off, and their faces are tattooed purple by shrapnel patterns.

Most everyone has a story about the day they blew up: the sucking silence before immolation, how the mouth filled with tar, the lungs with gas.

"First thing I said was, '[Expletive], that was my *good* eye,'" a soldier with an eye patch tells an amputee in the bar.

The amputee peels his beer label. "I was awake through the whole thing," he says. "It was my first patrol. The second [expletive] day in Iraq and I get blown up."

When a smooth-cheeked soldier with no legs orders a fried chicken dinner and two bottles of grape soda to go, a kitchen worker comes out to his wheelchair and gently places the Styrofoam container on his lap.

A scrawny young soldier sits alone in his wheelchair at a nearby table, his eyes closed and his chin dropped to his chest, an empty Corona bottle in front of him.

Those who aren't old enough to buy a drink at the bar huddle outside near a magnolia tree and smoke cigarettes. Wearing hoodies and furry bedroom slippers, they look like kids at summer camp who've crept out of their rooms, except some have empty pants legs or limbs pinned by medieval-looking hardware. Medication is a favorite topic.

"Dude, [expletive] Paxil saved my life."

"I been on methadone for a year, I'm tryin' to get off it."

"I didn't take my Seroquel last night and I had nightmares of charred bodies, burned crispy like campfire marshmallows."

Mologne House is afloat on a river of painkillers and antipsychotic drugs. One night, a strapping young infantryman loses it with a woman who is high on her son's painkillers. "Quit taking all the soldier medicine!" he screams.

Pill bottles clutter the nightstands: pills for depression or insomnia, to stop nightmares and pain, to calm the nerves.

Here at Hotel Aftermath, a crash of dishes in the cafeteria can induce seizures in the combat-addled. If a taxi arrives and the driver looks Middle Eastern, soldiers refuse to get in. Even among the gazebos and tranquility of the Walter Reed campus in upper Northwest Washington, manhole covers are sidestepped for fear of bombs and rooftops are scanned for snipers.

Bomb blasts are the most common cause of injury in Iraq, and nearly 60 percent of the blast victims also suffer from traumatic brain injury, according to Walter Reed's studies, which explains why some at Mologne House wander the hallways trying to remember their room numbers.

Some soldiers and Marines have been here for 18 months or longer. Doctor's appointments and evaluations are routinely dragged out and difficult to get. A board of physicians must review hundreds of pages of medical records to determine whether a soldier is fit to return to duty. If not, the Physical Evaluation Board must decide whether to assign a rating for disability compensation. For many, this is the start of a new and bitter battle.

Months roll by and life becomes a blue-and-gold hotel room where the bathroom mirror shows the naked disfigurement of war's ravages. There are toys in the lobby of Mologne House because children live here. Domestic disputes occur because wives or girlfriends have moved here. Financial tensions are palpable. After her husband's traumatic injury insurance policy came in, one wife cleared out with the money. Older National Guard members worry about the jobs they can no longer perform back home.

While Mologne House has a full bar, there is not one counselor or psychologist assigned there to assist soldiers and families in crisis—an idea proposed by Walter Reed social workers but rejected by the military command that runs the post.

After a while, the bizarre becomes routine. On Friday nights, antiwar protesters stand outside the gates of Walter Reed holding signs that say "Love Troops, Hate War, Bring them Home Now." Inside the gates, doctors in white coats wait at the hospital entrance for the incoming bus full of newly wounded soldiers who've just landed at Andrews Air Force Base.

And set back from the gate, up on a hill, Mologne House, with a bowl of red apples on the front desk.

Into the Twilight Zone

Dell McLeod's injury was utterly banal. He was in his 10th month of deployment with the 178th Field Artillery Regiment of the South Carolina National Guard near the Iraqi border when he was smashed in the head by a steel cargo door of an 18-wheeler. The hinges of the door had been tied together with a plastic hamburger-bun bag. Dell was knocked out cold and cracked several vertebrae.

When Annette learned that he was being shipped to Walter Reed, she took a leave from her job on the assembly line at Stanley Tools and packed the car. The Army would pay her $64 a day to help care for her husband and would let her live with him at Mologne House until he recovered.

A year later, they are still camped out in the twilight zone. Dogs are periodically brought in by the Army to search the rooms for contraband or weapons. When the fire alarm goes off, the amputees who live on the upper floors are scooped up and carried down the stairwell, while a brigade of mothers passes down the wheelchairs. One morning Annette opens her door and is told to stay in the room because a soldier down the hall has overdosed.

In between, there are picnics at the home of the chairman of the Joint Chiefs of Staff and a charity-funded dinner cruise on the Potomac for "Today's troops, tomorrow's veterans, always heroes."

Dell and Annette's weekdays are spent making the rounds of medical appointments, physical therapy sessions and evaluations for Dell's discharge from the Army. After 19 years, he is no longer fit for service. He uses a cane to walk. He is unable to count out change in the hospital cafeteria. He takes four Percocets a day for pain and has gained 40 pounds from medication and inactivity. Lumbering and blue-eyed, Dell is a big ox baby.

Annette puts on makeup every morning and does her hair, some semblance of normalcy, but her new job in life is watching Dell.

"I'm worried about how he's gonna fit into society," she says one night, as Dell wanders down the hall to the laundry room.

The more immediate worry concerns his disability rating. Army doctors are disputing that Dell's head injury was the cause of his mental impairment. One report says that he was slow in high school and that his cognitive problems could be linked to his native intelligence rather than to his injury.

"They said, 'Well, he was in Title I math,' like he was retarded," Annette says. "Well, y'all took him, didn't you?"

The same fight is being waged by their friends, who aren't the young warriors in Army posters but middle-age men who left factory jobs to deploy to Iraq with their Guard units. They were fit enough for war, but now they are facing teams of Army doctors scrutinizing their injuries for signs of pre-existing conditions, lessening their chance for disability benefits.

Dell and Annette's closest friend at Mologne House is a 47-year-old Guard member who was driving an Army vehicle through the Iraqi night when a flash of light blinded him and he crashed into a ditch with an eight-foot drop. Among his many injuries was a broken foot that didn't heal properly. Army doctors decided that "late life atrophy" was responsible for the foot, not the truck wreck in Iraq.

When Dell sees his medical records, he explodes. "Special ed is for the mentally retarded, and I'm not mentally retarded, right, babe?" he asks Annette. "I graduated from high school. I did some college. I worked in a steel mill."

It's after 9 one night and Dell and Annette are both exhausted, but Dell still needs to practice using voice-recognition software. Reluctantly, he mutes *The Ultimate Fighting Challenge* on TV and sits next to Annette in bed with a laptop.

"My name is Wendell," he says. "Wendell Woodward McLeod Jr."

Annette tells him to sit up. "Spell 'dog,'" she says, softly.

"Spell 'dog,'" he repeats.

"Listen to me," she says.

"Listen to me." He slumps on the pillow. His eyes drift toward the wrestlers on TV.

"You are not working hard enough, Dell," Annette says, pleading. "Wake up."

"Wake up," he says.

"Dell, come on now!"

For Some, a Grim Kind of Fame

No one questions Sgt. Bryan Anderson's sacrifice. One floor above Dell and Annette's room at Mologne House, he holds the gruesome honor of being one of the war's five triple amputees. Bryan, 25, lost both legs and his left arm when a roadside bomb exploded next to the Humvee he was driving with the 411th Military Police Company. Modern medicine saved him and now he's the pride of the prosthetics team at Walter Reed. Tenacious and wisecracking, he wrote "[Expletive] Iraq" on his left leg socket.

Amputees are the first to receive celebrity visitors, job offers and extravagant trips, but Bryan is in a league of his own. Johnny Depp's people want to hook up in London or Paris. The actor Gary Sinise, who played an angry Vietnam amputee in *Forrest Gump,* sends his regards. And *Esquire* magazine is setting up a photo shoot.

Bryan's room at Mologne House is stuffed with gifts from corporate America and private citizens: $350 Bose noise-canceling headphones, nearly a thousand DVDs sent by well-wishers and quilts made by church grannies. The door prizes of war. Two flesh-colored legs are stacked on the floor. A computerized hand sprouting blond hair is on the table.

One Saturday afternoon, Bryan is on his bed downloading music. Without his prosthetics, he weighs less than 100 pounds. "Mom, what time is our plane?" he asks his mother, Janet Waswo, who lives in the room with him. A movie company is flying them to Boston for the premiere of a documentary about amputee hand-cyclers in which Bryan appears.

Representing the indomitable spirit of the American warrior sometimes becomes too much, and Bryan turns off his phone.

Perks and stardom do not come to every amputee. Sgt. David Thomas, a gunner with the Tennessee National Guard, spent his first three months at Walter Reed with no decent clothes; medics in Samarra had cut off his uniform. Heavily drugged, missing one leg and suffering from traumatic brain injury, David, 42, was finally told by a physical therapist to go to the Red Cross office, where he was given a T-shirt and sweat pants. He was awarded a Purple Heart but had no underwear.

David tangled with Walter Reed's image machine when he wanted to attend a ceremony for a fellow amputee, a Mexican national who was being granted U.S. citizenship by President Bush. A case worker quizzed him about what he would wear. It was summer, so David said shorts. The case manager said the media would be there and shorts were not advisable because the amputees would be seated in the front row.

"'Are you telling me that I can't go to the ceremony 'cause I'm an amputee?'" David recalled asking. "She said, 'No, I'm saying you need to wear pants.'"

David told the case worker, "I'm not ashamed of what I did, and y'all shouldn't be neither." When the guest list came out for the ceremony, his name was not on it.

Still, for all its careful choreography of the amputees, Walter Reed offers protection from a staring world. On warm nights at the picnic tables behind Mologne House, someone fires up the barbecue grill and someone else makes a beer run to Georgia Avenue.

Bryan Anderson is out here one Friday. "Hey, Bry, what time should we leave in the morning?" asks his best friend, a female soldier also injured in Iraq. The next day is Veterans Day, and Bryan wants to go to Arlington National Cemetery. His pal Gary Sinise will be there, and Bryan wants to give him a signed photo.

Thousands of spectators are already at Arlington the next morning when Bryan and his friend join the surge toward the ceremony at the Tomb of the Unknowns. The sunshine dazzles. Bryan is in his wheelchair. If loss and sacrifice are theoretical to some on this day, here is living proof—three stumps and a crooked boyish smile. Even the acres of tombstones can't compete. Spectators cut their eyes toward him and look away.

Suddenly, the thunder of cannons shakes the sky. The last time Bryan heard this sound, his legs were severed and he was nearly bleeding to death in a fiery Humvee.

Boom. Boom. Boom. Bryan pushes his wheelchair harder, trying to get away from the noise. "Damn it," he says, "when are they gonna stop?"

Bryan's friend walks off by herself and holds her head. The cannon thunder has unglued her, too, and she is crying.

Friends from Ward 54

An old friend comes to visit Dell and Annette. Sgt. Oscar Fernandez spent 14 months at Walter Reed after having a heart attack in Afghanistan. Oscar also had post-traumatic stress disorder, PTSD, a condition that worsened at Walter Reed and landed the 45-year-old soldier in the hospital's psychiatric unit, Ward 54.

Oscar belonged to a tight-knit group of soldiers who were dealing with combat stress and other psychological issues. They would hang out in each other's rooms at night, venting their fury at the Army's Cuckoo's Nest. On weekends they escaped Walter Reed to a Chinese buffet or went shopping for bootleg Spanish DVDs in nearby Takoma Park. They once made a road trip to a casino near the New Jersey border.

They abided each other's frailties. Sgt. Steve Justi would get the slightest cut on his skin and drop to his knees, his face full of anguish, apologizing over and over. For what, Oscar did not know. Steve was the college boy who went to Iraq, and Oscar figured something terrible had happened over there.

Sgt. Mike Smith was the insomniac. He'd stay up till 2 or 3 in the morning, smoking on the back porch by himself. Doctors had put steel rods in his neck after a truck accident in Iraq. To turn his head, the 41-year-old Guard member from Iowa had to rotate his entire body. He was fighting with the Army over his disability rating, too, and in frustration had recently called a congressional investigator for help.

"They try in all their power to have you get well, but it reverses itself," Oscar liked to say.

Dell was not a psych patient, but he and Oscar bonded. They were an unlikely pair—the dark-haired Cuban American with a penchant for polo shirts and salsa, and the molasses earnestness of Dell.

Oscar would say things like "I'm trying to better myself through my own recognizance," and Dell would nod in appreciation.

To celebrate Oscar's return visit to Walter Reed, they decide to have dinner in Silver Spring.

Annette tells Oscar that a soldier was arrested at Walter Reed for waving a gun around.

"A soldier, coming from war?" Oscar asks.

Annette doesn't know. She mentions that another soldier was kicked out of Mologne House for selling his painkillers.

The talk turns to their friend Steve Justi. A few days earlier, Steve was discharged from the Army and given a zero percent disability rating for his mental condition.

Oscar is visibly angry. "They gave him nothing," he says. "They said his bipolar was preexisting."

Annette is quiet. "Poor Steve," she says.

After dinner, they return through the gates of Walter Reed in Annette's car, a John 3:16 decal on the bumper and the Dixie Chicks in the CD player. Annette sees a flier in the lobby of Mologne House announcing a free trip to see Toby Keith in concert.

A week later, it is a wonderful night at the Nissan Pavilion. About 70 wounded soldiers from Walter Reed attend the show. Toby invites them up on stage and brings the house down when he sings his monster wartime hit "American Soldier." Dell stands on stage in his uniform while Annette snaps pictures.

"Give a hand clap for the soldiers," Annette hears Toby tell the audience, "then give a hand for the U.S.A."

A Soldier Snaps

Deep into deer-hunting country and fields of withered corn, past the Pennsylvania Turnpike in the rural town of Ellwood City, Steve Justi sits in his parents' living room, fighting off the afternoon's lethargy.

A photo on a shelf shows a chiseled soldier, but the one in the chair is 35 pounds heavier. Antipsychotic drugs give him tremors and cloud his mind. Still, he is deliberate and thoughtful as he explains his path from soldier to psychiatric patient in the war on terrorism.

After receiving a history degree from Mercyhurst College, Steve was motivated by the attacks of Sept. 11, 2001, to join the National Guard. He landed in Iraq in 2003 with the First Battalion, 107th Field Artillery, helping the Marines in Fallujah.

"It was just the normal stuff," Steve says, describing the violence he witnessed in Iraq. His voice is oddly flat as he recalls the day his friend died in a Humvee accident. The friend was driving with another soldier when they flipped off the road into a swamp. They were trapped upside down and submerged. Steve helped pull them out and gave CPR, but it was too late. The swamp water kept pushing back into his own mouth. He rode in the helicopter with the wet bodies.

After he finished his tour, everything was fine back home in Pennsylvania for about 10 months, and then a strange bout of insomnia started. After four days without sleep, he burst into full-out mania and was hospitalized in restraints.

Did anything trigger the insomnia? "Not really," Steve says calmly, sitting in his chair.

His mother overhears this from the kitchen and comes into the living room. "His sergeant had called saying that the unit was looking for volunteers to go back to Iraq," Cindy Justi says. "This is what triggered his snap."

Steve woke up in the psychiatric unit at Walter Reed and spent the next six months going back and forth between there and a room at Mologne House. He was diagnosed with bipolar disorder. He denied to doctors that he was suffering from PTSD, yet he called home once from Ward 54 and shouted into the phone, "Mom, can't you hear all the shooting in the background?"

He was on the ward for the sixth time when he was notified that he was being discharged from the Army, with only a few days to clear out and a disability rating of zero percent.

On some level, Steve expected the zero rating. During his senior year of college, he suffered a nervous breakdown and for several months was treated with antidepressants. He disclosed this to the National Guard recruiter, who said it was a nonissue. It became an issue when he told doctors at Walter Reed. The Army decided that his condition was not aggravated by his time in Iraq. The only help he would get would come from Veterans Affairs.

"We have no idea if what he endured over there had a worsening effect on him," says his mother.

His father gets home from the office. Ron Justi sits on the couch across from his son. "He was okay to sacrifice his body, but now that it's time he needs some help, they are not here," Ron says.

Outside the Gates

The Army gives Dell McLeod a discharge date. His days at Mologne House are numbered. The cramped hotel room has become home, and now he is afraid to leave it. His anxiety worsens. "Shut up!" he screams at Annette one night, his face red with rage, when she tells him to stop fiddling with his wedding ring.

Later, Annette says: "I am exhausted. He doesn't understand that I've been fighting the Army."

Doctors have concluded that Dell was slow as a child and that his head injury on the Iraqi border did not cause brain damage. "It is possible that pre-morbid emotional difficulties and/or pre-morbid intellectual functioning may be contributing factors to his reported symptoms," a doctor wrote, withholding a diagnosis of traumatic brain injury.

Annette pushes for more brain testing and gets nowhere until someone gives her the name of a staffer for the House Committee on Oversight and Government Reform. A few days later, Annette is called to a meeting with the command at Walter Reed. Dell is given a higher disability rating than expected—50 percent, which means he will receive half of his base pay until he is evaluated again in 18 months. He signs the papers.

Dell wears his uniform for the last time, somber and careful as he dresses for formation. Annette packs up the room and loads their Chevy Cavalier to the brim. Finally the gates of Walter Reed are behind them. They are southbound on I-95 just past the Virginia line when Dell begins to cry, Annette would later recall. She pulls over and they both weep.

Not long after, Bryan Anderson also leaves Mologne House. When the triple amputee gets off the plane in Chicago, American Airlines greets him on the tarmac with hoses spraying arches of water, and cheering citizens line the roads that lead to his home town, Rolling Meadows.

Bryan makes the January cover of Esquire. He is wearing his beat-up cargo shorts and an Army T-shirt, legless and holding his Purple Heart in his robot hand. The headline says "The Meaning of Life."

A month after Bryan leaves, Mike Smith, the insomniac soldier, is found dead in his room. Mike had just received the good news that the Army was raising his disability rating after a congressional staff member intervened on his behalf. It was the week before Christmas, and he was set to leave Walter Reed to go home to his wife and kids in Iowa when his body was found. The Army told his wife that he died of an apparent heart attack, according to her father.

Distraught, Oscar Fernandez calls Dell and Annette in South Carolina with the news. "It's the constant assault of the Army," he says.

Life with Dell is worsening. He can't be left alone. The closest VA hospital is two hours away. Doctors say he has liver problems because of all the medications. He is also being examined for PTSD. "I don't even know this man anymore," Annette says.

At Mologne House, the rooms empty and fill, empty and fill. The lobby chandelier glows and the bowl of red apples waits on the front desk. An announcement goes up for Texas Hold 'Em poker in the bar.

One cold night an exhausted mother with two suitcases tied together with rope shows up at the front desk and says, "I am here for my son." And so it begins.

The War Inside

JUNE 17, 2007

By Dana Priest and Anne Hull

Army Spec. Jeans Cruz helped capture Saddam Hussein. When he came home to the Bronx, important people called him a war hero and promised to help him start a new life. The mayor of New York, officials of his parents' home town in Puerto Rico, the borough president and other local dignitaries honored him with plaques and silk parade sashes. They handed him their business cards and urged him to phone.

But a "black shadow" had followed Cruz home from Iraq, he confided to an Army counselor. He was hounded by recurring images of how war really was for him: not the triumphant scene of Hussein in handcuffs, but visions of dead Iraqi children.

In public, the former Army scout stood tall for the cameras and marched in the parades. In private, he slashed his forearms to provoke the pain and adrenaline of combat. He heard voices and smelled stale blood. Soon the offers of help evaporated and he found himself estranged and alone, struggling with financial collapse and a darkening depression.

At a low point, he went to the local Department of Veterans Affairs medical center for help. One VA psychologist diagnosed Cruz with post-traumatic stress disorder. His condition was labeled "severe and chronic." In a letter supporting his request for PTSD-related disability pay, the psychologist wrote that Cruz was "in need of major help" and that he had provided "more than enough evidence" to back up his PTSD claim. His combat experiences, the letter said, "have been well documented."

None of that seemed to matter when his case reached VA disability evaluators. They turned him down flat, ruling that he deserved no compensation because his psychological problems existed before he joined the Army. They also said that Cruz had not proved he was ever in combat. "The available evidence is insufficient to confirm that you actually engaged in combat," his rejection letter stated.

Yet abundant evidence of his year in combat with the 4th Infantry Division covers his family's living-room wall. The Army Commendation Medal With Valor for "meritorious actions...during strategic combat operations" to capture Hussein hangs not far from the combat spurs awarded

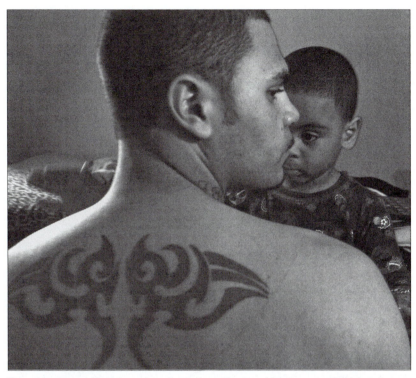

"I'm pushing the mental limits," says Jeans Cruz, a former Army specialist who saw combat in Iraq. He cares for his parents and 4-year-old son, Jeans Jr., in the Bronx while struggling with post-traumatic stress disorder. Veterans Affairs has denied his request for disability compensation. (Photograph courtesy of Michel du Cille/*The Washington Post*)

for his work with the 10th Cavalry "Eye Deep" scouts, attached to an elite unit that caught the Iraqi leader on Dec. 13, 2003, at Ad Dawr.

Veterans Affairs will spend $2.8 billion this year on mental health. But the best it could offer Cruz was group therapy at the Bronx VA medical center. Not a single session is held on the weekends or late enough at night for him to attend. At age 25, Cruz is barely keeping his life together. He supports his disabled parents and 4-year-old son and cannot afford to take time off from his job repairing boilers. The rough, dirty work, with its heat and loud noises, gives him panic attacks and flesh burns but puts $96 in his pocket each day.

Once celebrated by his government, Cruz feels defeated by its bureaucracy. He no longer has the stamina to appeal the VA decision, or to make the Army correct the sloppy errors in his medical records or amend his personnel file so it actually lists his combat awards.

"I'm pushing the mental limits as it is," Cruz said, standing outside the bullet-pocked steel door of the New York City housing project on Webster Avenue where he grew up and still lives with his family. "My experience so far is, you ask for something and they deny, deny, deny. After a while you just give up."

An Old and Growing Problem

Jeans Cruz and his contemporaries in the military were never supposed to suffer in the shadows the way veterans of the last long, controversial war did. One of the bitter legacies of Vietnam was the inadequate treatment of troops when they came back. Tens of thousands endured psychological disorders in silence, and too many ended up homeless, alcoholic, drug-addicted, imprisoned or dead before the government acknowledged their conditions and in 1980 officially recognized PTSD as a medical diagnosis.

Yet nearly three decades later, the government still has not mastered the basics: how best to detect the disorder, the most effective ways to treat it, and the fairest means of compensating young men and women who served their country and returned unable to lead normal lives.

Cruz's case illustrates these broader problems at a time when the number of suffering veterans is the largest and fastest-growing in decades, and when many of them are back at home with no monitoring or care. Between 1999 and 2004, VA disability pay for PTSD among veterans jumped 150 percent, to $4.2 billion.

By this spring, the number of vets from Afghanistan and Iraq who had sought help for post-traumatic stress would fill four Army divisions, some 45,000 in all.

They occupy every rank, uniform and corner of the country. People such as Army Lt. Sylvia Blackwood, who was admitted to a locked-down psychiatric ward in Washington after trying to hide her distress for a year and a half; and Army Pfc. Joshua Calloway, who spent eight months at Walter Reed Army Medical Center and left barely changed from when he arrived from Iraq in handcuffs; and retired Marine Lance Cpl. Jim Roberts, who struggles to keep his sanity in suburban New York with the help of once-a-week therapy and a medicine cabinet full of prescription drugs; and the scores of Marines in California who were denied treatment for PTSD because the head psychiatrist on their base thought the diagnosis was overused.

They represent the first wave in what experts say is a coming deluge.

As many as one-quarter of all soldiers and Marines returning from Iraq are psychologically wounded, according to a recent American Psychological Association report. Twenty percent of the soldiers in Iraq screened positive for anxiety, depression and acute stress, an Army study found.

But numbers are only part of the problem. The Institute of Medicine reported last month that Veterans Affairs' methods for deciding compensation for PTSD and other emotional disorders had little basis in science and that the evaluation process varied greatly. And as they try to work their way through a confounding disability process, already-troubled vets enter a VA system that chronically loses records and sags with a backlog of 400,000 claims of all kinds.

The disability process has come to symbolize the bureaucratic confusion over PTSD. To qualify for compensation, troops and veterans are required to prove that they witnessed at least one traumatic event, such as the death of a fellow soldier or an attack from a roadside bomb, or IED. That standard has been used to deny thousands of claims. But many experts now say that debilitating stress can result from accumulated trauma as well as from one significant event.

In an interview, even VA's chief of mental health questioned whether the single-event standard is a valid way to measure PTSD. "One of the things I puzzle about is, what if someone hasn't been exposed to an IED but lives in dread of exposure to one for a month?" said Ira R. Katz, a psychiatrist. "According to the formal definition, they don't qualify."

The military is also battling a crisis in mental-health care. Licensed psychologists are leaving at a far faster rate than they are being replaced. Their ranks have dwindled from 450 to 350 in recent years. Many said they left because they could not handle the stress of facing such pained soldiers. Inexperienced counselors muddle through, using therapies better suited for alcoholics or marriage counseling.

A new report by the Defense Department's Mental Health Task Force says the problems are even deeper. Providers of mental-health care are "not sufficiently accessible" to service members and are inadequately trained, it says, and evidence-based treatments are not used. The task force recommends an overhaul of the military's mental-health system, according to a draft of the report.

Another report, commissioned by Defense Secretary Robert M. Gates in the wake of the Walter Reed outpatient scandal, found similar problems: "There is not a coordinated effort to provide the training required to identify and treat these non-visible injuries, nor adequate research in order to develop the required training and refine the treatment plans."

But the Army is unlikely to do more significant research anytime soon. "We are at war, and to do good research takes writing up grants, it takes placebo control trials, it takes control groups," said Col. Elspeth Ritchie, the Army's top psychiatrist. "I don't think that that's our primary mission."

In attempting to deal with increasing mental-health needs, the military regularly launches Web sites and promotes self-help guides for soldiers. Maj. Gen. Gale S. Pollock, the Army's acting surgeon general, believes that doubling the number of mental-health professionals and boosting the pay of psychiatrists would help.

But there is another obstacle that those steps could not overcome. "One of my great concerns is the stigma" of mental illness, Pollock said. "That, to me, is an even bigger challenge. I think that in the Army, and in the nation, we have a long way to go." The task force found that stigma in the military remains "pervasive" and is a "significant barrier to care."

Surveys underline the problem. Only 40 percent of the troops who screened positive for serious emotional problems sought help, a recent Army survey found. Nearly 60 percent of soldiers said they would not seek help for mental-health problems because they felt their unit leaders would treat them differently; 55 percent thought they would be seen as weak, and the same percentage believed that soldiers in their units would have less confidence in them.

Lt. Gen. John Vines, who led the 18th Airborne Corps in Iraq and Afghanistan, said countless officers keep quiet out of fear of being mislabeled. "All of us who were in command of soldiers killed or wounded in combat have emotional scars from it," said Vines, who recently retired. "No one I know has sought out care from mental-health specialists, and part of that is a lack of confidence that the system would recognize it as 'normal' in a time of war. This is a systemic problem."

Officers and senior enlisted troops, Vines added, were concerned that they would have trouble getting security clearances if they sought psychological help. They did not trust, he said, that "a faceless, nameless agency or process, that doesn't know them personally, won't penalize them for a perceived lack of mental or emotional toughness."

Overdiagnosed or Overlooked?

For the past 2½ years, the counseling center at the Marine Corps Air Ground Combat Center in Twentynine Palms, Calif., was a difficult place for Marines seeking help for post-traumatic stress. Navy Cmdr. Louis Valbracht, head of mental health at the center's outpatient hospital, often

Lt. Sylvia Blackwood, right, an Army reservist, served two tours in Iraq; when she returned, paranoia and panic set in. For months she sought no help, but after she contemplated suicide she went to Veterans Affairs. She spent a harrowing week in a psychiatric ward in Washington, then ended up at a VA clinic in Kentucky with individual and group therapy. (Photograph courtesy of Michel du Cille/*The Washington Post*)

refused to accept counselors' views that some Marines who were drinking heavily or using drugs had PTSD, according to three counselors and another staff member who worked with him.

"Valbracht didn't believe in it. He'd say there's no such thing as PTSD," said David Roman, who was a substance abuse counselor at Twentynine Palms until he quit six months ago.

"We were all appalled," said Mary Jo Thornton, another counselor who left last year.

A third counselor estimated that perhaps half of the 3,000 Marines he has counseled in the past five years showed symptoms of post-traumatic stress. "They would change the diagnosis right in front of you, put a line through it," said the counselor, who spoke on the condition of anonymity because he still works there.

"I want to see my Marines being taken care of," said Roman, who is now a substance-abuse counselor at the Marine Corps Air Station in Cherry Point, N.C.

In an interview, Valbracht denied he ever told counselors that PTSD does not exist. But he did say "it is overused" as a diagnosis these days, just as "everyone on the East Coast now has a bipolar disorder." He said this "devalues the severity of someone who actually has PTSD," adding: "Nowadays it's like you have a hangnail. Someone comes in and says, 'I have PTSD,'" and counselors want to give them that diagnosis without specific symptoms.

Valbracht, an aerospace medicine specialist, reviewed and signed off on cases at the counseling center. He said some counselors diagnosed Marines with PTSD before determining whether the symptoms persisted for 30 days, the military recommendation. Valbracht often talked to the counselors about his father, a Marine on Iwo Jima who overcame the stress of that battle and wrote an article called, "They Even Laughed on Iwo." Counselors found it outdated and offensive. Valbracht said it showed the resilience of the mind.

Valbracht retired recently because, he said, he "was burned out" after working seven days a week as the only psychiatrist available to about 10,000 Marines in his 180-mile territory. "We could have used two or three more psychiatrists," he said, to ease the caseload and ensure that people were not being overlooked.

Former Lance Cpl. Jim Roberts' underlying mental condition was overlooked by the Marine Corps and successive health-care professionals for more than 30 years, as his temper and alcohol use plunged him into deeper trouble. Only in May 2005 did VA begin treating the Vietnam vet for PTSD. Three out of 10 of his compatriots from Vietnam have received diagnoses of PTSD. Half of those have been arrested at least once. Veterans groups say thousands have killed themselves.

To control his emotions now, Roberts attends group therapy once a week and swallows a handful of pills from his VA doctors: Zoloft, Neurontin, Lisinopril, Seroquel, Ambien, hydroxyzine, "enough medicine to kill a mule," he said.

Roberts desperately wants to persuade Iraq veterans not to take the route he traveled. "The Iraq guys, it's going to take them five to 10 years to become one of us," he said, seated at his kitchen table in Yonkers with his vet friends Nicky, Lenny, Frenchie, Ray and John nodding in agreement. "It's all about the forgotten vets, then and now. The guys from Iraq and Afghanistan, we need to get these guys in here with us."

"In here" can mean different things. It can mean a 1960s-style vet center such as the one where Roberts hangs out, with faded photographs of Huey helicopters and paintings of soldiers skulking through shoulder-high elephant grass. It can mean group therapy at a VA outpatient clinic during work hours, or more comprehensive treatment at a residential clinic. In a crisis, it can mean the locked-down psych ward at the local VA hospital.

"Out there," with no care at all, is a lonesome hell.

Losing a Bureaucratic Battle

Not long after Jeans Cruz returned from Iraq to Fort Hood, Texas, in 2004, his counselor, a low-ranking specialist, suggested that someone should "explore symptoms of PTSD." But there is no indication in Cruz's medical files, which he gave to *The Washington Post*, that anyone ever responded to that early suggestion.

When he met with counselors while he was on active duty, Cruz recalled, they would take notes about his troubled past, including that he had been treated for depression before he entered the Army. But they did not seem interested in his battlefield experiences. "I've shot kids. I've had to kill kids. Sometimes I look at my son and like, I've killed a kid his age," Cruz said. "At times we had to drop a shell into somebody's house. When you go clean up the mess, you had three, four, five, six different kids in there. You had to move their bodies."

When he tried to talk about the war, he said, his counselors "would just sit back and say, 'Uh-huh, uh-huh.' When I told them about the unit I was with and Saddam Hussein, they'd just say, 'Oh, yeah, right.'"

He occasionally saw a psychiatrist, who described him as depressed and anxious. He talked about burning himself with cigarettes and exhibited "anger from Iraq, nightmares, flashbacks," one counselor wrote in his file. "Watched friend die in Iraq. Cuts, bruises himself to relieve anger and frustration." They prescribed Zoloft and trazodone to control his depression and ease his nightmares. They gave him Ambien for sleep, which he declined for a while for fear of missing morning formation.

Counselors at Fort Hood grew concerned enough about Cruz to have him sign what is known as a Life Maintenance Agreement. It stated: "I, Jeans Cruz, agree not to harm myself or anyone else. I will first contact either a member of my direct Chain of Command…or immediately go to the emergency room." That was in October 2004. The next month he signed another one.

Two weeks later, Cruz re-enlisted. He says the Army gave him a $10,000 bonus.

His problems worsened. Three months after he re-enlisted, a counselor wrote in his medical file: "MAJOR depression." After that: "He sees himself in his dreams killing or strangling people.... He is worried about controlling his stress level. Stated that he is starting to drink earlier in the day." A division psychologist, noting Cruz's depression, said that he "did improve when taking medication but has degenerated since stopping medication due to long work hours."

Seven months after his re-enlistment ceremony, the Army gave him an honorable discharge, asserting that he had a "personality disorder" that made him unfit for military service. This determination implied that all his psychological problems existed before his first enlistment. It also disqualified him from receiving combat-related disability pay.

There was little attempt to tie his condition to his experience in Iraq. Nor did the Army see an obvious contradiction in its handling of him: He was encouraged to re-enlist even though his psychological problems had already been documented.

Cruz's records are riddled with obvious errors, including a psychological rating of "normal" on the same physical exam the Army used to discharge him for a psychological disorder. His record omits his combat spurs award and his Army Commendation Medal With Valor. These omissions contributed to the VA decision that he had not proved he had been in combat. To straighten out those errors, Cruz would have had to deal with a chaotic and contradictory paper trail and bureaucracy—a daunting task for an expert lawyer, let alone a stressed-out young veteran.

In the Aug. 16, 2006, VA letter denying Cruz disability pay because he had not provided evidence of combat, evaluators directed him to the U.S. Armed Services Center for Research of Unit Records. But such a place no longer exists. It changed its name to the U.S. Army and Joint Services Records Research Center and moved from one Virginia suburb, Springfield, to another, Alexandria, three years ago. It has a 10-month waiting list for processing requests.

To speed things up, staff members often advise troops to write to the National Archives and Records Administration in Maryland. But that agency has no records from the Iraq war, a spokeswoman said. That would send Cruz back to Fort Hood, whose soldiers have deployed to Iraq twice, leaving few staff members to hunt down records.

But Cruz has given up on the records. Life at the Daniel Webster Houses is tough enough.

After he left the Army and came home to the Bronx, he rode a bus and the subway 45 minutes after work to attend group sessions at the local VA facility. He always arrived late and left frustrated. Listening to the traumas of other veterans only made him feel worse, he said: "It made me more aggravated. I had to get up and leave." Experts say people such as Cruz need individual and occupational therapy.

Medications were easy to come by, but some made him sick. "They made me so slow I didn't want to do nothing with my son or manage my family," he said. After a few months, he stopped taking them, a dangerous step for someone so severely depressed. His drinking became heavier.

To calm himself now, he goes outside and hits a handball against the wall of the housing project. "My son's out of control. There are family problems," he said, shaking his head. "I start seeing these faces. It goes back to flashbacks, anxiety. Sometimes I've got to leave my house because I'm afraid I'm going to hit my son or somebody else."

Because of his family responsibilities, he does not want to be hospitalized. He doesn't think a residential program would work, either, for the same reason.

His needs are more basic. "Why can't I have a counselor with a phone number? I'd like someone to call."

Or some help from all those people who stuck their business cards in his palm during the glory days of his return from Iraq. "I have plaques on my wall—but nothing more than that."

A Wife's Battle

OCT. 14, 2007

By Anne Hull and Dana Priest

Michelle Turner's husband sits in the recliner with the shades drawn. He washes down his Zoloft with Mountain Dew. On the phone in the other room, Michelle is pleading with the utility company to keep their power on.

"Can't you tell them I'm a veteran?" asks her husband, Troy, who served as an Army scout in Baghdad and came back with post-traumatic stress disorder.

"Troy, they don't care," Michelle says, her patience stretched.

The government's sweeping list of promises to make wounded Iraq war veterans whole, at least financially, has not reached this small house in the hills of rural West Virginia, where one vehicle has already been repossessed and the answering machine screens for bill collectors. The Turners have not been making it on an $860-a-month disability check from the Department of Veterans Affairs.

After revelations about the poor treatment of outpatient soldiers at Walter Reed Army Medical Center earlier this year, President Bush appointed a commission to study the care of the nation's war-wounded. The panel returned with bold recommendations, including the creation of a national cadre of caseworkers and a complete overhaul of the military's disability system that compensates wounded soldiers.

But so far, little has been done to sort out the mess of bureaucracy or put more money in the hands of newly disabled soldiers who are fending off evictions and foreclosures.

In the Turner house, that leaves an exhausted wife with chipped nail polish to hold up the family's collapsing world. "Stand Together," a banner at a local cafe reminds Michelle. But since Troy came back from Iraq in 2003, the burden of war is now hers.

Michelle has spent hundreds of hours at the library researching complicated VA policies and disability regulations. "You need two college degrees to understand any of it," she says, lacking both. She scavenges information where she can find it. A psychotic Vietnam vet she met in a VA hospital was the one who told her that Troy might be eligible for Social Security benefits.

Michelle Turner's husband, Troy, a former Army scout, returned from the Iraq war profoundly changed. Disabled by severe post-traumatic stress disorder, he now relies on his wife for everything. "He can't deal with every-day stresses of living," Michelle says. (Photograph courtesy of Michel du Cille/*The Washington Post*)

Meanwhile, there are clothes to wash, meals to cook, kids to get ready for school and a husband who is placidly medicated or randomly explosive. Besides PTSD, Michelle suspects that Troy may have a brain injury, which could explain how a 38-year-old man who used to hunt and fish can lose himself in a three-day *Scooby-Doo* marathon on the Cartoon Network.

"He can't deal with everyday stresses of living," Michelle says. "He can't make decisions. He is a worrywart. Fearful. It's like they took Troy and put him in a different person."

As thousands of war-wounded lug their discharge papers and pill bottles home, more than a quarter are returning with PTSD and brain trauma. Compensation for these invisible injuries is more difficult and the social isolation more profound, especially in rural communities where pastures outnumber mental health providers. Troy's one-year war has become his wife's endless one.

His Illness, Her Full-Time Job

The Turners live in a small rental house in the northern tip of West Virginia, surrounded by enormous blue sky and the dark spine of South

Branch Mountain. There is a VFW tavern in town, but Troy doesn't bother. After one of his distraught soldier buddies from Iraq got so drunk he wrapped his motorcycle around a tree, Troy stays away from alcohol. Still, the techniques he learned to calm his PTSD in Army and VA treatment programs—tai chi meditation and classical music—seem like distant remedies in this county of farm equipment and Ford pickups.

Michelle thinks Troy's anxiety and depression are worsening, and she tells anyone who will listen—her pastor, doctors and counselors at VA. His speech is sometimes soupy from mood stabilizers. The meds give him tremors. He used to cut the grass and bring home a paycheck, but now he stays inside like a perpetual patient. His memory is shot, and he relies on Michelle for everything.

"What is the name of the doctor who looks at knees?" he asks one day.

Michelle takes a breath. "Orthopedic," she says. "Troy, *please try.*"

At 31, her eyes are hollowed by worry and her brown hair is turning gray. The Turners live 80 miles from the Martinsburg VA Medical Center, where Troy receives his care, and sometimes they go once a week. The all-day journey requires a babysitter for the kids—ages 10 and 11, both from previous marriages—and burns $25 worth of precious gas.

"This is the part you don't see on TV," Michelle says.

One hot morning, they set out for Martinsburg yet again. Troy recently screened positive for possible traumatic brain injury—he was exposed to multiple blasts in Iraq—and the hospital wants him back for more comprehensive testing. Troy and Michelle are quiet on the ride into Martinsburg. A Bible rests on the back seat. The cornfields and emerald hills spread out from the two-lane highway. Troy's pill box is between them, along with the silence.

Finally Troy says he thinks his new medication is making him less aggressive.

Michelle is skeptical. "You don't have an 'off' button anymore," she says.

Troy, in the passenger seat, keeps his eyes on the road. "They broke it off when I was over there."

He served with the 3rd Infantry Division during the 2003 invasion of Iraq. Before that, he spent a decade with the National Guard, pulling a tour in Bosnia. A laconic country boy with a plug of tobacco in his cheek, Troy was a cavalry scout with the 3rd Battalion, 15th Infantry Regiment that pressed into Baghdad. His platoon sergeant was decapitated by a rocket-propelled grenade, and others he knew were obliterated.

Troy's problems started after his tour. While he was on home leave from Fort Stewart one weekend, Michelle found him sitting on the bed with a bottle of pills. He said he couldn't go back. Michelle drove him to the Martinsburg VA hospital, which shipped him to Walter Reed for three weeks of psychiatric care.

He was sent back to Fort Stewart and returned to duty, a reality he could not cope with. Twice he tried to commit suicide and was hospitalized at Winn Army Community Hospital before being medically discharged for PTSD in 2004. After 13 years in uniform, Troy got nearly the lowest disability rating possible, a $11,349 severance check and no benefits.

Michelle was dating Troy at the time. She had visited him at Walter Reed. When he asked if she wanted out of the relationship, she said she would stick by him as long as he continued to treat her well. They were married on Valentine's Day in 2005.

For 18 months Troy worked as a truck driver until his symptoms began to worsen. He imagined he saw Army vehicles on the interstate, causing him to shake and panic. His family needed the $2,600-a-month salary, so Troy kept driving and Michelle rode in the truck with him. Finally VA doctors increased Troy's medication, and he became too zonked to drive.

VA rated Troy's disability level at 50 percent, resulting in $860 a month in compensation. Like many wounded soldiers, he was clobbered by a fine-print government regulation known as "concurrent receipt," which prevents double compensation. That meant before he could receive his VA disability check, Troy had to pay back the $11,349 he received when he left the Army. For 13 months, VA withheld his check until the Army amount was reimbursed.

The Turners' foothold in working-class America completely slid away when Michelle—who has worked as a teacher's aide and an inventory-control specialist at Wal-Mart—developed health problems and was forced to quit her job. Now her full-time job is Troy.

His illness has eroded their marriage, but on the morning they arrive at the Martinsburg VA hospital, she leads the charge on his behalf. The concrete behemoth serves 129,000 vets from West Virginia, Maryland, Virginia and Pennsylvania. It is at once efficient and numbingly bureaucratic.

Michelle and Troy move down the hallways, passing a room near the PTSD residence where a group of young vets, some tattooed and still muscled from the desert, are playing a game of ring toss. The cafeteria smells of bleach and canned peaches.

In the small lobby of the neuropsychological department, Troy leans over the sign-in clipboard, pen in hand, staring at the sheet. Michelle tells him what day it is. They sit together on the hard chairs until Troy's name is called.

With two hours to kill, Michelle wanders into the hallway and runs into a Vietnam vet she has befriended. A former Marine with ramrod posture, the vet has PTSD and an encyclopedic knowledge of VA procedures. "Don't take no for an answer," he tells Michelle. "Huntington [a VA regional office] says you are his fiduciary, right?"

"They say they need to come out and do a home study," Michelle says.

The vet shakes his head angrily. "Don't let these people get over on you!"

She returns to the waiting room. A flier on the bulletin board catches her eye: "Coming Soon, Help for Veterans and Families." A door opens, and one of Troy's doctors asks her to step into his office. When Michelle emerges 15 minutes later, she stands alone in the waiting room, twisting the handle of her purse. The doctor said Troy is getting worse.

Not knowing where else to go, Michelle heads upstairs to the PTSD offices. Troy has already done one 45-day stint in the residential program, and Michelle has been trying to get him in again. She knocks on the door of a counselor, a big, bald, friendly man who does not wave off the intrusion.

"You think he's violent at this point?" the counselor asks.

Michelle dodges the question. "He's not getting any counseling," she says, leaning against the door.

The counselor explains that all 50 beds in the program are full and the waiting list is 25 deep. "I apologize for not being able to get him in right away," he says.

Michelle's voice breaks. "I know you are doing the best you can," she says. "Anymore, he's just ashamed. I wish I had a video camera set up to show the people at the VA: This is what an average day looks like."

She goes back for Troy, who has finished his tests. He is yawning and tired. He tells Michelle how hard he tried, and she smiles and touches his arm. They go upstairs to make an appointment with Troy's psychiatrist. The clerk tells Michelle that unfortunately the doctor is on leave for the next month. The first available slot is five weeks out, at 8:30 a.m.

"Is there anything later than 8:30?" Michelle asks, politely. "We have a three-hour drive."

Nine o'clock is the best they can do. The appointment is for 20 minutes.

The last stop of the afternoon is the travel reimbursement office on the first floor. The government has promised to care for its wounded, but the proof is often in cramped places such as this, where disabled veterans stand in line to get their mileage reimbursed. The VA mileage rate has not changed since 1977. While a federal worker gets 48.5 cents per mile, a disabled veteran is still paid 11 cents a mile.

Michelle steps to one window and gets a receipt for $14.52. At the next window, $6 in government "deductibles" are taken out, bringing the grand total to $8.52.

On the way home, Michelle pulls into a Flying J truck stop, pumping gas in the hot breeze, watching the numbers spin higher.

'Ain't a Scratch on Me'

Money became so desperate this spring that Michelle contacted Operation Homefront, a national organization that gives emergency assistance to deployed service members and the returning wounded. In a sign of the deepening financial crisis faced by many back from war, Operation Homefront has provided $2 million in bailout funds to 4,300 families so far in 2007, double last year's caseload.

The Turners received $4,500 to cover three months of late car payments, rent and various other bills, and a grocery card for food. Troy was angry and embarrassed, but Michelle told him they had no other choice. The $860 VA disability check barely covers expenses.

Michelle has been pushing to have VA reevaluate Troy in hopes of getting his disability rating raised and his compensation increased. He can't drive, he can't work, he can barely function without her. A Black Hawk model set is next to his recliner, a therapeutic hobby made impossible by the shaking in his left arm.

The house is small, and the blare of Nickelodeon from the TV chokes the day.

"I am at the end of my rope," Michelle says. But at least now she has the help of an assistant officer with the West Virginia Division of Veterans Affairs in a little office in Moorefield, about 30 miles from Romney. The officer submits the right paperwork to have Troy reevaluated.

Doctors find that his condition has worsened and that his PTSD is "chronic and severe." Michelle gets copies of the medical records and sits down with them on her living room floor. Wearing an Army T-shirt that says "Got Freedom?" she begins reading. The documents are a gold mine of information that validate what she has said all along. But instead of feeling exonerated, she feels sickened.

He has nightmares frequently, two to three times a week, in which he sees himself back in Iraq . . . and Baghdad. He sees himself fighting, sees dead bodies, parts of bodies, blood rushing from bodies. In the dreams he smells blood and burnt flesh and he hears bullets passing over his head. He is fearful and scared and wakes up in cold sweats. Flashbacks are also frequent, 2 or 3 times a week, triggered by helicopters passing over, burn flesh smell, barbecue, current Iraq news and sometimes seeing military vehicles brings flashbacks.

Michelle goes page by page. Troy is in his recliner holding the remote control. From time to time she looks up at him, then her eyes go back to the records.

He has a lot of guilt feelings that he could not save his sergeant.

She comes to a page that lists Troy's problems.

Hearing loss.

Tremors.

Obesity.

PTSD.

Depressive disorder.

Michelle calls out to Troy. "They are saying your memory is extremely low," she says. "And here's another thing. 'Hearing loss. Exposure to artillery and machine gun fire.'"

VA concludes that Troy's worsening condition merits an increase of his disability rating to 70 percent, raising his monthly check to $1,352 a month. According to VA, he doesn't meet the criteria for 100 percent because his impairment is not "persistent," with "persistent delusions" or a "persistent danger of hurting himself or others." He is still able to perform his own hygiene.

From Michelle's point of view, Troy can hold a toothbrush, but he can't hold a job. "Even at 70 percent, you can't raise a family," she says. She has a year to appeal the rating.

But there is good news: The VA hospital in Martinsburg finds a bed for Troy in the PTSD residential rehab program.

Michelle is relieved. Troy will get help and she will get a respite. Troy packs his small suitcase with resignation. He doesn't want to go. During the intake session in Martinsburg, he is withdrawn and sullen. When the doctor asks if he has been having suicidal thoughts, he says yes. The news punches Michelle in the gut.

Troy is allowed to come home on weekends, so Michelle makes the four-hour round trip to pick him up on the first Friday night. On Sunday, he refuses to go back. He says he has been through it before. Michelle pleads with him to get in the truck but he won't, and he loses his spot in the program.

Troy returns to his recliner. VA tells Michelle that a contract counselor who visits rural counties will be in touch to schedule time with Troy. Two weeks later, Troy has his first appointment. Whatever is discussed in the 60-minute session causes him to cry the next day.

The Turners decide to pack up and leave their $475-a-month rental house for a $450-a-month mobile home in Moorefield to save money and be near Troy's mother for help. They are strained beyond belief. Still, there are moments of gallows humor. "I have PTSD, what's your excuse?" Troy kids Michelle.

"I have a husband with PTSD," she says.

Before they leave, someone from Hampshire County's Heritage Days parade calls to see if Troy wants to ride on the veterans float. Troy declines. It's not just the crowds.

"Other people got wounded, and all I got was a mental thing," he says.

Michelle raises an eyebrow. "It's still an injury."

"I think about that doctor down there," Troy says, referring to a psychologist at Fort Stewart who suggested he was faking it. "Plus, the fact that guys are missing arms and have bullet holes and everything else. Ain't a scratch on me."

To remember who Troy used to be, Michelle keeps a photo of him hidden in her camera case. In the picture he is smiling and eager, ruggedly at home in his Army fatigues. Now she looks at the man in the recliner. "It's people like you that made our country," Michelle says. She goes back to filling out forms, and Troy goes back to Nickelodeon.

Staff researcher Julie Tate contributed to this report.

To read more stories from the Walter Reed investigation, go to www. poynter.org/bnw2009/resources.

X-Ray Reading

By Ben Montgomery

The writers' use of ironic detail, dialogue and cinematic techniques help a pounding investigation hit home.

An excerpt from
The Other Walter Reed, Part 2: The Hotel Aftermath

By Anne Hull and Dana Priest

The guests of Mologne House have been blown up, shot, crushed and shaken, and now their convalescence takes place among the chandeliers and wingback chairs of the 200-room hotel on the grounds of Walter Reed Army Medical Center.

Oil paintings hang in the lobby of this strange outpost in the war on terrorism, where combat's urgency has been replaced by a trickling fountain in the garden courtyard. The maimed and the newly legless sit in wheelchairs next to a pond, watching goldfish turn lazily through the water.

But the wounded of Mologne House are still soldiers— Hooah!—so their lives are ruled by platoon sergeants. Each morning they must rise at dawn for formation, though many are half-snowed on pain meds and sleeping pills.

In Room 323 the alarm goes off at 5 a.m., but Cpl. Dell

We've just been shown an "establishing shot" in which the writers give us a sweeping view of the human suffering we're about to explore.

Suddenly, we're in a room. Not just any room—Room 323. And we're watching a small piece of daily drama unfold, with the help of specific details—like "instant oatmeal"—and sharp bits of dialogue. Note that the reporter was in the room at 5 a.m., when Annette wakes up. It's hard to imagine the trust-building that went on in order for the reporter to get this type of access.

McLeod slumbers on. His wife, Annette, gets up and fixes him a bowl of instant oatmeal before going over to the massive figure curled in the bed. An Army counselor taught her that a soldier back from war can wake up swinging, so she approaches from behind.

"Dell," Annette says, tapping her husband. "Dell, get in the shower."

"Dell!" she shouts.

Finally, the yawning hulk sits up in bed. "Okay, baby," he says. An American flag T-shirt is stretched over his chest. He reaches for his dog tags, still the devoted soldier of 19 years, though his life as a warrior has become a paradox. One day he's led on stage at a Toby Keith concert with dozens of other wounded Operation Iraqi Freedom troops from Mologne House, and the next he's sitting in a cluttered cubbyhole at Walter Reed, fighting the Army for every penny of his disability.

McLeod, 41, has lived at Mologne House for a year while the Army figures out what to do with him. He worked in textile and steel mills in rural South Carolina before deploying. Now he takes 23 pills a day, prescribed by various doctors at Walter Reed. Crowds frighten him. He is too anxious to drive. When panic strikes, a soldier friend named Oscar takes him to Baskin-Robbins for vanilla ice cream.

Notice how the use of the verb "stretched" makes this a sharper sentence, versus, say, "He's wearing an American flag T-shirt." It reaffirms the soldier's size, a point that will be used again in a few paragraphs.

The reporter tucks an important bit of character data behind an action. Rather than throwing the clause into a boring structure— like, "Dell, who has been a soldier for 19 years, reached for his dog tags"—we get the information in the middle of the open-ended action.

Anne Hull calls lines like these "gold nuggets," and she and Dana Priest sprinkle them throughout the story to keep the reader moving. And remember the references to his size above? The payoff is that the reader sees a big man who is scared.

Another fantastic, pointed detail. He takes 23 pills, not the more general "many" or "dozens."

"They find ways to soothe each other," Annette says.

Mostly what the soldiers do together is wait: for appointments, evaluations, signatures and lost paperwork to be found. It's like another wife told Annette McLeod: "If Iraq don't kill you, Walter Reed will."

After Iraq, a New Struggle

The conflict in Iraq has hatched a virtual town of desperation and dysfunction, clinging to the pilings of Walter Reed. The wounded are socked away for months and years in random buildings and barracks in and around this military post.

The luckiest stay at Mologne House, a four-story hotel on a grassy slope behind the hospital. Mologne House opened 10 years ago as a short-term lodging facility for military personnel, retirees and their family members. Then came Sept. 11 and five years of sustained warfare. Now, the silver walkers of retired generals convalescing from hip surgery have been replaced by prosthetics propped against Xbox games and Jessica Simpson posters smiling down on brain-rattled grunts.

Two *Washington Post* reporters spent hundreds of hours in Mologne House documenting the intimate struggles of the wounded who live there. The reporting was done without the knowledge or permission of Walter Reed officials, but all

The reporters shoot back up the ladder of abstraction for another sweeping statement, which is really the nut paragraph. They are saying where this story will lead and challenging readers to come along.

Another gold nugget.

Lends this the eyewitness integrity that takes readers to another level.

those directly quoted in this article agreed to be interviewed.

The hotel is built in the Georgian revival style, and inside it offers the usual amenities: daily maid service, front-desk clerks in formal vests and a bar off the lobby that opens every afternoon.

But at this bar, the soldier who orders a vodka tonic one night says to the bartender, "If I had two hands, I'd order two." The customers sitting around the tables are missing limbs, their ears are melted off, and their faces are tattooed purple by shrapnel patterns.

Most everyone has a story about the day they blew up: the sucking silence before immolation, how the mouth filled with tar, the lungs with gas.

"First thing I said was, '[Expletive], that was my good eye,'" a soldier with an eye patch tells an amputee in the bar.

The amputee peels his beer label. "I was awake through the whole thing," he says. "It was my first patrol. The second [expletive] day in Iraq and I get blown up."

When a smooth-cheeked soldier with no legs orders a fried chicken dinner and two bottles of grape soda to go, a kitchen worker comes out to his wheelchair and gently places the Styrofoam container on his lap.

A scrawny young soldier sits alone in his wheelchair at a nearby table, his eyes closed and

---

Margin notes:

There are a few things similar about the quotes so far. First, they're each short, digestible and powerful. A long quote high in a story can stop readers cold. Second, each quote is delivered by someone inside a scene: Annette, Dell, and, now, a soldier at a bar. There are no detached voices floating in from the atmosphere.

Nice verb.

With so much emotional material to this point, this line is like a splash of cold water. And it smacks so real.

Details should reveal something. Here we have grape soda reminding us how young this "smooth-cheeked soldier" is.

his chin dropped to his chest, an empty Corona bottle in front of him.

Those who aren't old enough to buy a drink at the bar huddle outside near a magnolia tree and smoke cigarettes. Wearing hoodies and furry bedroom slippers, they look like kids at summer camp who've crept out of their rooms, except some have empty pants legs or limbs pinned by medieval-looking hardware. Medication is a favorite topic.

"Dude, [expletive] Paxil saved my life."

"I been on methadone for a year, I'm tryin' to get off it."

"I didn't take my Seroquel last night and I had nightmares of charred bodies, burned crispy like campfire marshmallows."

This nice, quiet, peaceful metaphor sets us up for some heavy, violent, high-impact details.

Mologne House is afloat on a river of painkillers and antipsychotic drugs. One night, a strapping young infantryman loses it with a woman who is high on her son's painkillers. "Quit taking all the soldier medicine!" he screams.

Pill bottles clutter the nightstands: pills for depression or insomnia, to stop nightmares and pain, to calm the nerves.

Here at Hotel Aftermath, a crash of dishes in the cafeteria can induce seizures in the combat-addled. If a taxi arrives and the driver looks Middle Eastern, soldiers refuse to get in. Even among the gazebos and tranquility of the Walter Reed campus in upper Northwest Washington,

Did you notice we get a statistic here? The beauty of this sentence is that this number, 60 percent, and the necessary but bland attribution, are followed by an interesting detail and image. It's like taking medicine with a spoonful of sugar.

manhole covers are sidestepped for fear of bombs and rooftops are scanned for snipers.

Bomb blasts are the most common cause of injury in Iraq, and nearly 60 percent of the blast victims also suffer from traumatic brain injury, according to Walter Reed's studies, which explains why some at Mologne House wander the hallways trying to remember their room numbers.

Some soldiers and Marines have been here for 18 months or longer. Doctor's appointments and evaluations are routinely dragged out and difficult to get. A board of physicians must review hundreds of pages of medical records to determine whether a soldier is fit to return to duty. If not, the Physical Evaluation Board must decide whether to assign a rating for disability compensation. For many, this is the start of a new and bitter battle.

Months roll by and life becomes a blue-and-gold hotel room where the bathroom mirror shows the naked disfigurement of war's ravages. There are toys in the lobby of Mologne House because children live here. Domestic disputes occur because wives or girlfriends have moved here. Financial tensions are palpable. After her husband's traumatic injury insurance policy came in, one wife cleared out with the money. Older National Guard members worry about the jobs they can no longer perform back home.

While Mologne House has a full bar, there is not one counselor or psychologist assigned there to assist soldiers and families in crisis—an idea proposed by Walter Reed social workers but rejected by the military command that runs the post.

After a while, the bizarre becomes routine. On Friday nights, antiwar protesters stand outside the gates of Walter Reed holding signs that say "Love Troops, Hate War, Bring them Home Now." Inside the gates, doctors in white coats wait at the hospital entrance for the incoming bus full of newly wounded soldiers who've just landed at Andrews Air Force Base.

And set back from the gate, up on a hill, Mologne House, with a bowl of red apples on the front desk.

Into the Twilight Zone

Dell McLeod's injury was utterly banal. He was in his 10th month of deployment with the 178th Field Artillery Regiment of the South Carolina National Guard near the Iraqi border when he was smashed in the head by a steel cargo door of an 18-wheeler. The hinges of the door had been tied together with a plastic hamburger-bun bag. Dell was knocked out cold and cracked several vertebrae.

The reporters use Mologne House as the touchstone for this story, the place that hosts the core of the action. So if something happens outside Mologne, the reporters quickly offer a point of reference. They move the camera "outside the gates," then back "inside the gates." This technique—typically used in moviemaking—helps readers develop a sense of location.

Another shift.

When Annette learned that he was being shipped to Walter Reed, she took a leave from her job on the assembly line at Stanley Tools and packed the car. The Army would pay her $64 a day to help care for her husband and would let her live with him at Mologne House until he recovered.

They lead us back down the ladder of abstraction here, to the interesting details of the experience of one soldier and his wife.

Opposing details stacked side-by-side reveal the paradox.

A year later, they are still camped out in the twilight zone. Dogs are periodically brought in by the Army to search the rooms for contraband or weapons. When the fire alarm goes off, the amputees who live on the upper floors are scooped up and carried down the stairwell, while a brigade of mothers passes down the wheelchairs. One morning Annette opens her door and is told to stay in the room because a soldier down the hall has overdosed.

Notice also that while we've met and heard from many soldiers, the reporters don't want to confuse readers with a bunch of names. We have Annette and Dell, and that is all. Other characters may enter and exit, but the story is wrapped tightly around the couple in Room 323.

In between, there are picnics at the home of the chairman of the Joint Chiefs of Staff and a charity-funded dinner cruise on the Potomac for "Today's troops, tomorrow's veterans, always heroes."

Dell and Annette's weekdays are spent making the rounds of medical appointments, physical therapy sessions and evaluations for Dell's discharge from the Army. After 19 years, he is no longer fit for service. He uses a cane to walk. He is unable to count out change in the hospital cafeteria. He takes four Percocets a day for pain and has gained 40 pounds from medication and inactivity. Lumbering and blue-eyed, Dell is a big ox baby.

Annette puts on makeup every morning and does her hair, some semblance of normalcy, but her new job in life is watching Dell.

"I'm worried about how he's gonna fit into society," she says one night, as Dell wanders down the hall to the laundry room.

The verb "wanders" is loaded with meaning in this instance. He's lost. He's slow. He's sheepish. Imagine replacing "wanders" with "walks" or "strolls." It deflates this sentence. The right verbs add power and meaning to a sentence.

The more immediate worry concerns his disability rating. Army doctors are disputing that Dell's head injury was the cause of his mental impairment. One report says that he was slow in high school and that his cognitive problems could be linked to his native intelligence rather than to his injury.

"They said, 'Well, he was in Title I math,' like he was retarded," Annette says. "Well, y'all took him, didn't you?"

The same fight is being waged by their friends, who aren't the young warriors in Army posters but middle-age men who left factory jobs to deploy to Iraq with their Guard units. They were fit enough for war, but now they are facing teams of Army doctors scrutinizing their injuries for signs of pre-existing conditions, lessening their chance for disability benefits.

Dell and Annette's closest friend at Mologne House is a

We meet another character here, but the reporters give us the details only to add a touch of context to the point they're trying to make. Again, no name. They don't want readers to dwell on this character.

47-year-old Guard member who was driving an Army vehicle through the Iraqi night when a flash of light blinded him and he crashed into a ditch with an eight-foot drop. Among his many injuries was a broken foot that didn't heal properly. Army doctors decided that "late life atrophy" was responsible for the foot, not the truck wreck in Iraq.

When Dell sees his medical records, he explodes. "Special ed is for the mentally retarded, and I'm not mentally retarded, right, babe?" he asks Annette. "I graduated from high school. I did some college. I worked in a steel mill."

It's after 9 one night and Dell and Annette are both exhausted, but Dell still needs to practice using voice-recognition software. Reluctantly, he mutes *The Ultimate Fighting Challenge* on TV and sits next to Annette in bed with a laptop.

"My name is Wendell," he says. "Wendell Woodward McLeod Jr."

Annette tells him to sit up. "Spell 'dog,'" she says, softly.

"Spell 'dog,'" he repeats.

"Listen to me," she says.

"Listen to me." He slumps on the pillow. His eyes drift toward the wrestlers on TV.

"You are not working hard enough, Dell," Annette says, pleading. "Wake up."

"Wake up," he says.

"Dell, come on now!"

This bit of dialogue takes us into their world and gives us an inside look at the frustration they face. It goes much further toward reflecting the reality of the situation than having them explain it in an interview.

For Some, a Grim Kind of Fame

No one questions Sgt. Bryan Anderson's sacrifice. One floor above Dell and Annette's room at Mologne House, he holds the gruesome honor of being one of the war's five triple amputees. Bryan, 25, lost both legs and his left arm when a roadside bomb exploded next to the Humvee he was driving with the 411th Military Police Company. Modern medicine saved him and now he's the pride of the prosthetics team at Walter Reed. Tenacious and wisecracking, he wrote "[Expletive] Iraq" on his left leg socket.

Amputees are the first to receive celebrity visitors, job offers and extravagant trips, but Bryan is in a league of his own. Johnny Depp's people want to hook up in London or Paris. The actor Gary Sinise, who played an angry Vietnam amputee in *Forrest Gump,* sends his regards. And *Esquire* magazine is setting up a photo shoot.

Bryan's room at Mologne House is stuffed with gifts from corporate America and private citizens: $350 Bose noise-canceling headphones, nearly a thousand DVDs sent by well-wishers and quilts made by church grannies. The door prizes of war. Two flesh-colored legs are stacked on the floor. A computerized hand sprouting blond hair is on the table.

One Saturday afternoon, Bryan is on his bed downloading

There is always a point of view to help readers retain a sense of position. When the reporters switch characters, they show us physically where the character is.

Here we have a long sentence full of reported facts, followed by a short and beautifully harsh bit of the reporter's voice. *The door prizes of war.* It's like three singles and a grand slam.

music. Without his prosthetics, he weighs less than 100 pounds. "Mom, what time is our plane?" he asks his mother, Janet Waswo, who lives in the room with him. A movie company is flying them to Boston for the premiere of a documentary about amputee handcyclers in which Bryan appears.

Representing the indomitable spirit of the American warrior sometimes becomes too much, and Bryan turns off his phone.

Perks and stardom do not come to every amputee. Sgt. David Thomas, a gunner with the Tennessee National Guard, spent his first three months at Walter Reed with no decent clothes; medics in Samarra had cut off his uniform. Heavily drugged, missing one leg and suffering from traumatic brain injury, David, 42, was finally told by a physical therapist to go to the Red Cross office, where he was given a T-shirt and sweat pants. He was awarded a Purple Heart but had no underwear.

David tangled with Walter Reed's image machine when he wanted to attend a ceremony for a fellow amputee, a Mexican national who was being granted U.S. citizenship by President Bush. A case worker quizzed him about what he would wear. It was summer, so David said shorts. The case manager said the media would be there and shorts were not advisable because the amputees would be seated in the front row.

This may be the best sentence in the story. Two tiny details that, alone, would bear little fruit. Together, though, they summarize the bizarre world inside Mologne House.

"'Are you telling me that I can't go to the ceremony 'cause I'm an amputee?'" David recalled asking. "She said, 'No, I'm saying you need to wear pants.'"

David told the case worker, "I'm not ashamed of what I did, and y'all shouldn't be neither." When the guest list came out for the ceremony, his name was not on it.

Still, for all its careful choreography of the amputees, Walter Reed offers protection from a staring world. On warm nights at the picnic tables behind Mologne House, someone fires up the barbecue grill and someone else makes a beer run to Georgia Avenue.

Bryan Anderson is out here one Friday. "Hey, Bry, what time should we leave in the morning?" asks his best friend, a female soldier also injured in Iraq. The next day is Veterans Day, and Bryan wants to go to Arlington National Cemetery. His pal Gary Sinise will be there, and Bryan wants to give him a signed photo.

Thousands of spectators are already at Arlington the next morning when Bryan and his friend join the surge toward the ceremony at the Tomb of the Unknowns. The sunshine dazzles. Bryan is in his wheelchair. If loss and sacrifice are theoretical to some on this day, here is living proof—three stumps and a crooked boyish smile. Even

This great sentence creates an illusion with some smart wordplay. By pairing the word "choreography" with amputees, then following that with "a staring world," we have the hints of a staged performance.

the acres of tombstones can't compete. Spectators cut their eyes toward him and look away.

Suddenly, the thunder of cannons shakes the sky. The last time Bryan heard this sound, his legs were severed and he was nearly bleeding to death in a fiery Humvee.

Boom. Boom. Boom. Bryan pushes his wheelchair harder, trying to get away from the noise. "Damn it," he says, "when are they gonna stop?"

Bryan's friend walks off by herself and holds her head. The cannon thunder has unglued her, too, and she is crying.

Ben Montgomery is a reporter with the St. Petersburg Times.

BEHIND the STORY

Winner's Q&A

An Interview with Anne Hull and Dana Priest

This edited e-mail interview was conducted by Al Tompkins, Poynter Institute Broadcast/Online Group Leader, with Anne Hull and Dana Priest, winners of the ASNE Distinguished Writing Award for Local Accountability Reporting.

AL TOMPKINS: How did you hear about this story? What started your investigation?

DANA PRIEST: A friend of an acquaintance called up, asked for a lunch date and shared a tiny corner of this problem. In this sense it was a classic tip, one that has been rare in both of our careers.

Much has been said and written about how difficult this story was to tell. Had the Army and/or the hospital known that you were working on this story, you certainly would have been shut out. How did you get access to the patients and their rooms? How did you introduce yourself to people you met along your journey at Walter Reed? Were you prepared to lie to gain access?

ANNE HULL: Working beneath the radar was crucial because we needed to see the problems at Walter Reed with our own eyes. We needed to roam around the 113-acre facility at various hours of the day or night and talk to soldiers and Marines without the interference of Army public affairs. We needed to connect with wounded soldiers who were not preselected by the Army.

So we bypassed the normal protocol of requesting permission to visit Walter Reed and be accompanied by an escort. We simply went onto post on our own. We never lied about our identity. We presented our driver's licenses at the guard gates as all visitors do. Once on the post, we made sure to not bring attention to ourselves while reporting. We tried to never put ourselves in the position where someone might ask, "Who are you?" As with any reporting, you try not to stand out from your subjects.

If reporting involves multiple rings, we started at the outer rings first and slowly worked our way closer to the center. We began by doing lots of observation at Walter Reed. We hung out in the hotel that housed wounded soldiers. We spent time in the bar at the hotel. We sat outside where soldiers congregated. We mostly listened.

A general pattern of complaints emerged: long waiting periods to see doctors, bungled paperwork, uncaring administrative staff and platoon sergeants and tough living conditions for some soldiers who'd been stranded at Walter Reed for as long as two years. One of the most common complaints was how little the Army was willing to pay out in disability benefits for wounds suffered in Iraq. This ticked many soldiers off and made them more willing to speak out.

While lots of news reports had focused on the inpatient population at Walter Reed—the great care the amputee soldiers received, for instance—there had been very little on the vast and massive outpatient population literally stuck at Walter Reed for months and years. This is the group we targeted, and eventually we identified soldiers and wives and girlfriends who might be willing to talk.

We approached them carefully and introduced ourselves as reporters interested in writing about some of the problems they were experiencing. In this fashion, we moved from the "outer" rings to the "middle rings" and finally to the inside tensions of the story by gaining access to a patient's life and medical records. It was a tedious and time-consuming process but necessary to amass a network of sources.

How can you explain why it took so long for journalists to find this story? You have spoken of a "petting zoo"—an area where other journalists were taken to see Walter Reed.

ANNE HULL: Most of the media's coverage of the war-wounded focused on the great efforts of military medicine, credited with saving countless lives because of new technology and selfless dedication. But as the war dragged on, the number of wounded soared and the military was simply not prepared to handle the cascading physical, mental and financial problems that developed among outpatients. The Army's multiple layers of bureaucracy and inability or refusal to "staff up" to address these problems resulted in the mess at Walter Reed.

But the Army public affairs agenda was to keep steering journalists toward the outstanding medical care, Purple Heart ceremonies and state-of-the-art rehab facilities for amputees. The larger and more ominous story in the background was harder to see, in part because it was hidden by the Army and in part because it's more difficult to get. I think there was also a certain mythology about Walter Reed that dissuaded reporters from looking more closely.

The term "petting zoo" was used by a wounded Marine to describe the spit-polished areas of his base where public affairs officials brought members of the media. He said this during testimony before the presidential commission appointed to examine military health care in the wake of the Walter Reed stories.

Dana, you have said, "We're in an era of journalism where a lot of journalists are doing the talking. The art of listening is so fundamental to what we do. If you have a heightened ability to do that, you can pick up so much." What are some of the elements of this "heightened ability" that you mentioned? What do great listeners hear that others miss? Can you give me examples of how "just listening" turned out to be key to this project?

DANA PRIEST: The "heightened ability" is soaking in body language, facial expressions, things not spoken. Mostly, though, if you know the context in which you are operating, you can judge the people you are interviewing so much better. Do they feel reluctant about something? Can you reassure them to make things easier? Do they feel intimidated by your presence? There are many, many ways to put people at ease with a non-judgmental manner, with clothes and demeanor that fit in to the surroundings.

"Just listening" steered us in so many important directions. We didn't understand the dimensions of post-traumatic stress disorder, for example. But listening carefully gave us clues, right away, to people whose emotions were "off," either a little or a lot. This eventually led us to be able to probe an area that is highly personal—intimate, really—to ask questions about depression and the sleeplessness and sadness and suicide.

Listening also clued us in to just how widespread the problem at Walter Reed was. No one just came right out and said that right away. Everything was couched in Army terms, or in terms of a single soldier's experience. No one wanted to speak for anyone else. And yet so many of the stories that soldiers related were about the bad care of their fellow soldiers—the young private who killed himself down the hallway because no one was paying attention; the guy who kept forgetting his appointment because he didn't have a family member living with him to remind him.

The two of you came to this project with different skills. Priest is an investigator, Hull a narrative storyteller. What did you learn from each other?

ANNE HULL: While we both describe ourselves as reporters, how we approach a story or tell it is very different. Dana has spent much of her life examining broken or negligent systems or institutions. I have focused on the people being crushed or forgotten by those institutions. One thing I learned from her is the value in casting something in black and white. Often I'm carried away by the gray. Instantly, Dana can figure out the mission statement or promise—"only the best of care for our nation's wounded"—and juxtapose it with the brokenness of something, such as Building 18. She is an accountability reporter and relentless about her obligation as a journalist. She believes that if the press doesn't hold an institution accountable, no one else will. It's hard to convey how strategic and steely she is. Those are things you can't really learn but can only hope might rub off a little.

DANA PRIEST: Anne's approach is not direct. She's just willing to not know where a person is going to lead her, and for a much longer time than I generally have the patience for. And then she likes to sink into a subject and not emerge for days on end. And then, if that weren't frustrating enough for a daily beat reporter, just when I thought we had something figured out and knew where we were going, she'd say: "Well, this is just the start, we have to see where it takes us." I wanted to pin down as many moving parts as possible, as quickly as possible, and she wanted to do the opposite—to let a thousand flowers bloom, slowly, at their own, slow-as-molasses, natural pace. What she draws from this is a rare intimacy, and because she is such a great writer, she can then put that on the page for all to feel.

Beyond that, one of the great things I learned was the notion of "unpacking" the writing, letting it breathe like a good bottle of red wine. This, too, requires patience and a confidence that if you are giving readers a nice ride, they will stick with you beyond the third paragraph. As a beat reporter, my goal was usually to cram the most important things into a two- or three-paragraph suitcase. Beyond that, I learned how much fun and thought-provoking it can be to team up with someone who comes at a subject so differently.

Part One of the project ("Soldiers Face Neglect, Frustration at Army's Top Medical Facility," Feb. 18, 2007) opens this way:

Behind the door of Army Spec. Jeremy Duncan's room, part of the wall is torn and hangs in the air, weighted down with black mold. When the wounded combat engineer stands in his shower and looks up, he can see the bathtub on the floor above through a rotted hole. The entire building, constructed between the world wars, often smells like greasy carry-out. Signs of neglect are everywhere: mouse droppings, belly-up cockroaches, stained carpets, cheap mattresses.

Why do you pack nine descriptions (a torn wall, black mold, a hole in the shower ceiling, rotted hole, the greasy smell, mouse droppings, belly-up cockroaches, stained carpets, cheap mattresses) into the opening two sentences? After all you saw during four months of observation and investigation, why did these nine descriptions stick out to you as so important that you would lead your series with them?

DANA PRIEST: We wanted to get you into the room. We wanted you to smell the place, to understand that something's not right, that what's not right resides in a weighty historical context. Those nine descriptions are also just plain visceral, and they are everywhere: on the wall, on the ceiling, in the shower, in the air, on the floor, even on the thing he sleeps on. Because they are so small and visceral, the contrast to the lofty (honor, courage, and sacrifice of war) are all the more stark.

I want to point toward the opening of the June 17, 2007, story "The War Inside," about post-traumatic stress disorder (PTSD):

Army Spec. Jeans Cruz helped capture Saddam Hussein. When he came home to the Bronx, important people called him a war hero and promised to help him start a new life. The mayor of New York, officials of his parents' home town in Puerto Rico, the borough president and other local dignitaries honored him with plaques and silk parade sashes. They handed him their business cards and urged him to phone.

But a "black shadow" had followed Cruz home from Iraq, he confided to an Army counselor. He was hounded by recurring images of how war really was for him: not the triumphant scene of Hussein in handcuffs, but visions of dead Iraqi children.

In public, the former Army scout stood tall for the cameras and marched in the parades. In private, he slashed his forearms to provoke the pain and adrenaline of combat. He heard voices and smelled stale blood.

Why was it important to say he was from the Bronx? Why was it important to say his parents were from Puerto Rico? Why describe "silk parade sashes"? What is the power of using the last line, "He heard voices and smelled stale blood"?

DANA PRIEST: "The Bronx" says he's an everyman, a typical soldier. "His parents in Puerto Rico" says he was honored far from the Bronx, all the way in almost another country. Having to say it was his parents' home town was a burden, but we couldn't figure out how not to say it if we wanted to use Puerto Rico. The silk parade sashes, like the honors in Puerto Rico, are meant to give you the sense of the one world—celebrations, honors, silk ribbons—I contrast to another, which begins in the second to the last sentence and ends with the last, tough sentence. Hearing voices lets you know something is wrong with him. Smelling stale blood lets you know he's been bloodied, or in combat. It's very intimate. That he even knows to call it stale blood is the point.

To me, the following is among the most powerful passages. I would like for you to X-ray read it for me and tell me the thought process behind how you wrote it. (Excerpt from "The Other Walter Reed Part 2: The Hotel Aftermath," Feb. 19, 2007):

Thousands of spectators are already at Arlington the next morning when Bryan [Anderson] and his friend join the surge toward the ceremony at the Tomb of the Unknowns. The sunshine dazzles. Bryan is in his wheelchair. If loss and sacrifice are theoretical to some on this day, here is living proof—three stumps and a crooked boyish smile. Even the acres of tombstones can't compete. Spectators cut their eyes toward him and look away.

Suddenly, the thunder of cannons shakes the sky. The last time Bryan heard this sound, his legs were severed and he was nearly bleeding to death in a fiery Humvee.

Boom. Boom. Boom. Bryan pushes his wheelchair harder, trying to get away from the noise. "Damn it," he says, "when are they gonna stop?"

Bryan's friend walks off by herself and holds her head. The cannon thunder has unglued her, too, and she is crying.

You chose active verbs here. The sunshine DAZZLES, thunder SHAKES, spectators CUT, Bryan PUSHES. How do you think about the verb choices you use in your sentences? How do verbs affect the reader's experience and understanding?

You also chose stark and contradictory descriptors: "three stumps and a crooked boyish smile." Why did you use those phrases next to each other?

You compared the cannons to thunder in an earlier sentence, then you come back to thunder in the closing sentence. What is the value of this foreshadowing technique?

ANNE HULL: Bryan Anderson and another soldier allowed me to go with them to Arlington for the annual Veterans Day ceremony. Bryan was one of the war's few triple-amputees and a young man with incredible guts and optimism. The image of him in his wheelchair among the acres of headstones at Arlington provided a powerful image, so I asked to go—not knowing what I'd get or if we'd even use it. We got there along with tens of thousands of others who were paying their respect. Bryan was used to being stared at. But at Arlington—on hallowed grounds that represented sacrifice—it was the opposite: People saw him and looked away.

As soon as the cannons started, he became anxious and upset. The loud percussion reeled him back to Iraq and the day he was hit. You can't say why a writer picks certain words or descriptions other than the pure emotions that well up within you when you are witnessing something. Here was this boyish young man cut down so brutally by his injuries, yet he always had a smile. The innocence—that crooked smile—was juxtaposed with the horrors of war. There was the added dimension of his presence in a sea of dead. It was a multiplicity of truths that all collided at this very historic place.

Mentioning the "thunder of cannons" the first time wasn't really foreshadowing; it was just explaining what was happening in sequential order of action. Cannon thunder. Bryan gets upset. The cannon thunder also upsets his fellow soldier.

How do you take notes while working undercover? How do you organize your notes, which must have amounted to volumes after four months? Did you write as you reported or did you complete your reporting, then sit down to write?

ANNE HULL: Working "discreetly" is a more accurate way to describe the reporting. We were careful to avoid detection. We were discreet about how we took notes in public spaces. Both of us are copious note-takers who would probably use a stick to write in the dirt if we had to. We stayed on top of our notebooks, which meant we tried to transcribe our notes or scraps of paper as quickly as possible so as not to fall behind. We organized our notes by source (or "character") and made sure to download to each other constantly so we would both know what we had in our notes in order to make connections, i.e., five soldiers we talked to who lived in Building 18 all had mental problems, so that meant Walter Reed was sticking psychologically fragile soldiers in a crummy building outside the fortress of the post. Because we were alleging neglect, we had to document instances of neglect and look for common patterns. After three months of reporting, we decided it was time to write, but that didn't stop the reporting, which continued right through until the eve of publication.

Describe the "showdown" interviews that you had to have with the Army and Walter Reed just before the publication. You finally started asking the hospital questions the early part of the week before the Sunday that the first story ran. But even then, the Army did not know that you had spent time in Building 18. What ethical issues did you see embedded in your tactics, and how did you navigate around them?

DANA PRIEST: The right thing to do was to ask for a response on every point in the story and that is what we did. In this sense, the showdown interview was fairly standard, except that it came as such a big surprise to them when we posed the questions in the first place. This was done first by e-mail. As for Building 18: They had had about six months (from the time we first learned of it) to clean it up. I never thought that sorry building would make it into the story. I thought for sure they would clean it up along the way because it would not have taken much to do so. When they didn't, their negligence just skyrocketed in my book. And capturing it could only be achieved by not allowing them time to clean it up before we published.

For a newspaper that has such a strong Web and multimedia presence, this project did not include videos from inside those rooms in Building 18. Why not? What else do you wish you could have done with the story in a multimedia/online way?

ANNE HULL: We didn't involve the Web site until the very end of the process. We wanted to work beneath the radar for as long as possible, and that included our own colleagues. In hindsight we should have collaborated earlier. While we had still photos of Building 18 and audio recordings in our Web presentation, we didn't have video. My dream online stuff always involves a mash-up of cinematography and documentary: blending still photos with archival photos and montage video accompanied by the actual music the soldiers are listening to. A real creative tour de force that "says" something as opposed to augments the text story.

Dana, you have told audiences that this story, at times, brought you to tears. What was it that touched you? Why is it important for journalists to still allow themselves to be touched by the stories they are reporting?

DANA PRIEST: The depth of the injuries and the road to repair seemed so overwhelming for some of these soldiers and their families. Each story was the same, yet it was completely different; a different body part gone, a different, awful nightmare, a different set of burdensome family or financial problems. The fact that they were living in such silence in the midst of all the thunderous clapping on their behalf was so powerful. "Allow" is a difficult word to deal with. Even though some of these people may have brought me to tears and to the point of red-faced anger, when it came to writing the stories, I was totally cautious and diligent in not overstating anything. In this sense I didn't allow the emotions to do anything but help tell the objective story before us—in all its outrageousness.

Anne, you have said, as a result of this project: "For the first time in my life I realized the true power we have, as journalists, to create change." What do you mean by that?

ANNE HULL: As a journalist you go about your daily work life trying to get a story out or make someone's life better or shine a light on wrongdoing. Most of us don't seek to entertain, we seek to illuminate. Still, the chances to play a role in creating reform are rare. The Walter Reed stuff landed with a ferocious wallop. Washington—Congress, the Pentagon, the White House—all reacted in dramatic fashion. It was a reminder to everyone in the *Post* newsroom that journalism is still this mighty tool for good. You always think you know this basic fact but seeing it unfold so viscerally is a powerful reminder.

Writer's Workshop

Talking Points

1. Dana Priest and Anne Hull establish an authoritative voice in their writing: The "outpatients in the Other Walter Reed encounter a messy bureaucratic battlefield nearly as chaotic as the real battlefields they faced overseas." "Disengaged clerks, unqualified platoon sergeants and overworked case managers fumble with simple needs...." "Soldiers, family members, volunteers and caregivers who have tried to fix the system say each mishap seems trivial by itself, but the cumulative effect wears down the spirits of the wounded...." "This world is invisible to outsiders." Discuss the kind of reporting that can lead to such an authoritative tone. Debate whether any of these conclusions need attribution, or whether the story supports the conclusions. Can you find examples in the story that support these conclusions?

2. In an interview with Poynter's Al Tompkins, Anne Hull says: "We needed to connect with wounded soldiers who were not preselected by the Army. So we bypassed the normal protocol of requesting permission to visit Walter Reed and be accompanied by an escort. We simply went onto post on our own. We never lied about our identity. We presented our driver's licenses at the guard gates as all visitors do. Once on the post, we made sure to not bring attention to ourselves while reporting." Discuss why Hull and Priest took this reporting approach. Could the Walter Reed stories have been pursued any other way?

3. In several of the Walter Reed stories, the wives of the wounded soldiers are depicted as strong, spirited women who, though exhausted, continue to fight for their husbands' medical care. These include Annette McLeod in "The Hotel Aftermath" and Michelle Turner in "A Wife's Battle." Discuss what you learn about these women in the storytelling. Why do you think the reporters chose to focus not only on the soldiers, but on their relationships with their spouses and families?

Assignment Desk

1. From the very start of the series, Priest and Hull use strong imagery to put the reader at Walter Reed: a torn wall, black mold, a rotted hole, mouse droppings, belly-up cockroaches. As an exercise, pick a room where you work or live, and identify five details that convey a sense of place.

2. Hull and Priest use snatches of dialogue in their stories, based on conversations that they have observed. For example, at the beginning of "The Hotel Aftermath," the writers describe a scene in which Annette McLeod is cautious about waking up her husband.

   "Dell," Annette says, tapping her husband. "Dell, get in the shower."

   "Dell!" she shouts.

   Finally, the yawning hulk sits up in bed. "Okay, baby," he says.

   As an exercise, observe a conversation between two of your friends and take notes. Reconstruct part of the conversation based on your notes.

The Charlotte Observer

Finalist: ASNE Local Accountability Reporting
Finalist: Pulitzer Prize for Public Service

Binyamin Appelbaum, Lisa Hammersly Munn, Ted Mellnik

Sold a Nightmare

MARCH 18, 2007

Mark and Lea Tingley bought a new home in 2001 in a subdivision called Southern Chase. Photos on the family computer show a smiling young couple holding a baby girl in a bare room.

They recall feeling surprised they could afford a house. And thrilled. It was their first home, their largest investment, in the neighborhood where they planned to raise a family.

Beazer Homes USA built the Tingleys' home. Southern Chase was a new kind of subdivision for Beazer, an experiment in selling low-cost homes to low-income families.

The strategy was a financial success for Beazer.

But the neighborhood fell apart.

Seventy-seven buyers have lost homes to foreclosure in a subdivision of 406 homes. That's about one in five, more than six times the national rate.

Some homes sat empty. Others became rentals. Prices dropped.

Standing in his side yard last fall, Mark Tingley pointed to holes in his siding, garbage in neighboring yards, overgrown lawns, junked cars. He feels angry, cheated and trapped.

"We were just so happy," he said. "Now, no one is happy."

The buyers in Southern Chase share responsibility for the decisions they made.

But an *Observer* investigation found Beazer acted in ways that made a high rate of foreclosures inevitable. Beazer not only built the homes in Southern Chase, it arranged mortgage loans for two-thirds of the buyers.

Lea and Mark Tingley look over mortgage papers at their home in the Southern Chase subdivision. They struggle to make their monthly payments. They would like to sell but can't. "We owe more on the house than what we can sell it for," Lea said. (Photograph courtesy of Christopher A. Record/*The Charlotte Observer*)

The company used that control to arrange larger loans than some buyers could afford. That allowed it to include the cost of financial incentives in the price of homes.

Some of Beazer's actions violated federal lending rules, the *Observer* found.

Beazer said its practices in Southern Chase were "in strict compliance with federal, state and local laws and regulations." The company said in a written statement that the foreclosures were mostly due to economic difficulties experienced by the buyers.

"Beazer is committed to providing quality homes of superior value," the letter read in part.

The company's CEO, Ian McCarthy, declined to speak with the *Observer*.

The Federal Housing Administration, which insured most of the mortgage loans, failed to address the problems. The government has paid more than $5 million to cover defaulted loans in Southern Chase. It continues to insure new Beazer loans.

The Department of Housing and Urban Development, which administers the FHA program, told the *Observer* it was not aware of the problems in Southern Chase and did not plan to investigate the loans it insured for buyers there.

Demand 'Hot as a Match'

The night before Southern Chase opened in 1997, people camped outside the sales office, waiting to pick the best lots.

Home prices started below $80,000, roughly half the Charlotte-area average. Demand was "hot as a match," said Barry Helms, the sales agent who greeted them. He remembers selling six or seven homes the first day.

The unusually low prices were a strategic decision for Beazer. Too many companies were building homes in the Charlotte area for traditional first-time owners, the company said in its 1997 annual report. Beazer's answer was to build and sell homes for less.

Beazer also was responding to opportunity. The federal government was pushing to expand home ownership. It was encouraging mortgage lenders to relax standards, to make loans available to many lower-income families for the first time. The FHA offered to insure the loans: If the borrower didn't pay, the government would.

Beazer, which operated in the Carolinas at the time as Squires Homes, chose a site off N.C. 49 in Concord, where land was still relatively cheap.

The subdivision is 15 minutes from Lowe's Motor Speedway, so Beazer gave racing names to the streets: Winners Circle, Rockingham Lane. It built vinyl-sided homes on small lots, mostly one story, an average of 1,327 square feet.

Contractors did the building. Beazer focused on marketing. It held pizza parties at nearby apartment complexes. It took tenants to see homes.

"We believe in the dream," read a Beazer flier distributed to apartments in Concord. "We believe that everyone deserves to own their own home."

But as the company pushed to find new buyers, it increasingly crossed the line between selling to people who could barely afford homes, and selling to people who couldn't.

Plunging In

Lea and Mark Tingley were not looking to buy a home in early 2001. They had little savings.

Lea made $11 an hour weighing trucks at a Martin Marietta rock quarry. Mark made a little less as a forklift operator at a building supply store.

They heard about Southern Chase from Lea's brother, who had just put a deposit on a home there. If he could afford a house, Lea recalls thinking, I can, too. The Tingleys drove out the next day from their Concord apartment.

They say the sales agent told them Beazer would arrange the down payment. The company also would arrange a mortgage. It would even help with the monthly payments for the first two years.

Lea remembers the sales agent saying, *Let's just do this. You're pregnant. You need a home of your own.*

She returned the next day with a $600 deposit.

The company spent about $9,000 on financial incentives for the Tingleys, including the down payment, most of the closing costs and help with the mortgage payments. The company offered similar financial incentives to most buyers from 2001 to the end of sales in 2004.

As Beazer's costs rose, the company raised the price of new homes in Southern Chase by an average of 10 percent per square foot between 2000 and 2002. That was twice the price increase for similar homes elsewhere in Cabarrus County.

The model the Tingleys purchased, the Talladega, had a base price of $96,490 on a 1999 price sheet. By 2001, Beazer had raised the base price for the same model with the same square footage to $108,990.

Buyers needed larger loans to pay the higher prices. Beazer arranged the loans through a subsidiary, Beazer Mortgage, which acted as a mortgage broker, matching customers with lenders for a fee of several thousand dollars. From 2001, Beazer Mortgage arranged loans for 84 percent of the buyers in Southern Chase.

Almost all of the loans were insured by the Federal Housing Administration. That meant Beazer and the lender had little to lose if the borrower could not afford the loan.

Beazer assured borrowers it was acting in their interest.

One buyer saved a brochure from Beazer's mortgage business that reads in part, "There are no salespeople in this office. The people you work with are working for you, to secure the best possible deal on your behalf."

Costly Loan Maneuvers

The Tingleys moved into their new home in April 2001. Lea cleared out her 401(k) to pay $2,500 toward closing costs.

The keys came in a manila envelope with instructions on the front:

"1) Dump on table.

2) Place key on ring.

3) Do the 'Happy Dance' (*Jump up and down shouting wildly.*)"

The thrill did not last.

Lea had applied for the loan without Mark because he had credit problems.

She omitted from her application a monthly payment of $350 on a leased Dodge Avenger.

Lea said a Beazer employee told her to do it because the application also didn't include Mark's income.

"At the time it made sense to me and I was just excited about owning the home," Lea said. She says she knows she shouldn't have omitted the payment, but she trusted the employee.

Loan documents show that Beazer Mortgage prepared a final version of Lea's application before the closing. On that final version, Lea's monthly income was overstated by $187. It had been correct on the original application Lea signed. It is unclear when the number changed.

FHA rules required Beazer to document the borrower's income and debts. Lea's credit report and W-2 show the accurate numbers.

Knowingly falsifying information on a loan application is a federal crime.

Lea says she didn't notice the change until the *Observer* pointed it out this fall.

The company did not respond to the *Observer*'s written questions about the loan.

The changes allowed Lea to qualify for the loan she needed.

But in the summer of 2001, three months after buying the home, Lea called the dealership and asked to have the Avenger repossessed. She could not afford the car and the mortgage.

Buydown Balloon Inflates

The Tingleys' monthly mortgage payments started low because Beazer had agreed to pay part of the bill for two years. The company arranged similar deals, called interest-rate buydowns, for 146 other buyers in Southern Chase.

Under FHA rules at that time, paying part of the loan allowed Beazer to arrange larger loans than buyers could otherwise get. But Beazer had to document that buyers likely would have enough money to make the full payment by the third year. The Tingleys say they were never asked.

Other buydown recipients in Southern Chase included a clerk in an accounting office, a nursing home assistant and a trash collector. There was little chance their income would increase sufficiently. They also say they were never asked.

In June 2002, the Tingleys' monthly mortgage payment climbed from $675 to $744. Their income did not keep pace. Mark had quit work to care for the couple's daughter. They were unable to pay the full amount.

One year later, the monthly payment went up again, to $856, and the Tingleys fell further behind.

The bank that made the loan, National City, let them keep the home— but only if they made larger payments to catch up.

They sold their furniture and replaced it with furniture from Goodwill. They sold gold coins given to Lea by her father. They ate Oodles of Noodles and lots of peanut butter.

They held on. Many of their neighbors did not.

2004 was the first year in which many buyers were making a full mortgage payment without Beazer's help.

The overwhelmed owners might have sold their homes to pay their debts. But prices in the neighborhood had dropped.

Too many homes were for sale. Foreclosed homes were available for 80 cents on the dollar. There were newer subdivisions nearby.

Many remaining residents owed more than they could sell their homes for, and they lacked the savings to pay the difference.

Martin and Jill Higginbotham tried to sell their home for two years after Martin took a job in Tennessee. Finally, Martin mailed in the keys and called the lender.

"Do what you have to do," he remembers saying.

The lender foreclosed in early 2004. Twenty-nine other owners lost their homes that year.

Mark Tingley took a part-time job. An auction house paid him to tend three foreclosed homes once occupied by his neighbors.

Can't Afford to Stay or Go

The Tingleys had a plan when they moved to Southern Chase. They would sell after five years and move to a larger home.

By last fall, their daughter was 5, their son was 3 and the 1,410-square-foot house felt small. But the Tingleys owed more than $115,000 on a house valued for tax purposes at less than $108,000.

They talked with real estate agents, who quoted even lower prices.

The Tingleys were struggling to pay their mortgage. The monthly bill had climbed to $1,091, including catch-up payments. They didn't have the savings to sell the home at a loss.

"We can't afford it, we can't sell it and we're hurting ourselves just trying to keep it," Lea said.

Her credit has become so bad she said she can't open a bank account.

She and Mark worry they will lose the home the next time they fall behind on the mortgage payments.

They worry the home is falling apart: There is mold in the carpet where it meets the walls. Vinyl siding is cracking and popping. Wooden trim is rotting.

They could walk away and accept foreclosure.

But they say they're not ready.

They worry most of all that this will be the last home they ever own.

This was the first of several stories in The Charlotte Observer *that examined the subprime mortgage crisis. Other members of the series team included Liz Chandler, Stella Hopkins, Gary Schwab and Patrick Scott. To read more, go to www.poynter.org/bnw2009/resources.*

BEHIND the STORY

Lessons Learned

By Binyamin Appelbaum

This story is about one neighborhood where almost 100 people have lost homes to foreclosure.

It is not an anecdote in a broader effort to explain the thousands of other foreclosures in Charlotte, N.C., or the hundreds of thousands nationwide. Instead of trying to wrap our arms around that task, we chose to authoritatively answer a smaller question. We wrote the story of one neighborhood.

By maintaining an extremely local focus, *The Charlotte Observer* made a singular contribution to the understanding of a national crisis. Any local paper, and perhaps only a local paper, can do the same.

Our narrative approach had three additional advantages. Reporters working on entirely different subjects may realize the same advantages by writing a narrative case study instead of a traditional investigative story:

To make the story tangible.

I once asked the great *New York Times* business reporter David Cay Johnston to explain how he writes stories about tax policy that are both understandable and entertaining. What I remember from his answer is that any transaction, however complicated, can be expressed in terms of a dollar. A 20 percent increase, for example, is the difference between $1 and $1.20.

We borrowed that technique in writing about a family and a neighborhood. We traded the impact of large numbers for the impact of intimacy. Instead of "mortgage companies," there was Beazer Mortgage. Instead of "borrowers," there were Mark and Lea Tingley.

The risk of this approach is that readers judge the broader issue by judging those subjects. Their judgments may be overly harsh or overly sympathetic. Or, if their own experience is inconsistent with the subjects', they may judge the story to be irrelevant.

The opportunity, however, is to connect with readers on a personal level. This narrative described choices in purchasing a home that were familiar to many readers. One person who called to thank us said, "You told my story."

To convince readers the story is true.

Investigative stories tend to make an argument and then support it with the fruits of careful research: anecdotes and quotes, statistics and facts. The goal is to compel the reader to accept the conclusion.

Readers are primed to accept certain arguments, such as the classic "Government agency wastes money, fails in stated purpose." Our central finding, by contrast, was something many readers were likely to view with suspicion: that people who voluntarily bought homes were victimized by a company whose employees mostly acted lawfully.

Rather than making that argument, we decided to tell a story.

The power of a good narrative is that it gives readers a sense of first-hand knowledge. It feels like experience. It allows the reader to draw conclusions. To be clear, we were trying to shape those conclusions; we chose to tell a particular story. Our hope was that the narrative would lead readers to a conclusion they might otherwise reject.

The Internet played a key supporting role, allowing readers to see and hear the main characters telling their own stories.

To portray the human element.

A narrative also allowed us to show people making irrational decisions. Readers could see that the numbers didn't work. The buyers didn't make enough money to pay their mortgages. But in the moment, the numbers made sense. The buyers believed the homes were affordable. The narrative let readers follow the Tingleys as they suspended their own disbelief and bought a home.

In the process, we tried to give readers a more nuanced answer to the question of responsibility. The buyers and the company had collaborated in a fiction. Their roles were not equal—the company led, the buyers followed—and that was part of the story, too.

Notwithstanding these advantages, it's important to note the limits of narrative. On the page and online, this story was surrounded by material that explained, justified and elaborated on some of its authoritative statements. The story told what we knew. The surrounding material told how we knew it. The separation allowed us to engage readers first, and it allowed readers to choose the depth of their immersion.

We added one more layer on the Web. An interactive map enabled people to see and explore every foreclosure in Charlotte. That proved hugely popular for the same reason as the narrative: Readers could use the data to reach their own conclusions.

Binyamin Appelbaum started covering the banking industry for The Charlotte Observer *in 2005. His reporting on mortgage lending culminated in a series that included this story. The series won the 2007 George Polk Award for Economic Reporting and was a finalist for the 2008 Pulitzer Prize for Public Service. Appelbaum now covers residential real estate for* The Boston Globe.

The Detroit News

Finalist: Local Accountability Reporting

David Josar

Tax Breaks for Needy Abused

OCT. 19, 2007

A little-known city committee empowered to give property tax exemptions to needy residents has awarded tax breaks worth thousands of dollars to apparently well-to-do homeowners, a three-month investigation by *The Detroit News* has found.

In some of the most egregious cases, people who own multiple houses, drive luxury vehicles and live in homes worth more than $500,000 have been granted "hardship exemptions" by the nine-member committee, which is appointed by the Detroit City Council.

The Hardship Committee keeps no notes, meets in private, has no staff and conducts no investigations of applicants. It has granted more than 14,000 applications totaling $15 million in tax exemptions over the past seven years.

In many cases, the hardship claims are legitimate and have provided tax relief to people living well below the poverty line. But in other instances, the committee has taken the word of well-off residents who have pleaded poverty.

"This is very, very serious," Councilwoman Sheila Cockrel said Thursday. "Even if we have to take criticism, I'll do my part that this is dealt with."

Among *The News'* Findings:

- The program is intended for property owners whose income is below the federal poverty guidelines and with assets of $5,000 or less, but that requirement is routinely waived or ignored by committee members.

- More than 300 residents who pleaded poverty drive luxury vehicles such as Cadillacs, Lexuses, Land Rovers and Corvettes. In five cases, people receiving exemptions had four or more cars; three had boats.
- More than 100 either did not live at the homes for which they obtained tax breaks, or owned other properties as well.
- 350 of those who received reprieves this year have gotten the breaks each year for the past seven. In some other Michigan communities with hardship programs, exemptions are capped at two consecutive years.
- 70 senior citizens got tax breaks even though they had received reverse mortgages with an average lump-sum payment of $120,000. Those who get reverse mortgages make no payments on them until the homeowner dies, sells or moves.
- More than half of the people who claimed they couldn't afford their taxes nonetheless met mortgage requirements—many for loans worth more than the purchase price of their homes.
- While a home may be owned by several people, some applicants listed just the poorest owner. In other cases, only one owner was listed, and the wealthier party's assets weren't disclosed. One owner of a home in the Woodbridge Historic District, for example, lived in an $800,000 Bloomfield Hills condo and drove a Corvette; the co-owner and applicant, who lived in the home on Avery, earned less than $20,000 a year.
- Tax breaks were granted to homes owned by five people who had been dead at least three years.
- Since 2001, the earliest that records were available, to 2006, the number of exemptions has grown 139 percent. Of the 2,919 applications the city received from January through mid-May this year, just 17 percent were rejected by the board, according to city records.

After getting wind of *The News'* investigation this week, the Detroit City Council scheduled a private meeting with its lawyers today to discuss the Hardship Committee.

The tax exemptions, originally intended to help the needy save their homes, have never been audited.

"We just have to go by what people tell us," said Mattie Johnson, 83, who has been on the committee for eight years. "We can't do any investigating."

When asked how a person can afford to drive a Cadillac Escalade, yet be exempt from taxes, Johnson said: "Poverty is measured different ways. Just because you have a Cadillac doesn't mean you're rich."

Representatives of the mayor's office are concerned by some of the tax breaks, but said their hands are tied. Detroit's projected deficit for the fiscal year that ended in July is nearly $70 million, according to a City Council estimate this month.

"We have no say over who gets the exemptions," said Linda Bade, the city's chief assessor. "This is all City Council." The mayor has no say in appointing Hardship Committee members and he cannot veto any exemptions they grant.

Lawyers to Reveal Findings

Through the Freedom of Information Act, *The Detroit News* reviewed records of people who had gotten tax breaks, as well as their addresses and the amount of forgiven taxes dating to 2001. The city provided heavily redacted copies of a handful of actual applications; city attorneys said much of the information they contained—such as household income and the number of people living at an address—is personal and cannot be released.

As part of the probe, *The News* also gathered information from county and court records.

After *The News* requested city records, attorneys in the city law department began inquiring about the program, too. At today's closed-door meeting, the lawyers will reveal what they found, and outline the council's options for addressing those findings.

Today's meeting was called by Councilwoman JoAnn Watson on Tuesday, a day after *The News* contacted her appointee to the Hardship Committee, Roslyn Trotter, to ask how Trotter's attorney, Bobby Joe Frierson, ended up with a $6,128 tax break on his $335,000 home in Sherwood Forest—one of the city's most fashionable neighborhoods. Its previous owner was ex-Detroit school superintendent Eddie Greene.

Frierson is representing Trotter, a Detroit Institute of Arts board member, in a civil case.

Bobby Joe Frierson's wife, Santranina Frierson, got the exemption after she made a sworn statement to the Hardship Committee that she was widowed. But Bobby Joe Frierson, who is listed as Santranina Frierson's husband on their mortgage documents and property deeds, is not dead. He was in Wayne County Circuit Court on Oct. 12, representing Trotter.

Trotter was one of two Hardship Committee members who approved the exemption for Frierson's home. Neither Trotter nor the Friersons returned repeated telephone calls seeking comment.

The nine members of the Hardship Committee break into teams of three to evaluate whether a person will get an exemption; two votes are needed.

In 2004, Karla Harper bought a $160,000 home in the 14000 block of Rutland, putting down 10 percent and borrowing the rest. Later that year, she briefly shared ownership of the property with Sean Tidwell, who continues to register a business to that address. Tidwell characterized the transaction as inadvertent and described Harper as a friend.

Later, Tidwell was appointed to the Hardship Committee by Councilwoman Martha Reeves. In 2006 and 2007, Harper applied for and was awarded a $5,657 tax break by the committee, although Tidwell did not vote on her application. Tidwell said Harper, who did not return phone calls, has been sick in recent years.

Home 'Is All I Have'

In 1980, the Michigan Legislature passed a well-intentioned law giving communities the discretion to temporarily suspend property tax bills for homeowners with incomes at or below the federal poverty level. Today, that benchmark is $20,650 for a family of four.

Leomy Smith, 74, is almost certainly the kind of person lawmakers had in mind.

Her home on Parkside in Detroit's University District, which she has owned since 1978, "is all I have, even though it's the worst house in the block," Smith said.

Her storm door is broken, the blinds are torn, windows are cracked and the mail slot has been mangled. There is little furniture in the home that Smith shares with her unemployed daughter, two teen-aged grandsons and a mentally disabled nephew.

"If I didn't get it [the exemption] I'd lose my house and I don't know where I'd live," Smith said.

Her tax break, which she has been receiving since at least 2001, is worth $4,800 a year. Her annual income, she said, is under $8,000 a year.

A Kenilworth Exemption

Pia Robertson's case isn't so clear. Robertson drives a 2006 Land Rover and owns a home in the 300 block of Kenilworth with an above-ground pool and a television satellite dish. She was awarded a $4,413 tax break in 2006, and says she deserves it.

"I'm needy," Robertson shouted as she walked out of her home and rode off in a 2007 cream-colored Escalade with temporary plates.

Robertson, who earned a degree from Wayne State, bought the house for $60,000 in 2003 with a $6,000 down payment. In 2005, she paid off the home loan, took out a new $100,000 mortgage and got the tax exemption the next year.

"I don't have to explain anything," Robertson said when asked why she couldn't pay her taxes.

Her neighbor, retired cafeteria worker Meredith Kominsky, 77, is puzzled by Robertson's tax break.

"There is no way this is fair," said Kominsky, who pays $1,000 a year in taxes.

She believes taxes are high in Detroit—and at 69 mills, they are—but says paying them is a part of civic responsibility.

"I could use the extra $1,000 a year to buy me some extras, but that's my duty," she said. "I get police protection. I get my street cleaned. I get my trash picked up. That stuff ain't free."

City Council's Role

Until sometime in the 1980s or 1990s—no one seems to know, exactly— the Detroit City Council vetted hardship applications itself. But it handed that duty to the committee, whose members are paid $200 per meeting.

Other Michigan communities imposed restrictions on hardship exemptions, such as limiting the number of tax-exempt years; capping the value of homes that can be exempted; and setting a ceiling on the assets that an applicant can have and still get an exemption.

But in Detroit, City Council oversight of the process is lax and the definition of who should get a tax exemption is vague. The applicants' income threshold is routinely waived, and unlike other communities, Detroit does not set a maximum limit on the value of homes seeking tax forgiveness.

The most expensive home pardoned from the tax rolls during the period reviewed was in 2004—a mansion in Detroit's upscale Palmer Woods neighborhood that sold in February 2005 for $525,000.

According to Detroit's application guidelines, a property owner may have assets, in addition to the home, of no more than $5,000. But in their notarized applications, many property owners failed to list additional homes, vehicles or cash they received from reverse mortgages, home equity loans and other financial instruments.

Jasper and Constance Williams, who live just north of New Center in a run-down brick home, did not report that they owned a rental home on the west side. They drive a late-model Escalade and a Cadillac STS.

Oscar Lucas, the 76-year-old owner of a home in an upscale section of West Outer Drive, did not disclose he had gotten a check for $247,500 in a reverse mortgage for his home—money that only must be repaid if he moves or dies. He slammed the door on a reporter asking about his tax break.

Charleszetta Lynn Cotton, 53, lives in a well-maintained, 4,000-square-foot, three-bath home on Atkinson in Boston-Edison. Since 2003, she's gotten tax breaks totaling $15,268.

She says looks can be deceiving. "I'm entitled to help when I need it," said Cotton, explaining that she was laid off from her job at General Electric in 2000 and can't work due to asthma.

"I'd lose this house if I didn't get the break."

Cotton shares the brick home with her husband, Tyrone, 46, and her daughter, Jamayea Cheeks, 32. Neither works, Cotton said.

On her 2007 application for the tax break, Cotton wrote that she was separated from her husband and didn't know where he was. When a reporter stopped by this week, her husband—who she said can't work because of a bad back—was in the living room, watching a wall-size color TV.

She said she and her daughter together lease the 2005 Chrysler Pacifica in their driveway.

Cotton said ongoing renovation projects were accomplished by getting contractors to install materials she found on clearance at Lowe's.

"We're struggling. I still have funeral expenses from when my sister died in January," she said.

Council President Kenneth V. Cockrel Jr. said Thursday he is "concerned" about the Hardship Committee's work and the questions raised by *The News'* investigation, but added there was little he can say pending advice from the city's law department and the possibility of a criminal investigation.

"We're committed to finding out all the facts," he said.

BEHIND the STORY

Lessons Learned

By David Josar

When I saw a report called "Hardship Tax Exemptions" on the Detroit City Council agenda, I became curious. I had been a city hall/urban affairs reporter for more than a decade, but I had never heard of a program that wipes away poor people's property taxes.

That's what this bare-bones report covered. There was a chart showing that property tax exemptions had grown to the point that they cost the city about $6 million a year in lost revenue. A city council staffer raised some questions, but the report was never discussed in the meeting and it was quietly filed away.

For the next six months, I picked away at the story while covering my daily beat. I filed public records requests, negotiated with city attorneys, took photos of houses, crisscrossed Detroit to survey properties and pulled property and other records to show that many of the people pleading poverty were living in luxury.

Here's what I learned in the process.

Be curious about obscure documents, and be patient and vigilant in following up on them. The Detroit City Council gets dozens of reports each week. I block out time to go through them because they may lead to a good story.

Do your legwork and use your knowledge of the community. My first break came when the city gave me a list of 28 recipients of tax breaks, along with their addresses and the value of their exemptions. Instead of relying on public documents, I opted to do an in-person survey to get details that couldn't be found otherwise. Some of the homes on the list were so run-down, they had to be uninhabitable. Others were immaculate, well-maintained and had luxury vehicles parked in the driveway. Out came my digital camera, and I snapped photos that would be part of the final project.

Break down a large project into smaller, manageable tasks. I eventually obtained a two-foot stack of documents identifying more than 5,000 properties that received tax breaks. I couldn't physically survey each home.

Instead I bird-dogged the properties in the most upscale neighborhoods and those that received the largest tax breaks.

In about a month, while still producing daily stories, I came up with a list of 24 properties that would be the backbone of the articles. For each property, I created a file with a photo of the home, tax documents, lawsuits, mortgages and deeds. These folders helped me pitch the story to my editor. Later, during the final editing, they served as quick guides to ensure all my details were correct.

Negotiate for records. In my initial inquiries, I was told that the public body that approves the tax breaks kept no minutes or public records. That made no sense because government entities are required to take some sort of minutes of their deliberations. I filed numerous public records requests for hardship applications and supporting documents.

The city lawyer who handles public records requests became an ally. She helped me get portions of tax rolls as a substitute for the nonexistent meeting minutes. She and I worked out a deal that got me selected batches of records when it would be too costly for the paper to pay for retrieving and copying the entire set.

Interview and observe. The public records, coupled with the photographs of the houses, were the bones of the story. The homeowners' interviews put the meat on that skeleton. Although time-consuming, I opted to interview in person the 24 people I had focused on. That's how I found the details that made the story come alive: the woman who explained why she needed a poverty tax break even as workmen renovated her house and her husband watched a wide-screen TV; the family living in the broken-down home that was nearly devoid of furniture; the woman who shouted, "I'm needy" as she drove off in her Cadillac Escalade.

Decide when more is better. Four months before the stories were printed, I had done enough reporting to write a solid story about the abuses involving the 24 properties I had selected. I also had records of more than 5,000 properties granted tax breaks. It was nearly impossible to research each of these property owners.

Still, an editor and I decided to run abbreviated public records checks on the roughly 2,000 properties and individuals granted breaks for one year. This would give a broader picture than just the 24 homes. For the next two months, I spent about half of my workdays checking mortgages, delinquent taxes and ownership of boats and vehicles. In the end I could list definitively, during one year, how many of the tax-break recipients owned luxury autos, took second mortgages to get cash out of their homes and owned multiple properties.

David Josar is now in his second term at The Detroit News, *where he covers Detroit city government. From 1995 to 2000, he wrote about Wayne County government, organized crime and federal courts. In the interim, Josar was the Stuttgart, Germany, bureau chief for the European edition of* Stars and Stripes. *He lives in a restored house that he bought from the city of Detroit for $438 in back taxes.*

The Free Lance-Star

Finalist: Local Accountability Reporting

Pamela Gould

Clues Point to Serial Killer: Evonitz Not Checked in Unsolved Slayings

NOV. 18, 2007

If federal authorities had pursued serial killer Richard Marc Evonitz as relentlessly as they pursued Darrell Rice, at least three families could know whether Evonitz killed their daughters.

Five years ago, relying predominantly on forensic testing, investigators announced that overwhelming evidence showed Evonitz killed 16-year-old Sofia Silva, 15-year-old Kristin Lisk and 12-year-old Kati Lisk.

In the final days of his life in June 2002, while fleeing from authorities into Florida after abducting and raping a South Carolina teen, Evonitz told one of his sisters he had committed "more crimes than he could remember," police said.

Whether it was an idle boast remains to be seen.

On Aug. 13, 2002, with the local, state and federal law enforcement officials of the Lisk-Silva Task Force behind him, then-Spotsylvania County Sheriff Ron Knight pledged they would do all they could to determine every crime the former sailor and salesman committed in his 38-year life.

That hasn't happened.

That pledge for a definitive investigation into Evonitz's criminal activities has been either forgotten, aborted or blocked.

The FBI was to create a timeline of Evonitz's life and then notify police agencies around the country—if not the world—to see if they had any crimes the former Spotsylvania resident might have committed. As they have done with other serial killers, the FBI's profilers planned to then host a meeting of investigators to discuss their cases.

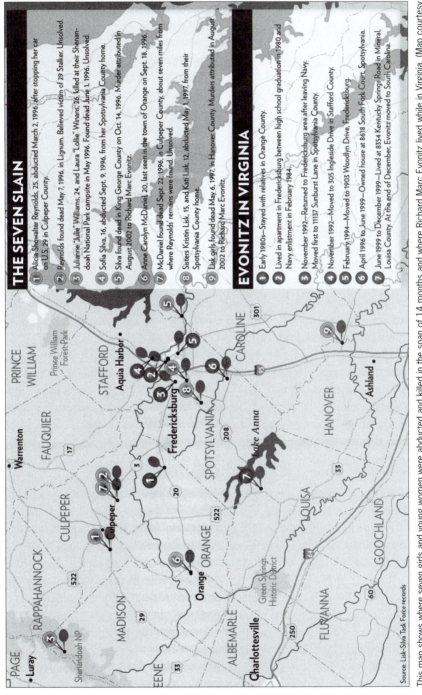

THE SEVEN SLAIN

1. Alicia Showalter Reynolds, 25, abducted March 2, 1996, after stopping her car on US. 29 in Culpeper County. Reynolds found dead May 7, 1996, in Lignum. Believed victim of 29 Stalker. Unsolved.

2. Julianne "Julie" Williams, 24, and Laura "Lollie" Winans, 26, killed at their Shenandoah National Park campsite in May 1996. Found dead June 1, 1996. Unsolved.

3. Sofia Silva, 16, abducted Sept. 9, 1996, from her Spotsylvania County home. Silva found dead in King George County on Oct. 14, 1996. Murder attributed in August 2002 to Richard Marc Evonitz.

4. Anne Carolyn McDaniel, 20, last seen in the town of Orange on Sept. 18, 1996. McDaniel found dead Sept. 22, 1996, in Culpeper County, about seven miles from where Reynolds' remains were found. Unsolved.

5. Sisters Kristin Lisk, 15, and Kati Lisk, 12, abducted May 1, 1997, from their Spotsylvania County home.

6. Lisk girls found dead May 6, 1997, in Hanover County. Murders attributed in August 2002 to Richard Marc Evonitz.

EVONITZ IN VIRGINIA

1. Early 1980s—Stayed with relatives in Orange County.

2. Lived in apartment in Fredericksburg between high school graduation in 1980 and Navy enlistment in February 1984.

3. November 1992—Returned to Fredericksburg area after leaving Navy. Moved first to 11137 Sunburst Lane in Spotsylvania County.

4. November 1992—Moved to 305 Ingleside Drive in Stafford County.

5. February 1994—Moved to 1903 Woodlyn Drive, Fredericksburg.

6. April 1996 to June 1999—Owned house at 8618 South Fork Court, Spotsylvania.

7. June 1999 to December 1999—Lived at 8354 Kentucky Springs Road in Mineral, Louisa County. At the end of December, Evonitz moved to South Carolina.

Source: Lisk-Silva Task Force records

This map shows where seven girls and young women were abducted and killed in the span of 14 months and where Richard Marc Evonitz lived while in Virginia. (Map courtesy of Scott Carmine/*The Free Lance-Star*)

The timeline was finally finished in the summer of 2006 after the FBI got Evonitz's Navy records. But plans for the meeting have been scrapped.

And despite saying they would forensically check Evonitz against crimes nationwide, the FBI and Virginia State Police didn't pursue those tests for unsolved homicides in Evonitz's own backyard.

Beginning in March 1996, seven girls and young women were killed in a 14-month span—all within the region where Evonitz was known to troll for his victims.

Four of those slayings remain unsolved.

Starting in 1997—five years before Evonitz surfaced—and still today, federal authorities have relentlessly pursued Darrell David Rice, a computer programmer from Maryland with mental health problems. His most serious crime before he became the focus of investigators' attention was using illegal drugs.

They pursued Rice as a suspect in the March 1996 death of Alicia Showalter Reynolds, a 25-year-old graduate student who was abducted by a man in a pickup while traveling along U.S. 29 in Culpeper County.

They pursued him in the May 1996 deaths of 24-year-old Julianne "Julie" Williams and 26-year-old Laura "Lollie" Winans, killed at their campsite in Shenandoah National Park.

They checked him as a suspect in the abductions and deaths of Sofia Silva in September 1996 and sisters Kristin and Kati Lisk the following May.

And Culpeper Sheriff H. Lee Hart called him a suspect in the September 1996 slaying of Orange County resident Anne Carolyn McDaniel, whose body was found a few miles from Reynolds' remains near the community of Lignum.

Coming Up Empty

Rice was 29 years old at the time investigators began considering him in the series of slayings.

He was arrested July 9, 1997, minutes after trying to grab a woman bicyclist in Shenandoah National Park and asking her to expose her breasts.

Even Rice's attorneys admit it made sense to check him in Reynolds' death and the Shenandoah park slayings the year before. He had tried to abduct a woman, he drove a pickup, his father had a home in Culpeper and Rice looked similar to one of the composites created after Reynolds' death.

But the attorneys say it shouldn't have taken long to eliminate the Columbia, Md., resident as a suspect.

Witnesses who saw Reynolds on the shoulder of U.S. 29 reported the man talking to her had a black pickup with lots of chrome, probably a

Nissan. The same description was given by most of the women who were flagged down in the weeks before Reynolds' disappearance by a man claiming they were having car troubles.

And women who got into the truck with the so-called "29 Stalker" said the truck was tidy and had an automatic transmission mounted on the steering column and an in-dash radio.

Rice's truck was bright blue, not black; a Chevy S-10, not a Nissan. It had a stick shift on the floor, was littered with items and had a tape player on the seat that dangled from the dash by electrical wires.

In addition, state police asked one of two women used repeatedly to screen suspects to look at a lineup including his photo within weeks of Rice's arrest and she didn't identify him.

The Shenandoah slayings were committed by someone able to control two experienced outdoorswomen without drawing any attention along a trail a third of a mile from Skyline Drive and the busy Skyland Lodge.

The killer subdued both women and sliced their throats without Winans' dog—which wasn't harmed—creating a commotion.

If it was Rice, he did it without leaving a single bit of forensic evidence.

That was of particular note given that the lead investigator, FBI Agent Peter C. Groh, looked at Rice's truck after his 1997 arrest and said it appeared it hadn't been cleaned since the time of the slayings and would likely provide evidence.

Not only did the truck not provide any link, nothing else did, either— not belongings from Rice's home, his computer, his father's car, his father's home or even his DNA.

Not one bit of forensic evidence linked Rice to the Shenandoah slayings.

And not one bit of forensic evidence linked Rice to Reynolds' death or to any of the women who had contact with the 29 Stalker.

Who Is the 29 Stalker?

The one thing women who were stopped by the 29 Stalker consistently said was that he was smooth, seemed sincerely concerned about their safety and came across as nonthreatening—so much so that three women besides Reynolds got into the truck with him.

Two of them—including the second woman used to screen suspects— looked at a photo lineup that included Rice's picture and didn't identify him.

The third woman picked a Virginia state trooper from the first lineup she viewed. Six years later, after Rice's photo appeared in newspapers and on TV, that woman picked him from a six-person photo spread.

One year later, she reportedly told a private investigator Evonitz was the man who abducted her.

That woman, Carmelita Shomo, isn't the only person to open up the possibility that Evonitz could be the 29 Stalker. At least three other people make a case for that to be fully explored.

• Ann Ferguson Swibold of Orange told *The Free Lance-Star* that Evonitz was the man who tried to stop her in February 1996 by suggesting she was having car problems.

Swibold told state police that on Feb. 26, 1996, a man in a large, dark sedan followed her along State Route 230—a 10-mile stretch connecting U.S. 29 in Madison County to U.S. 15 in Orange.

She said he came up behind her and flashed his lights until both cars reached U.S. 15. When she turned right, he pulled beside her and mouthed for her to pull over because something was wrong with her car, the police report from March 12, 1996, shows.

All of that—apart from the vehicle—is identical to what other women who encountered the 29 Stalker reported to police.

Swibold said she didn't pull over because she knew she didn't have car problems.

She saw Rice's photo and said it wasn't him.

When she first saw Evonitz's photo, she said she had no doubt.

"I'm 101 percent sure," she said.

"I don't remember too many names, but I don't forget a face," she added.

• Amy Adrian Ates contacted the FBI in 2002 after seeing Evonitz's picture in the news.

Interviewed before Evonitz was confirmed as the Spotsylvania girls' killer, she told state police Special Agent David A. Russillo that Evonitz was the man who followed her home from work along U.S. 29 in Culpeper in either August or September 1999.

She told police the driver was a clean-cut white man with brown hair and a neatly trimmed goatee. The car was a "cherry red two-door coupe."

"Ates advised when she saw the photo of Evonitz on the television she became very scared because he looked exactly like the individual that followed her," the police report states.

Evonitz lived in the Fredericksburg area from 1992 to '99, moving to Louisa County after he lost his Spotsylvania home to foreclosure in June 1999, according to information assembled by the Lisk-Silva Task Force.

While living in Louisa, Evonitz worked out of rental space there at Centurion Tools.

On July 24, 2002, Centurion Tools President Fred Fitzsimmons told state police Senior Special Agent David M. Riley and Spotsylvania sheriff's Detective Joseph Cagnina of the Lisk-Silva Task Force that Evonitz sometimes associated with four former co-workers from Walter Grinders in Spotsylvania.

He specifically mentioned one who owned a red Pontiac Fiero, and said Evonitz may have driven his colleague's car sometimes.

A Fiero is a small two-door coupe.

• Walter Grinders' co-worker Lyell Chapman said Evonitz often took long midday breaks, and told him of trying to pull over women drivers.

"He just went on and on about how you can flag 'em down in traffic and tell them there's something wrong with their car. Then they think you're a nice guy," Chapman told *The Free Lance-Star.*

"One day he came in mad as hell. He pulled up alongside one woman in traffic. She got in the center turn lane and he caught the red light. He was some kind of mad about that."

Walter Grinders is a machine-tool business in Spotsylvania, located just minutes from Evonitz's South Fork Court home.

Chapman said Evonitz, who was in customer service and sales, would come to his work area in the late afternoon and tell him about his fascination with the idea of raping and strangling women and his admiration for serial killer Ted Bundy.

Chapman told police Evonitz said Bundy "was probably the most intelligent man on the planet" and "no matter what Bundy did, you've got to admire his brilliance because he manipulated and got control of so many women without getting caught for a very long time."

• On July 3, 2002, Chapman told Spotsylvania Detective Cagnina and state police Senior Special Agent Riley that Evonitz "acted as though he could come and go as he pleased at the company and didn't have to account for his time like the non-salaried employees."

Evonitz created Walter Grinders' time-keeping system in Excel software. He filled out his own time sheets on an honor system.

The 29 Stalker incidents occurred at various times and on various days of the week.

Alicia Reynolds was abducted on a Saturday morning. Evonitz claimed he was working that day from 9:25 a.m. until 12:10 p.m.

Chapman said he never knew Evonitz to work on Saturdays.

Bonnie Jose, Evonitz's wife at the time, was astounded at even the suggestion that he worked Saturdays. As a hair stylist, she said, she worked every Saturday but never knew him to work that day.

• Despite what is depicted in the 29 Stalker composites released to the public, many women reported the man had facial hair, some saying he may have had a mustache. One composite circulated among law enforcement officials shows a man with a goatee. Evonitz sported at least a mustache at the time, and also had a goatee at some point.

• Handwritten notes found in Evonitz's locked footlocker inside his home place him in the Lignum area of Culpeper where both Reynolds' and McDaniel's bodies were found. The notes also place him on the road that leads to Shenandoah National Park.

Evonitz's widow, Hope Crowley Evonitz, told King George County sheriff's Capt. Steve Dempsey and state police Agent William Hicks that she and her husband both enjoyed driving back roads. Specifically, she said they drove back roads in Culpeper.

• Though Evonitz never owned a pickup, Chapman said he saw him driving one. A friend owned a Nissan truck, and his first wife told the FBI Evonitz knew how to hot-wire cars, having done it as a teen to take joy rides.

• Police noted that many of the women flagged down by the 29 Stalker were petite, in their 20s, with long, dark hair. Sofia Silva and the Lisk sisters were petite with long, dark hair, a point law enforcement stressed in suggesting Evonitz was attracted to a particular "type" of victim.

In the park slayings, FBI profilers said Julie Williams was likely the focus of the attack. She was 24, tall and thin, with dark hair.

Similar Crimes?

Based on witness accounts and other information, the Spotsylvania Sheriff's Office attributed two sexual-assault cases to Evonitz in addition to the Lisk and Silva slayings.

The first was a May 1994 incident that began in the parking lot of the Massaponax McDonald's.

An 18-year-old woman was assaulted after a man talked her into giving him a ride in her pickup. Once inside the truck, the man threatened her with a knife and forced her to drive to two Spotsylvania sites where he assaulted her.

The second case was the rape of a Spotsylvania teen inside her home in June 1995. Two girls, ages 13 and 11, were home alone when a man broke in between 1 and 2 p.m. The older girl was raped and the younger was fondled, according to police reports.

Those cases share similarities with Evonitz's known crimes, as well as with the unsolved slayings of Williams, Winans and Reynolds.

• As was the case when he abducted Sofia Silva and the Lisk sisters, police don't believe Evonitz worked the day of the June 1995 rape.

Evonitz also was off work four days during the week when Williams and Winans were believed to have been killed in Shenandoah National Park. The date of their deaths is unknown.

• In the Spotsylvania break-in, he came prepared with a sports bag that included scissors and surgical gloves. He cut a sheet at the house into strips to bind the younger girl.

Clothing from the Shenandoah slaying victims was used to gag them and to bind Winans' ankles. Their killer also used duct tape he is believed to have brought with him to bind their wrists. That tape was cut, not torn, according to an FBI Laboratory report.

FBI profilers said in an October 1996 analysis of the Shenandoah slayings that the killer "came prepared and with sufficient time to act in a calculated and concerted rather than frenzied, spontaneous fashion."

• No seminal fluid was found with the young rape victim, nor was any found in the cases of Sofia Silva, Kati Lisk, Kristin Lisk, Julie Williams or Lollie Winans. Initial forensic tests in the Reynolds case showed the only such evidence there likely came from her husband, who is not a suspect.

Evonitz was experiencing sexual dysfunction in 1996 and 1997. By the time he abducted and raped the South Carolina teen in 2002, he had been prescribed Viagra.

FBI profilers said in their analysis of the Shenandoah slayings that the "lack of evidence of sexual assault by the offender may be the result of his inability to perform due to sexual dysfunction."

The South Carolina assault and Lisk-Silva cases also offer parallels to the Shenandoah slayings.

• Evonitz stuffed a rolled-up paper towel into the South Carolina victim's mouth to keep her quiet after abducting her. Crime scene investigators found a flattened and blood-soaked roll of toilet paper at the Shenandoah scene.

• Evonitz used sexual devices in assaulting the South Carolina teen and had a wide assortment of them in his belongings. The same kind of device was found at the Shenandoah slaying scene, where both victims were found naked.

• Evonitz owned oils as part of his cache of sexual items. An oil was detected inside both young women during their autopsies. Its source was not among their belongings.

• Intricate knots were used to tie rope around the blanket that covered the body of Sofia Silva. Police said Evonitz's Navy training may have been employed in tying the knots. He served in the Navy from February 1984 through October 1992.

The first expert consulted by the FBI in the Shenandoah slayings said the knot used in the ligature on Winans' ankles was a "midshipman's hitch," something "commonly used aboard ships."

She said it requires training and generally is "associated with the Navy, Coast Guard or water craft," according to her Aug. 23, 1996, letter to the FBI.

• As with Silva, who had been wrapped in a blanket, the bodies of Williams and Winans were cocooned. They were left naked inside their sleeping bags.

Failure on Forensics

Law enforcement officials have not turned a blind eye to Evonitz.

Following his June 27, 2002, suicide, they gathered hundreds of pieces of evidence from all of his vehicles, from his last residence in South Carolina, from his former home in Spotsylvania and from his body during his autopsy.

They interviewed his mother, father, sisters, widow, ex-wife, colleagues, co-workers and supervisors.

They sent an electronic communication about Evonitz to police agencies across the country, and later sent letters to jurisdictions he was known to have visited.

They created a timeline that juxtaposed his work schedule with the 29 Stalker incidents. And they've long had a preliminary timeline of his life and know much about the places he lived, worked and traveled.

But what they have not done is taken what some would argue is the simplest step—pursuing science as far as they can.

Rice was indicted in April 2002 on federal capital murder charges in the May 1996 slayings of Williams and Winans, without any forensic link.

Four months later, police said forensic evidence showed conclusively that Evonitz was the Lisk-Silva killer.

In the ensuing months, additional forensic testing in the park slayings strengthened Rice's claims of innocence while raising questions about whether Evonitz could have been the killer.

• In September 2003, after confirming none of the Shenandoah slayings evidence was from Rice, FBI Lab hairs-and-fibers expert Douglas Deedrick checked two head hairs from the Shenandoah slayings scene against hairs from Evonitz and noted microscopic similarities.

The hairs were then forwarded to the lab's mitochondrial DNA analysis unit.

• In October 2003, FBI Lab scientist Constance Fisher reported that mitochondrial DNA analysis showed Evonitz could not be ruled out as the source of the two crime-scene hairs.

• In January 2004, federal prosecutor Tom Bondurant hired an outside lab to test DNA from the Shenandoah slayings scene using a new forensic test called Y-STR.

But he didn't ask that it be checked against Evonitz, *The Free Lance-Star* found.

Y-STR analysis is useful because it isolates the male portion of DNA from a mixed sample and produces a profile based on the Y chromosome that is unique to men.

Bondurant said the results provided the final impetus for dropping charges against Rice on Feb. 25, 2004. But he refused to release the results.

A review of the evidence, the timing of the analyses and what remains undone in the evaluation of Evonitz leaves many questions. It specifically raises the issue of why each time forensic tests could have furthered—if not answered—the question of whether he killed Julie Williams, Lollie Winans or Alicia Reynolds, those steps weren't taken.

Given the timing, the answer appears to be because of one man—Darrell Rice.

More precisely, the pending prosecutions of Darrell Rice.

This story was part of the first chapter of a six-chapter package that ran in a special section on a single day. The other chapters detailed the years-long efforts to link Darrell Rice to three local slayings, the conflicting interests that blocked forensic testing of a local serial killer for those killings and the reaction of victims' families to these revelations. To read more from the package, go to www.poynter.org/bnw2009/resources.

BEHIND the STORY

Lessons Learned

By Pamela Gould

A defense attorney's job is to mount the best defense possible, but until I covered the abduction trial of Darrell Rice I had never heard a lawyer declare his or her client innocent outright.

Rice wasn't accused of just one abduction. State and federal prosecutors suspected him of being the Route 29 Stalker, a pickup-truck driver who flagged down dozens of female drivers and ultimately killed graduate student Alicia Showalter Reynolds. Prosecutors also suspected Rice in the murders of two other young women but were forced to withdraw federal capital murder charges against him.

As pretrial proceedings in Rice's abduction trial grew contentious, my editor agreed we would dig deeper regardless of the verdict. But we didn't foresee how complicated that venture would be.

We started out trying to determine whether Reynolds' slaying could be solved. We ended up evaluating five unsolved murder cases, analyzing the years-long pursuit of Rice, educating ourselves about every form of DNA analysis, and, in the process, discovering that law enforcement on all levels had reneged on a pledge to run scientific tests to evaluate a serial killer for the unsolved slayings.

One challenge was finding a way to make sense of a mountain of information. I used a spreadsheet to analyze the contents of dozens of reports from women who reported contact with the 29 Stalker. The spreadsheet enabled me to group similar information from a variety of sources and check it for consistency. That's how I recognized that Rice was younger than the 29 Stalker described by witnesses, and that Rice's truck was different from the one they described.

The critical tool to understanding the big picture, though, was a timeline. By merging the key steps of all the investigations into a comprehensive timeline, I could see what detectives knew and when. The timeline exposed the connections among the investigations. It showed that federal officials had sought capital murder indictments for Rice despite five years of forensic tests that failed to link him to the crime. And while the time-line couldn't assign motive, it led me to one reason investigators might not have wanted to check serial killer Richard Marc Evonitz against evidence from the unsolved slayings: The serial killer surfaced two months *after* Rice was indicted.

The more I investigated, the more I realized the breadth of law enforcement's failure to check evidence for links to Evonitz. That reminded me of a fundamental of watchdog reporting: If public officials say they'll do something, check back to see whether they do. I didn't simply ask them; I pored over scores of documents, determined they hadn't and then confronted them.

Proving something didn't happen is trickier than showing it did. I took key statements made by law enforcement and sought to prove or disprove them. For instance, one official contended no physical evidence linked Evonitz to the unsolved murders. Yet I learned no tests had been conducted to check for a link.

It's critical to understand the details in order to recognize the big picture. Here I relied on DNA experts who taught me the science and evolution of DNA testing and helped me assess what had been done and could be done with evidence from the unsolved cases.

Specifically, I learned which DNA tests were used to produce the genetic profiles in the state DNA database. That was key because Evonitz's DNA profile had been run through the database after he was identified in 2002, but the crimes in question had occurred six years earlier.

When I learned the DNA profiles stored in the database were created with tools implemented in the summer of 1997, and that evidence from the unsolved slayings hadn't been reanalyzed since 1996, I realized Evonitz's profile couldn't have been compared to the evidence because the evidence wasn't in the database.

Throughout my investigation, I turned to forensic experts, people familiar with law enforcement practices and my editor. I had to be sure I understood things correctly, that I had every report and that I hadn't missed anything that would contradict my reporting. I called some sources again and again until I was certain I had the science, timing and facts straight.

Overall, the project drove home one critical point: Don't forget your mission.

Journalists, not unlike law enforcement, have a duty to seek truth and pursue justice—even if that means abandoning their original assumptions. Law enforcement officials' erroneous statements about the Evonitz investigation and their relentless pursuit of Rice despite numerous red flags

254 Investigative Journalism

suggested that they had lost sight of their mission—to find justice for these young women, with no agenda other than truth.

Pamela Gould has spent the last nine years of her 22-year journalism career as a general assignment reporter at The Free Lance-Star *in Fredericksburg, Va. Prior to that, as an editor at the* Potomac News *in Woodbridge, Va., she led an award-winning investigation into a state crime lab error that caused the wrong man to be arrested for a young woman's murder. That young woman's death was eventually linked to Richard Marc Evonitz, the serial killer in these stories.*

PART 4

Feature Writing

Lane DeGregory

With the reputation for storytelling that Lane DeGregory has, people understandably ask her how she does it. What does she tell them?

"Talk to strangers."

"Read the walls." (That means read cereal boxes, classified ads, *anything.*)

"Eavesdrop." "Get people to go for a walk." "Listen for dialogue, not quotes."

And most importantly, "Look for stories *everywhere.*"

For Lane DeGregory, "everywhere" often leads her to people whose lives seem undeserving of coverage—until she discovers the universal connections that exist between all of us. Connections such as ambition, pride, greed.

Such connections jump off the pages of the stories in DeGregory's prizewinning entry for this year's ASNE nondeadline writing category. Maybe none of us has jumped a motorcycle over 13 tour buses in front of 90,000 spectators, but we can relate to Evel Knievel's fear of aging, his concern for his image. Most of us have not participated in an interracial adoption, but we can feel Nancy Bostock's pain as a mother watching her child—and her family—suffer.

Accurately identifying those connections, DeGregory will tell you, is essential to the storyteller's success. Ignore them, and you merely convey information. But communicate them effectively, and you offer readers a chance to find meaning in their world.

A graduate of the University of Virginia, DeGregory wrote for *The Virginian-Pilot* in Norfolk for 10 years before moving to the *St. Petersburg Times* in 2000.

Her stories have won more than a dozen national awards, including the 2007 Ernie Pyle Award from the Scripps Howard Foundation for human interest writing; second place in the 2007 National Headliner Awards for feature writing; finalist in the 2006 American Society of Newspaper Editors Awards for nondeadline writing; second place, 2006 American Association of Sunday and Feature Editors award for general feature writing; and first place, 2000 National Association of Black Journalists' Salute to Excellence. Her work has appeared in the 2000, 2004 and 2006 editions of *Best Newspaper Writing*.

Ask DeGregory why she tells stories, and she talks about helping her readers *feel.* That means:

Helping her readers discover that they have a lot in common with Steve Stanton, a transsexual.

Helping her readers notice the remarkable people in their neighborhoods like Eric Wills, the lawn-mowing postman. (This story is reprinted in Part 7.)

Helping her readers appreciate how a mother's decision to give away her child can be an act of love.

"Evel Knievel, Steve Stanton and Nancy Bostock had been in the paper hundreds of times," DeGregory said in an interview for this book, "but there's a whole other layer to them—no one had ever asked them their personal stories. I try to do that."

"I want to make people real, so readers can relate."

—Butch Ward, Distinguished Fellow, The Poynter Institute

What Goes Up

AUG. 5, 2007

By Lane DeGregory

The old daredevil tips back in his recliner, nursing a blue lollipop. His small white dog, Rocket, slumbers in his lap.

On the Food Network, a chef is shouting. Evel Knievel grabs the remote, fumbles with the buttons. "Blasted thing," he growls. "I can't turn it down." He slams the clicker on the table beside him. Buries his face in his hands.

"I spend my days right here, mostly," he says, without lifting his head. It's been three weeks since his second stroke. He is always tired, sometimes addled. Knievel is 68 but has the body of—well, of a man held together with pins and plates.

"I used to go all over the world," he grumbles. "I used to travel eight months a year. Now I can't even drive."

He takes 11 pills in the morning, a dozen at night. They keep his blood flowing and his transplanted liver working. They ease the arthritis that burns his back, arms and legs. It hurts like hell, being mortal.

It's a hot morning in July. In two weeks he is supposed to fly to his hometown of Butte, Mont., for the annual festival in his honor: Evel Knievel Days. He'll wave from the passenger seat of a pickup, sign some autographs, try to impersonate the man he used to be.

"This is my last performance," he says. "If I make it."

If I make it. How many times do you think Evel Knievel has said those words?

Usually he did make it, piloting his motorcycle over cars, snakes, sharks, buses. But we remember him just as well for the times his cycle came up just a teensy bit short. Knievel scattered pieces of himself at Caesars Palace, in Wembley Stadium, in San Francisco's Cow Palace.

He was the first Jackass.

His aim was uncertain, but his timing was exquisite. In the mid-1970s, America was booing its returning soldiers and booting its president. In vroomed Knievel, wearing a red, white and blue leather jumpsuit, a hero's cape and a showoff's thick gold chains.

"Evel was the king of bling," his friend Bill Rundle says. "And they didn't even know what bling was back then."

A painting of Evel Knievel in his daredevil heyday hangs in his Clearwater condo. That Knievel is long gone. Today, at age 68, he is ailing. He has had two strokes and a liver transplant, and still reels from the injuries he incurred during his career. "He was such an icon," friend Bill Rundle says. "You don't believe icons can get old." (Photograph courtesy of Melissa Lyttle/*St. Petersburg Times*)

He gave Americans someone to cheer for, or at least provided a welcome distraction. Twelve days after Richard Nixon resigned, Knievel jumped 13 Mack trucks. On Oct. 25, 1975, more than half the country watched him leap over 14 Greyhound buses in Ohio—more than watched the "Thrilla in Manila" fight between Joe Frazier and Muhammad Ali. Knievel had money, fame and—he doesn't mind telling you—"oh God, more than 1,000 women."

And now here he is, struggling just to breathe. White wisps are all that's left of the thick hair that once spilled from his helmet. After weeks in the hospital, his golf course tan has paled. Gone are the gold chains, the diamond pinky ring, that swagger.

If life delivered neat endings, Evel Knievel would have gone out in a flash of glory, at the far end of a row of buses, or maybe in the bottom of the Snake River Canyon, which he famously failed to clear in 1974. Instead, after two marriages, four kids, a liver transplant, lung disease and a couple of strokes, the old daredevil sees this year's annual Evel Knievel Days as his ending. It will have to do.

"He was such an icon," Rundle says. "You don't believe icons can get old."

* * *

His wife, Krystal, 38, calls him by his given name, Bob.

They live with two spoiled Maltese in a modest Clearwater condo. You have to punch in a code to get through the lobby. The name above their code is an alias. When it said Knievel, drunks kept coming by late at night, buzzing their number.

An oil painting of Evel dominates his front hallway. A bronze statue of him stands on a bookshelf, surrounded by photos of his 11 grandkids.

The dog is snoring in Knievel's lap. Another chef is yelling on TV. Evel turns to a visitor and says, "Why don't you get up and get yourself a beer?"

It's 11 a.m. The visitor declines, thanks him. Knievel barks, "Then why don't you go get me one?"

"Christ almighty," he grouses when he finally gets his Michelob Ultra. He takes a swig.

"Forgive me," he says, "for using the Lord's name in vain."

* * *

"Okay, ask your questions. Hurry up. I don't have all day."

He doesn't want to waste whatever time he has left repeating things everyone already knows. For God's sake, people have written books about him. George Hamilton played him in a movie. The Bionic Woman wrapped her arms around his waist on an episode of her show.

He is tired of people pestering him, asking stupid questions.

What kind of questions? "That's a dumb question."

What was your favorite jump? "Jesus. Any jump I landed was my favorite."

What does it feel like to crash? "What the hell do you think it feels like? Christ almighty. It hurts."

Why did you do what you did? "Because I could. I could do the impossible. And it sure beat selling insurance."

Was it worth it? "What kind of stupid question is that? I'm still here, aren't I?

"Now hurry up. I'm running out of air."

* * *

From the time he could pedal a bike, Robert Craig Knievel wanted to fly.

He was born in 1938, in the desolate mining town of Butte. His parents divorced before he was 2 and left him and his younger brother to be raised by grandparents. "Bobby" was 8 when he got his first wheels. He taught himself to ride, then jump. By 12, he'd totaled four bikes and moved on to motorcycles. Everyone around Butte knew Bobby. He'd race through flower beds, leap curbs, pop wheelies through parking lots.

He wanted to be as flashy as Liberace, as brave as Roy Rogers, as beloved as Elvis. The legend goes that when he got tossed in jail for—what else?—reckless driving, a judge nicknamed him Evil Knievel. Later, Evel changed the spelling so he wouldn't seem so bad.

He worked as a hunting guide, then sold insurance and Hondas. If you beat him at arm wrestling, you won a free motorcycle. Some say he scammed people with a security guard business.

"A lot of Butte people really resent him to this day," says Mike Byrnes, who went to school with Knievel and now runs Butte Tours. "He's the most famous guy to come out of Butte. But we don't have any Evel sites on our tours.

"We've got a T-shirt, though. 'Butte, Montana: Birthplace of Evel Knievel. We apologize.'"

Knievel was 27, married and a father, when he set out to become a professional daredevil. He did everything: built the ramps, booked the venues, promoted the show. Pay him $500 and he'd jump two cars.

Then sponsors began upping the ante. Think you can jump six cars? We'll give you $1,500. Try seven—we'll make it $2,000.

Soon Knievel was coming up with his own stunts. How much would you pay me to jump buses? Sharks? The Grand Canyon?

"He always figured he'd at least try," says Rundle, who traveled with Knievel's entourage.

"This one time at the Cow Palace, he knew his bike wasn't getting up enough speed to make the jump. But Evel would never back down. He jumped anyway. That one broke him up pretty good."

Rundle was with Knievel in 1974 when the federal government said he couldn't jump the Grand Canyon. So Knievel had to settle for the Snake River Canyon. Promoters promised him $6 million.

For a week before the jump, ABC showed specials on how the stunt could go wrong, why the "Skycycle"—more rocket ship than motorcycle—wouldn't make it.

"They kept going over all the ways he could die," Rundle says. "And I don't think Evel thought he'd make it, either. But you know he'd just sit there watching all the reports and he never said anything to anyone. He never seemed to react. It was eerie."

* * *

Knievel needs oxygen. He lifts the dog from his lap, heaves himself out of the recliner.

He shuffles across his living room in white socks, past the Evel Knievel light-switch plate in his bedroom hall, past the photo of his second wedding, at Caesars Palace, where he once crashed so badly he spent a month in a coma.

Knievel opens his closet and pulls out the tubes that tether him to a tank. He flips on the machine, drinks in the air.

On the way back to the living room, he passes a table piled high with fan mail. A guy from St. Paul, Minn., sent an old photo of Evel leaping in front of a Ferris wheel. "I'm just wondering how you're doing," the man wrote. "You're extremely brave. I respect you." Knievel answers every inquiry—as long as he gets a self-addressed envelope, with postage.

"I never thought the empire would last this long," he says, easing back into his chair. He closes his eyes. The shadow of a smile seems to tug at his mouth.

Then he looks up, confused. "What year is it again?"

* * *

In the winter of 1976, Knievel wiped out after jumping a tank of live sharks, crushing both arms and his collarbone and suffering a severe concussion. He also smashed into a cameraman, who eventually lost an eye.

He did a few exhibitions after that—some with his son Robbie, now a grownup daredevil—then quit. He spent his time on golf courses and in casinos, gambling on everything, sometimes $100,000 on a football game.

Years later, after the IRS took some of his homes, Knievel cruised the highways in his custom RV, visiting car dealerships and Harley shops, towing a trailer filled with his past: the rocket he'd ridden into the canyon, five motorcycles, a skeleton illustrating the 35 bones he'd shattered. His appearances helped sell cars, put money in his pocket.

Then came liver disease and the strokes. Knievel can't go on the road anymore. He still does a few endorsements: Mini Coopers, a slot machine, a line of custom motorcycles. Last year, Evel toys were re-released. Even so, money is tight now; Knievel is trying to sell his custom RV.

These days, he says, he doesn't need an adrenaline rush. "The most joy I get now is waking up and wrapping my arms around my wife," he says. "But sometimes she sleeps way over on the other side of the bed and it's hard to get to her. Especially with the dogs between us."

More and more, he thinks about the life after this one. He says he knows God has a place for him. "My grandmother who raised me, she lived to 103, she'll be there waiting for me. And I hope she'll forgive me for all I put her through," Knievel says.

"She'll point her finger at me and say, 'I told you so, Bobby. I told you everything you wanted to do in life, you could. You can fall many times, but as long as you keep getting up, you'll never be a failure.'"

* * *

Evel Knievel needs a nap.

It's a couple of hours into the interview and he's talking about a stunt he never got to do. He wanted to jump out of a plane without a parachute and land in a haystack.

"They never let me do it," he says. "That's the only…"

He nods off. Ten seconds go by, then 20. The dog licks his hand.

When Knievel wakes and sees the visitor still sitting there, he gets angry. He's embarrassed, frustrated, in pain. "You have to go," he says, narrowing his eyes. "I have been known to have quite a temper. And I'm taking medication to stop it. But now I've got to get some sleep."

He's yelling now, pointing a crooked finger. "You gotta go. NOW!"

As the visitor exits, Knievel waves. "Thanks for coming," he calls. "Maybe I'll see you in Butte."

* * *

A couple of weeks later Knievel makes it to Montana, but barely. Instead of staying with his daughter or in a hotel, he checks into an assisted living facility because he's weak and having trouble breathing.

"He's not doing very well," says his old friend, Bill Rundle. "But he says he'll hold on, at least long enough to lead the parade."

Rundle created Evel Knievel Days in 2002 as a way of honoring his buddy. The event brought bikers from across the West. Rundle hired stunt cyclists and built a dirt ramp in the middle of town and even got Robbie Knievel to be there for his dad.

Last year, about 30,000 people packed Butte for Evel days. More than 100 paid $100 each to dine with "Himself," as the program calls him. Organizers had sold tickets to this year's event long before Knievel had the stroke.

The day before the festival, Rundle is concerned. "We had a tearful two-hour conversation last night," he says. "Evel says he's not going back to Florida. He's going to get through this last show. Then he wants to die right here in Butte."

* * *

Late Friday afternoon, more than 1,000 cycles—Hondas and Harleys, trikes and choppers—fill the street in front of the Finlen Hotel. A white pickup is parked at the head of the pack. It's striped with red and blue, sprinkled with stars. Even the leather seats are custom Evel. This is his ride.

Soon Rundle slides into the truck. He looks tired and worried. Are those tears in his eyes?

The bikers follow, revving their engines. The ground seems to tremble.

"Where's Evel?" people in the crowd keep asking.

Four teenagers climb into the painted pickup. Turns out they're Evel's grandchildren. The truck pulls forward, without Knievel.

Evel misses his own parade.

* * *

That night in the hotel banquet room, Evel images are everywhere. Plastic place mats show a blurry Knievel in his Skycycle. A mannequin in his jumpsuit is propped by the bar.

The head table is empty.

"Ladies and gentlemen," Rundle says. "Welcome to the Evel Knievel social." He pauses. A few people clap. "Evel wasn't feeling too well tonight. They had to take him to the hospital to find out what's wrong.

"But you know him. He just called. He's already checked out. He's on his way back here to join you," Rundle says.

"He doesn't want anyone saying they want their money back."

The salads have just been served when Knievel limps in, leaning on two friends. He sits down gingerly, then waves. The hospital band is still around his wrist.

"Everyone, please, let's enjoy our dinner," he says. "I just had a little spell with blood pressure. I think it was too much heat and overexertion on my part. But I'm okay now. Let's eat."

Breathing heavily, pausing between bites, Knievel shovels salad into his mouth while people walk up to shake his shaking hand.

After the entree is served, Knievel summons one of his helpers. He pushes back his chair, leans on the handle of his oxygen tank. "Thank you all very much. I had a tough day," he says.

He unfolds a small square of paper, thanks his doctors and his sponsors, says he has a new custom motorcycle company and there's a rock opera being written about him. It's like that time at Wembley Stadium, where he crashed and broke everything and got up and talked to the crowd anyway.

"I hate to duck out right now," he says. "But I just have to. Thank you so much for coming to see me. God bless all of you."

When he stands up the audience does too, clapping and chanting "Evel, Evel, Evel!" Forty-two minutes after he arrived, Knievel makes his way to the door, propped up by a friend, but still standing.

Introducing Susan

MAY 13, 2007

By Lane DeGregory

She couldn't sleep. She lay for hours in the dark.

In the morning, she would pose for her first portrait, at age 48. All her life, she had dodged and wavered and contemplated every avoidance, even suicide. Now, 12 hours to go.

She got up at 1 a.m., made coffee. She took a mug into the den of her Largo home, pulled out her red journal and started to write:

So here I sit. Alone in the early morning hours. Waiting for the rest of my life to begin.

She had spent years planning for this day. In the last month, she had frantically built a wardrobe, learned makeup, fretted over her too-short hair. She thought she looked good. Pretty. Professional.

Her debut would come after four decades of self-examination, in the dust of a leader's best-laid plans, in the remnants of her family. It glowed with the promise of possibility. Like new skin.

But what if others didn't see her the way she saw herself?

She had already lost her job, her friends and her home—the things that gave her an identity—for admitting she wasn't the person they knew. Now that she was showing them a second self, would they reject that person too?

She knew that some people would never even see Susan Ashley Stanton.

They would see a man in a dress.

Shedding a life usually means starting over, quietly, somewhere else. Slip town. Get a new job in a place no one knows your name.

For Steve Stanton, that wasn't an option.

He had been Largo's city manager for 14 years. He had rappeled with the firefighters and broken his nose with the SWAT team. When he decided to become a woman, he told only a few people. His wife knew, his son did not. But in February, someone told the newspaper.

Then came the speedy firing, and then CNN, *The Daily Show* and Larry King. Then came the pack of lesbian lawyers telling him whom to talk to, what to say.

As Steve, he was forceful, powerful in a governmental, almost dorky kind of way. Now he took orders. He waffled.

In the weeks after he was fired, and before he introduced the world to Susan, Steve went running in a Largo park every morning. After his jog, he would pull his red journal from his Jeep and write at one of the picnic tables. (Photograph courtesy of Jim Damaske/*St. Petersburg Times*)

No one really wanted Steve anymore. They wanted Susan. But who was she? She was a celebrity no one fully knew. Not even Steve.

Atlanta's Gay Pride Parade asked Susan to be grand marshal. A Chicago transgender convention invited her to speak. The city of Sarasota named Susan a finalist for its city manager job.

Tiptoeing through this transition is Steve-Susan. He is a thinner, longer-haired version of his former self, wearing too-big suits and folding his hands in a girly way.

On Tuesday, things change. Susan will meet with Congress members to lobby for transgender rights.

Paparazzi will mill around the Capitol. Gone is the carefully crafted plan of how to control the image of Susan. When she emerges in Washington, her photo will likely hit the AP wire and be transmitted around the world.

I always thought Susan's first appearance would be climbing the steps to Largo City Hall, Susan wrote in her journal. *Instead, I'll be climbing the steps to Congress.*

She consulted with her handlers, and, against their advice, agreed to head off the paparazzi with a hometown newspaper portrait taken Wednesday. She still had some control.

* * *

In 1998, Steve had a dream he was Susan and everyone could see it—and he woke up in a panic. Soon after, he wrote his first journal entry in Susan's voice. In the spring of 2007, Steve finally showed the world Susan— and posed for her first public portrait. (Photograph courtesy of Douglas R. Clifford/*St. Petersburg Times*)

When Donna woke, Steve had to put aside Susan. His wife knows Susan but doesn't want to live with her. Once Steve is Susan full time, he has to move out.

So Steve padded around their kitchen in running shorts and a tank top, scrambling eggs for their 13-year-old son. Travis still hasn't met Susan. He's only seen a blurry photo, snapped with a tripod and self-timer.

"Is it going to take two hours for you to get ready now too, Dad?" Travis asked. "Once you're her?"

The pronoun thing is hard, even in the Stanton house. Steve drives Travis to school. Susan goes shopping. Steve-Susan has been sleeping in the guest room for years.

One afternoon, running late, Susan had to change into Steve in the car. She forgot to take off her mascara. So he wore sunglasses to Travis' school.

A few days ago, Susan called home to say she was on her way. She was wearing a peach tank top and white capris. Having a good hair day.

"I'm coming home as Susan," she told Travis. "I want you to meet her." Travis hid in his room.

* * *

Finding Susan was as indelicate as renovating a house. It was spackling, painting and draping. For years, Steve needed a helmet wig, pancake makeup and foam breasts to be a woman. Lately there's been peeling and stripping—shedding the wig, the beard, letting the hormones transform him into a size 10 and a B cup.

To some, it seemed fake. A macho man wearing a bra? They labeled him a liar. Steve said he was just trying to find his true self.

But how can you be authentic—how can you even know who you are—when you haven't been allowed to try?

Steve has never felt like a man. "What kind of man would want to cut off his b——?" he asks.

He doesn't know if he feels like a woman. How could he?

He supposes he's somewhere in the middle.

"I'm still me," he says.

Susan still wants to scale walls with firefighters. She still loves Gator football and driving her Jeep. She has a softer handshake than Steve. She tries to remember to soften her voice, and still talks like a city manager, peppering long sentences with words like "absolutely" and "typically."

Hormones, she says, have softened her biceps and her personality. Steve could be a jerk, she admits. "I'd have probably fired me too."

Since Steve was fired, none of his former employees—his friends—have called. He had always thought that if he left Largo, they would give him an award.

So last week, he went to the engravers and picked out a trophy: blue, 16 inches with a marble base. On the plaque, he wrote the words he had hoped someone else would write: *To Steve Stanton: The World's Greatest City Manager.*

He needed a tangible reminder of his legacy in Largo. Before he becomes a full-time woman, he needed to acknowledge that he had been a good man. Soon, that $135 trophy will be all that's left of Steve.

* * *

Susan spread her new outfit on the guest room bed. She still had a hard time accessorizing. Men's suits were so easy. And boring.

Steve's closet had been a sea of gray and black. He liked pink shirts and coral ties. Now pink and coral tops crushed against the suits. Twenty pairs of women's shoes—size 8 1/2—cluttered the floor.

Steve never understood the shoe thing. Susan does.

"Shoes make the look. It's like washing your car and not Armor All-ing your tires," she says. She laughs. "Is that a guy thing to say?"

To choose her look, she had navigated International Plaza with her wardrobe consultant—her electrologist—and tried on at least 60 women's suits.

Even with her new shape, nothing fit right. She still has no hips. Her square shoulders felt squeezed in the narrow jackets.

She finally chose a charcoal gray jacket, a flowing skirt, and a rose colored knit shell. (No shirts with collars, her handlers said. Too mannish.)

The clothes are Steve's colors, the muted hues of a librarian, of a government wonk.

Steve-Susan loved evening gowns. Steve-Susan loved the clothes a man would choose for a woman. New Susan is learning to dress for herself.

That morning, she studied her image in the mirror. At first, all she saw was her face. She could not stop smiling.

She checked her watch: 8 a.m. Only two hours to do her hair.

* * *

Steve had gone to the same barber since he moved to Largo. He couldn't tell the guy who had given him the perfect side-part for 17 years that he aspired to highlights and shoulder-length layers.

He was rescued by the police chief's wife. For months, Diane Aradi trimmed Steve's growing hair, taught him to finger curl it into loose waves.

The morning of the photo shoot was Susan's first attempt at doing it on her own.

She armed herself with a blow dryer. Dug out her new round brush. But she couldn't get that lift like Diane did. Four times, she wet it down and started over.

By 9:30 a.m., Susan flopped on the bed in tears. Steve would have never cried over his hair.

"I can't do this," she moaned into the pillow. "I don't know how to be Susan."

Two more tries, then she dialed hair 911. She told the chief's wife: "This is an emergency."

* * *

Are they going to laugh? Should she even show up?

On the way to the photo shoot, she stopped at Barnes & Noble to browse. Books calm her. That's one reason she chose The Poynter Institute, a school for journalists that owns the *St. Petersburg Times,* as the location for the portrait. It's semiprivate, intellectual.

At the bookstore, she flipped through the biographies. Someday, she hoped to see her own story on the shelves. An agent is already peddling Susan's autobiography. By January, those journals she has been keeping since high school could become a book.

She checked the cafe's clock: 10:50 a.m.

The drive to the photo shoot was too short. Nervous, she parked blocks away. As she got out, she peeked in the mirror one last time.

* * *

It was over in a couple of hours. After all the primping and posing, trying to figure out what to do with her hands, crossing and uncrossing her legs, sitting and standing, turning side to side, tilting her head, and working her way from stiff and scared to relaxed and chatty, she asked for a paper towel to blot her makeup.

Someone gave her a bottle of water. The photographer opened his laptop and said she could see herself.

She leaned in. Scanned frame after frame.

That was her? That woman with the great hair?

"I look so happy."

* * *

She wanted to shop. She still needed another suit for her trip to D.C. But it was getting late. Travis had an appointment with the orthodontist.

Time to go back to being Dad.

As she steered her Lexus up the interstate, listening to Celtic folk music, her smile, so bright in the photo, began to fade.

Turns out, after all of that, this was the toughest part. After the years preparing, after she finally felt good about the way she looked, after she finally made her public debut—and no one laughed!—she drove slowly.

She didn't want to go home.

She wasn't ready to hang Susan back in the closet.

Breaking Point

NOV. 4, 2007

By Lane DeGregory

On good nights—there were some—bedtime in the Bostock home began around 8:30, when Nancy called her three kids to put on their pajamas.

Her husband often traveled for business, so she was used to running the routine alone.

She'd let her older daughter, 13, watch TV while she snuggled with her younger daughter, who's 9.

Then came her 11-year-old son. He would cringe when Nancy tried to hug him, so she'd sit on the floor beside his bed. The boy would say, "Tell me my story."

"There was a woman who had a very special baby growing in her belly," the story starts. She picked out his name and gave him his handsome looks, his infectious smile. And she loved that baby and wanted him to grow up safe. When he was born, she couldn't take care of him. So she gave her baby to a social worker, who took him to a foster home. Then one day, when he was 4, his parents found him and brought him home.

"And that's how you came to live here with us," Nancy told her son. "We're your forever family."

Though he asked for his story almost every night, the boy seldom reacted to it. Nancy would kiss his forehead, smooth his Lion King sheets, lock his closet so he couldn't shred his clothes. She'd turn on the baby monitor. "Good night," she'd whisper. "Sweet dreams."

Then she'd make sure the kitchen knives were locked up and drag the sofa into the hall between her kids' rooms. She kept a sleepy vigil all night on that couch, trying to keep everyone safe from her son.

Two weeks ago, Nancy made the front page when she told a state senate committee she was giving up her adopted son.

He tried to kill her, she said.

To get him the help he needs, she said, she has to turn the sixth-grader back to the foster system.

"I'm his mom and I will love him forever," she told Florida's Committee on Children, Families and Elder Affairs. "I don't want my son to come out as some sort of villain. He was born into this. ... He's a hurt child."

How can a mom give up her own son? Especially a mom like Nancy?

The Bostock family prays before dinner in 2004, when their son was 8 and their daughters were 10 and 7. Now, the boy who loved SpongeBob and Game Boy is back in state custody. (Photograph courtesy of Dirk Shadd/*St. Petersburg Times*)

❝ We just kept thinking if we're firm, loving and consistent," Nancy said, "eventually he'll come around and want to be part of this family. ❞

A former social studies teacher, Nancy, 39, has served on the Pinellas County School Board since 1998. She works with Head Start, volunteers as a Guardian Ad Litem to protect foster children. She has better credentials, better knowledge of resources than most parents. "If I can't find the help he needs," she said, "who could?"

Her husband, Craig, 43, said he feels like a failure. They've exhausted every option. "There will always be people who think we could've done a better job," he said. "But I don't know how."

What happened in that home?

How could parents who set out to give a little boy a forever family decide he would be better off without them?

* * *

On Nancy and Craig's third date, at the University of Florida, he told her he had been adopted as an infant and, some day, he wanted to adopt.

Three years after they married, Nancy gave birth to a daughter. Three years later, they adopted a 3-day-old girl. They started searching for another child almost right away.

Gender and race didn't matter. Craig and Nancy are white, but they'd bought a two-story home in a racially diverse neighborhood so a child of another ethnicity would feel more like he fit in.

Nancy was drawn to dozens of little faces, but for two years, they couldn't make a match. Finally, on a Web page of foster kids, Craig found a 4-year-old African-American boy.

The boy's mother had done drugs and drank while pregnant, his caseworker told them. He was developmentally delayed, had ADHD and had been bounced through at least seven foster homes.

"We thought, 'He's only 4. We're a stable, loving family,'" Nancy said. "'How bad could it be?'"

They visited him at his Polk County foster home, where he lived with a single mom and eight other foster boys. He was loud and wild, then quiet and withdrawn. They fell in love with his shy smile.

When they strapped their new son into his car seat to take him home, "He was like a feral animal," Nancy said. Clawing, kicking, shrieking.

In hindsight, Nancy said, he acted like he was being kidnapped.

* * *

In adoption classes, they'd been warned: The first year will be hard. They braced for temper tantrums and time outs. No one could have prepared them for the furor of their small son.

Right away, he called them Mom and Dad. And ugly and stupid. The worst words he knew.

Nancy had filled his new room with a train and farm set, a puppet who looked like him. She even found an African-American doll for the Fisher-Price dollhouse. But her new son turned every toy into a weapon.

He hurled trucks at his sisters, tore up video games, punched the walls until they looked like Swiss cheese. The smallest things would set him off: Put on your shoes, brush your teeth.

He would say: I can take care of myself. I don't need you!

Therapists diagnosed him with Reactive Attachment Disorder, a condition some doctors don't acknowledge. The disorder is said to be caused when infants are shuttled from home to home, making it impossible for them to bond, trust or accept affection. These children often fail to develop a conscience. They can be friendly to strangers but lash out at those closest to them.

"He'd grown to depend on himself. So if you asked him to do something, he just wanted to fight," Craig said.

There were good times, family dinners, trips to Disney World. They took him to Busch Gardens, fishing and to church. They took him to social workers, psychologists and pediatricians. They tried all sorts of pills, punishments and rewards. They talked to their pastor. They called the police.

"We just kept thinking if we're firm, loving and consistent," Nancy said, "eventually he'll come around and want to be part of this family."

I hate you. I don't want to live here, the boy screamed. For five years.

* * *

By age 9, the boy was taller than his mom. Nancy couldn't catch him when he ran. She dreaded even taking him to Publix; he always broke something or acted out. She wasn't embarrassed, she said. But she knew how things must seem. Here she was, a School Board member, and she couldn't control her own kid.

Her son had never had any real friends, she said. Soccer teams and scout troops didn't help him bond. At his own birthday party, he stood alone, watching the other kids splash in the pool.

To strangers, he often seemed polite and withdrawn. At school, in special education and mainstream classes, he behaved better. Until one day when Nancy was out of town and Craig got a call at Honeywell, where he works.

Their son had run out of class and was raging through the school office, tearing things off shelves, ignoring the counselor's pleas. "That's the first time I'd seen that cold look of defiance directed at someone other than me or Nancy," Craig said. "Things were different after that."

He started kicking the dog. He threw a brick at his sister's head. That summer, the family went to Hawaii. When Nancy took the kids to get ice cream, her son body-slammed his cousin. Back in the van, he reached from the back seat and pulled his mom's seatbelt across her neck. Tight.

"All of a sudden, everything got quiet and I couldn't see," Nancy said. "I don't know how I got the car pulled off the road."

In Florida, Nancy found Carlton Manor, a residential treatment program for boys with behavioral issues. The yearlong program ran five days a week. She could bring him home on weekends.

She thought that was a good thing.

* * *

In October 2005, Nancy helped her son pack. He moved into a dorm-like room with another boy. On weekends, his whole family was supposed to follow the program's strict rules.

If he challenged his parents' authority, they were to withhold all privileges. But how do you tell your daughters they can't go to the movies because their brother has been sitting on the time-out sofa for eight hours, refusing to brush his teeth? "He would rather defy us," Nancy said, "than do anything else."

One weekend in June 2006, the 10-year-old tacked a suicide note to his door. Nancy caught him in the kitchen and wrestled a butcher knife from his hand. He started sneaking out at night. Craig had to put an alarm on their front door.

On the advice of another therapist, they disbanded almost all rules. If their son didn't want to brush his teeth, fine. He went days without showering, Nancy said. He started to smell.

He spent 16 months at Carlton Manor, much longer than his allotted year. In January, his therapist said he wasn't ready to come home. But he could no longer stay there.

There had to be another place, another program. Three times, Nancy met with workers from the Department of Children and Families. Her son was too badly behaved for one program, they told her; not psychotic enough for another. He had been Baker Acted three times. The Bostocks had maxed out their insurance and spent thousands on treatment. They couldn't afford $60,000 a year for a private facility.

If parents have money, they can afford private placement; if they're destitute, the government will help. But for the middle class, there are few options. Finally, Nancy found the Attachment Trauma Network. Online, Nancy found 200 other parents, mostly of adopted children, struggling with the same behavior.

"It was such a backward relief, just to know we weren't the only ones," Nancy said. She searched for an expert on the subject, but couldn't find one. Time was running out.

In March, just before her son was to be discharged, Nancy had him in the car with her older daughter. Behind her, she heard a voice she didn't recognize saying, "I'm going to kill Mom."

Her daughter replied: You don't even have any weapons.

Oh yes I do, the boy said. I've got pencils, and they're really sharp, and some other stuff too.

When Nancy searched her son's room, she found a pack of pencils and a power cord stashed in a hole he'd kicked below the window. "In some ways, I looked at his little plan to kill me with something bordering on admiration," Nancy said. "I mean, that took a lot of planning and organization, which is something he doesn't normally show us."

She started sliding the sofa into the hall at night, to keep an eye on his door.

* * *

If the Bostocks had fostered the boy instead of adopting him—if he had stayed in the system—he would qualify for help. Finally, his therapist suggested: Maybe you should send him back.

Nancy was shocked. She had never thought of giving up her son. What kind of mother would?

"It was the opposite of everything I thought was right," she said.

Some kids, the therapist said, actually do better without someone loving them—or at least, without someone who expects to be loved back.

On March 17, Nancy asked the DCF committee for help one last time. She says they told her: Take him home. After he hurts you, we can help.

Nancy could have tried to have him declared mentally ill, so he could be sent to an institution. She could have charged him with abuse, had cops cart him off to a juvenile detention facility.

Instead, she called the child abuse hotline—on herself. "I can no longer keep my son safe," she said. He was leaping out of the car, sprawling in the street, perching on the balcony.

The system is set up to protect kids from parents, not parents from kids. For the state to take a child, the parents have to be charged with neglect, abuse or abandonment. Craig and Nancy consented to abandonment. A judge agreed to let them visit their son.

When officers came to take him, Nancy expected the boy to rage or—maybe—cry and beg to stay. He bolted. "He didn't want to go with them," Nancy said. "But he didn't want to stay."

Craig chased him and brought him back. The boy picked up his bags, turned to the people who had been his parents for seven years and asked, "Why can't I take the PlayStation?"

* * *

On good days—there are more now—Sundays in the Bostock home include a trip to see their son at his new foster home.

He's been back in state custody for eight months. The last time he was home was August, for his little sister's birthday. Holes still pock the walls; his Lion King sheets are still on his bed.

Next year, the Bostocks will have to decide whether to terminate their parental rights. They don't want to. They're still hoping someday their son can come home.

"It feels better, now, when we're with him," Nancy said. "With him out of the house, we don't have the constant battles."

Last Sunday, Nancy took her son to Sonny's Bar-B-Que. They talked for two hours.

When it was time to drop him off, she reached to hug her little boy. He stiffened as usual. "It's all right," she said. "You don't have to."

She stepped aside, to give him space. To her surprise, he sidled next to her. He tipped his head, just slightly, until it touched her shoulder.

He's the Guy—No Ifs, Ands or Buts

JUNE 12, 2007

By Lane DeGregory

At the end of the rodeo, Lee Greenwood's anthem blares through the speakers at Westgate River Ranch: "I'm proud to be an American…"

The crowd stands. The music builds. As the singer asks God to bless his country, four horsemen gallop into the dusty arena, unfurling seven-foot-long flags.

The flags are red, with white letters rimmed in blue sequins. Each man gets a word: GOD. BLESS. THE. USA.

You wonder: Who's the THE guy?

Think about it. The dude two horses ahead gets to be GOD. The next rider is BLESS. The cowboy at the end is Mr. USA. The third horseman isn't even a noun or a verb. He's just an article. Superfluous—except for grammatical purposes.

Who is the THE guy?

* * *

You ask Leroy Mason, who runs the rodeo, if he knows him.

"Sure," Mason says. "He's my son, Grant."

So on a Saturday in June, you meet Grant and his parents for lunch at the ranch. They take off their cowboy hats. Grant blesses the chicken fingers.

He's 15, been riding horses since he was 2. He was homeschooled until last year, when he enrolled at Lake Wales High so he could join the ROTC. Finished the year with a 3.9 GPA. Wants to go to West Point.

He's not what you had in mind. You were expecting some lackey who wrangles calves and lives in a mobile home with his girlfriend, her kid and a bunch of dogs.

"Grant doesn't want to be a cowboy, and I'm thankful for that," says his dad, who used to be one. "Been on the road most of my life. We moved here so Grant wouldn't have to grow up like that. Now he has a permanent home, land, horses." Mason smiles at his son.

"He doesn't know how blessed he is."

* * *

You watch Grant get the animals ready for the rodeo. He works with a guy named Ike.

Grant's cowboy hat is white. Ike's is black. Grant doesn't shave yet. Ike has a droopy mustache. Grant's shirt has dry-cleaner creases; Ike's wilts with sweat.

The teenager and the ranch hand cover more than 300 acres on horseback, flushing bulls from pastures, driving cattle.

Mostly, the THE guy leads.

Ike brings up the rear.

* * *

A half-hour before the rodeo, you're waiting at the deli for a piece of pizza. Ike comes up and asks what sort of story you're doing. You tell him you're here to write about the guy who carries the THE flag.

Ike looks confused. "Well, that would be me."

What? you ask. How can Ike be the THE guy?

"It wasn't by choice," he tells you. "They just handed me that flag four years ago, and I've been carrying it ever since.

"But for some reason, tonight they asked me to carry BLESS. Usually, Grant's BLESS."

* * *

You find Grant's mom outside the ticket booth. Tell her about your conversation with Ike.

Judy Mason hesitates. "Oh, that Ike," she says softly. "He'll say anything to get in the paper."

* * *

As the rodeo riders get ready, you thread through them, asking: Who carries the THE flag?

Ike, says a bull rider. That would be Ike, says a trick rider. Ike, says a steer roper, then the rodeo clown. Barrel rider Caity Wall tells you she choreographed that closing number years ago. Her mom sewed the flags. Her husband is GOD.

"The THE guy?" she says, laughing. "Oh, that's always Ike."

At the end of the rodeo, as Greenwood's anthem blares through the speakers, GOD gallops into the arena.

Next comes Ike, bearing BLESS. Grant follows, gripping THE.

"I'm proud to be an American..."

* * *

Afterward, you track down Ike.

His last name is Stein. His horse is Topper. You had it about right: He's 25, lives with the girlfriend, her kid, three dogs.

During the week, Ike takes care of 2,500 cattle. Weekends, he works at the rodeo. He's the guy who opens the bull chutes and prods the steers.

"I'm just the grunt," Ike says. "You don't want to write about me. Write about Grant."

But Grant is BLESS (except when reporters come).

You're the bridge between God and country, Ike.

The genuine article.

X-Ray Reading

By Ben Montgomery

Lane DeGregory uses the pronoun "you" to suck readers into her quirky exploration. We follow along willingly because she promises a payoff and never bores.

He's the Guy—No Ifs, Ands Or Buts

By Lane DeGregory

At the end of the rodeo, Lee Greenwood's anthem blares through the speakers at Westgate River Ranch: "I'm proud to be an American…"

The crowd stands. The music builds. As the singer asks God to bless his country, four horsemen gallop into the dusty arena, unfurling seven-foot-long flags.

The flags are red, with white letters rimmed in blue sequins. Each man gets a word: GOD. BLESS. THE. USA.

You wonder: Who's the THE guy?

Think about it. The dude two horses ahead gets to be GOD. The next rider is BLESS. The cowboy at the end is Mr. USA. The third horseman isn't even a noun or a verb. He's just an article. Superfluous—except for grammatical purposes.

Who is the THE guy?

* * *

You ask Leroy Mason, who runs the rodeo, if he knows him.

In using the second-person pronoun "you," she takes the reader inside her head and is being cleverly transparent.

Check out this paragraph's pacing. Lane DeGregory starts with two choppy three-word subject-verb sentences, followed by a smooth longer sentence. She quickly sets the scene while building some anxiety about what happens next. And consider the action verbs she uses: "stands," "builds," "gallops." Movement.

"Sure," Mason says. "He's my son, Grant."

So on a Saturday in June, you meet Grant and his parents for lunch at the ranch. They take off their cowboy hats. Grant blesses the chicken fingers.

He's 15, been riding horses since he was 2. He was home-schooled until last year, when he enrolled at Lake Wales High so he could join the ROTC. Finished the year with a 3.9 GPA. Wants to go to West Point.

He's not what you had in mind. You were expecting some lackey who wrangles calves and lives in a mobile home with his girlfriend, her kid and a bunch of dogs.

"Grant doesn't want to be a cowboy, and I'm thankful for that," says his dad, who used to be one. "Been on the road most of my life. We moved here so Grant wouldn't have to grow up like that. Now he has a permanent home, land, horses." Mason smiles at his son.

"He doesn't know how blessed he is."

* * *

You watch Grant get the animals ready for the rodeo. He works with a guy named Ike.

Grant's cowboy hat is white. Ike's is black. Grant doesn't shave yet. Ike has a droopy mustache. Grant's shirt has dry-cleaner creases; Ike's wilts with sweat.

The teenager and the ranch hand cover more than 300 acres

She jumps back into the role of the narrator here, using "you" to put thoughts in our heads, to gently guide us toward her climax.

DeGregory uses "chicken fingers" instead of the more general "food." This gives readers a tactile image. You can smell the grease. Beyond that, it's a revealing detail that says something about this family.

This last quote— "how blessed he is"—is used ingeniously here, for reasons you'll understand later.

As these contrasts are laid out, we realize something is coming. In this simple description, DeGregory creates a sense of anxiety that keeps readers moving. We subconsciously want to know why these details about Ike are important, so we keep reading.

on horseback, flushing bulls from pastures, driving cattle.

Mostly, the THE guy leads.

Ike brings up the rear.

Subtle foreshadowing.

* * *

Notice these section breaks, by the way. This story is barely more than 700 words, yet it's broken into eight digestible sections, each its own mini-scene. This helps on two fronts: It eliminates the need for lame transitions, and it speeds up the action.

A half-hour before the rodeo, you're waiting at the deli for a piece of pizza. Ike comes up and asks what sort of story you're doing. You tell him you're here to write about the guy who carries the THE flag.

Ike looks confused. "Well, that would be me."

What? you ask. How can Ike be the THE guy?

"It wasn't by choice," he tells you. "They just handed me that flag four years ago, and I've been carrying it ever since.

"But for some reason, tonight they asked me to carry BLESS. Usually, Grant's BLESS."

By a stroke of luck, the scam is up. Remember dad's quote above?

* * *

You find Grant's mom outside the ticket booth. Tell her about your conversation with Ike.

Judy Mason hesitates. "Oh, that Ike," she says softly. "He'll say anything to get in the paper."

Another smart, ironic quote.

* * *

As the rodeo riders get ready, you thread through them, asking: Who carries the THE flag?

Ike, says a bull rider. That would be Ike, says a trick rider. Ike, says a steer roper, then the rodeo clown. Barrel rider Caity Wall tells you she choreographed that closing number years ago.

Her mom sewed the flags. Her husband is GOD.

"The THE guy?" she says, laughing. "Oh, that's always Ike."

* * *

Great line— another dab of humor in a rolling piece.

At the end of the rodeo, as Greenwood's anthem blares through the speakers, GOD gallops into the arena.

Next comes Ike, bearing BLESS. Grant follows, gripping THE.

"I'm proud to be an American..."

* * *

Again, check out the verbs she's using. "Blares." "Gallops." "Bearing." "Gripping."

Afterward, you track down Ike.

His last name is Stein. His horse is Topper. You had it about right: He's 25, lives with the girlfriend, her kid, three dogs.

During the week, Ike takes care of 2,500 cattle. Weekends, he works at the rodeo. He's the guy who opens the bull chutes and prods the steers.

"I'm just the grunt," Ike says. "You don't want to write about me. Write about Grant."

But Grant is BLESS (except when reporters come).

You're the bridge between God and country, Ike.

The genuine article.

It's worth noting that both "bridge" and "article" have double meanings. "Bridge" is meant in both a literal and figurative sense. And "article" is the technical designation for "the," which DeGregory sets up earlier.

Ben Montgomery is a reporter with the St. Petersburg Times.

BEHIND the STORY

Winner's Q&A

An Interview with Lane DeGregory

This edited interview was conducted by Poynter Institute Distinguished Fellow Butch Ward with Lane DeGregory, winner of ASNE's Distinguished Writing Award for Nondeadline Writing.

BUTCH WARD: Let's begin at the beginning, Lane. Can you talk about where you get your ideas? What gave you the idea to write about Evel Knievel now?

LANE DEGREGORY: A reporter who had recently retired from the *St. Petersburg Times* was in the bank in Clearwater and saw this old man get out of the line for a teller. She asked some people if he was all right, and they said, "Oh, that's Evel Knievel, we'll take care of him." Well, she had the presence of mind to get the bank manager's card and called my editor to say she had seen Evel.

When my editor told us the story, everyone said, "You mean he's still alive?" And we decided I'd try to interview him. So we e-mailed the bank manager, and asked if he thought Evel would be willing to be interviewed. I wrote the e-mail at 4:45 p.m. and left the office to pick up my kids from baseball practice. While I was sitting in line at practice, waiting for them, my cell phone rang. It was Evel. "I hear you want to write about me. Can you come over tomorrow?"

So I thought I'd just interview him at home—had no idea Evel Knievel Days even existed. But during the interview, he kept saying, "I hope I make it to Butte," and I realized this would be my only chance to get him with his fans. So I told my editor, Mike Wilson, "I've got to go to Butte!" And after hearing why, Mike agreed and told me to get a photographer involved.

I'm surprised to hear that Evel invited you over. In the story, he sounded pretty antagonistic.

He was. He'd scream at me to leave, then he'd hug me. I think he was embarrassed at his physical condition; he'd run out of breath and get embarrassed, and then his embarrassment would turn to anger.

So is there any one way in which you get most of your good ideas?

Most of the best ones come to me during my time off—someone in my life outside the office tells me a story. Other moms, for instance, or guys in my husband's band. If I hear a story and I like it enough to repeat it at dinner, I think, hey, maybe there's a story there worth looking into.

I also get ideas from subjects of other stories. When I finish a story about someone, I leave behind my card and cell phone number, and I tell them I'm always interested in good stories. I don't keep in touch with everyone, but I'm impressed by how often stories generate other stories. I think people feel empowered by my invitation to let me know when they have an idea.

For the lawn-cutting postman (Editor's note: This story is reprinted in Part 7), I had done a story about a little girl who had a brain tumor and who wanted to record an Elvis song in a real studio. So she got to record the song, and I did the story. After she died, I kept in touch with her mom by e-mail and about four years later, she called. You should do a story, she said, about our postman; he's making a difference in a lot of lives here in our neighborhood.

Let's talk about how you frame stories. You told the story of Susan Stanton by re-creating the day she appeared in public for the first time as a woman. Why pick that day?

After the story broke that Steve Stanton, the Largo city manager, had decided to become a woman, I teamed up with Lorri Helfand, the reporter who had broken that story, to do a big profile of Stanton. We began and ended the profile with Stanton's firing, and in between tried to explain the events that led up to it.

After the profile ran, my editor, Mike, and Joe Childs, who runs the Clearwater bureau, said, "We need to break the first picture of her when she comes out as a woman." So photographer Doug Clifford and I spent a month trying to convince Stanton that he didn't want to be "paparazzied" when he finally decided to become Susan. Finally we agreed that if he would guarantee the *Times* his first public photo, we would give him some control over the photo. Then Stanton told me she was going on this shopping trip, and I knew I needed to go with her. She agreed, but said no photographer, and I couldn't be writing in a notebook in public—I could just tag along.

Kelley Benham edited this story, and when I told her about that shopping trip, she suggested I frame the story around that outing because it was the day of Steve Stanton's transformation—and that's what this was about: Transformation. When Kelley heard that Stanton had agreed to let me go on this shopping trip, she said, "Just give me that day."

Okay, so you've already mentioned your editors 35 times. What role do editors play in your work?

Mike [Wilson] and I have worked together seven years now, and we've evolved like an old married couple. I always talk about my ideas with Mike before I do much reporting—he rejects about half of them—though if I feel passionately about one, I might do some reporting anyway and then try to convince him. We then talk again after I finish reporting—that's the most important conversation of all. Just five or 10 minutes over a Coke in his office or we take a walk. We discuss what the story is about, what it means in one or two words, what to include and what to leave out. Like in the Stanton story, Mike and Kelley and I all agreed it was about Transformation—so I didn't have to worry about anything else while I was writing. Just Transformation. Talking to Mike really helps me see the story that I want to tell before I even begin to write.

You clearly choose the scenes in your stories carefully. How do you decide which to include and which to leave out?

I struggle with that a lot, because I always over-report. So after I report, but before I talk with Mike, I make a list of 10 scenes and next to each one I write, "This scene was about…" and "These scenes were about…" And then I talk to Mike, and he might say, Well, I think you can only have three, and these two scenes are about the same thing—say, about love—and so you don't need both. So then I can whittle them down. I think this process has helped me get better at self-editing.

Several of these stories dealt with some very personal material. How did you convince the subjects in these stories to trust you?

I had never covered Steve Stanton when he was Largo city manager. So an editorial writer in the Largo bureau and the bureau's editor, Joe Childs, brokered my initial interview with him. They got me and the Largo city hall reporter together with Steve, stayed in the room for the first 20 minutes and then left us alone. I had brought with me some of my stories, including a transgender story, so Stanton could see that I knew how to handle a story on that issue with sensitivity. His trust in me grew from there.

With Nancy Bostock, sometimes the connections you make away from work have an impact later on the job. My kids went to the same summer camp as Nancy's, and so we didn't know each other really well, but I knew her well enough to approach her at one point and ask her—because she was school board chairperson—for advice on sending my children to middle school. When the story about her decision to return her son to the foster care system broke on Page A1, I said there's got to be more to this story, and I want to tell it. So I called and asked if she remembered me, and she said yes.

Eventually we talked four or five times that week—we'd meet for lunch, at a restaurant or her house, then talk again at night after both of us had put our kids to bed. And I interviewed her husband by phone.

You agreed not to name her adopted son or her other children. Why?

The hardest part of that story, for me, was that I couldn't talk to the adopted kid. I was really conflicted. Nancy didn't want him to be part of the story, and because she had returned him to the state, they had custody and the state said no way to an interview.

Mike said right up front that we weren't going to name the child under any circumstances. It just didn't seem fair, he said, to such a young, damaged child to put his name out there where Google could find it forever. And Nancy didn't want us to identify her other daughters, even though their names had been published elsewhere. After Mike and I talked with her a lot about it, we eventually agreed not to name them either.

Not being able to speak with the children actually changed the way I approached the story. I had originally thought of trying to capture the family dynamic and how it was affected by the son, but I couldn't get that. So Mike and I agreed, if we can't get the family dynamic, let's focus on the mother. And so it became, for me, a story about motherhood.

Kelley ended up editing this story, too, and she really helped me zoom in on certain scenes instead of broad-brushing the whole picture.

Your stories include lots of details. How do you decide what to include and what to leave out?

Once I know the scenes I'm going to use, I can decide. Some scenes I just want to fast-forward through, but others I want to linger in cinematically. So for those, I need a lot of detail—and sometimes I have to go back to get it. I spent enough time in Evel's condo to take notes on all of the things on the walls; but when I was out shopping with Susan, I had to duck into a restroom to write stuff in my notebook—since she wouldn't let me carry one in public.

When I was working on the Nancy Bostock story, I asked Nancy to walk me through her son's bedroom. It had already been completely dismantled—his things had been sent to his new home. So I walked her around the room, and I asked her about how things there had been before—like, what kind of sheets had been on his bed? When she told me he had Lion King sheets, I thought that was perfect, because it showed that, despite his frightening adolescent behaviors, he was still a little boy in many ways.

Then I asked her if they had a bedtime ritual, and she told me that was the worst time of all. So I asked her to describe it, and as I heard how horrible it was, I realized I had just received a gift I had no idea was coming: my lead.

Did you work on these stories for a long time?

I was never working on just one at a time—right now, for example, I'm juggling seven stories. During the week I worked on the "Adopted Child" story, I spent an hour or two each day when I was reporting and a day to write. I did the interviews in Evel's home and then did two other stories while I waited to go to Butte to finish it. The lawn-cutting postman (Editor's note: This story is reprinted in Part 7) took two days to report and write.

Do you get emotionally involved in your stories?

I cry when I write some of them. If I'm writing about someone who's crying, I start to cry. I think it helps me, because I want the reader to feel that. But if the story makes me angry, then I find it harder to write.

Evel made me angry. He treated me meanly, and I don't know why. When I got kicked out of Evel's, I felt berated for no reason. He made fun of every question I asked him. When I told Mike about it, he asked me if I had written all of that down. Yes, I said, because I was trying not to cry. He said, well, write it into the story. Really, I asked? Sure, he said; your interactions will help the reader understand Evel. So I did, and it ended up being one of the parts of the story people talked about the most.

Tell me how you write.

Want me to describe my process? Okay, here it is:

As I said before, after I finish reporting, I have a meeting with Mike and I take notes during that meeting. We agree on where the story will begin and where it will end. We agree on which scenes I'll use. And we agree on which characters will be most important. Then I gather up all of my notes and I leave the newsroom—because I can't write there.

I go home and spread all of my notes out on the dining room table and I create a timeline of the event—it's the closest I get to an outline. Now I have what I need: my scenes, my characters, my chronology, my beginning and my end.

I then go back and reread my notes. I don't transcribe them, but I take notes on my notes. For example, I'll write, "I want to make a scene out of this material." If I have three or four notebooks of material, I'll typically take three or four pages of notes on them.

Then I go into my closet-sized office and—without any notes—I start to write. I spend a lot of time on the lead, but then it goes pretty fast. I print out that draft and reread it with my notes. Then I return to the computer and revise.

You said earlier that during the conversation with your editor after you finish reporting, you try to find the one or two words that describe what your story means. The Stanton story, you said, was about Transformation. What was the Evel story about?

Aging, image.

The adopted child story?

Mike and I decided it was about Loving. Letting go. I always thought it was about Motherhood.

The lawn-cutting postman?

Giving.

Looking back on these stories, what do they reveal about your reason for telling stories?

I tell stories because I want to make readers feel. What newspapers primarily do is give people information, and I want to help you decide how it makes you feel, how you fit in with the rest of the world. You know, these stories are a bit unusual for me because I usually write about people you've never heard of. I prefer writing about folks no one knows, or doesn't notice. Evel Knievel, Steve Stanton and Nancy Bostock had been in the paper hundreds of times, but there's a whole other layer to them— no one had ever asked them their personal stories. I try to do that. I want to make people real, so readers can relate.

You said Evel made you angry. How did the others make you feel? What did they teach you?

Steve Stanton taught me that people like her are not freaks. Many people struggle with identity. I need to remember that: We're all unusual in our own ways, and some of the most seemingly mainstreamed "normal" people are hiding the strangest sides; while some of the biggest "weirdos" are actually the most normal. It's our job, as journalists, to get beyond character profiles and show people as whole humans.

The postman taught me I need to look at people I might never take time to look at. He's a metaphor for what all of us can be. I need to notice the quiet folks and their deeds more. They inspire the masses. Readers sent more than $4,000 to that postman to pay for gas, and that small daily story generated more than 200 e-mails and calls.

Nancy Bostock made me want to hug my kids.

BEHIND the STORY

Sources Say

An Interview with Nancy Bostock

This is an edited e-mail interview with Nancy Bostock, whose family was the subject of the story "Breaking Point."

What surprised you about being part of the story or the story itself?

NANCY BOSTOCK: Craig and I were very surprised at the level and intensity of interest in our family's situation. When we decided that I would speak at a meeting of the state Senate Committee on Children, Families and Elder Affairs, we did so knowing full well that I could wind up as part of a news story. I guess we thought that the *St. Petersburg Times* would cover the meeting in a perfunctory way and that, perhaps, I might be mentioned in the story.

We were happy at the thought of possibly contributing in some small way to bringing attention to needed reforms in our state's child welfare system. Never did we expect our family's situation to not only be the focus of that initial news story but also the impetus for additional news stories. Journalists from other local media outlets contacted us, and producers from ABC's *20/20* and CNN contacted us and wanted to cover "our story." Dozens and dozens of families and professionals from around the world contacted us, asking us for help, offering us help or sending us their support and encouragement. And dozens of additional interested citizens weighed in on the Internet through various blogs.

What surprised us about the story was the intensity of community interest in our family's plight. What, unfortunately, did not surprise us was that, even in the glare of intense public scrutiny, our child welfare system still couldn't help us. They are simply not prepared to help families in situations like ours.

What have you learned from this experience?

Over the past years, I have worked to access much-needed services for our son right along with my community efforts to improve our child welfare system for all children. I knew that sharing our personal family struggles through the newspaper article might in some small way help reform efforts by bringing public attention to the issues facing families raising children affected by attachment and trauma-related issues. I hoped that sharing our personal family struggles might comfort other families in similar circumstances. But what we learned is that sharing our personal family struggles in such a public way was both intensely stressful and incredibly therapeutic at the same time.

The stress came both from the initial telling of our story to Lane DeGregory over an hours-long breakfast/lunch and then from the subsequent conversations, over and over again, with supportive friends and new friends who contacted us as a result of the story. While it was wonderful to receive so much support, each conversation added another layer to our stress.

People who wanted to encourage us contacted us in every way imaginable: e-mail, phone, U.S. mail, through mutual friends, flower delivery and other small tokens and even a well-intentioned but awkward condolence card. People who wanted to criticize us used the Internet. Some of the postings were hateful. I reminded myself that for those folks who expressed such hateful comments, ignorance really is bliss. I told myself that I am actually happy for those folks, happy that they have no idea of the true struggle my family had been going through.

The folks with the hateful Internet comments were easier for me to deal with emotionally than the other families who contacted me for help with their own similar struggles. With each additional sad family story I heard, I wanted to scream, "Didn't you read the story? I don't know how to help you; I don't even know how to help myself!" My stress symptoms begin to flare even now, seven months later, just thinking about each of them and what they are going through. Shortly after the story ran, I had to stop returning e-mails and calls to these families. I know that I let a lot of good, hurting people down, but it was just too hard. Recently, though, I have been able to begin contacting some of them.

Dealing with the local media was manageable and dealing with Lane was wonderful. Dealing with the national media was not. [The] demands of the producers for access to our children, to old family photos and videos and some of the high-pressure tactics were just too much. It was very difficult to say no to such a potentially beneficial opportunity, but the potential harm to my children was just too great. We agonized for days over this decision but in the end saying no was a giant relief.

In contrast, Lane was so very understanding when we declined her request for a photograph with the kids and an interview with my son. Although she likely had access to a multitude of family pictures already in the public realm, she used very tasteful photographs that were respectful of our desire to spare what we could of our children's privacy. She never once pressured me or tried to go around me to child welfare officials for access to my son.

During the weeks immediately after this publicity, the foster care folks were threatening to move my son out of a therapeutic setting and into a regular foster home. We decided to fight the proposed move with what limited ability we had. During this multifaceted, intensely stressful period in our lives, my otherwise healthy, physically active 43-year-old husband suffered a stroke. He remained hospitalized for almost two weeks and eventually underwent a heart operation. I guess you could say he had a broken heart! This occurred in the weeks immediately preceding Christmas.

At the New Year, reflecting upon the previous year ... [we realized that] we had gained a greater understanding of our own journey and of our commitment to one another as a family, even a family that is not able to live together under one roof. It is true, it seems, the old saying, "That which does not kill us, makes us stronger."

What would you like to say to other journalists who cover similar fields or situations?

Emulate Lane, she is the greatest! She showed us such compassion and told our story with such finesse. She can do so much with so few words.

When you deal with families in crisis, whatever that crisis may be, try to understand the incredible stress they are under. Try not to add to that stress, no matter what your deadline. Some things are more important than your deadline.

Try to understand that whatever preconceived notion you may have of right or wrong in a particular situation ("I could never give up my child!") could change in an instant (What if it were necessary for the safety of your other children? What if it were in the child's own best interest?). Try to truly expand your concept of fairness. Surface-level facts are just that ("School Board Member Abandons Son!") but the true story is much deeper. (What drove a loving mother and father to pursue the drastic choice of legally abandoning their much-wanted son?)

If you try to emulate Lane, you will treat the family compassionately, tell their story with depth and objectivity and maybe even win your own award!

Writer's Workshop

Talking Points

1. Lane DeGregory said her story about Evel Knievel was a story about aging and image. Identify at least 10 details DeGregory used in that story to keep the reader focused on those themes.

2. Because she was unable to interview any of the children in the Nancy Bostock story, DeGregory abandoned her plan to write about the impact of a severely disruptive child on the family dynamic. Instead, she focused on the theme of motherhood. Assuming you had access only to the adults in her story, what other themes could you bring out?

3. On its surface, Steve Stanton's decision to become a woman is not a decision with which most readers can relate. Yet DeGregory said Stanton's story was about a search for identity—a search that many of us experience. What devices—scenes, details, dialogue, etc.—did DeGregory use to broaden Stanton's story into one that many readers could relate to?

Assignment Desk

1. Before she begins writing, DeGregory and her editor identify one or two words that capture "what my story is about." Review your last five stories and do this exercise: First, write a brief paragraph that tells what your story is about, then reduce the paragraph to one sentence, and finally to one or two words. Then reread your story to see how well it focused on those "meaning" words from beginning to end. Now, delete any passages that wandered from your focus. Is your new story more effective?

2. An essential ingredient in DeGregory's stories is her ability to reconstruct scenes that she did not witness. Select three events to which you referred generally in your recent stories and compile a list of questions you could use to reconstruct each of those scenes in detail.

3. DeGregory encourages storytellers to find ideas by "reading the walls"—by which she means reading anything and everything—and by "talking with strangers." Over the next week, make a list of story ideas you get by reading anything and everything, and by striking up conversations away from your beat—in the supermarket, on the bus, in a restaurant, at church. Make a list of which of those ideas you would not have gotten before.

Chicago Tribune

Finalist: Nondeadline Writing

Louise Kiernan

The Beekeepers, Part 1

OCT. 28, 2007

The men opened the hive and bees swirled up into the sky like sparks from a fire.

Bees flew through the weedy yard and past the chain-link fence. They flew into the alley, where a woman braced herself against the hood of a police car.

Bees flew toward the gas station, where the calls of hustlers selling drugs sliced the air. And beyond where the men could see them, bees scattered into the vacant lots and backyard gardens, parks and parking lots of Chicago's West Side, searching, as always, for nectar.

This sunny morning in September 2006 was warm, but a bite to the breeze signaled fall. A boy walked by, dressed in a white shirt and navy pants. School had opened today. It was time for a new start, time for what the people who work at the nonprofit agency on this corner in East Garfield Park had decided to call Sweet Beginnings.

The three men standing at the hive were learning how to become beekeepers. None had any experience at this job or, for that matter, much significant work history at all.

Tony Smith, a pug of a man with a broad face, moved with the graceful, contained gestures of someone accustomed to negotiating small spaces. At 30, he had spent half his life in prison.

Hovering uneasily behind him was Shelby Gallion, a 22-year-old former drug dealer. In an oversized T-shirt and jeans that blurred the outlines of his body, his expression unreadable, Shelby looked a little out of focus, as if he might eventually drift out of sight. He lived in a halfway house, still on parole.

At 49, Gerald Whitehead was trying to overcome a lifetime of crime and addiction by learning beekeeping in a program called Sweet Beginnings. (Photograph courtesy of José M. Osorio/*Chicago Tribune*)

Gerald Whitehead, the oldest member of the trio at 49, had been released from jail just a week before, after being cleared of a heroin-possession charge, the most recent stumble in the struggle to turn his life around after decades of violence and addiction. Gerald seemed intimidating, with his heavy-lidded eyes and thrust-out chin, but when he smiled, his face cracked open wide and bright.

The three men and 17 hives in this yard were the makings of a small experiment, an attempt to address one of the most stubborn and destructive problems in Chicago and other cities around the country: what to do with the hundreds of thousands of people released each year from prison.

Over the last three decades, harsher penalties for drug crimes and stricter sentencing laws have helped fuel explosive growth in the nation's prison population and, inevitably, in the number of inmates returning to society. In Chicago alone, roughly 20,000 ex-offenders come home each year.

Most end up in neighborhoods like this one, where unemployment is high, opportunity scant and the temptation of drugs and crime rarely more than a corner away. They don't stay long. More than half the state's prisoners find themselves back behind bars within three years of their release.

The Sweet Beginnings program kept its beehives behind the North Lawndale Employment Network's offices on Chicago's West Side, within sight of the Eisenhower Expressway and in the heart of a neighborhood struggling against poverty, unemployment and crime. The hives were an opportunity for the agency not just to help people find jobs, but to create them. (Photograph courtesy of José M. Osorio/*Chicago Tribune*)

Finding work can reduce someone's chances of returning to prison. Although getting a job with a criminal record is difficult, checking the conviction box on an application poses only one hurdle. Many former inmates face other problems, from poor education and little understanding of workplace rules to drug addiction or a lack of stable housing. And behaviors that help people thrive on the job—teamwork, communication—are often the opposite of those that ensure survival in prison.

For five years, the North Lawndale Employment Network, or NLEN, had helped ex-offenders find employment. With Sweet Beginnings, the agency decided to create its own jobs, in its own neighborhood, where people could learn how to work and build an employment history before they moved on. The idea attracted the attention of major philanthropies and companies, among them the MacArthur Foundation, Boeing Co. and Ben & Jerry's, each of which donated expertise or money to the effort.

Now, what may have once seemed like little more than a quirky venture—using former prisoners to produce honey in the ghetto—stood on the verge of transforming itself into a high-profile business.

Tony Smith (center) adds a honey mixture to a body cream base as he and his co-workers, Gerald Whitehead (left) and Shelby Gallion, learn how to make body-care products for the Sweet Beginnings business. The decision to make honey-based products such as lotion and lip balm was based on the desire to increase profits and create more job opportunities. (Photograph courtesy of José M. Osorio/*Chicago Tribune*)

Whether it would succeed depended in part upon the three men in the yard. The men measured success in starker terms. Failing, they feared, meant going back to the streets, going back to prison or getting killed.

During the coming year, through the bees' final foraging in fall, the threat of winter, promise of spring and richness of summer, the men and the enterprise of Sweet Beginnings would attempt nothing less than their own reinvention.

This morning's lesson was about survival. John Hansen, the beekeeper training the workers, showed them how to tilt the hives to get a sense of how much honey they contained. A heavy hive meant the bees had stored enough to make it through the winter. A lighter hive would need help.

The hives, with their unevenly stacked wooden boxes, called supers, looked like tipsy filing cabinets scattered among the clumps of goldenrod, Queen Anne's lace and clover.

The men moved among them, gently leaning each hive back and opening the lid to peer inside.

An elderly woman stopped at the fence. "What y'all got in there? Bees?" she asked.

"Yep," John answered, still bent over a hive.

"Oh, Lord, think I better get back."

After a minute or two, Shelby disappeared inside the building. John continued to make his way around the yard, Gerald and Tony in tow.

"Look at that," John cried out at Hive No. 2, lifting a frame thick with honey, each cell a stud of gold. At Hive No. 6, bees crowded the entrance, but the supers felt suspiciously light.

When they finished, John delivered his verdict.

"I think," he said, "we can bring them through the winter."

Second Chances

"To make a prairie it takes a clover and one
bee,—
One clover, and a bee,
And revery."

Emily Dickinson

In this pocket of the West Side, the past may fade or burn or erode almost to dust, but it persists. It holds on.

Like the Star of David that adorns the front of the Independence Boulevard Seventh Day Adventist Church, a remnant from the time when Chicago's Jews lived and worshiped in the neighborhood. Or the cracked patches of concrete in the overgrown lot at 1550 S. Hamlin Ave., where Martin Luther King Jr. lived for a short time in a rundown apartment to protest the way Chicago's blacks were housed.

Or, in the conference room at the North Lawndale Employment Network, the blotch of greenish ink on Tony Smith's right forearm, visible as he took notes in a narrow, slanting script. It had been a tattoo of a cobra until he removed what he could with lemon juice and a sewing needle.

The cobra is a symbol of the Mickey Cobras street gang, as is the "MC" inked on Tony's left shoulder. Police records say Tony belonged to this gang. He won't say much about that or anything else in his past.

What he will say is this: "I was a naive, snotty-nosed street kid who didn't care about himself or other people."

His first arrest came at age 9, for disorderly conduct. By the time he turned 13, he had been convicted in an attempted murder and was, according to a police officer who knew him, one of the most violent and feared gang members in the Cabrini-Green public housing complex. He marked his 16th birthday awaiting trial for beating three men with a gun and torturing two of them with a heated ice-chopper. That crime earned Tony a 30-year prison sentence.

He emerged almost 15 years later, having never used a cell phone or filled out a job application. When he talked about what he wanted to see for the first time with his own eyes, he named—after Navy Pier and Millennium Park—a Jet Ski.

Across the conference table, Shelby idly twirled one of the braids near his ear. Shelby's past was his shoes. The butterscotch Timberland boots imprinted with tiny hexagons or the candy-bright Bathing Ape sneakers. New shoes, like his new watch and new cell phone, the leather "Scarface" cell phone case—all accessories of the lifestyle he said he wanted to leave behind.

He began selling drugs about the time he started high school, and by his senior year, the money and all it bought had easily trumped education. Then came two stints in prison and, during the second one, nights spent lying on his cot, wondering what would become of his two young daughters.

That was why he had come to Sweet Beginnings. But he still thought about the old life. It took him a week at the agency to earn what he could have made in a matter of hours on the street.

And Gerald, standing at the kitchen window, staring out at the hives?

Gerald's past was the hovel of a building across the alley, where he had snorted $10 bags of heroin. And his grandmother's house three blocks away, where he had stayed as a child and sexually assaulted a young woman as an adult. The bar around the corner where he once got shot on his birthday. His past was the man crossing the street he knew from Narcotics Anonymous and the cap-shadowed teenager who walked in the door of the North Lawndale Employment Network and addressed him as "Brother Bone."

Gerald's past was everywhere.

His earliest memory was of being bitten by a dog. He bit the dog back.

Gerald wasn't sure whether he remembered this incident because it happened or remembered it because he was told it happened. It didn't matter. He became that story: the boy who would bite back.

He grew up with two older brothers and 10 younger sisters, a mother who worked as a live-in nurse and a father who was, as he put it, "kind of missing in action."

Gerald struggled in school. He never learned how to read or write well. The other children made fun of him. By 6th grade, he had basically stopped going.

"I started out making a career," he said. "Whatever I could steal to make a hustle."

At the same time, he joined the Unknown Vice Lords. In the gang, he could force respect from all the people who had once belittled him. He moved up to become an "elite," a top-ranking gang member and close associate of onetime Vice Lords kingpin Willie Lloyd.

From the age of 20, Gerald bounced in and out of prison, spending more time inside than out: armed robbery, home invasion, criminal sexual assault, burglary, aggravated battery, drug possession.

He was 43 before he decided he couldn't do the time anymore. He has his conversion story. One night in prison, he broke down. Was this all his life would ever be? Had God put him here for nothing more? He wanted to die.

Then, in his cell, he sensed the spirit of his late grandmother, who always gave him a meal when he was hungry and a bed when he was homeless, and he felt at peace.

He could try to change.

It proved difficult. He lost a job working in maintenance at a nursing home after a background check revealed his criminal record, he said. There was an arrest for domestic battery. He was using drugs too, crack and then heroin. He became a dope fiend, a hype.

That went on for years, until his mother persuaded him to check into a residential drug treatment program, where he stayed for five months. Not long after he got out, in the spring of 2006, he stopped by the fence at NLEN on his way to sell loose cigarettes at the gas station nearby. He knew the agency; the month before, he had gone through its four-week job-training program for ex-offenders.

A couple of men were setting up hives. Gerald asked if he could watch. Then he asked if he could help. He stepped into the yard and began handling the hives, as though, one of the men observed, he had been beekeeping all his life.

At first, Gerald worked for free. He did whatever needed to be done: fixing the lawn mower, pulling weeds, picking up the trash that blew in from the alley. It was somewhere to go every day. Soon, the agency began to pay him, $7.25 an hour.

Every day was a fight. Stay straight, go to work. Failing would be as easy as stumbling off the curb into the street.

"It's a wrassle trying to do good," Gerald said one afternoon. "You always got evil whispering in your ear."

He felt comfortable around the bees. He liked them. If you didn't know bees, he thought, they might scare you. But once you knew them, you came to respect them.

Gerald understood bees.

Finding Sweetness

The building that housed the North Lawndale Employment Network, near the corner of West Flournoy Street and South Independence Boulevard, had once been a duplex and still felt like someone's home.

Walk in and you might find a worker bouncing a toddler on her knee while she interviewed the child's mother or an old woman grumbling about delays on the Pulaski bus.

Most days, the center hummed with people who came for one of the agency's job-training programs, a computer class or to get help writing a résumé. Amid the bustle, the Sweet Beginnings employees set up bee-keeping class at whatever table happened to be free and began to learn about bees.

They learned there are three types of honeybees: the worker bee, which is female; the drone, which is male; and the queen bee, which mates with the drones and lays the colony's eggs.

They learned that a worker bee lives for about six weeks. They learned that it takes the nectar from 5 million flowers to make 1 pint of honey. They learned that pollen mixed with nectar is called bee bread.

During these lessons, Tony took notes on a yellow legal pad. Gerald tilted his chair back or leaned forward, head propped on his arms, always restless. Shelby occasionally cleaned his nails with a public transit card.

Their teacher, John Hansen, was 76 and white and jangled the change in his pocket. He had begun keeping bees 31 years before, after he saw a sign someone had posted on a bulletin board at the suburban publishing company where he worked, offering to sell two hives. He went on to become president of the Illinois State Beekeepers Association, and in his retirement, he still kept bees, sold honey and ran a small business managing hives and removing bees from people's homes.

Of everything John taught the men about bees, they found nothing as interesting or amusing as what they learned about drones.

When drones hatch, the worker bees help them out of their brood cells while the worker bees must emerge on their own. Drones that mate with the queen on what is euphemistically called the "nuptial flight" die because the act rips their sexual organs from their bodies. When winter approaches, worker bees drive the drones from the hive, to certain death.

One morning, Tony walked in with his heavily underlined copy of *Beekeeping in the Midwest,* the book they were assigned to read.

"It said male drones are like human males," Tony told John. "They don't do no work. I kid you not, that's what they said." The book doesn't compare men and bees; that was Tony's analysis.

In the beginning, the men's hands-on instruction mostly involved learning how to care for the hives and prepare them for winter. While they worked, they used a smoker, a metal can with attached bellows, to blow smoke into the hives to distract the bees. The smoke causes the bees to act as though their hive is on fire, and they eat honey to fortify themselves to flee, ignoring intruders.

Honey bees usually sting only if they feel threatened. Tony had never been stung, so John plucked a bee from a hive and stung him with it to make sure he wasn't allergic to the venom. Gerald hardly seemed to notice stings or care beyond issuing the occasional epithet. Shelby seemed the most leery, often hanging back while the others worked. But when Tony asked if the bees scared him, Shelby denied it.

In the early fall, the men learned how to extract honey, to harvest it from the frames where bees build the combs.

Because the Sweet Beginnings hives didn't contain enough honey to spare, John brought in eight frames from his own apiary. The frames, stacked in the kitchen of the resource center, looked a little like wood-frame screens, except that, instead of wire grids, the panels held hundreds of hexagons filled with honey.

As the men crowded around a large metal tank, a lone bee banged against the kitchen window.

"Do we have to actually do it?" Tony asked.

"Yeah, you guys are going to do it," John replied.

To extract honey, a beekeeper uses a knife to cut open the wax caps that seal the individual cells of honey in the frame. Then, the frames are placed in an extractor, which spins them to release the honey. The honey drips down the walls of the extractor and exits through a tap.

Slowly and delicately, Shelby slid the knife against the frame. Wax curled off in strips. A slight scent, sweet and floral, filled the kitchen.

"Just swipe it," Tony advised.

"Let it ride even and flat," Gerald said.

"You're doing fine," John said. "Just watch your fingers."

Tony and Gerald each took a turn. The knife, as it drew across the wax, made the thick, wet smack of a cartoon kiss. Sunlight warmed the honey in the frames to the color of amber, glowing against the black shadow of the blade.

"That honey look good, don't it?" Tony asked.

As the extractor spun, the air began to smell sweeter and sweeter. Thin streams ran down the inside of the tank. Minutes passed. A nickel-sized dollop of honey pooled on the filter atop the white bucket under the tap.

"There's the first drop," John said.

While the extractor whirred, the men went outside to check on the bees. Brenda Palms Barber, the exuberant black woman who served as the North Lawndale Employment Network's chief executive officer, joined them.

"I want to see how the babies are doing," she called out, standing at the hives, perfectly at ease in her gray suit while the others wore jackets with netted hoods.

More than two years before, Brenda had come up with the idea for Sweet Beginnings when she decided that the employment network needed to do more than help people find jobs; it needed to create them.

She considered a landscaping business or delivery service but worried that customers might be reluctant to allow ex-offenders in their homes. A friend suggested a honey co-op.

Brenda knew nothing about honey, but the idea intrigued her. She liked it even better when she learned that some people consider urban honey more flavorful than its rural counterpart because the bees can gather nectar from more varied flowers within a shorter distance. Imagine creating sweetness out of the asphalt and hardship of the West Side.

The agency launched Sweet Beginnings in the spring of 2004 with a grant from the Illinois Department of Corrections. Two years later, after parting ways with the original group of beekeepers working with the agency, the program started over with fresh bees and a new idea.

The bees came from Wisconsin, picked up and delivered by NLEN's chief operating officer, who had to roll down the windows of his Jeep Cherokee on the way back because the 30,000 bees generated so much heat and noise.

The new idea came from a business plan created by volunteers at Boeing, the chairwoman of the board of Ben & Jerry's and others. It called for Sweet Beginnings to shift its focus from selling honey to selling honey-based products such as lotion and lip balm. They hoped the move would increase profits and, with the expansion into manufacturing, packaging and marketing, the job prospects of its workers.

When Brenda and the beekeepers returned to the kitchen, about 4 inches of honey stood in the 5-gallon bucket.

She passed out plastic spoons and everyone dipped in to taste.

"Yum," she said. "It's really, really good."

She continued to talk, in a stream of words as smooth and unbroken as the honey pouring into the bucket. She talked about biscuits and business competition and hosting a honey cook-off and social purpose and making lip balm.

When she was almost done, she said, "That's some of the stuff we're thinking." Then she paused and said something else, slowly, as if the idea had just struck her.

"Our demographic," she said, "is the opposite of the people working on it."

Under Suspicion

"There is a Thief Amongst Us!" the signs announced.

"IS IT YOU!"

One sign was posted above the sink in the kitchen of the resource center. Another was taped to the bathroom door. More hung on the walls next to inspirational quotes from Eleanor Roosevelt and Gail Sheehy.

The signs went up in late September, after someone stole the agency's digital camera from a cabinet in the downstairs conference room. It was only the second theft in the two years since NLEN had moved into the building, and it hurt.

The agency prided itself on being the kind of place where visitors wandered back to the kitchen to help themselves to coffee and bought candy for school fundraisers by dropping a dollar on a desktop.

No doors barred the offices; no cameras peered down from the ceilings. The clients who came here already felt as though the world treated them like criminals; the people who helped them didn't want to do the same.

That trust disappeared with the discovery of a dented cabinet door.

Brenda felt betrayed. She didn't like thieves. She could find a job for a murderer before she could find one for a thief. Stealing was a crime of opportunity, and every time a thief saw something to steal, he had to decide not to steal it.

If the signs shouted the crime, other conversations in the building occurred in whispers.

Who would know the camera was kept in the basement conference room, in the cabinet with the VCR? The beekeepers, who watched videos for their classes. And Gerald? Well, he had been an addict, and everyone knows that hypes steal.

This was the first of a four-part series that followed three ex-felons through a workplace training program in Chicago. To read the rest of the series, go to www. poynter.org/bnw2009/resources.

BEHIND the STORY

Ethical Reporting

By Louise Kiernan

Gerald Whitehead and I sat on a stoop as the afternoon unfolded. We talked as kids drifted by on their way home from school and we talked as the people who worked at the building behind us let themselves out the chain-link gate and went home.

In the year I followed Gerald and two other men through a workplace training program that teaches ex-felons how to care for bees and make products from honey, we had many conversations, hard and easy. But I think most often about this discussion because it captured an essential dilemma in writing about ordinary people: the exhilaration that comes with unearthing a chunk of the truth, at getting closer to the heart of their story, and at the same time, the painful awareness of what telling that truth might mean for them.

I had learned that Gerald had been in jail on drug charges one day when he called in sick to work. I already suspected that despite his repeated denials, Gerald, a long-time addict, was still using.

We talked for more than two hours that day. At first Gerald denied using drugs, but I kept asking. Eventually, he confessed that he had been snorting heroin on and off for months. He understood I would include that information in my story, but when I told him I'd have to bring it up in my close-out interview with the head of the agency, he asked me for a favor: He wanted to tell her first. I agreed.

I'm used to writing about people who don't have experience with reporters. Those are the people who interest me. Over the years, I have worked hard to treat them with honesty, sensitivity and respect, and to make sure they understand what they're getting into when they agree to be written about. But this project proved challenging in ways I didn't expect.

The story began simply enough. When I proposed to the North Lawndale Employment Network's chief executive officer, Brenda Palms Barber, that I follow three trainees through the Sweet Beginnings program, she immediately signed on. "The good, the bad and the ugly," she told me more than once, and she kept her word.

Two of the three trainees, Tony Smith and Shelby Gallion, made it clear that they would cooperate with the photographer and me only while they were at work. Fortunately, Gerald, the most reflective and charismatic of the three men, soon emerged as our main character and he didn't mind where we followed him.

Sweet Beginnings had received some news coverage and would continue to attract attention while I worked on my story, but those articles were very different from what I wanted to do. Typically, a reporter would come out for a few hours, interview the men, spend some time in the apiary and write a quick feature. I realized the men were used to interviews; they weren't used to reporting.

I explained that I would check out what they told me, talk to their friends and family and read through their court records. What concerned them most was what I would learn—and write—about their criminal backgrounds. I gave them the simplest and best reason I could: We had to know where they had been to understand how far they had come.

I also told them that anytime I was with them, I was reporting my story and recording what they said and did. But if they wanted to go off the record, they only had to ask. That happened just once, when one of the men wanted to complain about the day's work.

Throughout the reporting, I kept my notebook and tape recorder visible so everyone was aware of what I was doing. I trusted that over time they would become comfortable enough with me that it wouldn't matter. Sooner or later, people can't help being themselves.

In fact, the biggest ethical struggle week in and week out was making sure everyone did remember I was there as a reporter, not a friend. Brenda wanted my opinion on the scents for the products. Gerald asked me for money. Many times I had to explain that I couldn't do anything that might affect the course of the story or make me part of it, no matter how trivial that action might seem. Sometimes, that meant fighting my impulses to intervene or comment upon what was happening around me.

Other issues surfaced as well. The men didn't always tell me the truth. Gerald neglected to mention his sexual assault conviction. Tony told me he didn't have any children, but he has a teenage daughter. In both instances, I had to talk with them about what I had learned and how I was going to handle it in the story.

When the series was almost ready to run, I met separately and privately with Tony and Gerald to run through my final questions and go over exactly, point by point, what the articles would say. I didn't want them to be surprised by anything that would appear in print. By that time, Shelby had been fired and dropped out of touch with the agency and me. Despite my best efforts, I couldn't track him down.

The day after the series started, I met Gerald at his new job to find out what he thought about the stories. He flashed that grin of his. "It's cool," he told me.

I wish this essay could conclude with that moment, but the complicated realities of stories like this one don't always allow for happy endings.

The next time I saw Gerald, a few weeks later, I gave him some extra copies of the stories. He talked proudly about the attention they had brought him. But his tentative grip on success was already slipping. He had gotten into trouble on the job. A month or so later, he accused the agency and his employer of abandoning him. They said they were doing what they could to help him but were hampered by his self-destructive behavior.

I wrote a follow-up story examining Gerald's claims and what had happened to him and the two other men, who recently had been arrested together on drug possession charges. Tony ultimately managed to get back his job at the agency. But Gerald was angry and out of work. He stopped returning my calls. I don't know what he's doing now or how he feels about the stories that once made him grin with pride, but I know I treated him fairly and honestly.

The last time we talked, he told me, "I'm just trying to do what I got to do to survive."

I hope he will.

Before becoming a senior editor at the Chicago Tribune, *Louise Kiernan worked for the paper's projects team. She wrote the lead article in a series that won the 2001 Pulitzer Prize for explanatory journalism and was a Pulitzer finalist in the same category that year for an individual project. She has worked at small papers in Oklahoma, Texas and Tennessee.*

Narrative Strategies

By Thomas French

Narrative opens us up. When we report inside other people's lives, immersing ourselves in the grand design and tiny details of their days and nights, we do everything we can to see through their eyes, feel what they feel, slip into their skin. As much as we can, we disappear inside them.

Such invisibility is hard enough. But the next step is even trickier, and just as important. After we've finished reporting and are ready to write, we have to rematerialize back inside our own skin. Sitting in front of the computer keyboard, our fingers ready to tap out the first paragraph, we have to detach ourselves from our subjects enough to render their stories with clarity and meaning and vivid power.

This combination of skills—almost supernatural empathy, paired with steely-eyed critical judgment—runs through the award-winning narratives in this volume. It's there in Dana Priest and Anne Hull's incendiary pieces on the wounded and forgotten at Walter Reed (reprinted in Part 3), in the quiet power of Louise Kiernan's series on the felons forging new lives as beekeepers and in David Finkel's remarkable war dispatches from Baghdad (reprinted in Part 8).

It's there, too, in the beautiful and startling stories of Lane DeGregory, my friend and colleague at the *St. Petersburg Times*. I have known Lane for many years—and even edited her for six months, awhile back—and can attest to the abundance of empathy she brings to every assignment.

Lane is one of the most open-hearted people I've ever known. Although she's too young to have been a hippie, she radiates peace and harmony. Her pod-mates in the newsroom often joke that she lives perpetually in the Summer of Love. She's relentlessly upbeat, with a smile on her face every day, a kind word for everyone she meets and a decided preference for writing mini-epics about downtrodden and forgotten souls no one else thinks to cover.

The carnie eking out his last days in the trailer park, the jilted woman clutching the little engagement ring her fiancé gave her before making his

exit, the garage mechanic who keeps a lemur near the front counter—
these are the subjects Lane is drawn to, again and again. If someone's crying in a smoky bar, she is there. If there's hay or straw on the floor, and a
one-eyed dog anywhere in the vicinity, she's already scribbling in her notebook. Once, I suggested that maybe it would be fun for her to profile a
bank president and find the wild child hidden inside the three-piece suit.

"Sure," she said, looking at me as if I'd lost my mind.

Lane's powers are in full display in her stories here. Who else could
have persuaded Steve Stanton, the former city manager of Largo who lost
his job after announcing he was becoming a woman, to let a reporter tag
along as he went shopping for a dress? Who else would have sat in the
bleachers at the rodeo, watching four horsemen gallop into the arena with
signs that said GOD BLESS THE USA, and wondered about the rider
who was stuck holding the unglamorous THE?

And yet, what struck me as I reread Lane's pieces was not just their
open-heartedness, but their toughness and rigor. When she decides to
track down the THE guy—a seemingly innocuous quest—she already is
imagining who he will be. Using the second-person, she shares her guess
with the reader:

> You were expecting some lackey who wrangles calves and lives in a
> mobile home with his girlfriend, her kid and a bunch of dogs.

Then Lane's search takes an unexpected turn, straight into what appears
to be a startling deception. Suddenly the story is no longer just about the
rodeo or patriotism, but about overweening pride and skewed priorities and
the pervasiveness of class in American culture—all revealed, as best we can
tell, through a cover-up in the most unlikely of settings.

In a muscular piece that doesn't waste a word, Lane reports every
detail with unflinching precision. She doesn't shy away from the darker
undertones. She also doesn't cloud the story with that finger-wagging,
prosecutorial tone that creeps into some investigative reporting. She just
lays it out, unadorned, and then leaves it to readers to make whatever
judgments they deem fit. Then she ends it with a grace note that reminds
us why she wanted to pursue this story in the first place. Once again, she
asks us to identify with someone who would otherwise be ignored.

> You're the bridge between God and country, Ike.
> The genuine article.

Her portrait of Evel Knievel is completely different, yet just as striking.
This time, Lane finds her way into the life of someone famous, not her

typical subject. But the man she meets is no longer the daredevil who rocketed above the Snake River Canyon. Now 68, Knievel is a ghost of his former self, aching and tired and struggling to breathe, barely hanging on. More than anything else, he's angry. He lashes out at Lane, mocks her, yells at her:

> He is tired of people pestering him, asking stupid questions.
> What kind of questions? "That's a dumb question."
> What was your favorite jump? "Jesus. Any jump I landed was my favorite."
> What does it feel like to crash? "What the hell do you think it feels like? Christ almighty. It hurts."

These are not the responses Lane usually hears. With her sunny personality, she typically charms her subjects. Not Knievel.

> Was it worth it? "What kind of stupid question is that? I'm still here, aren't I?
> "Now hurry up. I'm running out of air."

Lane has acknowledged that when she left the interview, she felt defeated and was fighting off tears. But then she talked to her editor, Mike Wilson—who also happens to be my editor—and he helped her see that Knievel's prickliness was a gift that took her into the heart of her story. Mike's insight was crucial, because it allowed Lane to take that step back and see what she really had. Working together, she and Mike were able to bring Knievel into focus.

> He takes 11 pills in the morning, a dozen at night. They keep his blood flowing and his transplanted liver working. They ease the arthritis that burns his back, arms and legs. It hurts like hell, being mortal.

It would be hard to find a more gorgeous summation of the story than that last sentence. Ultimately, it's what most of our stories are about—the reality of how we live out our own limited time on this earth.

As reporters, empathy gets us inside these stories. But critical thinking tells us what to make of them once we're back in the newsroom, staring at that blank screen.

Thomas French is a Writing Fellow at The Poynter Institute and a Pulitzer Prize-winning reporter at the St. Petersburg Times.

PART 5

Editorial Writing

Winner: Editorial Writing

Marie Dillon

Chicago Tribune

To get straight to the point, Marie Dillon writes funny editorials. Very funny.

Parsing humor for its component parts is a notoriously low-yield undertaking, and you won't get a lot of assistance from Dillon. She describes her method as defining a topic, doing a lot of reporting (not necessarily evident to the reader), figuring out what she has to say and then writing it in one take.

For starters, the topics in this entry are seriously droll in the right hands: librarians refusing to buy a prizewinning children's book in which a dog is bitten by a snake in a particularly sensitive place; academic double-talk in a report clearing the president of Southern Illinois University of plagiarism charges; City Council deliberations on rules for taking dogs to outdoor cafes and a new birth control pill eliminating menstrual periods.

Dillon would like to make clear that this is not all she does. As she puts it in a brief bio, she "covers mass transit, immigration and other weighty subjects but is grateful that the job allows her to indulge an occasional personal rant."

To these assignments, she brings writing that is consistently compact and flavorful, sentences with a sure sense of timing, language that presses the envelope of family newspaper accept-ability. And some other mysterious grace notes that Dillon insists are a bit of a mystery to her, too.

Indeed, while the Dillon editorials are flamboyant in an appealing way, Dillon on Dillon is understated.

She grew up an Air Force brat, settling in Mesa, Ariz., with hopes of becoming a veterinarian. She switched majors several times at Arizona State University, falling onto the journalism track, which she has stayed with ever since.

Though Dillon has 20-plus-years as a reporter and editor, she had just six months' previous experience as an editorial writer before joining the *Chicago Tribune* editorial board in February 2006.

"Pretty early on I knew I wanted to do it [write editorials]," Dillon said, "but I don't feel you can just step into it. People have defined roles on edi-torial boards, and once they get there, they tend to stay there."

After years of paying dues at all three major South Florida newspapers ("I may be the only person ever to trade in a car with all three parking stickers"), she landed a job writing editorials at the *Sun-Sentinel* in Fort Lauderdale. Six months later, in 2000, her husband, online expert Rich Gordon, accepted a job at Northwestern University's Medill School of Journalism, and she got to do six years of the preparation tour all over again at the *Tribune*. (The couple has an 11-year-old son, Conrad, whom Dillon describes as "the best writer in the family.")

Back in her reporting days, Dillon won a couple of prizes, "but nothing big, nothing great—and that was so long ago I've forgotten for what." Earlier this year, she did win the Beck award, an internal *Tribune* writing prize, "so February was a really good month for me."

Though she was consistently low-key and modest under direct ques-tioning, I found Dillon the quipster sneaking back into our side e-mail conversations. In the interview that follows, I had suggested (and Dillon politely rebuffed) the idea that great American humorists used to be mostly male but that she was part of a rising tide of wisecracking female voices.

Explaining a delay in setting up a phone interview, Dillon wrote that she had been sick, adding, "I'm writing about the Chicago Teachers Union pension fund today and not feeling much like a female humorist."

In one of our last exchanges, I said I didn't mean to badger her with my pet theory. I had been influenced by going to college in the late 1960s when feminism was picking up steam. Though I wouldn't claim the signif-icance of equal pay for equal work or a seat at the table in boardrooms and political circles, I thought it mildly interesting that women writers have clearly achieved humor parity.

To which Dillon replied, "Maybe you are right—I was born a little late to appreciate it. I think women broke into the writing game early in the struggle, long before the more important gains, such as getting guys to fold laundry."

—Rick Edmonds, Media Business Analyst, The Poynter Institute

Don't Let Your Kids Read This

FEB. 20, 2007

By Marie Dillon

The best children's book published last year begins with a passage about a rattlesnake that bit a dog named Roy right there on, um, the first page. Right there on…the passenger's seat of a '62 Cadillac. OK, OK. On the scrotum.

We'll venture that your reaction to finding the word "scrotum" on the editorial page is a lot like the average fourth-grader's reaction to finding it in the second paragraph of the 2007 Newbery Medal winner, *The Higher Power of Lucky.* A little gasp, maybe a snicker.

But you're still reading.

A number of school librarians apparently never got past page one of the book, though, and they don't think its targeted audience of 9- to 12-year-olds ought to, either. Many say they won't buy it for their shelves. "Because of that one word, I would not be able to read that book aloud," one of them explained, calling it "a Howard Stern-type shock treatment." We have three words for that: Oh, come on.

The Higher Power of Lucky is about a scrappy 10-year-old who eaves-drops on 12-step meetings as she struggles to take control of her listing life. It's a tale that could have been told without the word "scrotum," but it's pretty tame compared to the in-your-face potty humor of Dav Pilkey's wildly popular *Captain Underpants* series or *The Day My Butt Went Psycho* by Andy Griffiths.

Author Susan Patron, a 35-year veteran of the Los Angeles Public Library whose job is to select children's books, said she wanted to create characters that rang true to her young audience. The word "scrotum," she wrote, "sounded to Lucky like something green that comes up when you have the flu and cough too much," a perfectly pitched line even if it does sound a little like one of Pilkey's snot jokes.

"Scrotum" isn't a dirty word; it's a precise clinical word for a body part and a lot milder than the other words a 10-year-old (or Howard Stern) might use to describe that body part. Half the kids that age actually have a scrotum, and all of them are getting to the point where they're going to start asking questions. This is no time for the adults to get squeamish.

If librarians don't want to answer those questions, we have three more words to suggest: "Ask your parents."

'Infelicities in Attribution'

OCT. 12, 2007

By Marie Dillon

Any college student knows better than to turn in a term paper that contains passages lifted from another source. In this age of cut-and-paste Internet research, it's extremely easy to do—and easy to detect.

Even in the Dark Ages, circa 1984, students who cribbed from others' work did so at their peril. A teacher who found repeated examples of unattributed verbatim text could not be expected to accept a student's stammered explanation that it was all an accident. A student could expect no mercy.

But things were different at the state's second-largest university in those days, or so we're told. Standards were inconsistent, definitions were unclear and style manuals weren't mandatory at Southern Illinois University when Glenn Poshard, now the university's president, was laboring over his doctoral thesis.

That was the finding of a faculty committee that reviewed Poshard's 1984 dissertation after the president was accused of plagiarism.

Though it dances delicately around the charges—the *Best Euphemism for "Plagiarism" Award* goes to the review committee for coining the phrase "infelicities in attribution"—the report does conclude that Poshard committed "inadvertent plagiarism." Based on the report, SIU's board of trustees decided Thursday that Poshard can keep his Ph.D. and his job if he cleans up the paper and resubmits it.

The committee's findings are consistent with what Poshard has maintained all along, except that he doesn't think what he did should be called plagiarism. He admits his paper includes many sections for which he failed to credit the authors. Sometimes he left out the quotation marks; sometimes he forgot to do a footnote. But never on purpose! And besides, the instructors supervising his work never found fault with his citations.

Anyone can make a mistake. But 30 times in 111 pages? That's what SIU's student paper, *The Daily Egyptian,* reported in August. Some of the examples might have been a little nitpicky, but it does strain our credulity to imagine that Poshard simply forgot, all those times, that the words he was typing were not his own.

His apologists on the review committee chalk it up to "the academic culture in that period" and note that a style manual that spelled out the rules of proper citation was "available at the time but not required." Poshard clearly had a passing familiarity with those rules, since he sometimes followed them, sometimes not, and for that reason the committee decided his actions should be described as "inadvertent" instead of "uneducated" plagiarism.

After examining several papers written about the same time, the committee concluded that "quite a few" students employed deficient citation methods similar to those used by Poshard, and that these were accepted by dissertation committees.

All of this is supposed to make us feel better about the fact that a university president was awarded a doctoral degree based on a paper in which he copied the work of others, left and right, and presented it as his own. It doesn't. Instead, it spreads the blame to the institution in a way that undermines the value of all the diplomas earned at SIU, past, present and future.

The assertion that doctoral students and their professors were largely ignorant of the rules of attribution—and that such deficiencies can be remedied by patching up the footnotes decades later—is an unwarranted indictment of the school's academic standards and integrity. We'll wager that if we polled SIU alums who earned their degrees around the same time Poshard was earning his, we'd find little confusion about what is, or isn't, plagiarism.

Take Your Dog to Lunch Day

SEPT. 9, 2007

By Marie Dillon

It was news to a lot of people that dogs aren't allowed at sidewalk cafes in Chicago. It's hard to get a table on the patio in some neighborhoods without stepping around a golden retriever or on a Chihuahua.

Metromix, RedEye and other arbiters of hip hot spots regularly publish lists of bars and eateries that welcome dogs to their outdoor (and sometimes indoor) seating areas. The complimentary steak tartare doggy treats at Brasserie Jo have gotten a lot of ink. The Web site DogFriendly.com has an extensive listing of Chicago restaurants that allow diners to bring their dogs.

So it was a surprise when the City Council started talking about an ordinance to permit the practice, and an even bigger surprise that so many people—*cat* people, we suspect—were vehemently opposed. Dogs don't belong at eating establishments, they protested. They'll fight, they'll bite, they'll bark. They'll steal the burgers off our plates and relieve themselves on our shoes.

A Health Department official warned that dog hair and saliva would contaminate tables, floors and anything else that touches the dogs, including the wait staff. Dogs carry fleas and germs and "may have feces on their face," Frances Guichard, director of food protection, told a council committee.

Aldermen were grossed out, but their concern was fleeting, probably because they know the dogs are already under the tables and none of that scary stuff is happening. So beginning Jan. 1, it will be perfectly legal for Bowser to join you at the corner coffee klatch, just as he's been doing all along. Of course, now there are *rules*, but nothing worth growling about: Dogs can't sit on tables or chairs or eat off the china. Their vaccinations must be current. Employees must check the rabies tags but aren't allowed to touch the animals—how's that going to work?—and the restaurant must post a sign warning that dogs are allowed on the premises.

Chicago offers a lot of reasons to wag your tail, if you have one. There are bark parks and dog beaches, dog boutiques and doggy day-care centers. Some luxury hotels provide a pet concierge or set aside floors where dogs are allowed to roam freely. There are taxis that cater to four-legged passengers and real-estate networks that match renters with dog-friendly landlords. There are canine cruises along the Chicago River and the Lake Michigan shoreline. A whole industry has grown up around dog-walking, dog-sitting and dog-washing. There are even services that contract to pick up the poop in your yard. Some business districts have communal water bowls on every corner.

It's enough to make you wonder who's running this town—the dogs or the Democrats?—but in either case, it's pointless to fight the pack. If you don't want to dine with the dogs, then steer clear of the places that invite them, the same way vegetarians avoid steakhouses and Baptists avoid brew pubs. Everyone else can sit and stay.

So Long, Aunt Flo

JUNE 7, 2007

By Marie Dillon

Our Little Redheaded Cousin is here for another visit, if you know what we mean, and we are not happy about it. We are crampy, we are bloated, we are tired, and the next person who leaves a dirty glass in the sink instead of putting it in the dishwasher is either headed for divorce court or grounded for life and *don't you dare* suggest this has something to do with our "time of the month" or we'll set your hair on fire or cry.

Ahem.

Procter & Gamble has just the thing for days like this: a chirpy Web page that celebrates "being a girl," full of helpful hints about selecting the right feminine hygiene products and e-mailable postcards so you can "wish your friend a happy period." Really. We suppose the e-greetings could be faintly amusing, in a girlfriend-to-girlfriend, what-are-these-people-smoking kind of way. But guys, don't even think about it.

Wyeth Pharmaceuticals has a better idea: a curse-bursting birth-control pill called Lybrel. Instead of mimicking a 28-day cycle, complete with a fake menstrual period, Lybrel dispenses with the periods altogether. The U.S. Food and Drug Administration approved the drug last week, but women have been on to this fix for ages. Resourceful brides manipulate the dose of traditional birth-control pills to keep Aunt Flo from crashing the honeymoon. Female combat soldiers apply the same strategy to avoid sharing a foxhole with their Little Friend.

Still, the idea of putting Mother Nature on hold indefinitely gives some women pause. They forget that Mother Nature's plan was for women to spend their reproductive years either pregnant or breast-feeding, not shopping for maxi-pads. Thirteen menstrual cycles a year is at least 12 more than what Mother Nature had in mind.

All that menstruation causes problems most people never contemplate. A couple of years ago, Kotex introduced "quiet pad wrappers" to mute the incriminating crinkle caused by opening a feminine-hygiene product in a public restroom. Last year, the makers of a washable, reusable menstrual device promoted their Diva Cup as an earth-friendly alternative to the tons of disposable feminine products crowding our land-fills. Who knew?

So let's hear it for Lybrel, the first birth-control pill that prevents unwanted pregnancies, reduces noise pollution and fights global warming. Best of all, it ensures that you don't have to have a happy period unless you damn well feel like it.

X-Ray Reading

By Ben Montgomery

Marie Dillon's use of casual, common language helps readers connect with the editorial page.

So Long, Aunt Flo

By Marie Dillon

Our Little Redheaded Cousin is here for another visit, if you know what we mean, and we are not happy about it. We are crampy, we are bloated, we are tired, and the next person who leaves a dirty glass in the sink instead of putting it in the dishwasher is either headed for divorce court or grounded for life and don't you dare suggest this has something to do with our "time of the month" or we'll set your hair on fire or cry.

Ahem.

Procter & Gamble has just the thing for days like this: a chirpy Web page that celebrates "being a girl," full of helpful hints about selecting the right feminine hygiene products and e-mailable postcards so you can "wish your friend a happy period." Really. We suppose the e-greetings could be faintly amusing, in a girlfriend-to-girlfriend, what-are-these-people-smoking kind of way. But guys, don't even think about it.

Wyeth Pharmaceuticals has a better idea: a curse-bursting

Stop right here. Is this an editorial about a menstrual period? We're in on it from the very beginning for the simple fact that she's writing about something rarely discussed at the water cooler, much less on the editorial page.

Notice that the second sentence in this opening paragraph starts with three short clauses and three quick commas, then slips into a run of words that speed the pace of reading and offer insight into mood. You can hear this woman speak.

This short, funny clearing of the throat is fantastic after such a long run of words. The author is raging, then regaining her composure.

Nice adjective.

Dillon is setting the table with these two paragraphs. She is offering interesting context without slowing us down.

Nice description. We're taught to limit our adjectives, but she uses them to great effect throughout.

birth-control pill called Lybrel. Instead of mimicking a 28-day cycle, complete with a fake menstrual period, Lybrel dispenses with the periods altogether. The U.S. Food and Drug Administration approved the drug last week, but women have been on to this fix for ages. Resourceful brides manipulate the dose of traditional birth-control pills to keep Aunt Flo from crashing the honeymoon. Female combat soldiers apply the same strategy to avoid sharing a foxhole with their Little Friend.

Still, the idea of putting Mother Nature on hold indefinitely gives some women pause.

Notice the back and forth.

They forget that Mother Nature's plan was for women to spend their reproductive years either pregnant or breast-feeding, not shopping for maxi-pads. Thirteen menstrual cycles a year is at least 12 more than what Mother Nature had in mind.

Dillon gives nature a personality here by repeating "Mother Nature." The natural order becomes a character.

All that menstruation causes problems most people never contemplate. A couple of years ago, Kotex introduced "quiet pad wrappers" to mute the incriminating crinkle caused by opening a feminine-hygiene product in a public restroom. Last year, the makers of a washable, reusable menstrual device promoted their Diva Cup as an earth-friendly alternative to the tons of disposable feminine products crowding our landfills. Who knew?

She's slipping into sarcasm, and she does it in a simple, understated way.

Nice adjective.

So let's hear it for Lybrel, the first birth-control pill that prevents unwanted pregnancies, reduces noise pollution and fights global warming. Best of all, it ensures that you don't have to have a happy period unless you damn well feel like it.

———— Great closing.

Ben Montgomery is a reporter with the St. Petersburg Times.

BEHIND the STORY

Winner's Q&A

An Interview with Marie Dillon

This edited e-mail interview was conducted by Poynter Institute Media Business Analyst Rick Edmonds with Marie Dillon, winner of ASNE's Distinguished Writing Award for Editorial Writing.

RICK EDMONDS: I saw a picture of the *Tribune* editorial board recently, which looked to be 13 pretty serious people. Or is that 12 pretty serious people and you?

MARIE DILLON: I can't wait to tell them you said that.

Have you always been a class clown, or did you grow into it?

I have seven siblings (Irish Catholic). We're all pretty funny.

That's Maureen Dowd's explanation too—getting air time at a crowded dinner table. Talk a bit about where you find your ideas and the place of funny pieces in the editorial page mix.

Some of it is of course dictated by news, especially on the more serious topics (immigration, mass transit, Latin America, etc.).

Some of my best assignments are other people's suggestions. I love it when someone at the board meeting says, "I have an idea for Marie." I'll pretty much take any idea and run with it.

I get a lot of ideas just from life—I have a husband, a son, a dog, etc. I think I'm in a good demographic for this job at this moment: I'm one of the younger baby boomers and an "older" mom, so some of my peers are grandparents and some are in their late 20s and early 30s. I play tennis with some very smart women who have a lot to say about the world. And you'd be amazed at what comes up on the PTA message board.

I grew up in the Air Force, so we moved around some, and I've moved several times in my career, too. So I think I have an unusual diversity of experiences and acquaintances, and I'm finally getting old/wise enough to make something of them.

As for the place of funny editorials...if you want to know the truth, it's a little worrisome that those are my most popular pieces. For the record, while this entry is heavy on funny stuff, it's not necessarily a representative sample. But those are definitely the ones that get the feedback. Nobody ever says, "Great piece on tax increment financing!"

What portion of your work and the mix of the page goes to light pieces of this kind?

Well, that's hard to say. There's light, and then there's fluffy. Two of the most popular things I wrote last year were about an employment agency that told its rent-a-Santas not to say "ho" and a study that found women with big butts are smarter than women with small butts. Those were fluffy. I suppose "Aunt Flo" falls in that pile. I like to think the scrotum piece and the dog piece actually made a point in a funny way, and that there's more room for that sort of funny piece than for the frivolous funny piece. But sometimes I can't resist the fluffy ones.

How do you decide which subjects make the grade for one of your editorials and which do not?

Anything goes, as long as I can think of something new to say. I hate repackaging the same old opinion.

The pieces do not look as if they require much additional reporting. Or do they sometimes?

Actually I do TONS of reporting. You have to do a lot of research to form a good opinion. But that doesn't mean you have to oppress the reader with it.

Still, it must be all about, or mostly about, the crafting and writing?

Heck, no. Believe it or not, I've never had a job with tighter deadlines, so every day is a sprint. I find that the more time I devote to reporting, the less time it takes me to write because I don't have to B.S. my way through it.

Talk about how you handle drafts and rewriting.

I don't usually have time to rewrite. A lot of days I come out of the board meeting at 11 a.m. with an assignment that has to be filed by 4 p.m. Sometimes it's a subject I don't know much about. So I just write it as fast and as well as I can and hit the send button at 3:59. If I do have the luxury of not writing on deadline, I will tinker with it the second day and I'm usually glad I did. But I generally like to get it done and move on. As Linda Ellerbee once said, it's not brain surgery.

There is a cartoon I've had posted near my computer for years that helps me keep things in perspective. I'm including it here for your amusement:

These pieces read very polished. Can you provide an example or two of what you changed or ditched in getting to a final version?

These four are all pretty much first drafts. I did try to find a way to write "Aunt Flo" in something other than the first person, but it wasn't nearly as fun and I truly thought the piece was going to be spiked anyway, so I just went ahead and had my fun. Boy, was I surprised.

What role does your editor play?

My editor, Bruce Dold, is brilliant. He reads everything, knows everything, can preside over a very contentious discussion and then very calmly synthesize what the editorial ought to say. He can spell Condoleezza Rice without looking it up. He gives me a lot of freedom and encouragement. I'm sure he would save me from myself if I tried to go too far, but he likes to push the envelope, too. I can't tell you how much fun it is to work in that environment. In terms of actual line editing, he sometimes will change one or two words or add a transition and improve the piece by (I'm not kidding) 50 percent or more. It's amazing.

The banned book piece, particularly, struck me as exemplary for not a wasted word. Do you scan drafts ruthlessly for tightening or are you naturally concise?

I was an editor for many years, and I had to bust a lot of masterpieces to briefs. Sometimes that's a travesty, but often it's for the better. I try to keep it in mind.

That piece was especially sparing in its use of anything but the most basic of adjectives. The only ones I spotted were "scrappy 10-year-old," "her

listing life," and "squeamish." Some of the other pieces were more expansive, but do you achieve your plainspoken tone, in part, by sticking to nouns and verbs?

Yes. If you pick a strong noun or verb, it can do the work of several words.

I get the idea that you are not into deconstructing yourself. But can you give a specific example or two from these pieces of how you or an editor got from good to better in a passage? Or I would settle for what the writing process is in creating a graceful sentence like, "It's hard to get a table on the patio in some neighborhoods without stepping around a golden retriever or on a Chihuahua."

There's not a lot to deconstruct, is the thing. Sometimes I stare at my screen for a good long time before I type something, but the first thing to come out of my fingers is usually the last. That was the case with the dog sentence. I was thinking about the outdoor coffee shop in Rogers Park where I go with my tennis coach on Saturdays. There are a lot of dogs underfoot, including his two Chihuahuas. I'm always afraid someone is going to trip over one of those snoozing retrievers and step on Max or Sarah.

If I know what I want to say, then I rarely have trouble saying it. When I wrote about the librarians wigging out over the word "scrotum," I was thinking of my then-10-year-old son, who has a rich vocabulary. And I had such great material to work with on the plagiarism piece that John McCormick, who edited that one, actually stopped at one point and said to me, "Give back your paycheck!" By which he meant the editorial had obviously written itself.

I can give you an example from a piece that wasn't part of the entry. It was about the scene at a Bruce Springsteen concert now that the fans (and the band) are all getting kind of creaky. It wasn't at all like those four-hour Springsteen shows we went to in the '80s, where nobody sat down the whole time. What I wrote was that it was "scary to survey the seats in Chicago's United Center this week and see all those paunchy, jowly, graying (or balding) fifty-somethings who stayed out past their bedtime to see, gulp, Bruce Springsteen."

My editor, Bruce Dold, was at the same concert, and he didn't think "scary" was the right word; he thought the word was "fun." It changed the tone of the whole piece, made it sound lighthearted and affectionate instead of like it was written by some whiny boomer dumbstruck by the concept of aging. One word made that much difference! That's what a good editor can do for you.

When is the right time to go hog wild with puns (dogs at lunch) or euphemisms (Aunt Flo)?

Were there puns in that dog piece? Yikes. I hate puns. But you can't have too many euphemisms, ever.

You've got a point about puns. Here is what my colleague Roy Peter Clark had to say: "They are not technically puns. There is probably a name for them drawn from the excruciating exactness of Greek and Roman rhetoric, but no need to go there. They fall in the general category of 'wordplay.' Sometimes a writer will put a little spin or twist upon an expected phrase: for fun, I've called that effect not a cliché, but a touché."

There is some undercurrent of anger in the first two editorials at the lameness of fusty, do-good librarians or temporizing academicians. Is that the sort of thing that makes you mad?

I was good and mad about the Southern Illinois University plagiarism thing. I still am. As for the fusty librarians, God bless them. I wanted to come across as indignant, but I was secretly thrilled to be writing about scrotums.

Your editorials have a whole lot of voice—easy to identify but I imagine hard to achieve. What are your tests for making sure these sound like a Marie Dillon editorial?

I'm not trying to write Marie Dillon editorials. I'm writing for the board. I don't always care about or agree with what I'm writing, but I'll use whatever voice I need to make the point. I'm sure I wouldn't be asked to channel Lou Dobbs, for example, because immigration is something I do have strong feelings about. But on most subjects, I am happy to be a hired gun.

Though they are unsigned, do colleagues, friends and readers have a pretty easy time spotting which editorials are yours?

About half the time when someone tells me they loved "my" piece, it turns out it was written by Paul Weingarten or John McCormick. We are always getting blamed for each other's work.

One convention of editorials is that they include a "call to action." Yours don't seem to tell anyone to do anything (unless you count going to lunch with a dog). Is that a part of the strategy of offering lighter fare in the editorial page mix?

Well, again, this isn't a representative body of work. I've written a lot of those call-to-action things on immigration, Darfur or Cuba policy, for instance. You can see how well that's working.

Your bio talks about a lot of more conventional reporting and editing jobs. What was your career path from there to here?

I was managing a fast-food restaurant and attending Arizona State University when I got my first newspaper job at the *Mesa Tribune.* (I took a BIG pay cut, by the way.) It was a great first job because the Cox chain had just bought the suburban dailies on the east side of Phoenix, and they hired my favorite professor, Max Jennings, to run the *Tribune.* Naturally he hired a bunch of his students. For a couple of years there it was like we were still in college (and in fact, several of us were). I wrote features, covered religion, health, city hall and did a lot of general assignment stuff.

When I graduated, Max lobbied the editors at the *Dayton Daily News* (also a Cox paper) to hire me. I spent four years as a one-woman bureau, covering seven mostly rural counties north of Dayton. It was a great job, lots of cherry-picking. I got to do a lot of national stories, too. But it was a tough place to be single.

I became an editor sort of by accident. One day I got a call from Tom O'Hara, who was then at *The Palm Beach Post* (more Cox). He was recruiting editors. I think he thought I was one because my title was "bureau chief," but he hired me even after I disabused him of that. At the *Post* I met my husband, Rich Gordon, who is now a famous new media guru.

This was 1989 and the height of the great South Florida newspaper wars, and I guess I turned out to be a mercenary—I'm one of the few people I know who has worked for all three of those papers. From the *Post* I went to the state desk at *The Miami Herald,* then I jumped ship to do national and foreign editing at the *Sun-Sentinel.* But I always wanted to write editorials, and I got my chance at the *S-S*—for six months. I was rudely interrupted when Rich was hired to launch the new media program at the Medill School at Northwestern University. Lucky for me, the *Chicago Tribune* was kind enough to take me in. But it was back to editing.

I spent six years on the metro desk. My last job there was deputy metro editor/Sunday. But I had my eye on this job the whole time. Now that I have it, they're going to have to blow me out with dynamite.

Would you have any advice for younger journalists or journalism students who aspire to write pieces like yours?

What I would say to them, and they won't like it, is that they should concentrate on being a good reporter and writer and save the opinion stuff for when they're older. You need a lot of life under your belt before you start telling other people what to think. Much of what I wrote in my younger days is painfully embarrassing to me today.

Who are some of your models for editorial writing—or for good writing in general? And why?

When you see an editorial you like, you generally don't know who wrote it. There's someone I admire at *The Boston Globe,* but I have no idea who it is. And there's someone at the *Los Angeles Times,* and one really cranky *New York Times* writer (I actually have a theory about who that is). My favorite writer in the world is Calvin Trillin. There are a lot of great columnists here at the *Tribune,* far too many to mention without really stepping in it, but I especially admire Mary Schmich. Fred Grimm at *The Miami Herald* and Frank Cerabino at *The Palm Beach Post* are two other favorites. But column writing isn't as close to editorial writing as a lot of people think.

I've come across some surprisingly great nonfiction writers, and I think there are similarities between their work and what I'm trying to do. One is Dr. Elmer Grossman, a Berkeley physician who wrote *Everyday Pediatrics for Parents.* Obviously it's meant to be a parenting resource, but it's a great read. Another is Pat Blaskower, coauthor of *Women's Winning Doubles,* of all things. I also loved Vicki Iovine's *The Girlfriends' Guide to Pregnancy.* I disagree with almost everything Caitlin Flanagan has to say, but she is really fun to read. I hope there are people who say that about me.

Since you mentioned it, what are some of the relevant differences between columns and editorials?

Everyone knows who the columnist is. Their photo is right there! So they have to be themselves, or at least they have to remain true to whatever persona they've created. I'm not all that interested in letting the readers get to know me. I love the anonymity of editorial writing. It's a little like acting: You can step into a role just for that one piece. On the next piece, you can be somebody else.

My impression—or maybe my bias—is that historically there have not been a great many female humorists. But more recently we have been getting very funny stuff from the likes of wiseacre gals Maureen Dowd, Gail Collins and Miss Manners. Do you think of your pieces as feminine in tone and topic? Has this genre opened to women in a way it was not, pre-feminism?

Great female humorists, hmmm. There are some really funny women out there—Merrill Markoe, Linda Ellerbee, Cynthia Heimel, Anne Lamott— but I don't know if they count as humorists.

Here's something fun to ponder: We got exactly one complaint about the "Aunt Flo" piece, and that was from a woman who was sure it was written by a man. She was OK with it once she learned it wasn't.

Aside from "Aunt Flo," though, what's so feminine about the tone/topic of my stuff?

In my experience, the only place where you find reliably gender-specific voices is in the sports section. (On our editorial page, though, the two people who most often write about sports are both women.) I don't object to the suggestion that I write like a girl; I just don't know what it means.

What do you see yourself doing as a writer 10 years from now?

This question has always given me fits on my annual review. I always knew where I wanted to end up—on the editorial board! But if you asked me to articulate a career path, I couldn't do it. Unless there was a job opening that actually intrigued me, I usually didn't know what I wanted to do "next." I just kept reaching for fun jobs and waiting for this one.

Ten years from now? I'd love to say I'm going to be doing exactly what I'm doing now, but that's the sort of thinking that got our industry into this leaky boat. Let's just say I'd like to keep writing editorials for a good long time, and if that means I have to text-message them to your toaster, I'm there.

Writer's Workshop

1. Marie Dillon has several techniques common to excellent writers, but not so easy to master when you are starting out. She varies the length of her sentences, including many that are very short and some that are very long. Underline examples of each in the four pieces and discuss the effect she achieves. Why do you think all eight sentences in the next-to-last paragraph of the dog editorial are roughly the same length?

2. Check the direct quotes in these pieces. Dillon uses them sparingly and edits them down to what's essential—sometimes just a couple of words. In one of your own pieces or another, edit longer quotes to what is most worth quoting. Does the piece benefit in speed and concision?

3. While these editorials are appealing, in part, by being nontraditional, reread them and see if you can find in each an explicit statement of the main point Dillon is making. (Hint: It is never in the first or last paragraph but several times is close by.)

4. In the interview, Dillon said that there is more reporting behind the pieces than meets the eye but "that doesn't mean you have to oppress the reader with it." In the "take your dog to lunch" and "Aunt Flo" pieces, note how many statements were probably researched separately and then assembled.

5. Another convention Dillon avoids is the editorial "we." What do her pieces gain as a result? Does the practice work consistently, or are some of these opinion pieces in which it is hard to find the opinion? Why do you think she chose to break her pattern in the "Aunt Flo" piece, in which "we" actually means "I"? How does that choice turbocharge the humor? (Hint: Dillon says in the interview that she loves the anonymity of editorial writing because "it's a little like acting: You can step into a role just for that one piece. On the next piece, you can be somebody else.")

Assignment Desk

1. Dillon seems a case in point of the axiom, "If you want to write well, read a lot." Search for samples from several of the authors she cites in her interview. Then write a brief essay on what her style has in common with theirs.

2. Read your local or campus paper for a week and pick out a topic or two that might be suitable for the Dillon treatment. Then try writing it—or describe what would be needed to make such a piece funny while making a point.

3. Pick a topic for an opinion piece (it need not be funny). Then try the Dillon "non-method" method. Report a lot, more than you need. Think out in advance what you want to say (with an outline, if that helps). Then write it in a single take with only light revision. How did it work out? Or would you need to do more reporting and heavier rewriting to have a finished final draft?

THE ARIZONA REPUBLIC

Finalist: Editorial Writing

Linda Valdez

A Defining Moment

SEPT. 21, 2007

If you've lost a loved one, you've probably felt that aching void that grief carves into your heart.

How you fill that void says a lot about who you are, what you believe and what kind of life you want to live.

The Valley is grieving the murder of Phoenix police Officer Nick Erfle. He was a good man who deserved better. His death was an assault on law and order and our collective sense of security.

How the community responds to those emotions will say a lot about who we are, what we believe and what kind of community we want to inhabit.

These are not petty questions.

They should not be answered by a few loud voices that appeal to fear and anger.

But that's what is happening in our community.

Self-righteous radio talkers, angry letter writers and mad bloggers claim to know exactly the right lesson to take away from this horrible event.

The killer was an illegal immigrant, they say.

Most cop killers are illegal immigrants, they say.

Phoenix police policies coddle illegal immigrants, they say.

The first statement is true. The killer was an illegal immigrant. But he did not arrive recently with an armload of foreign ideas. He was brought here as an infant. He was a product of this society.

The other statements are not true.

Phoenix Police Chief Jack Harris says 10 Phoenix police officers have been killed in the past 20 years. Only Officer Erfle's murder and two others were committed by illegal immigrants.

Nor does Phoenix have a "sanctuary" policy that prevents police from turning criminal illegal immigrants over to Immigration and Customs Enforcement. In fact, Phoenix police detectives partner with federal immigration officers to investigate smuggling crimes, home invasions, gangs and other violent activity.

Erik Jovani Martinez, the man who shot Officer Erfle, had previously been arrested by the Phoenix police and had been deported as part of the criminal proceeding. He came back across a porous border that is the product of federal failures.

Martinez should not have been on the street the day he shot Officer Erfle.

He was there because of the federal government's broken immigration system.

For many years, this newspaper has called on Congress to fix it.

We continue to call on Congress to do the job only the federal government can do.

This can't be fixed by turning Phoenix police into ersatz immigration officers. But that's what some commentators want. As you listen to them, please remember that they were calling for such things even before Officer Erfle was killed. They shaped his murder into a tool for their propaganda even before he was cold. That's not respect. That's exploiting a tragedy.

As a practical matter, if police did routine immigration enforcement, it would endanger public safety. Cops would be processing illegal immigrants instead of responding to your call about the prowler in the back yard. Asking the police to do immigration enforcement duties would also change the very texture of our community. Latinos, who have helped to shape our traditions, our culture and our economy, would become subject to police challenge just because of their ethnic heritage.

That's not the kind of community we have.

The voices that are demanding you change it are passionate and insistent.

But as you listen to them, ask yourself what you believe about human dignity.

Think about what kind of community you want this to be.

BEHIND the STORY

Lessons Learned

By Linda Valdez

What can you learn from beating your head against a brick wall? In this case, I learned the value of saying, "Ouch!"

It began with what is cynically referred to as an Obligatory Editorial.

The shooting of a police officer in the line of duty is the kind of tragedy that often merits an editorial because of the perceived need to express a sense of the community's grief. Don't get me wrong. These are important editorials. But they are not generally memorable, and they are not popular assignments. They can be difficult to write because there often isn't much new to say. The purpose is to comfort, not to challenge; to reassure, not to provoke. Those who volunteer for such editorials usually are trying to curry favor with the boss or make amends for something.

I didn't volunteer to write an editorial about the shooting of Phoenix police Officer Nick Erfle. The task fell to me because my beat includes illegal immigration, and the accused cop killer is an illegal immigrant. This fact was immediately exploited by anti-immigrant factions in our community, who attempted to direct community outrage over a single criminal act at an entire class of people. *The Arizona Republic*'s editorial page was also the target of criticism due to our longstanding support of comprehensive immigration reform. The accused's criminal record would have precluded him from the kind of earned legalization we support, but such nuance was lost on our critics. Their irrational opposition is the brick wall against which we have continually made our argument for immigration reform. In this context, we were going to have to stick by that argument.

This editorial would be difficult to write, but not for the usual reasons. This time, there was something new to say. The editorial would have to provoke the community to take a hard look at how it was being manipulated, and it also would have to honor the fallen officer and express sympathy for his colleagues and friends.

I began with a few questions: How do I condemn those who are using tragedy to further their own agenda, without appearing to defend a cop killer? How do I share the community's grief while urging people not to let anger get the best of them?

I added a few more: How do I defend an editorial position on immigration reform without sounding defensive? How do I keep the focus on the immediate tragedy and still acknowledge the complexities of immigration policies?

I learned several things in writing this editorial. One is that simplicity is a powerful tool for expressing complex ideas. I kept my sentences short and to the point. I resisted the urge to offer long, philosophical arguments about the causes of illegal immigration and the consequences of current policies. Instead I focused on the fallen police officer and the community's response to his killing.

I also learned that tapping into one's own experience can be valuable. The discussion of grief at the beginning of the editorial came from my memories of coping with the deaths of people I loved. I also relied on my personal feelings to express anger at the senseless killing of this officer. Doing so gave the editorial a sense of humanity that works because it is authentic.

Objectivity is a journalistic tool. But it may not be the right tool for every assignment. In this case, detachment would have alienated the reader. People needed to know we cared. That's the "Ouch!" This hurt, and our editorial showed that.

I also learned something about the importance of idealism, which is too easily dismissed in our hard-bitten business. The call for the community to engage in some introspection and consider the long-term consequences of its reaction to this incident was based on a belief in basic human decency. It was blatant hope.

There may not be too many times when emotion is the best tool, but this editorial works because the "Ouch!" is as authentic as the clear commitment to continue the head banging.

Linda Valdez has been an editorial writer for The Arizona Republic *since 1993, focusing on social needs and the disadvantaged. She has written extensively in recent years about illegal immigration, a topic with personal connections—she is married to a Mexican immigrant and is the great-grandchild of an illegal immigrant from Ireland. Valdez was a finalist for the Pulitzer Prize in editorial writing in 2003 and has received numerous other awards.*

The San Diego

Union-Tribune.

Finalist: Editorial Writing

Ruben Navarrette Jr.

Our Hair Trigger

NOV. 23, 2007

Who is afraid of a little español? Apparently, there are some folks in a small town in Tennessee who prefer their Plato and Cervantes in English only. And they think you should, too. In fact, they insist on it.

The ruckus began at the Marshall County Memorial Library in the community of Lewisburg when an employee named Nellie Rivera came up with a radical and subversive idea. Rivera asked herself: Why not hold a bilingual story time where children hear tales read to them in Spanish?

Ay, caramba! You can imagine what happened next. When it comes to language, and especially when it comes to Spanish, a lot of Americans have a hair trigger. While people all over the world are busy learning two or three languages, many Americans seem almost proud that they speak only one. And they demand that everyone else speak exclusively English, too.

In this case, they say, how dare a library, whose mission, after all, is to educate the population by spreading information in a variety of ways, expose innocent children to a foreign language? What good could come of that? Well, besides imparting a valuable and extremely marketable skill that would help future generations navigate a highly competitive job market while making them more worldly and well-rounded? Besides that.

Yet, before long, some of the local townspeople were raising a fuss and demanding that any books purchased by Marshall County for the library be in English only and—get this—that any books donated to the library by private individuals be accepted only if they were in English.

Setting conditions on the use of public dollars is one thing, but extending those conditions to gifts? How do you say "ungrateful"—in German, French or Spanish?

This controversy isn't just about library books. It's not even just about language. It's the latest offshoot of the immigration debate, in which people are likely to get worked up not just by the fact that people are coming here but by what language they speak when they arrive. It's also a direct manifestation of the fear that many people have that their American culture is slipping away and being replaced by something bilingual and multicultural.

That's nonsense. It recalls the Know-Nothings, the anti-immigrant and anti-Catholic political party that enjoyed prominence in the 19th century by stoking fears and preaching intolerance.

The fact is that immigrant groups of today are assimilating as quickly and as thoroughly as they always have. Besides, those who demand cultural conformity never stop to think about the possibility that our culture is a delectable stew with all these different spices. Remove the spices, and it's no longer American.

And what do other folks in Lewisburg, and around the country, think of the controversy involving the library books? Apparently, not much. As word of this bilingual backlash got around, scores of local residents began whipping out checkbooks and making donations to the library specifically earmarked for buying Spanish-language books. Many of the donations were in honor of Rivera.

Now that's—what's a good English word?—chutzpah.

BEHIND the STORY

Lessons Learned

By Ruben Navarrette Jr.

As an editorial writer and columnist, you sometimes choose a topic because it's in your back yard. But not always. Sometimes, the events unfold clear across the country—but they resonate where you live.

Even though I live in San Diego, Calif.—which is a couple thousand miles away from Lewisburg, Tenn., (pop. 10,413)—I took an interest when I read about how that town's library had been dragged into the ugly and unproductive debate over English-only. Or, put more honestly, ongoing efforts to scale back the prevalence of Spanish.

Not every opinion writer in the country would see it that way. Some wouldn't have the faintest idea what was really going on here. They would find more diplomatic ways of presenting the events to avoid casting aspersions on the good people of Lewisburg. They might argue this was about free speech or setting community standards.

Not a chance. As someone who often writes about the immigration issue and related cultural controversies, I knew immediately what this story was about. And language is only part of it. It was about what sociologists call "cultural displacement"—the sense that a particular group is losing power because it's losing population and prominence.

The uproar in Lewisburg started when Nellie Rivera, an employee at the Marshall County Memorial Library, came up with a simple, and it turns out, subversive, idea: To hold a bilingual story time where children hear tales read to them in Spanish.

As I began to read the story, already I could see storm clouds on the horizon.

Sure enough. A portion of the Lewisburg community immediately raised a fuss and demanded that any books purchased by Marshall County for the library be in English only. It gets even more comical. The critics also demanded that any books donated as gifts to the library by private sources be accepted only if they were in English.

I can't say I was surprised. As not only an opinion writer but also a Mexican-American, I figured out long ago what the language debate in this country is really about and has always been about—not whether government documents should be printed in languages other than English or whether there should be bilingual education or bilingual ballots. No, what gets Americans fired up is that, suddenly, they have to "press 1 for English" or put up with Spanish-language commercials on English-language television networks or pass by Spanish-language billboards hawking everything from beer to burgers to banking.

And, of course, these concerns only become more acute in the midst of a national debate over immigration.

So I knew I had more than enough material for an editorial. In the course of writing it, I realized that what the townspeople in Lewisburg were really afraid of wasn't children's books, or even Spanish. It was something larger and more powerful. It was change—specifically, the changes seeping into our culture, the sense that many people have that English and those who speak it will someday take a back seat to bilingualism and multiculturalism. The inside joke is that Lewisburg isn't exactly Tennessee's version of "Little Mexico." It isn't even "Little San Diego." The Hispanic population there is miniscule, but growing. And no one knows that better than the town residents who tried to pressure the library to ban Spanish-language books as a way of turning back the clock and forestalling change.

Luckily, I learned, not everyone in Lewisburg shares that sense of dread. As word of the bilingual book ban got around, another group of town residents lined up on the other side of the issue. They resorted to a most interesting form of civil disobedience. They didn't march or hold sit-ins. They whipped out checkbooks and made donations to the library, specifically earmarked for the purchase of Spanish-language books. And here's the best part: Many of the donations were in honor of Nellie Rivera, the assistant librarian who started all this.

I concluded that the whole ruckus was silly and terribly unnecessary. Imagine reading Cervantes in English. Why should library books serve as a proxy for the immigration issue, I asked? After all, immigration—illegal or otherwise—doesn't just happen to a community. If the people of Lewisburg, Tenn., are tired of Mexican immigrants hanging around, they should stop hiring them and go back to cutting their own lawns, raising their own kids and cleaning their own homes. But, unfortunately, that won't leave much time for reading books—in any language.

Ruben Navarrette Jr. is on The San Diego Union-Tribune*'s editorial board and writes a nationally syndicated column. A graduate of Harvard College and Harvard's John F. Kennedy School of Government, he is the author of* A Darker Shade of Crimson: Odyssey of a Harvard Chicano. *He has been a general assignment reporter and a metro columnist for* The Arizona Republic *and an editorial columnist for* The Dallas Morning News.

PART 6

Covering Diverse Communities: Immigration, Race and Ethnicity

Winner: Diversity Writing

David Gonzalez

Growing up in the South Bronx, David Gonzalez remembers walking by storefront churches and listening to their worship—a blend of shouting, singing and drumming.

"They were strange places, since as Catholics we kept our distance," he recalled. "Part of me always wanted to see what led people to worship in these seemingly random temples."

He got his chance. Over several months, Gonzalez, a reporter at *The New York Times,* spent many of his nights and weekends immersed in the life of a Pentecostal church, most of whose members were from the Dominican Republic.

At the Ark of Salvation for the New Millennium, with the help of Pastor Danilo Florian, Gonzalez and photojournalist Ángel Franco gained the trust of a group of people who typically have been ignored by the media.

In his three-part series, "House Afire," Gonzalez tells the intimate stories of individuals at the church. He also sheds light on a global trend that he had noticed years earlier while covering Latin America.

"Though Pentecostalism…is often associated with the stereotypical 'holy rollers' of the Bible Belt, it has made deep inroads in Asia and Africa," he wrote in the first story of the series. "In this hemisphere, its numbers and growth are strongest among Latinos in the United States and in Latin America, where it is eroding the traditional dominance of the Roman Catholic Church."

For his series, Gonzalez won the Freedom Forum/ASNE Award for Distinguished Writing on Diversity.

"While these churches are commonplace in many minority neighborhoods, I suspected that many of our readers dismissed them as not quite serious places...," he said in an e-mail interview. "My thesis was that these places are reflecting a global change that will have lasting implications for urban America."

Gonzalez's interest in immigrants, religion and community comes from his roots. His parents came to New York from Puerto Rico. His father worked as a handyman in an office building. His mother worked at a public school cafeteria.

"The whole time, I was in Catholic schools, which I am convinced helped make me who I am today," he said. "The priests never coddled us as poor little kids who could not accomplish anything because we were in 'bad' neighborhoods or came from migrant families.... They expected—and got—excellence from us....

"All of these experiences shaped me as a writer," he said. "My parents gave me the gift of a second language, and an appreciation of the sacrifices people make to ensure their children succeed. My neighborhoods gave me roots, and an appreciation for working-class, ethnic New York. Of course, Catholic schools gave me an understanding of the real role of religion in daily life."

Gonzalez earned a bachelor's degree in psychology from Yale University and a master's degree in journalism from Columbia University. Before entering journalism, he worked for several nonprofit agencies in New York's Latino and African-American communities, and he was project coordinator for a Bronx-based arts group supporting emerging Latino photographers.

He taught photography at a middle school in an "utterly devastated" neighborhood—and noticed "from my classroom, busloads of tourists descending...to photograph the rubble," he said. "That had an indelible impact on me: My kids took pictures of everyday life devoid of rubble or despair. The outsiders preferred rubble devoid of everyday life."

Gonzalez joined the *Times* in 1990, where he has worked as Bronx bureau chief, Metro religion reporter and Caribbean and Central America bureau chief. He has written the biweekly "Citywide" feature since returning to New York in 2004.

He is passionate about writing about overlooked communities. "Too often, reporters look at places in turmoil and decide they know the narrative already, rather than delving into the nuances and intricacies of these places," he said.

"I like to go to places off the radar and see what I can find there," he said. "It is not a matter of—ugh—giving voice to the voiceless. That is such an arrogant statement. They can speak just fine. The question is: Are reporters listening?"

—Thomas Huang, co-editor of *Best Newspaper Writing*

A Sliver of a Storefront, A Faith on the Rise

JAN. 14, 2007

By David Gonzalez

The storefront, it turned out, was more front than store: a drug den masquerading as an auto-sound business. And the sight of six hoodlums being paraded out in handcuffs was sadly familiar among the brick tenements of west Harlem.

But for Danilo Florian, who stumbled upon the police raid in November 2002, it was nothing less than a revelation.

"This could be a church," he muttered. "Lord, that is the place."

Mr. Florian, a factory worker by day and a pastor by night, was desperate to find a home for his small congregation, which faced eviction from its dank basement sanctuary. In a lucky confluence of real estate and religion, he tracked down the storefront's building manager, cajoled him into a five-year lease at a nice rent and even talked him into joining the church.

Now, on most nights when the neighborhood winds down to rest, the fluorescent lights inside the room flicker to life, and the spartan, whitewashed space rattles under a sonic barrage of prayers, yelps and tambourines. As a teenage band pounds out bouncy Latin rhythms, men in crisp business suits that belie their dreary day jobs triumphantly pump their fists. Women in flowing skirts shout, stomp and gyrate wildly. The air crackles.

The congregation, made up mostly of immigrants from the Dominican Republic, has grown to about 60, and they are bent on converting many more. For they are living Pentecostalism, the world's fastest-growing branch of Christianity, with a fervor and sense of destiny that resonate in the grand name they have chosen: the Pentecostal Church Ark of Salvation for the New Millennium.

Among them are reformed drug dealers and womanizers, cafeteria workers who earn barely enough to pay the bills and women whose sons or husbands are in prison. What they share inside this unlikely temple on Amsterdam Avenue near 133rd Street is a faith in God, in miracles and in one another. Religion here is not some sober, introspective journey or Sunday chore, but a raucous communal celebration that spills throughout the week.

The Pentecostal Church Ark of Salvation for the New Millennium, at 1463 Amsterdam Avenue, near 133rd Street in Harlem. The congregation, which has about 60 members from all over Upper Manhattan and the Bronx, moved into the storefront four years ago after the pastor seized an unusual opportunity: a police raid that had shut down a drug den there. (Photograph courtesy of Ángel Franco/*The New York Times*)

Storefront churches like this have become part of the streetscape in New York and around the globe in recent decades. Tiny and makeshift, they sprout up almost overnight, wedged in among the bodegas and take-out counters. Just in these few blocks of Harlem, there are at least seven others.

Yet "los aleluyas," as the Pentecostals are called by their neighbors, sometimes dismissively, remain mysterious to outsiders—their intensity scary to some, comical to others. They can dress plainly, shun the simplest pleasures and warn of imminent catastrophe for those who are not born again. Children preach like adults, and adults wail like children. Here one day, their churches may be gone the next.

This is the story of one such church: its people, its pastor, their fight to survive and the emotional, sometimes extreme religion that fires them night after night.

It is also the story of Hispanic faith in the 21st century, seen in tight focus. Though Pentecostalism, a strain of evangelical Christianity, was born a century ago in Kansas and is often associated with the stereotypi- cal "holy rollers" of the Bible Belt, it has made deep inroads in Asia and Africa. In this hemisphere, its numbers and growth are strongest among

Latinos in the United States and in Latin America, where it is eroding the traditional dominance of the Roman Catholic Church.

Experts believe there are roughly 400 million Pentecostals worldwide, and this year, the number in the city is expected to surpass 850,000—about one in every 10 New Yorkers, one-third of them Hispanic. Precise numbers, however, are hard to come by because there are scores of denominations and no central governing body.

Although several large Pentecostal organizations like the Assemblies of God have bureaucracies, colleges and legions of missionaries, about 80 percent of all Pentecostals belong to small or independent congregations. They have aggressively courted the poor, and imparted a work ethic that is nudging their members into the middle class and beyond.

Here, in cramped storefronts like Ark of Salvation, people whose lives are as marginal as their neighborhoods discover a joyful intimacy often lacking in big churches. They find help—with the rent, child care or finding a job. As immigrants, they find their own language and music, as well as the acceptance and recognition that often elude them on the outside.

They find the discipline and drive to make a hard life livable.

To spend a year with this congregation is to see a teenage single mother and party girl discover the strength to go to college, marry in the church and land a job. It is to see a former political radical and brawler pray over alcoholics in the park. It is to see the 50-year-old pastor roaming the city, driving the church's van to gather members for Bible class or trolling for converts outside an upper Broadway subway station—to keep the Ark afloat, and growing.

That growth could have profound implications. The Ark and other storefronts are already draining Catholic and mainline Protestant churches of the urban immigrants who have long filled their pews. Their striving members could refigure the political calculus of New York or even the nation, turning a historically liberal Hispanic population into a force for conservatism.

Then again, any of these churches could vanish, victim to a rent increase, a fickle landlord or a financial setback. They are trying to thrive in New York, of all places, where poor neighborhoods are gentrifying and housing prices are soaring, where strangers can be hostile and, on this block, dangerous. Their demanding creed, with its rigid moral code and almost daily churchgoing, can split families and alienate friends.

The souls who worship at 1463 Amsterdam Ave. have gotten by for six years on their faith, their wits and whatever breaks—even a drug bust—come their way. As they chase outsize dreams of a bigger building and a far bigger flock, they are guided only by Scripture and a quiet man who assures them that the meek really shall inherit the earth.

"We are not complacent," Pastor Florian explained. "We are more ambitious than Rockefeller."

The Spirit of a Crusade

Pass through the drab metal doorway, behind the tightly drawn blinds, and the storefront starts to look like a church. Heavy green drapes flank a worn pulpit. Packed tightly below are dozens of chipped wooden chairs cadged from a Midtown bar.

And much of the worship here looks like any Christian service, if several notches higher in volume and passion. One recent Sunday, quiet prayers in Spanish gave way to singing, Bible readings and testimony from the congregation, then a collection, a sermon and a final blessing from the pastor.

But during the blessing, the band's hypnotic beat quickened. Prayers became cries of "Glory to God!" The crowd pressed forward, and a thicket of hands strained to touch the pastor's outstretched arm. Some women began to quiver and shake, their ponytails whipping from side to side.

The room grew hot, and a strange sound came rumbling from up front.

"Omshalamamom!" shouted Lucrecia Perez, her hand thrust into the air, her eyes clenched shut. "Shambalashalama."

She was speaking in tongues, an ecstatic and indecipherable flood of syllables that often erupts during intense worship—brought on, the faithful believe, by the presence of the Holy Spirit, part of the divine Trinity. Though uncommon or unheard of in most other Christian churches—even dismissed as hokum by some ministers—it is celebrated here as the very mystery that gives the faith its name.

On the day known as the Pentecost, according to the New Testament, the Holy Spirit descended on the disciples after Christ's resurrection, allowing them to speak in languages unknown to them. Later, Christians occasionally broke into garbled prayer or prophecy, to the approval or alarm of church authorities, but it took nearly 2,000 years for the phenomenon to light a spark.

On New Year's Day in 1901, a woman in Topeka, Kan., began speaking in tongues during a Bible-school prayer vigil and did not let up for three days. Pentecostal groups formed, and in 1906, a preacher named William J. Seymour started a series of jubilant meetings in Los Angeles, called the Azusa Street Revival, that are now credited with propelling the faith throughout the world.

Like other evangelicals, Pentecostals assert the Bible's word-for-word authority, the need to accept Christ and the duty to share that faith with others before the end days, when the born-again will be whisked up to heaven in what they call the rapture.

But they differ in their intense conviction that the Holy Spirit descends on believers and blesses them with extraordinary gifts, especially the power to speak in tongues, that prepare them for those dark days, when everyone else will be left behind to suffer.

The message can be grim. The strictest Pentecostals—and Ark of Salvation has several "rajatablas," as they are called—can come across as humorless scolds, dressing severely and rejecting any distraction from God: television, popular music, even too much work.

If that were all Pentecostalism offered, the storefronts would be empty.

But the gloom is tempered by a noisy, collective joy born of the belief that the faithful will be blessed in this world and the next. That joy lends a sense of freedom, and often abandon, to services at the Ark, where people break into song or their own spur-of-the-moment prayers.

Music flows through everything—not solemn hymns, but brassy Caribbean tunes. In fact, some sound exactly like the songs that hard-core members condemn—the pop and salsa on Spanish-language radio—but with religious lyrics that are repeated so breathlessly that some singers faint.

That ability to harness the local music and culture is one reason for Pentecostalism's swift spread around the world.

"It takes in everything and absorbs it," said the Rev. Dale T. Irvin, president of the New York Theological Seminary. "You get as a result this extraordinary emergence of churches."

In New York, the ranks of Pentecostals have grown 45 percent since 1995, said Tony Carnes, president of the International Research Institute on Values Changes in New York City, an independent group financed largely by foundations that has been surveying churches since 1989.

Pentecostals became the city's largest group of born-again Christians in the mid-1990s, and within a few years, a new storefront church was opening every three weeks in the South Bronx, he said. The 9/11 attacks set off a fresh growth spurt.

Another factor in that growth worldwide is the way the faith reaches out to people on society's edges and gives them vital roles. Unlike Catholics and some evangelical Christians, Pentecostals let women preach and lead; Mr. Florian's co-pastor is his wife, Mirian. The humblest member can take the pulpit to share testimony, a prayer or a poem. Recently,

Pastor Danilo Florian stood before the congregation as a visiting pastor took to the pulpit. (Photograph courtesy of Ángel Franco/*The New York Times*)

an 8-year-old girl preached excitedly to a rapt congregation, then laid her hands in blessing on a new convert.

Mr. Florian himself has few credentials other than three years of night-school Bible classes and a wrenching sense of duty. A lapsed Catholic from the Dominican Republic, he joined a small Pentecostal church 16 years ago after his 7-year-old daughter survived a grave bout with encephalitis. Six years ago he and eight others left that church and founded the Ark in the basement of a building riddled with rats.

The congregation, which draws members from all over Upper Manhattan and the Bronx, moved to its street-level space four years ago thanks to the drug raid, and a willingness to seize on opportunities. That pragmatism is also reflected in its religious practices, which are more moderate than in many other storefront churches.

While the Ark forbids smoking, drinking and dancing and discourages flashy clothes and jewelry, it issues few other edicts. While its members believe that Satan—the enemy, they call him—is as real as God, they conduct no exorcisms, as in some churches.

While some members speak in tongues, most do not, including Pastor Florian, a low-key man who explained the experience in surprisingly down-to-earth terms. "It is like a fax talking to another fax," he said. "Tongues are not a human language. It is your spirit speaking with God."

And while nearly everyone in the congregation works and puts something into the brass bowls that are passed around at every service, Mr. Florian makes none of the urgent appeals for money—or promises of windfalls or miracles—that drive some churches. The pastor, who still works his factory job decorating expensive handbags, takes no salary from the church.

Not that the Ark celebrates poverty. Members are told that hard work and frugal living will be rewarded, perhaps not lavishly, but adequately. The dress code for services is decidedly white collar: suits for the men, long skirts for the women. Children are urged to excel in school, and the pastor boasts of the several college graduates in the church—refuting what he says is the notion that born-again Christians are simple-minded.

"When you are a professional, people have no idea how you can be a believer," he said. "The Gospel is not just for the poor. God is not a God of the ignorant."

The poor do get help, from the church's meager savings account or from other members; it is not unusual to see a small wad of cash passed from hand to hand after services. But unlike many larger churches, the Ark has neither the mission nor the money to dispense charity to the needy outside—except as a means to convert them.

And its members, proud and stoic, are reluctant to accept handouts. When Ms. Perez, the woman who spoke in tongues, had her hours as a home health aide cut back, she and her daughter Genesis moved into a homeless shelter for eight months. For weeks before their eviction, she asked the congregation for prayers, but barely hinted at her plight.

"I can't ask them for money," said Ms. Perez, 46. "They don't have it to lend. They need what they have for a new church."

Last April, Pedro Garces, the building manager and a church member, found her an affordable studio. Whatever happens, members are constantly reminded, the Ark will bear them up.

"We will never be alone," Pastor Florian said one night during Bible study. "That is God's promise."

Hotheads and Warm Hearts

The first to arrive, as usual, was Ramón Romero. On a Thursday evening in July that was still hot and sticky at 6:30, he walked slowly from his apartment to the church, past reminders of the life he had left behind. Two laborers lounged on a grimy stoop, sipping beer, as men outside a bodega argued politics, and raunchy reggaeton music thumped from passing cars.

Mr. Romero, a handsome man of 73 and a founding member of the Ark, rolled up the church's metal gate and slipped into the silence inside. The others would soon arrive—with their own reasons for coming and their own styles of worship—but this was his time and his way. He knelt and clasped the slatted back of a wooden chair, his lips emitting no more than a low rasp.

That rasp, which can rise to a growl, is one hint that this stern, stony-faced man was once a scrapper. A strict father, he let his wife coddle the children, as he put it, while he wielded the strap. He was tough outside the home, too, active in leftist politics and unions in the Dominican Republic before he moved here in the mid-1960s.

"I was someone who did everything except stain my hands with blood," Mr. Romero said. "I was a hothead."

He paid for it. His efforts fighting the dictatorship of Rafael Trujillo landed him in jail for seven months, he said. While driving a Pepsi-Cola route in the Dominican Republic, he helped workers unionize and strike for fair pay, but the bottling company lured everyone back to work, he said, then fired him—with the support of the same workers he had organized.

Years later, feeling betrayed by politics and worried about his wife's depression, he let a nurse bring her pastor to their home one night to pray. Mr. Romero converted quickly, with the same intensity he had brought to politics.

His wife, Esperanza, took longer to let go of her Roman Catholicism, particularly the room she had filled with statues of saints—worthless idols, according to Pentecostals, who believe that people should pray directly to God. Mr. Romero persuaded his wife that the statues had to go.

"I went in that room with a hammer, and I broke every saint that was there," he recalled. "I smashed a table, a fountain full of water, an expensive one. I broke it all. I tied it up in a bag and tossed it in the farthest dump."

He paused at the memory. "And nothing happened to me."

His wife died in 1999, but her name is still on the downstairs buzzer. In their sparely furnished apartment, Mr. Romero passes the time reading the Bible and, with a tinge of guilt, watching sports. His five children— some live nearby, and one is in the congregation—hardly talk to him. He wonders if he may have been a bit too strict.

But no matter. This night, as he settled into his regular seat near the front, he had achieved a kind of peace.

By then he had been joined by another early bird, Ramona Campaña, who enjoys the church's sociability as much as its spirituality. As others entered, Ms. Campaña, 73, looked up from her Bible, smiled and extended a hand. An elegant woman, she wore a long skirt and matching jacket whose only embellishment was a golden brooch bearing a cross and a lamb, the church's logo.

When she arrived in New York from the Dominican Republic 35 years ago, she worked in a hotel laundry, ironing until her eyes stung from the steam. Her lunch included a bottle of Heineken stashed in her purse. She played the numbers. And, she said, she practiced the sort of once-a-week Catholicism that was more habit than conviction.

"You can sit next to me, and when the service is over you don't even know my name," she said. "You don't ask, 'How are you?' It's foom, and you're out."

That ended one day in the Bronx that was so jarring she still recalls the date: June 12, 1993. Ms. Campaña and her daughter had gone to the wake of a relative who had converted to Pentecostalism on his deathbed. Most Christian wakes focus on the deceased, but the faithful at this service turned away from the open coffin and crusaded for new members, offering a stark choice: Accept Christ or spend eternity in hell.

Moved by the congregation's passion—"I saw unity in them," she said— she joined a Pentecostal group. After moving to 141st Street years later, widowed and alone, she heard about a new church in a nearby basement and went out asking, "Where are the aleluyas?" until she found the Ark.

"It's good," she said, "to be in a place where they see you not by how you look, but by what's in your heart."

As this evening's service started, Ms. Campaña lost herself in song, smacking a battered tambourine and swaying in rhythm. Like several other women, she was so taken with the prayers and music that she doubled over, feet stomping and arms flailing, until her neighbors eased her back up.

But others' worship was as varied as their lives. Young mothers sang cheerily alongside their fidgeting children. Grandmothers prayed aloud nonstop, as if in a running conversation with the Almighty. Two teenage boys exchanged a laugh. Near the front, Roy Guzman, a 25-year-old engineer who works for an international consulting company, sat motionless, immersed in his Bible.

"I don't just want to *feel* this," he said later, a little sheepishly. "That could be a flaw, but I like to have an intellectual knowledge of what I'm doing."

And then there was his cousin Chislen Peña, a normally soft-spoken young woman who fairly explodes when her time comes to preach.

Dressed austerely—long black skirt, pulled-back hair, no earrings or makeup—she paces the narrow stage with nervous energy, shouting, slapping her Bible and tossing her head back. She will pause, freeze the congregation in her gaze, then break into a grin and yell, "Aleluya!"

She is joyful—fiercely, severely joyful—even if her life has been anything but.

Ms. Peña, 28, had her first child when she was 14, with a man who ended up in prison for murder. She had a daughter with another man who was deported for dealing drugs. She married for the first time soon afterward, only to divorce when her husband told her he had HIV. Her brother is in jail for murder.

"I once tried to kill myself," she said. "I heard little voices telling me to do it."

She found her faith through an uncle, and like other Pentecostals, she preaches about her life to show that no one is beyond help. In the pulpit at one service, her voice hoarse and her forehead sweaty, she told of waiting for the results of her HIV tests.

"I said forgive me—He forgave me," she said, to rising applause. "Praise the Lord! And the tests kept coming back negative! And negative! And negative!"

After the service, people lingered for conversation and food, hugging and thanking her. They all knew she had returned to school, earned a college diploma and found a job as a counselor in a drug treatment center.

Remarried in 2004 to a fellow Pentecostal, she was expecting her third child, a boy they planned to name after an Old Testament prophet who warned of impending punishment.

Just saying the name made her smile.

"Jeremiah," she said.

Saving 'el Mundo'

The end is near. This is actually good news at Ark of Salvation: At the start of the earth's final days, they believe, a trumpet blast will herald the rapture. But for those left behind, the Book of Revelation and sermons at the church lay out a litany of horrors that will follow: plagues, poisoned rivers, smoke that will pour from the earth and blot out the skies.

The Ark's ultimate mission, then, is to save the nonbelievers—not just for their sake, but for the church's. To keep going, Pastor Florian says, the Ark must grow.

So as much as its members mistrust and revile the secular world—"el mundo," as they call it—they must leave the church's embrace to spread the word to anyone, anywhere, anytime.

"God sometimes sends you to places you do not want to go to—like you have to go somewhere where you can be robbed," the pastor reminded them one night with a smile, shrieking in mock terror: "Oh, no! Not 134th Street!"

Congregants from other churches joined in a service. (Photograph courtesy of Ángel Franco/*The New York Times*)

They exhort relatives and friends, schoolmates and co-workers, with promises of hope or warnings of damnation. They hold weekly services in people's apartments and invite neighbors. In good weather, they haul out the drums and amplifiers and preach on the sidewalk. They walk up to strangers in parks and supermarkets.

Eneida Vasquez was window-shopping at a 99-cent store one day when she spotted Kenia Ledesma, a sad-eyed woman with three young daughters and a rocky marriage. She walked up to the stranger, told her she was not alone and hugged her. Ms. Ledesma joined the church that week.

But the congregation leaves little to chance. One July afternoon, three teenagers sat in the church, neatly sorting piles of religious tracts. One girl stamped the Ark's address onto the leaflets, which are printed in Spanish with color photos and graphics.

"We order them from the Dominican Republic, 10 for a penny," Pastor Florian explained. "They are bigger and different from the ones you usually see around here. That way, when someone gets it they can't say, 'Oh, I saw this already.'"

Before the teenagers headed out in small groups, he gave them precise instructions: Approach the person with a smile. Hold out the tract with the cover facing up. Leave with a "God bless you."

The payoff, however, was slim. Everyone could see the aleluyas coming, by their dress, their smiles, their persistence. Some neighbors were polite, but from others they got snubs, catcalls or worse.

Outside El Mundo, a store on Broadway that sells $100 suits and $10 dresses, a drunken man glared at Frankie Lora and Stephanie Dionisio, both 16. He cocked his head and leered at Stephanie.

"You good?" he taunted. "You good?"

She fumbled for a tract, the one that said drunkards will never enter heaven. As he staggered off, cursing, Stephanie turned to Frankie. "Tell him Jesus loves him," she pleaded. "Tell him!"

On days like this, members console themselves with the knowledge that they did their duty. Maybe, they speculate, the person they approached in the park joined another storefront—for there is little sense of competition among the neighborhood's many Pentecostal congregations, which sponsor events together and visit one another.

That camaraderie, however, does not extend to the institution that once loomed large in so many members' lives: the Catholic Church. Pentecostals believe that Catholics and many Protestants will not be joining them in the rapture. Only born-again Christians, they say, will be saved.

Pastor Florian does not preach much about other faiths, and in fact his three children have attended Catholic schools on scholarships. But his feelings are clear. The day after Pope John Paul II died in April 2005, the pastor began his sermon with a pointed remark.

"We are not sad," he said. "Our leader is not dead. Our leader is Jesus Christ. And he is alive!"

Around the corner is the Church of the Annunciation, a thriving Catholic parish where Mexicans and Dominicans make up most of the roughly 1,100 worshipers who fill its sanctuary on Sundays.

Its pastor, the Rev. Jose Maria Clavero, knows that the Catholic Church has lost many Latinos to Pentecostalism, but he sees those converts as nominal Catholics who were never part of any parish. "If they are taking in people who were not anywhere, blessed be God," he said. "At least they are in church."

He and other priests, remembering when large parishes were the vibrant heart of New York immigrant life, give the small storefronts credit for building intimate, supportive communities in some of the city's most forlorn neighborhoods. And Annunciation, like many Catholic and mainline Protestant churches around the world, has even embraced Pentecostalism's ardent worship style, as part of the charismatic renewal movement that began in the 1960s.

A small charismatic group meets for prayer every Monday, and Father Clavero makes a point of attending. At first it was to keep the group in check; he was alarmed by what he saw as an overemphasis on healing and miracles—the same sort of zeal that makes Pastor Florian nervous.

But the group has matured, the priest said, and its exuberant songs echo through the church each Sunday.

"It lifts you up," he said. "You'd have to be a stone not to feel it. They give life."

The Politics of Purity

The sidewalks along St. Nicholas Avenue were thick with weekend shoppers and booming with music. Slowly, a faint background rumbling grew into a roar as 200 people strode into the middle of the street, part of the annual "Great March for Christ" in Washington Heights.

"A Christ who is against adultery!" hollered a Pentecostal preacher leading the procession. "A Christ who is against homosexuality! That is the Jesus we represent."

The marchers—including a delegation from Ark of Salvation—prayed, sang and urged repentance. Some scurried to hand out tracts and invitations to a religious rally.

But while they wooed the public, one figure was courting them. Adriano Espaillat, a Democratic assemblyman then running for Manhattan borough president, stood among them, casting for votes, not souls.

"God bless you," Mr. Espaillat said with a quick handshake to each marcher. "God bless you."

Pastor Florian turned his back on him.

"He is a politician," he said curtly. "I cannot even look at him."

The prevailing image of evangelical Christians in America is one of militant churches and politically ambitious leaders, like the Rev. Jerry Falwell and Pat Robertson, who have built a national base of like-minded Christians determined to shape public policy, especially on sexual issues.

But while Pentecostals strongly oppose abortion and gay marriage, they have a long history of shunning political involvement. Though some notable Pentecostals have run for office—John Ashcroft on the right and the Rev. Al Sharpton on the left—most politicians are seen as agents of the secular world.

"I think Pentecostals realize ultimately their trust is in God and not in politics," said Loida Martell-Otero, a theology professor at Palmer Theological Seminary in Pennsylvania. "The people in power have traditionally rendered them powerless."

That has not stopped political leaders from trying to convert them, especially in cities like New York, where Latino Pentecostals are seen as a large and growing bloc that could turn to either party. Republicans invoke causes like banning abortion and gay marriage, while Democrats promote economic programs for the poor who fill so many storefront churches.

Pentecostals do vote, and are eager for more involvement, according to a study released in October by the Pew Forum on Religion and Public Life, which found that 79 percent of Pentecostals wanted religious groups to speak out on political issues.

In New York, the poverty and independence of many Pentecostal churches have kept them from coalescing, said Mr. Carnes, whose International Research Institute on Values Changes has studied their growth. But Pentecostals are teaching a tireless work ethic, he said, that will vault them—especially their children—into more professional and managerial jobs in coming years, and make them a major economic and social force.

The next step, Mr. Carnes said, could be leveraging that force into political clout. "The key for these pastors will be to connect up with disaffected leaders in the centers of power—some councilman or businessman looking for something different," he said. "You could have a huge change in the city."

Now, though, many pastors are torn.

Mr. Florian would love to have a soup kitchen or an after-school center for teenagers, and the congregation turned to its city councilman, a Democrat, for help in finding a bigger building to house them. But they dropped the effort after the councilman invited them to help out at a neighborhood health fair, and the pastor learned they would not be allowed to preach there.

"I only want to do things for the Lord," Mr. Florian said. "I do not like to ask any man for favors."

He and other storefront pastors would seem natural allies for the Republican Party, which has courted Latino Pentecostals, political analysts say, with government grants for churches that run "faith-based" social services. But the Ark, like most small churches, has neither the space nor the staff for such programs.

Mr. Florian says he supports President Bush "for his principles," and has urged his congregation to vote for candidates who share their moral values. But he cannot vote; though he is a legal resident and says he intends to become a citizen as his wife did, he has not assembled the paperwork.

And unlike many Christian ministers, he has little to say about most public issues: Iraq, terrorism, even immigration. He and others at the Ark are busy enough with the troubles they see in their own streets and homes: crime, drugs, splintered families.

In fact, before abortion and gay rights dominated political discourse, Latino Pentecostals in New York invariably supported liberal candidates who reached out, as they did, to the poor and forgotten.

Today, the Rev. Ruben Diaz, one of the first Pentecostals to venture into New York politics, pursues evangelicals with a mix of social-spending liberalism and family-values conservatism. A Democratic state senator from the Bronx, Mr. Diaz warns that his party's support for gay marriage and abortion rights could alienate his religious constituents.

"The evangelical churches will be the Achilles' heel of the Democratic Party," he said, "unless it opens the door to a segment of the population who does not think exactly like them."

There is no doubt where the Ark stands. Yet even on the moral issues that matter most to the congregation, Pastor Florian has little faith that a political party or sprawling bureaucracy can get the job done. He is even wary of close ties to other religious groups with their own agendas.

So for now, at least, the Ark will go its own way—the slow way—as it tries to save the world and realize its Rockefeller ambitions. Praying and singing. Supporting one another. Approaching strangers on the street. Changing minds and hearts, one by one.

After one fruitless afternoon handing out tracts, a girl in the congregation ran up to tell Pastor Florian that a woman had promised to visit the church. His face lit up.

"Do you know what it is to save a soul?" he asked. "Just one soul? Priceless."

Building a Church, and Paying Off a Sacred Debt

JAN. 15, 2007

By David Gonzalez

As his 7-year-old daughter lay near death, Danilo Florian raged. The doctors could do no more. His prayers—a desperate turn to the religion he had abandoned long ago to pursue a successful jewelry business—seemed equally futile.

He had come to New York years earlier from the Dominican Republic with nothing but the desire to prosper as a family man and businessman. Now, as it all fell apart in a Manhattan hospital, he sought a few moments of silence in a dimly lighted room off the intensive care ward.

Then it happened. Out of nowhere, he says, came a voice.

"Do business with me," it demanded.

Sixteen years later, the girl is a young woman, and Mr. Florian is keeping his end of the bargain. The jewelry business is long gone. He abandoned it to heed the call to serve God, plunging into Pentecostalism and founding Ark of Salvation, a shoebox of a storefront church in west Harlem that explodes most nights with prayer and song.

Today, the word "pastor" hardly describes this dynamo who propels a flock of 60—most of them Dominican immigrants of modest means—round the clock and through the week. Teacher, chief cheerleader and social director, he is even the chauffeur who ferries them to services all over town in a secondhand airport van, usually after eight hours at a factory job making luxury handbags.

To the adults, he is the confidant who counsels them through crises. To the teenagers, he is the surrogate father who praises them and takes them on outings. To the needy, he is the benefactor who slips them a little cash. To all, he is the leader who promises a glorious future in a grand new church, even though they have saved a small fraction of the fortune it would cost.

"Pelea, pelea, pelea," he murmured one night as he made his rounds in the church van, mouthing the words to a hymn. Fight, fight, fight.

The battle is not just for this storefront. In thousands of tiny, sometimes fly-by-night churches around the globe, men like Pastor Florian get

Pastor Danilo Florian with his flock after Sunday service at Ark of Salvation, a storefront church in Harlem. His days are long, he says, but rewarding. (Photograph courtesy of Ángel Franco/*The New York Times*)

things started and keep them going against tremendous odds. Their success or failure may decide whether Pentecostalism continues growing faster than any other Christian group.

They work largely on their own, without the hierarchies or resources that sustain the clergy of other faiths. Many are self-taught and self-supporting. Mr. Florian, 50, who takes no salary from his church, has only a few years of night-school Bible classes, no pastoral training and no ambition to join a larger denomination, as some storefront pastors do.

His ministry reflects the startling intimacy that has been Pentecostalism's essence since it began a century ago: What matters the most—even for a leader of souls—is a transforming personal encounter with God.

Like many storefront ministers, Pastor Florian lives modestly in the same kind of rough-edged neighborhood as his members. But unlike his peers who hurl brimstone or promise miracles, he is cautious and quiet. A serene figure even when worship is frenzied, he can silence the crowd with a raised hand.

He is also human. Disorganized and absent-minded, he loses cell phones, gets lost driving, forgets appointments and would miss even more

if his wife and co-pastor, Mirian, did not keep careful watch. At the end of his hectic days, exhaustion tugs on his sturdy frame.

And though he is too private to discuss it much, he struggles with disappointment. Although he believes that the deal he struck with God saved his daughter, his two younger children have drifted away from the faith.

For a man who sees himself in so many ways as a father, that is painful. For a storefront pastor, it is also useful, allowing the people who walk through the church doors on Amsterdam Avenue to see themselves in him.

"It unites us, because he is human," said Lucrecia Perez, who recently spent eight months in a homeless shelter. "He has to work like us. He has gone through need."

A Business Proposition

Father figures always let him down.

His father was a businessman, making a nice living running cockfights, a taxi service and a bodega in the Dominican towns where Mr. Florian grew up, the oldest of five children. But by his teenage years, he says, his father had squandered it all on bad bets, strong drink and frequent affairs.

The boy thought he had found someone to look up to in Padre Camilo, the pastor of the Roman Catholic church where he was an altar boy. But one day the rumors flew that the priest had gotten drunk in a bar and begun shooting his pistol.

"I didn't believe it because I admired him and loved him," Mr. Florian said. "Whether it was true or not, I still don't know. But it got into my mind."

His faith vanished as the family's tumbling fortunes forced them to a poor neighborhood in Santo Domingo, the sprawling capital, where his mother ran a candy store and a fruit stand. Their comedown was humbling: He had to sell ice cream to his high school classmates at recess.

"They would look at you like you were really poor," he said. "Like we were less."

Like any adolescent adrift, he searched for something or someone to rely on. He found both when a friend invited him to a crusade led by Yiye Avila, a fiery traveling preacher from Puerto Rico who is now one of the most popular Pentecostal evangelists in the Americas. He converted that night.

But his new faith was tenuous. After juggling two jobs to help pay for college, he followed his family to New York in 1979 and found a job at a jewelry factory that consumed his time. He even met Mirian, a Roman Catholic, through a factory friend. They married in 1982 and had a daughter, Dianne, the next year.

His labors began to pay off. After he started a lucrative business making buttons and medals at home, a client in Mexico hired him to set up a factory there, and in 1990 proposed a huge deal: commemorative jewelry that churches would sell for Pope John Paul II's visit that year to Mexico City.

Then Dianne fell ill with encephalitis, an inflammation of the brain, ending up in the intensive care ward at St. Luke's Hospital. For 10 days, her body was racked with convulsions.

One afternoon after Christmas, Mr. Florian said, doctors told him they could do nothing for the little girl who lay comatose, tethered to tubes and surrounded by religious statues his wife's family had brought. That evening, he sought quiet in a room off the ward.

"There's no hope," he recalled thinking. "She's only 7. Who could help? I did everything possible."

Then, as he tells it, came the voice.

"Work with me," he heard.

He looked around. He was alone, and frightened.

"Do business with me," the voice commanded. "Reconcile with me."

He thought of the jewelry business that had consumed him, and of the religious medals that would make him even more money. Ambition and greed had brought him to this, and he felt shame.

He tried pushing the matter out of his mind. But the voice returned, he said, warning that if he did not agree in 15 minutes, the girl would die.

"It was a strong voice," he said. "Like a horn. I thought I was going crazy. I cried, I cried and I cried. And in my mind, I left everything."

Tranquility washed over him, though it was fleeting as he returned to his daughter's bedside. A nurse scrambled from the room, and a stench wafted through the air. He thought Dianne had died.

"She was sitting up in the bed," he said. "She had vomited something black. But she sat up."

The child recovered and, sticking to the bargain, the Florians searched for a congregation. Mirian felt unwelcome at the local Catholic church, and they faded into anonymity at a busy Pentecostal congregation. Then they found Exodo, a small Pentecostal group near their apartment on Amsterdam Avenue.

Mr. Florian insists he had no intention of becoming a preacher. But his playfulness and patience with young people led to his being named co-pastor. In 2000, upset with how Exodo was being run, he and eight others went looking for a place to pray until they could join another congregation.

One of them, Ramón Romero, discovered a basement room on 134th Street that was crawling with rats inside and drug dealers outside. He and Mr. Florian drove out the rats with a machine that blasted high-pitched noise. The landlady was so relieved to see Christians instead of crack addicts that she provided the space free.

On the street one day, someone called Mr. Florian "Pastor." He laughed it off, but Mr. Romero did not. "You will be our pastor," he declared. "We do not need to find another church."

On the cusp of 2001, they chose a big name for their little sanctuary, befitting the year and their quest: the Pentecostal Church Ark of Salvation for the New Millennium. For Danilo Florian, the work had just begun.

A Home Divided

Sunday is no day of rest for Pastor Florian. On this particular one, he was deep into his sermon, preaching about hope and home life. "If anyone is the enemy of the family, it is Satan," he said. "Every family has to struggle against the beast in the home."

A reminder of those trials was slumped in the back row. His teenage son, Danilito, glumly played with his cell phone and held hands with his girlfriend, an older girl who had a baby by a previous boyfriend.

"How glorious it is when a father can say, 'There is my child,'" the pastor continued. "How joyful a child would feel to hear you say, 'I am proud of you.'"

Danilito, chatting with his girlfriend, ignored him.

Family is a pillar of any church's life, and even more so at Ark of Salvation. The day the Florians converted, their three children joined them at the altar, and went on to sing or play music at services.

But at the Catholic schools they have attended, they have been exposed to different beliefs. As teenagers, they have pulled away from their parents and sometimes their faith.

Dianne, now 23 and fully recovered from her illness, remains the stalwart. Until her student teaching in New Jersey made increasing demands on her time in recent months, she was a fixture at services, singing with a throaty growl. On New Year's Eve, she was married at the storefront, with her father officiating.

She is not shy. During Bible study at church, she has sparred with her father over women's role in marriage. One summer, she drew her parents' ire for spending too much time at a catering job. She treasures her independent streak, which she credits to the Jesuits who taught her in grade school and at St. Peter's College in Jersey City.

But her assertiveness is tempered by a feeling that because she is the pastor's daughter, the congregation watches her every move. "You try to live your life in the right way," she said, "so people don't say things to other people."

And her life, after all, is intertwined with her father's conversion. She says a big reason she stays in the fold is the debt she owes—and the gratitude she feels—for her recovery.

Her father puts it far more bluntly. "The Lord gave her her life back," he said. "If she leaves, she could die."

He and his wife were less strict with Dianne's 22-year-old sister, Danitza, now a senior at St. Peter's. Last summer she moved in with her boyfriend. Her father now wishes he had kept her at home.

Until recently, Danitza attended church sporadically. One Sunday, she showed up in a tight T-shirt with the word "sexy" emblazoned across the chest. But she respectfully joined the line of supplicants waiting for a final blessing.

The pastor handing out religious tracts on the street. (Photograph courtesy of Ángel Franco/*The New York Times*)

As her mother anointed the girl's forehead with oil, Pastor Florian stood to the side and sobbed.

Tearful moments like that are the few public hints that all is not well with his family. One Saturday, as he plopped down on the parlor sofa for an interview at their house in Bedford Park in the Bronx, the quiet was broken by giggles behind the locked door of his son's room.

Danilito, who at 18 looks like a younger version of his father, was inside with his girlfriend, Silka. Although the congregation agreed that Danilito was a gifted drummer and singer, his father had expelled him from the church band.

"Someone who is sinning cannot touch the instruments that are used to adore the Lord," Pastor Florian said, moments after the boy cracked open the door, grabbed his sneakers and dashed off with Silka.

Danilito has since taken up with a new girl, but he has also flirted with real danger. Last summer, he hung out with friends outside a nearby building where neighbors suspected that drugs were being sold.

"It fills me with such shame," his father said. "The image everybody here has of my family is of my daughters going to college with God's help. Now they see him with those boys. It's like he threw everything to the gutter."

The pastor pleaded with him to stay away, but he refused—until September, when one friend was shot dead.

Out of respect, the congregation says nothing about the family's troubles. And though Pastor Florian wishes he could confide in someone besides his wife, he keeps his feelings to himself.

"I can't talk to anyone because there would be gossip," he said, "and that destroys a church."

The children of many pastors, he says, fall away from religion. "Maybe because you do not give them as much time as you should, since you have to spend time with the other children," he speculated. "They could become jealous."

He and his wife take comfort in believing they have done all they could for their children. "They have a foundation," he said. "God will call them like he called me."

'I Don't Sleep Anymore'

The streets of Bedford Park are mercifully quiet at 6 a.m. when Pastor Florian gets up, pulls on a polo shirt, khakis and sneakers and walks to the D train for the 45-minute commute to the garment district.

He has worked in factories since arriving in New York, spending the last dozen years at Judith Leiber, where he polishes stones and precious metals for intricately jeweled handbags that fetch thousands of dollars. The bags may be delicate, but the work is exacting. When he gets home around 5 p.m., he trudges up the creaking stairs.

Then his real job begins.

He rests for a few moments, grabs a snack and dons a natty suit, tie and shined shoes. His wife by his side, he climbs into the church van to round up the congregation for that night's services, driving all over the Bronx and Upper Manhattan. Whatever they do, he is with them, even if he is not preaching. He must set an example.

"You can't say, 'I go to church once a week' and leave it closed the rest of the week," he explained. "When I have a church, it is open seven days a week."

Ark of Salvation almost meets his ideal: There are no services on Monday. Bible class is on Thursday, youth services on Friday and adult services on Wednesday. Tuesdays and Saturdays, a small delegation conducts a service in someone's apartment or visits another church, as far away as Queens or Brooklyn. Sunday is the week's highlight, as the Florians preside over three hours of song, testimony and preaching.

Afterward, the couple linger to counsel people. They help clean and repair the storefront. Intent on keeping the teenagers off the streets during the summer, Pastor Florian leads day trips to the Delaware Water Gap in Pennsylvania or quick jaunts to Yonkers for hot dogs and video games.

The fact is, from the moment he wakes to when he dozes off 20 hours later after reading Scripture or researching sermons, he hardly pauses.

"I've always worked," he said, shrugging. "That's why I don't sleep anymore."

Despite the unending demands, he is calm and cheerful, almost unnaturally so. Annoyance flashes across his eyes when he looks down from the pulpit at a paltry turnout. But if more is bothering him, he seldom lets on. "A pastor always has to have a happy face and be in his glory," he said.

Yet not too happy or too glorious. While other Pentecostal ministers shake or shout, Pastor Florian prefers to pray quietly. He is careful how he acts in church, especially after visiting revivals where preachers made wild claims.

"If someone says they are going to heal the sick, leave," he warned his congregation. "For a miracle to happen, people need faith. Their faith heals them. Man does not do miracles."

And because he knows that some preachers care more about lining pockets than saving souls, his appeals for money are few and understated. Inside his home, he pauses to make something clear: "Everything I have, I had before becoming a pastor."

The Florians' boxy house is tucked into a neighborhood whose noisy fringes are plagued by drugs and violence. The pastor has been stopped by the police and questioned, but he says those slights bring him closer to the lives of his congregation.

He dotes on the house, painting or ripping up carpets. Proud of his self-taught craftsmanship, he showed off a new door he had installed.

"Give a Dominican a piece of thread, and he'll make you an airplane," he said with a laugh. "Ever since I came to New York, I was told that if they ever ask you at a job if you have experience, say yes."

His wife and her mother run a day care center in a warren of colorful rooms on the second floor. She is a whiz at multitasking, feeding one child while comforting another and answering her phone.

Small wonder that the pastor relies on her at home and in church, where she is known as Pastora. For years she drove a school bus, and still navigates the city better than he. In those days, she imagined they would be living in Miami by now, easing into a slower and more affordable life.

"I knew if he became pastor, that would be it for Miami," she said. "It's not easy."

Beyond the Storefront

The church van smelled of quickly eaten fried-chicken dinners as Pastor Florian cruised up Amsterdam Avenue with a dozen people crammed inside. As always on a Saturday night, they were visiting another church. As always, something was on his mind besides the traffic and the sermon he was about to give.

Real estate.

"There was a place on 152nd Street for $580,000," he told his wife. "There is another place available on 156th Street. The owner used to have a cafe downstairs and prostitutes upstairs."

As the van passed building after building, he rattled off the history of each one that fit the bill for his ideal church. Mirian's eyes widened when she saw a meticulously restored brick structure on 126th Street. "That would be good for a church," she said. "The first floor!"

He said nothing, but smiled faintly.

This is how he found the Ark's current home: traveling the streets, keeping his eyes open. But today that rented storefront hardly meets the congregation's needs.

Last spring, they were homeless for two weeks after an upstairs neighbor left the bathtub running and the ceiling collapsed. The room is cramped, with no space for all the community services Pastor Florian feels he needs to attract new members and keep the church growing: a soup kitchen, youth programs, immigration counseling and activities for the elderly.

So even as he tackles his overstuffed schedule, he always has one unfinished job, and it is his biggest ever: finding a permanent home where his congregation—not some landlord—can control its future. A place where it can graduate from storefront to institution.

That means money, and lots more than the church has in its anemic savings account. Collections bring in about $2,500 a month, half of which covers the rent. On average, $1,000 goes for insurance, utilities, gasoline and help for people in a pinch. If they are lucky, maybe a few hundred dollars remains.

At that rate, it will take decades to raise the $200,000 down payment Pastor Florian estimates they need to buy a new place. So far they have only $13,000, from special collections and food sales.

Time may be running short. The neighborhood is gentrifying, pushing real estate prices higher. One nearby storefront congregation has already been forced to move in with another.

Even the pastor's own finances are in peril. His employer has told him he will be let go next month, joining dozens of workers laid off since last summer.

Yet that setback and the church's meager finances do not seem to faze Pastor Florian, who reassures his congregation that God will provide. Somehow, faith will trump finances.

"We are not guided by logic," he told them one Sunday. "Having a temple in New York is difficult. We may not have the resources, but we have faith we will get one."

And as strange as it may sound, he harbors a small hope that the storefront will be their last earthly home.

Just as God's voice came to him in the darkness 16 years ago, he lives each day awaiting a second call: the trumpet blast announcing the rapture, the day when most Pentecostals believe they will be summoned to heaven—rising out of their busy factories, church vans and frantic schedules.

The sidewalk outside the Ark was rank and grimy one Wednesday night in May. Scraps of food spilled from trash bags that had been picked clean of cans and bottles to redeem. The usual clutch of men in the bodega argued about politics and baseball.

But inside the church, the walls thumped with music. Several congregations from other parts of town were crammed into the seats, and more people squeezed in through the narrow doorway.

The room was unbearably hot. The noise was deafening. Pastor Florian was beaming.

"I am full of joy," he said. "It does not matter if you are from Brooklyn or Queens, for wherever we are, God has called us to be one people."

He peered over the top of his reading glasses.

"I wish the Lord would come tonight," he said. "After the service is over, I'd love to hear that trumpet sound."

A Church's Challenge: Holding On to Its Young

JAN. 16, 2007

By David Gonzalez

When Frankie Lora chuckles, his bass guitar bounces and he loses the beat. Sometimes the pianist next to him stumbles and can't keep up with the choir. And one singer gets so emotional that she veers off into tearful shouts of praise.

If music is the motor that drives Pentecostal worship, the band and choir at Ark of Salvation for the New Millennium, a little storefront church in west Harlem, could use a tuneup. Ragged and off-key at times, they are easily out-classed when they sit in with the seasoned musicians at other churches.

Yet they grab attention for one simple reason: They are often the only teenagers in the room.

As Pentecostalism advances across the world, winning converts faster than any other Christian denomination and siphoning believers from more established faiths, it is also suffering its own slow leak: young people who are falling away from the faith.

Mainline Christian churches have grappled with the problem for years. And recently, evangelical leaders in the United States sounded an alarm over "an epidemic of young people leaving."

But the loss is doubly distressing for Pentecostals, evangelical Christians who can be especially zealous in seeking new members and rejecting the secular culture they feel is luring adolescents away from religion.

Against that backdrop, Ark of Salvation is an unusual success. Unlike most of the other Pentecostal churches they visit, this 60-member congregation has attracted a devoted core of teenagers—more than a dozen—who sing and pray at every service. This is no accident.

When the first of them showed up two years ago at the austere storefront on Amsterdam Avenue, dragged along by friends or family, they had little inclination toward religion or music. But Pastor Danilo Florian saw in them the seeds of his church band. More important, he saw in this motley bunch of knockabout youngsters the future of his fledgling church.

He gave them instruments. He paid for music lessons. And he lavished gifts that few of them had ever known, growing up in fractured families and on dangerous streets: Attention. Praise. Expectations.

After an emotional baptism, Ramón Romero and Eneida Vasquez carried a limp Jessica Marte from the Delaware River. (Photograph courtesy of Ángel Franco/*The New York Times*)

Today, they are thriving. The bassist, Frankie Lora, looks as if he may defy his mother's fears that he will end up like his brother, who is serving a life sentence for murder. The pianist, Juan Carlos Matias, once lonely and aimless, is studying to become an engineer. And the singer, Jessica Marte, who was cutting class and fighting at age 12, now dreams of opening a clothing store for Christian girls.

They have also embraced a strict—and sometimes strait-laced—moral code, which they are urged to spread to friends and strangers.

But they are still teenagers, living in a city filled with temptations for quick pleasure and easy money that the founders of Pentecostalism a century ago never imagined. At school, they have classmates who live only for the latest music, gadgets or fashions, or friends who sell drugs. At home, some have parents who ridicule their faith.

And being teenagers, they have their own doubts and questions about their newfound religion's many rules and rituals. Frankie still recalls his disbelief when he saw people shouting, crying and twitching at his first service. "I was looking at them like they were retarded," he said. "I never saw jumping like that in the street."

Reaching these young people took a lot of work. Keeping them in church as they enter the wider world may prove even harder.

For the pastor and the other adults who lead the congregation's youth group, that means striking a balance between keeping them in line and letting them find their own way. It means shielding them not only from the evils of the world, but also from the excesses of some other churches.

And for the teenagers, it means navigating a tricky adolescence in which the boundaries are strict, but not always understandable. They can have cell phones and video games, but are told not to watch television. They can date, but preferably only other Pentecostals and then sometimes only with a chaperon. Dancing is taboo, but they can gyrate in religious ecstasy. Horror movies are bad, yet preachers regale them with gruesome visions of the apocalypse.

These young people struggle. They sometimes bend the rules, or drift away from religion altogether. But for now, at least, most have their faith in God, and something else just as powerful: the feeling that for the first time, someone has faith in them.

Frankie's Fight

Frankie lives the way he plays his bass—trying mightily to get it right.

He stopped screaming at his parents and has cut back on cursing, but sometimes the words still slip out. His grades are improving, but Italian class still vexes him. "I might have to copy from a friend," he joked.

Sometimes he prays to be strong. He certainly looks it, with a bruiser's thick arms and barrel chest, and a scowl to match. Just three years ago, Frankie ran with a rowdy pack. At 14, he was arrested and handcuffed to a pole at the local station house for stealing Pokémon cards from a Barnes & Noble. His mother grounded him for a year.

She was not overreacting. She knew what could happen to neighborhood boys like Frankie when they turned 16. "The same age my brother was when he started killing," he said.

Until his mother died of cancer in November, Frankie's new faith was the lifeline she clung to, hoping he would not turn out like his older brother, Jose, who is in prison for two murders.

In the mid-1990s, their stretch of 109th Street was awash in cocaine and bullets. Jose and his crew killed a rival dealer and later avenged the murder of his father's friend. They called themselves Natural Born Killers.

"My brother had beef with everybody on the streets," Frankie said. "My mother would hear gunshots, and she would go downstairs looking for him to see if he was alive or dead."

For years, she refused to let Frankie leave their apartment, finally letting him go outside, he said, only after "everybody got locked up." On evenings when she was away, he hung out with friends at a bodega, bragging about fights, sex and girls. They rode their bikes around Manhattan all night, or drank rum and beer.

"We were the baddest ones in the neighborhood," he said. "Crazy stuff."

The Loras went to Sunday Mass, but weekends were better known for family parties filled with music and liquor. Nobody blinked when the boys tipped a few beers.

Two years ago, Frankie and his cousin Juan Carlos Matias visited an older cousin, Roy Guzman, who was excited about a new storefront church he had just joined. The three were close, playing basketball and video games. But Roy grew serious that night, warning that if Christ returned, the two boys would be damned.

That message, from an admired older cousin, nudged them to visit the Ark. A week later, they joined.

Up front, their future beckoned: a keyboard and drums, untouched since the pastor's son was expelled from the band after taking up with an older girl. Jefferson Abreu, a friend Frankie had invited to church, asked to play the drums, and Juan Carlos began noodling on the keyboard. Frankie was already studying the bass.

Today, his calm demeanor defies both his looks and his past. Pastor Florian connected with him. "The pastor is cool," he said. "He doesn't lie to us. He is a little kid, like us."

Frankie enjoys a joking camaraderie with his bandmates, sometimes cupping his hand over his mouth to stifle a laugh or rolling his eyes at a sour note. But seeing his old friends can be awkward. When they curse, he laughingly tells them to stop. When they talk about fighting or sex, he stays quiet.

He tried getting them to visit the church.

"They're now selling drugs, hustling," he said of the boys on the block. "I tell them to think about God. They say, 'Yeah, it's true.' But they don't feel like coming. They got to make money."

His home life has been hectic. Before she died, his mother, Altagracia, had been hospitalized repeatedly for gallbladder cancer, returning home weak and needing care. His father, Francisco, he said, insults the Ark, calling it a scam to fleece them of what little money they have.

A rough-looking man, Francisco Lora is the only family member who has not converted to Pentecostalism. He scorns the congregation's belief that their prayers kept his wife alive through years of surgery and chemotherapy. And he scoffs at his son Jose's conversion in prison last year.

Jefferson Abreu, the band's drummer, kept the beat as Pastor Florian's daughter Dianne led a hymn. (Photograph courtesy of Ángel Franco/*The New York Times*)

"What is the use if you already killed a lot of people?" he snarled while mopping at the bodega where he works. "If you do something bad, you should think about God before. But they look for God afterward."

Frankie tries to ignore his father's rage, focusing instead on all that has to be done: schoolwork, practicing the bass and praying for his brother's release—even though Jose is ineligible for parole until 2054.

"I wish he was out," Frankie said. "To see what it feels like to have a brother."

'We Are the Bridge'

Frankie is not the only teenager yearning for an older brother or sister. So when Pastor Florian looked for someone to start a youth group and nurture his congregation's future, he picked the man who had brought Frankie into the church—his cousin Roy Guzman—and Roy's wife, Giselle.

A newlywed couple in their mid-20s, the Guzmans are old enough to be confident in their beliefs, yet young enough to remember being city kids confused about school, dating or friends who think your religion is crazy.

"Most of the people at the church are very mature, very old," said Giselle, a petite, bubbly woman who easily passes for a high school student. "We are the bridge between both generations. If young people have questions, they are not going to ask the elders. They're going to ask us."

Not that the elders are stingy with advice. Ramón Romero growls that the young musicians rush through prayers to spend more time practicing. Eneida Vasquez warns them about watching anything on television. Jeans in church or earrings anytime are forbidden, and the pastor even discouraged one boy from buying a pink shirt.

Sometimes the thou-shalt-nots seem endless. When the teenagers trooped one evening into Juan 3:16, a basement church celebrating its 37th anniversary, festive music and balloons promised a party. Instead, a glowering, skeletal woman—a visiting preacher—railed against reggaeton music and even country outings.

"You do not replace God with the garbage of this world," she shouted indignantly. "You cannot contaminate yourself in the world. We need to be apart!"

Giselle, who helped her husband lead the youth group, was horrified. "She said it was wrong to go to amusement parks," she recalled in their walk-up on 109th Street, where the irreverent sitcom *Arrested Development* droned in the background. "That you have to be in church 24/7."

The temptation to keep a tight rein on the young is strong in storefront churches. Pablo Polischuk, a Pentecostal minister and psychologist in Boston, cautions that these man-made prohibitions can be so severe that they deny normal teenage impulses. That, in turn, can backfire.

"The philosophy is to insulate and isolate to preserve them from a toxic environment, but it does not prepare them to face that environment with dignity," Dr. Polischuk said. "When you try to protect them so much, the end result is the first germ that goes through them spoils them."

So the Guzmans try to accommodate the young people, going to movies and playing video games with them. Once a month, in a variation on a slumber party, the teenagers stay overnight at church, watching Christian movies and chatting.

"People think Christians have to be boring," Roy said. "That's not true."

Pastor Florian takes them swimming, biking and on trips to amusement parks. When one boy got a weekend job that kept him from services, the pastor went easy on him because the boy needed the money.

And though his sermons sometimes condemn the secular world, the pastor holds up the Guzmans as examples of well-educated Christians who have succeeded in that world. Both have degrees in engineering and mathematics from New York University and Stevens Institute of Technology. Roy works for the technology and consulting firm Accenture, while Giselle now works for a construction company.

In fact, Pastor Florian sometimes sees danger for the teenagers in religion.

One summer afternoon, Roy, Frankie and the others piled excitedly into the church van for the Youth Explosion, a revival meeting at St. Mary's Park in the South Bronx. But the stage and the audience were dominated by adults, some with a hard-edged look from their hell-raising days.

The presiding preacher promised to heal people with cancer and AIDS. Waving his hand like a sideshow psychic, he said he sensed there were teenagers in the audience whose lives were imperiled: a young man with a dragon tattoo, a suicidal girl, a gun-toting teenager. As if on cue, they rose and went up to pray.

But even before the prayers ended, Pastor Florian hustled his teenagers back into the van. "That was all just a show," he said later. "It gave me such embarrassment."

The ceaseless vigilance is hard, but every so often it pays off.

For the young people of the Ark and their mentors, the transforming moment came in June 2005. After a year of prayer, study and noisy nights in the storefront, the congregation gathered one tranquil Saturday morning along the haze-shrouded banks of the Delaware River in Pennsylvania.

The Guzmans joined a procession of seven white-clad teenagers and three other adults, down a boat ramp to the gravelly shore. As they lined up in silent anticipation, Pastor Florian asked: "Who does not want to be baptized? You still have time."

No one wavered. Slowly, the pastor, his wife and two other preachers waded chest-deep into the river. They turned to the crowd on shore and beckoned.

Frankie was among the first. Pastor Florian cradled his beefy shoulders, whispered urgently into his ear, dunked him backward and gently lifted him back up. The dazed teenager staggered to shore and clutched his weeping mother.

Juan Carlos emerged from the water heaving with sobs. Roy, who was last, punched the air victoriously. When they regrouped on shore, soaked and shivering, Pastor Florian reminded the teenagers that they were no longer children from the block, but missionaries to the world.

"Now," he said, "you are workers."

A Hard Sell

The work started soon enough. One night just a month after the baptism, Genesis Mora, all of 13 years old, paced a stifling living room crammed with young people. Four girls sat near the back, and she fixed her gaze on these potential recruits.

"You think your friends are going to be there for you when you have problems," she told them, dismissively shaking her head. "But when problems and tribulations come, they distance themselves." Christians, she said, are different.

Earlier, her fellow teenagers from the Ark—prompted by the pastor— each stepped up to tell how their faith made them stronger, how their grades had improved.

It is a measure of how much the pastor expects of these young people that they are entrusted with preaching to outsiders. And it is a measure of how much he wants to attract even more that he regularly arranges home visits to seek converts in a relaxed setting.

This night, a family in the congregation had offered its west Bronx apartment, a half-hour drive from the church, and invited neighbors, who spilled into the hallway. Pastor Florian—trading his suit for a polo shirt and khakis—sat among them, keeping his young charges on message.

"When you study, God is there with you, too," he chimed in. "He sees what you study and records it in your mind."

The teenagers from the Ark were friendly yet persistent. The invited girls listened quietly. Afterward, Jessica Marte and another girl flanked one, asking her to the Ark.

The girl hesitated. "I feel my heart beating," she said, nervously.

"That is Jesus talking to you," Jessica said.

As peer pressure goes, it was gentle but unmistakable. In the end, however, none of the girls visited, standing up the pastor when he went to pick them up. Indeed, the youth group's efforts are often met with blank stares, smirks or empty promises.

But this is how the congregation attracted the teenagers it has—through invitations from cousins and classmates—and the pastor keeps telling them they must bring in more. Much of his mission is offering alternatives for the young people he sees sitting bored on stoops every day or running wild in the night. And one of his biggest dreams is an after-school center where they could study, play—and convert.

"Imagine if we had a place where they could play basketball," he said. "We could play some Christian music in the background, too. I promise you, after a week like that, you will see changes."

Still, the biggest changes in the teenagers have been prompted not by social events or preaching, but by one another. Jessica, whose mother dragged her to services, says she was finally won over by watching Frankie, a tough guy turned tender.

"I was amazed at him," she said. "It was cool that I could see other kids like me, who had problems in school like I did and used to hang out. I saw how they changed."

Jessica, 15, was an unlikely convert. Two years ago she was rowdy on the streets, defiant at home and about to drop out of the eighth grade. Now she is in church every night. Long ago, she put away her earrings and began wearing skirts.

"My friends were like, 'Oh, my God! What are you doing?'" she laughed.

Yet any limits she has placed on herself have been matched by new expectations. She wants to open a store for Christian girls offering fashionable skirts that are neither too short nor too long. And though she still quarrels with her mother, she seems to channel that emotion into religious fervor.

One night, Jessica arrived at church fuming because her mother wanted her to babysit. Soon, she was singing so intensely that she trembled violently and collapsed to the floor, almost banging her head on the pulpit.

The service stopped.

The congregation gazed in awe at this Pentecostal rite of passage: In their eyes, the girl before them had just received the Holy Spirit. A friend gently stroked Jessica's hair while one woman jumped and shook next to the girl's motionless body.

Jessica soon stirred awake and was lifted to her feet. When the service ended, the other girls rushed up to her and pressed for details, as if she had just come home from a date. What had happened? What was it like?

Bewildered and tired, Jessica said she really couldn't explain it, but she felt peaceful. She felt loved. She felt different.

"You know what I say," she said later. "You'll never be the same as when you came in."

'God Doesn't Do Things Quick'

The pastor looked a little sad as Frankie and the others trickled into church one evening last April. Even though the congregation had attracted a few new teenagers, he feared it was not enough.

Some others had visited but never returned. And one mainstay was drifting away: a 16-year-old who had stopped attending regularly, just before she was to preach her first sermon—and around the time her father went back to prison.

Pastor Florian was particularly worried about one boy who liked hip clothes and sweet cologne and was friendly with even the toughest guys on the block. The boy was troubled. The task was daunting. The pastor turned to Roy—who had converted Frankie and others—to pray for him every day.

"You cannot let him go," the pastor implored.

Just in case, he assigned a second adult to pray for the boy.

But Roy's life was becoming complicated. He and his wife were expecting their first child, and he had started a job with an international consulting firm that has kept him away from home during the week.

Three other adults now lead the youth group, and attendance at meetings has grown spotty.

Frankie still shows up. At 17, he is still not quite sure where he is headed, especially since the chilly November day when the congregation crowded into a funeral parlor in Washington Heights. His mother was laid out in a silver coffin, dressed in white with a lacy veil gracing her head.

"Now I'm left here to suffer," Frankie said. "But if she's in heaven, I'm OK. She's watching over me."

Others may be watching as well. His bandmates still count on him to make time for practice. One woman promised his dying mother she would make sure he didn't stray from church. His father is looking to him to help pay the bills.

Frankie said he might have to enroll in night school so he could work during the day. But his brother, Jose, hopes Frankie will heed his urgent—though unlikely—career advice.

It started when Frankie visited him in prison recently and encouraged him to turn to God for help. "He said God doesn't do things quick," Frankie recalled.

Instead, Jose is depending on Frankie. He told him to become a professional baseball player so he could get a signing bonus, get a lawyer and get him out.

Chalk it up to teenage bluster or blind faith, but Frankie said he might try out for his school team, even though he hasn't stepped on a ball field in two years. Maybe, he said, he could find a baseball camp upstate where a scout could discover him.

"Right now I'm depending on baseball," he said. "I'm only depending on baseball."

Pastor Florian, however, is depending on Frankie. For his future. For his faith. For his church.

What he whispered into the boy's ear just before baptizing him in the Delaware River was this: You are destined to become a preacher.

BEHIND the STORY

An Interview with David Gonzalez

This edited e-mail interview was conducted by Thomas Huang, co-editor of Best Newspaper Writing *and an assistant managing editor at* The Dallas Morning News, *with David Gonzalez, winner of the Freedom Forum/ASNE Award for Distinguished Writing on Diversity.*

THOMAS HUANG: Where did the idea for the series come from?

DAVID GONZALEZ: One Friday evening near the end of 2004, Joe Sexton, the Metro editor, casually asked me if I had ever thought of writing about a storefront church. As a former Metro religion writer, I had once wanted to explore that world, one that I vividly remembered from my childhood in the South Bronx. I used to walk by these storefronts, hearing the raucous sounds of worship as shouts, drums and singing blended together. They were strange places, since as Catholics we kept our distance. Part of me always wanted to see what led people to worship in these seemingly random temples.

Also, as a former foreign correspondent in Central America and the Caribbean from 1999 to 2003, I had witnessed the huge growth of evangelical Christianity, especially Pentecostalism, in the region. From the teeming metropolis of San Salvador to the tiniest villages in Guatemala, I would always come across these congregations, which managed to attract all sorts of marginalized individuals. They had also reconfigured the religious (and political) maps, challenging the centuries-long dominance of the Catholic Church.

To me, the series was a way to explore the local consequences of a global phenomenon. While these churches are commonplace in many minority neighborhoods, I suspected that many of our readers dismissed them as not quite serious places that they could safely ignore. My thesis was that these places are reflecting a global change that will have lasting implications for urban America.

How did you decide what the focus of the series would be?

There were several factors at work. The immediate challenge was deciding what kind of congregation and where. I decided to focus on a Pentecostal congregation, since it was the world's fastest growing branch of Christianity. Since I wanted it to be reflective of larger movements—i.e., the role of the developing world and its diaspora as carriers of this faith—I was looking for a Latino immigrant congregation. Similarly, I wanted a church whose pastor had a day job, since few of these churches have full-time paid staff.

A couple of other factors came into play, too. I wanted a church that was relatively new so that the dynamic of an unclear future would be built into the series. Also, to illustrate the larger problem facing these churches as institutions confronting secular urban culture, I wanted a congregation that had a sizeable number of teenagers.

There was also a major logistical consideration: I would be reporting the series mostly at night, while also writing my regular biweekly "Citywide" column. Consequently, I wanted to find a congregation that was easily accessible from my home. As a result, I forgot about possible churches in Brooklyn and focused on Harlem, Washington Heights and the Bronx. Ultimately, I found one in west Harlem.

How did you organize the series, and how did you determine what the focus would be for each installment?

Pretty straightforward, actually. Originally we thought of a five-part series: an overview of the church, the pastor, youth, politics and money. It was only after the reporting was winding up that I sat down and combed over my notes to discuss with my editors the scope of what we had. We decided that the politics part could be made part of the overview, as could the congregation's approach to money.

This is not to say that their political views or approach to money/poverty was not interesting. It was, but it would not work as stand-alone chapters in a narrative series. (I could go on at length in a more traditional analytical story filled with scholars and other commentators, but that would not have fit in with the tone of the series.) Ultimately, the decision was made to do three pieces: the church, the pastor and the youth.

What role did your editor play in conceiving and shaping the series?

Joe Sexton, the Metro editor, thought the topic was worthy of setting me loose for months to see what I found. He had general questions that guided my reporting: Why do people go to these churches, what goes on inside them, etc. We had some long talks about what we were looking for in the early stages. Then he stepped back a bit while I did the reporting.

During the writing and editing process, he would step in at key moments to assess my drafts—did we have the right tone, scope, etc.—and offer suggestions.

I spent a year writing and rewriting the series. Patrick Farrell, one of the ablest editors I have ever worked with anywhere, was my direct editor on this. In the early stages of writing, he and Sexton would sit down with me and we would discuss the thrust of each chapter, before sending me off to write a top for each story.

As the writing progressed, Patrick and I would scope out the arc of sections of each chapter, and I would go off and write. (Each day's installment had five or six chapters, and that is how I wrote them—in sequence, a chapter at a time.)

What was the revision process like?

Endless—and worth it. I spent tons of time immersed in this world, where the divine is seen in the everyday. At night I would be among people who spoke in tongues or would twitch and swoon during worship. On weekends, I would be at revivals where preachers screamed and cried as they cast out demons. It became commonplace for me to witness this and not think twice about it. I found myself humming their hymns when I was in the office. What started out as something alien and sometimes scary had become totally natural to me. As a result, I needed to get some distance between me and the subject again. To step back and see it as an outsider, if you will.

That is where Patrick's editing and my rewriting became crucial. The earliest versions of the story were packed with intense detail and way too much religious-speak. While it all made sense to me—since I had spent so much time in that milieu—it no doubt would have turned off a casual reader. Still, I had to write my way through those intense initial versions that assumed too much of the reader until I got to a point where I was able to lay out the narrative simply and directly.

What, if any, ethical questions came up in the course of reporting and writing the series? How did you resolve them?

We were able to gain the trust of many of the people in the congregation because we were willing to listen to them without judgment. In some cases, I was honest with them about my own religious beliefs, which put them at ease somewhat (though not totally, since as a Catholic, they saw me as being in the wrong theological camp).

At one point, a member of the congregation confided in us (me and the photographer, Ángel Franco, who was a total partner in this) that she and her daughter were going to be evicted from their apartment. We knew this three months before anyone else in the church knew. While I told her of a community group in the neighborhood I thought might be able to help, I could do no more for her. So, I waited for the inevitable, which resulted in her and her daughter moving into a homeless shelter for eight months.

Sometimes, people would confide in us their criticisms of others in the church. While we thought it was unfair to use that in reference to an easily identifiable person, we did use it to inform our understanding of the tensions that existed in the church, especially between the generations.

Another time, I learned that the organizer of a youth revival had reportedly run off with money and had gotten hooked on drugs again. This revival had been something the church's young people had seemed to enjoy (though it would turn out the pastor had serious misgivings about it). I was able to track down the organizer's former roommates, who confirmed the broad details of the story, which I wound up using in the series to show the abuses of this type of faith.

One of the trickiest dynamics to deal with was the church's bluntness about wanting to convert us. They prayed for us the first day we showed up. They prayed for our family members when ill. They prayed for us when we were writing the series. They made no secret of wanting to convert us. I tried to deflect those appeals, by changing the topic or just saying I was happy with my religion. But I can pretty much guess they are still praying for us.

How was the series presented online, and was it accompanied by any other components (audio, video, slideshows, timelines, documents)?

We decided to do something special—and a first for the *Times*—a fully bilingual multimedia show. We settled on three chapters—one for each day— that explored an aspect of the story, rather than just repeat whatever ran that day. We wanted to bring the reader into the world of this church, so we used video and audio of services, home visits and even a baptism, where they could see and hear the church members describe their experiences. It involved minimal narration, used a lot of stills and video, and proved to be effective in giving these folks a very real face. (A link to the *Times'* online package can be found at www.poynter.org/bnw2009/resources.)

What steps did you take to learn more about the Dominican culture? How important was it to do that before diving deeply into the reporting?

Having had some familiarity with Dominican life here (as a Puerto Rican New Yorker) and there (as a foreign correspondent), I knew some of the prevailing currents of the culture, especially as it related to work, family and language.

My own ability to speak Spanish was perhaps the biggest asset. The vast majority of my reporting was done in Spanish, and it gave the series a cultural intimacy that would have been impossible to attain if the interviews had been done in English. The fact that the photographer and I spoke Spanish—Puerto Rican Spanish, to be exact—put them at ease, too, since it let them know that we had in common some aspects of Caribbean culture. They did not have to explain themselves—or edit their behavior, if you will—since they knew we understood the rhythms of their lives and speech. After a while, I could even mimic their accents.

I cannot stress enough that the photographer's cultural fluency helped make this project happen. Like me, he is a New York-born Puerto Rican. Together, we were able to have people relax around us in a way that allowed magic to happen before us.

Immigration, religion and community have been important subjects for you as a journalist. Why is that, and what draws you to these subjects?

Cities are always changing, and newcomers are always arriving to revive and redefine old neighborhoods. I think a good city reporter has to understand that basic fact, and explore that change. Immigrants have ALWAYS been here in New York, so it would be foolish to just dismiss any real and nuanced coverage of that change as a mere "minority" story. It is THE urban story.

Within that context, I try to look at how people make sense of this new world. How do they form community? How do they build and sustain those invisible bonds that exist in a neighborhood?

I grew up in the South Bronx when it was burning. The fact is that a lot of the devastation was countered by one force that refused to budge in the face of devastation: the church. During the 1960s and 1970s, church-based community organizers helped people band together to hold politicians, officials, banks and landlords accountable. While others ran, the church and its people stood their ground. I witnessed this in my life and have never forgotten that. Never.

What approach did you take to find the church you wanted to write about? Why did you choose the Ark of Salvation for the New Millennium?

I spent two months searching for the right congregation that met my criteria. Like a good reporter, I spoke with seminary officials, leading pastors and scholars. It got me nowhere.

An offhand comment/lament/panic attack to an Episcopal priest I know in Harlem resulted in him telling me that a storefront had just opened up around the corner from his church. I immediately went over, and luckily two members of the congregation were inside cleaning the place. They gave me the pastor's number and I arranged to meet him the next day.

Having had some Pentecostal friends, including a roommate at Yale, I knew that my appearance mattered. Before meeting the pastor I cut my hair, put on a white shirt and clean khakis and pressed blazer. I did this more out of respect for him and his church.

We met the next day and I laid out my intentions: I wanted to spend a lot of time reporting on the reality of this church. I was honest about my own religious background. I also told him that—as he well knew—a lot of outsiders think that Pentecostals are "crazy" and that the series would be a fair portrayal of their world.

He agreed. I later found out that he consulted a member who said that a newspaper story about her old church in Albany brought in some needed donations.

How did you gain access to the Ark, and what barriers lay in your way?

Pentecostals are amazingly open and welcoming of total strangers—it is part of their religious DNA. They are also open about their lives—after all, their services are often built around searing individual testimony about hardship and hope.

The photographer and I spent the first couple of weeks just sitting in the back during the services. We did not take notes or pictures. We both wanted to get a sense of the flow of the service and what each section of worship meant. I also wanted to understand who were the key figures in the church, the people whose trust I would have to earn if I was going to get into the story in a deep way.

As the reporting commenced in earnest, the biggest challenge was to get beyond the "God talk"—in other words, to get people to talk about their lives in more or less nonreligious ways. This is not to dismiss their faith, but to cast it in plain language. I wanted to get to a point where I would be able to portray their lives in a way and with events the nonreligious reader could understand.

Some barriers we never overcame: Pastors of other churches we would visit would visibly react with displeasure when they saw us coming through the doors. One congregant—a former drug dealer who escaped deportation by a miracle or a bureaucratic mix-up, depending on your point of view—avoided us completely.

How much time did you spend at the church and with the community? How important was it to immerse yourself in that environment?

For the first seven months, at least four nights and one afternoon a week, with each visit lasting at least four hours. Afterward, three or four visits a month.

Immersion was the only way to even begin to understand this. While I did not participate, I was with them at services, after school, in their homes and on the street. The mere act of accompanying them in their routines gave me an insight and feel that would have been impossible in a regular feature story. It's not that every reported detail made it into the story. But having known those details gave me a mental framework that informed my writing.

Did you have to juggle your year's work on the project with other stories? How did you balance all of that?

I reported the series on nights and on weekends, so I was able to do my column during the daytime. The fact that I could get to and from the church in 15 minutes tops helped a lot, especially when it came to working nights: I could spend more time reporting at the church instead of commuting. For comparison's sake, had I chosen a church in East New York (as someone suggested), I would have spent a total of two hours commuting alone. That said, when it came to writing, I put my column aside and focused solely on the series.

People like Ramón Romero, Ramona Campaña and Chislen Peña play important roles in your stories. What did you see in them, and why did you focus on them?

They were the most devoted, the most serious and the ones who the pastor relied on in different ways. These churches delegate responsibility, so they played crucial roles with the women, the youth or with counsel. They are also the ones that others look up to. I knew that I had to get through to them if I was to understand the church. So my first interviews were with the three of them (individually).

Overall, what stereotypes did you hope to shatter?

That these people were crazy, deluded and waiting for some heavenly reward after enduring a lifetime of earthly suffering. I wanted to present them as human beings trying to get by—and thrive—in an unfamiliar, unfriendly or outright dangerous city. I also wanted to convey a sense of the passion that flows through these services. Passion, not cacophony. That somehow they have been moved in a very real, though perhaps mystifying, way.

Danilo Florian's personal story lies at the heart of the series—his faith, his hopes, his frustrations. What first drew you to him? How open was he about his life and his family? How did you persuade him to open up?

He was actually very moderate in his religious views (compared with other Pentecostal preachers we met in the course of the reporting). He was soft-spoken, endearingly forgetful and sincerely interested in young people. Of course, the great irony is his own children have by and large left the faith.

He was actually quite open about a lot of it. Other things—like what happened with his son—we did not so much discuss at first than observe. We visited his home many times, and we accompanied him as he drove out to pick up the congregation.

The more we got to know him, the easier it got to ask him hard questions. I realized we had gained his trust when he showed us the church's finances before we even had a chance to ask (and that was something I had dreaded asking about, mind you).

What kind of response did you get after the series was published—from the church, from readers, from others?

The series attracted a lot of attention across a wide spectrum: from traditional Pentecostals to progressive theologians, Latinos and non-Latinos, etc.

The church itself was somewhat stunned by the reaction, especially since one big photo of the awning had the pastor's home number printed on it. As a result, people were calling him for weeks on end to ask for prayers or to offer help. I think they never imagined the depth of reaction. (The pastor wound up not being laid off from his job, by the way. I suspect his bosses saw the series and decided to keep him.)

Much of the reaction from Pentecostals and other evangelical Christians expressed both thanks and astonishment that *The New York Times* published a nuanced take on the church and its members. Many said they were touched by the humanity of the people I wrote about, that I got beyond the stereotypes of piety to portray people trying to make sense of an unfriendly world. At the same time, they thanked me for not holding back, but also showing some of the pitfalls of this kind of faith, too.

The bilingual multimedia portion was well-received too, resulting in e-mails from people in Latin America who were able to enjoy that part of the series.

Actual letters to the editor were few: about four, all of which were dismissive of—if not outright hostile to—the series and its premise. One writer lamented, and I paraphrase: *I turn to* The New York Times *for insight on the events of the day at a time when the nation is at war and the president's policies are failing. Instead I see you put on the front page an article about Dominican Pentecostals in Harlem. Did you abdicate your news judgment? What made this story more important than others?*

What amazed me, however, was that the letter was written by the chairperson of the history department at a well-known college. I was dumbstruck by how a historian (!) saw zero value in writing about the role Pentecostals play in 21st-century America. Indeed, if she supposedly was more concerned about the war and President Bush, how could she be so dismissive of a religious movement that is very much supportive of the president and his policies?

If anything, that reaction underscored the need for the series: As others have noted, cultural elites have nearly no direct experience with these groups and tend to dismiss them as insignificant. But they do so at their own peril. These groups have a bigger impact than others want to admit (or even know).

What other lessons did you learn from reporting and writing the series?

One: The value of rewriting.

Two: The value of re-rewriting.

Three: The importance of having a great editor as a colleague.

Those things helped me gain some distance on the series—after spending a year reporting, you need someone who can tell you to step back to a point where others can understand rather than be overwhelmed.

Four: Taking the time to get to know a subject, reporting all the time. Even though I hardly used the bulk of my reporting, all of it helped set the context. Because I had so many notes, I felt totally comfortable taking the story in any direction I needed.

Five: Get out of the way and just tell the story. Too often topics like this can elicit some of the purplest, most-cliché-ridden, sentimental copy around. When you have a subject as powerful as this, there is no need to adorn it with writing tricks that tell you nothing about the subject (but a lot, unfortunately, about the writer's ego).

Writer's Workshop

Talking Points

1. In the first 20 paragraphs of his first-day story, David Gonzalez sets up the "House Afire" series by weaving together descriptions of the Ark of Salvation for the New Millennium, a history and explanation of the Pentecostal movement and statistics related to that movement. He also introduces Danilo Florian, the church's pastor. Focusing on the first section, describe what each paragraph contributes to setting up the series.

2. While reporting, Gonzalez faced an ethical issue: He learned that a congregant and her daughter were going to be evicted from their apartment. "While I told her of a community group in the neighborhood I thought might be able to help, I could do no more for her," he said. "So, I waited for the inevitable, which resulted in her and her daughter moving into a homeless shelter for eight months." Discuss what you would have done in that situation. Why was it important for Gonzalez to limit his assistance? Are there any other situations in which you would have offered more help?

3. Gonzalez says that Ramón Romero, Ramona Campaña and Chislen Peña played crucial roles in the church and that congregants looked up to them. Identify the anecdotes that Gonzalez chose to tell about these three people. What do we learn about them? Why do you think Gonzalez chose the anecdotes that he did?

Assignment Desk

1. Gonzalez says that ever since he was a child in the Bronx, he was curious about Pentecostal churches. "I used to walk by these storefronts, hearing the raucous sounds of worship," he said. "Part of me always wanted to see what led people to worship in these seemingly random temples." Choose a street in your city or town that teems with people, preferably from diverse cultures. Spend an hour walking up and down the street. How many story ideas can you jot down in your notebook?

2. In "House Afire," Gonzalez and photojournalist Ángel Franco worked closely together from the start of the project. If you are a reporter, ask a photographer to lunch. If you are a photographer, ask a reporter to lunch. Sit down and come up with five story ideas you might be interested in working on together. Talk about how you would approach reporting the stories.

Hartford Courant.

Finalist: Diversity Writing

Monica Polanco

Success, at a Price

JAN. 28, 2007

Delia Guajardo wipes the infirmary walls at Choate Rosemary Hall, a prep school of America's elite.

Guajardo was once an experienced and respected public administrator in Mexico, with a secretary assigned to bring her paperwork and coffee. She now spends her days cleaning counters and door handles, dusting air vents and mopping floors. Walking through a student's dorm room, she spies a paper clip on the floor, bends and retrieves it.

Guajardo arrived in Wallingford 18 years ago for what was supposed to be a short visit, but she stayed for her children's sake. The sacrifices have been worth it, with one daughter on her way to becoming a teacher and the other studying to be a doctor. Though Guajardo makes less than $10 an hour, her husband, Juan Guajardo, earns as much as $60,000 a year at the local steel mill. His work is more grueling, but it pays.

The Guajardos are part of a thriving but reclusive community of about 500 Mexican families who moved to Wallingford from Lagunillas, a small, agrarian town in the Mexican state of Michoacán. They came, like many immigrants, for opportunity and money. Most of them are legal and naturalized citizens—for all appearances the archetypical immigrants who walked off Ellis Island and into a Norman Rockwell frame.

But these are reluctant Americans.

They fled no oppression. They are not tempest-tossed, wretched refuse, yearning to breathe free. They remain exuberantly Mexican, even though many have lived in the United States for decades. They would much rather live in México lindo, beautiful Mexico, the land that blew life into their lungs and sunned their caramel skin. For them, U.S. citizenship is not a political ideal, but a convenience that makes it easier to travel home.

Jacqueline Serna is escorted from Most Holy Trinity Church in Wallingford, Conn. As part of her quinceañera, or 15th birthday celebration, Serna is accompanied by her dance partners, José Soto, 18, at left, and his brother, Jonathan Soto, 17, at right. (Photograph courtesy of Patrick Raycraft/*The Hartford Courant*)

The American dollar allows them to flourish. Few first-generation, unskilled immigrants drive Cadillac Escalades earned by the sweat of their brow.

They keep a low profile in Wallingford and are careful not to engage the larger community, either socially or politically. They tolerate the punishing conditions at the steel plant, and the chore of vacuuming at Choate—accepting the kinds of jobs some people say American workers don't want.

"This is the best opportunity I've had in the United States," said Luís Yánez, a Mexican metallurgist who has worked at the steel plant for four years. "We don't take anybody's job away. We are really part of this economy," he said.

They cling to their Mexican culture, celebrating rites of passage as they would in Lagunillas, with live bands, steaming plates of rice, beans and beef, and generosity from friends and relatives.

Each December, the steel mill shuts down, allowing dozens of families to desert Wallingford and make the trek to Lagunillas, Michoacán's smallest town. They stay for as long as a month, visiting aging parents and celebrating Our Lady of Guadalupe, Patroness of the Americas, with a townwide Mass. They host a rodeo and revel at the fiesta de los norteños, a blowout party organized by the Northerners for their town.

For that one month, they can forget their jobs manipulating metal or cleaning up after privileged students. But when the calendar commands them back to Connecticut, Lagunillas once again becomes sad and quiet, as do its departing norteños.

Recasting an Age-Old Narrative

The Mexican presence in Connecticut is growing rapidly—from 8,393 in 1990 to 35,800 in 2005, according to U.S. Census figures. And Connecticut, which has long been a Puerto Rican enclave, now has the largest population of Mexicans in New England.

Undocumented workers make up the largest share of recently arrived Mexican immigrants, but Wallingford's Mexicans don't fit the picture of day laborers waiting on a street corner. They seem to be recasting an age-old narrative that portrays immigrants as eager to exchange one nationality for another.

"Everyone comes here and fits in this linear line from migrant to American citizen," said Mark Overmyer-Velázquez, an assistant history professor at the University of Connecticut. "That's the story that we've all heard, the heroic story." The Mexican community in Wallingford, Overmyer-Velázquez said, really complicates the story.

Several factors seem to play a role in the Lagunillans' reluctance: They are politically disengaged and financially autonomous, relatively few learn English, and they maintain strong family networks and cultural traditions across the border.

History, though, suggests that the Lagunillans, or their children, will slowly become part of the American fabric. Their immigrant narrative is still evolving.

"Part of what's happening in terms of the immigration debates," said David Lindstrom, an associate sociology professor at Brown University, "is that people are looking at only the very recent immigrants—and in the case of Mexico, there's a lot of very recent immigration from Mexico—then making the false conclusion that Mexicans don't want to integrate and be part of the United States."

All for the Children

Delia Guajardo's happiness peaked in Mexico.

"My dream was my career, my profession," she said.

A respected administrator in her home state of Michoacán, Guajardo was surrounded by family and the people she describes as her true friends.

That life slipped out of her hands after the devaluation of the Mexican peso in the 1980s. Guajardo was safe from the onslaught of layoffs, but her husband, an agricultural engineer trained in land and water conservation, quit his low-paying job before he could be laid off and sought work in the United States in 1988.

"My husband wanted to try his luck here," she said. "I thought he would stay six months and return."

But Juan Guajardo had savored the taste of the dollar. Spitting it out was not an option. Delia Guajardo and her daughters, then 4 and 2, arrived in Wallingford the next year for what was supposed to be a three-month visit. She had a return ticket home, but Juan had other plans.

She would have celebrated her 27th service anniversary this year at the Instituto Mexicano del Seguro Social, the national health insurance system, and would have qualified for full retirement benefits. If someone had described to Guajardo what her life would become, she would have dismissed it as fiction.

"Assume that I exchanged an entire world for that family unity," she said. "I left my career, my job, my friends, my personal evolution."

Like many of the men who work at the steel mill, Juan Guajardo moved to Wallingford first, then acquired visas for his wife and two daughters to join him. Their only son, the family's first American citizen, was born here in 1990.

Today, Delia and Juan Guajardo are homeowners, and their children are tallying their own successes. Ana, 20, spent a semester in France and earned a full scholarship from Eastern Connecticut State University, where she is a biology major and French minor; 22-year-old Brenda, the oldest, is completing her master's degree in teaching at the University of Connecticut and has worked with international students studying English at Choate; Juan Luís Guajardo, 16, began high school last year.

Delia Guajardo has kept a loving archive of her children's pasts: Brenda's uniform from her partial schooling in Mexico, awards, certificates, poems and videos of the girls' quinceañeras—their 15th birthday celebrations.

The girls still watch those videos, and they still ask their mother to braid their hair. It is during these moments that Delia seems happiest. She shares her love of poetry with Brenda Guajardo, who was first introduced to meter and rhyme in the womb.

"In writing a poem, what one has tucked inside blossoms," Delia Guajardo said.

During an impromptu reading of the anonymous "I Gave You Life," Brenda's and Delia's voices stream in and out as they take turns reciting the verses from memory. The sadness that manacles Delia releases her for a few precious moments.

She arrives at her favorite poet, Manuel Acuña, whose final poem, "Nocturno a Rosario," stands as a testament to the pain of unrequited love. Guajardo recites the lines with the intensity of a man willing to end his life rather than live without love, as Acuña did in 1873.

"I have to tell you that I adore you," she incants. "That I suffer very much, that I cry very much.... With a cry, I implore you, I implore you and I speak to you in the name of my last illusion."

The soliloquy could easily express Guajardo's relationship with Mexico, her homeland, and the United States, her keeper and tormentor.

U.S. citizenship is a loaded topic in her home. For Delia and Ana Guajardo, even dual citizenship isn't palatable; they consider themselves Mexican and intend to stay that way. Brenda became a naturalized citizen about three years ago to obtain student financial aid. "It made me angry," Brenda says.

While taking a break at Choate's infirmary waiting room, Delia reveals that her husband is once again tapping into his persuasive abilities. This time, Juan Guajardo wants to convince her that they should become U.S. citizens.

Juan tells his wife that he won't become a citizen without her—a ploy—but Delia flushes the idea out of her system. U.S. citizenship, she said, would dilute the blood that runs through her veins.

"I am a very sincere person—very frank," she says. "I don't like to do things without feeling them. My blood is Mexican, and I want to continue feeling Mexican."

The Quinceañera

If the Lagunillans are reluctant, so too is Wallingford.

The Mexicans are practiced at fading into the crowd, but they are unmasked when their outsized celebratory style overwhelms the neighborhood.

The quinceañera, an homage to blossoming womanhood, is one of many Mexican traditions the Lagunillans have preserved.

The 15th birthday party is a window into the Americanization of the youth of Lagunillas and the tension between the quietude of Wallingford and the boot-stomping joy the Lagunillans long to feel, even if for just one night.

On a cool fall evening, Jacqueline Serna is in her backyard rehearsing a choreographed waltz for her quinceañera. José and Jonathan Soto and four other teens take their places. They are Jacqueline's chambelanes, her dance partners. The festivities will include a Mass with a mariachi band, a white limo and a party that will draw about 400 guests.

Gloria Rodríguez, a family friend who has been teaching the teens the choreography, cues the music. A swooning arpeggio, a broken chord played on a harp-like instrument, fills the air and a man begins to sing in Spanish.

"While visiting your garden, 1,000 butterflies began to say beautiful things," he warbles. "The prettiest of the 1,000 kissed a rose and then went to you, marvelous."

The boys tap their feet, right to left, left to right, lightly scraping the concrete. Jacqueline unceremoniously spins toward the boys and they each take turns twirling her with upturned pinkies.

Later, the boys try to create a dance routine to Shakira's "Hips Don't Lie" to complement the sentimental waltz. For a moment, they lose all self-consciousness, gyrating their hips and gesticulating with their hands.

From the edge of their makeshift stage, they look like children, freed from the demands of their evolving identity. Later, they deny that any enjoyment took place.

On the day of the party, they are at the Hungarian Community Hall, stomachs in knots, as 400 people turn to watch them. Jackie, in a pink, poofy dress, is waiting for her cue. Her dark hair is curled around a gold crown.

Juan Rodríguez Jr., one of Jackie's dance partners, is not sure if they will have enough space to dance.

"I'm really nervous," he says.

The performance is perfect, except for a moment when Gloria Rodríguez thought a candle was going to set Jackie's dress on fire.

Everyone who contributed to the event drinks a toast and the party gets under way.

Couples dance in each other's arms. Fathers and mothers hold their babies as they dance with their spouses.

For a few moments, cultures mix. The crowd line dances to the song "Achy Breaky Heart" in Spanish. The younger guests form a loose circle and begin dancing to a pulsing beat. They are wearing glow sticks around their necks and doing their best tricks, spinning on their backs and doing the wave with interlocked fingers, moves that were invented on the streets of New York City before they were born.

Culture Clash

Someone has called the police about the music pulsing from the Hungarian Community Hall.

At 10:50 p.m., two police officers work their way through the crowded hall. They approach a man near the stage, exchange words, then walk up the steps to the stage and talk to a musician.

After a few moments, the man makes an announcement: The party's over. The audience boos. He repeats, offering condolences to those who planned to stay until 2 a.m.

People slowly slip on their coats and file to the front exit, passing the empty Bud Light cans on the tables.

Gloria Rodríguez turns and, as delicately as she can, says it's actually better to end the party early. This way, people go home before they're too drunk, she says, pointing out that at the last quinceañera, someone got into a fight on the dance floor.

"There's too many small children," she says.

But the men have a different take. It's hard to tell how much of their anger has been prodded by the free-flowing alcohol, but the community's reserved nature collapses nonetheless. They each bear similar expressions of anger and frustration. The scrutiny of the outside world has crashed their party.

Alfonso Serna, Jacqueline's father, lashes out at what he describes as the officers' superior attitude. He wants to know why they didn't come to him first.

He had accompanied them outside and tried to convince them to let the party continue. He darts between indignation and an inexplicable laugh. Serna's wife sweeps as he vents.

"I live here," he says. "I own my house. I never complain about the cops, ever. Why do they treat us like this?"

Someone floats a question: Why don't the Mexicans set an acceptable noise level with the police department before holding a party?

In a moment of bravado, Serna says he will file a complaint with the department the next day, a Sunday.

José Antonio Ávila, who was hired to film the party, documented the conversation between Serna and the police. One of the officers shined his light into the camera, distorting the images. Ávila kept his distance, fearing further reprisals. Though Ávila is a U.S. citizen, he is stymied by fear.

At home, in Lagunillas, the quinceañera would have been open to the whole town. Everyone would have felt a sense of ownership in the revelry.

But here, it's different. The Hungarian hall is in a residential neighborhood and the music has been pumping through the powerful sound system since about 3 p.m.

About 12 years ago, when these parties first began, fewer Mexicans lived in town, Ávila says. The officers who were dispatched to the parties were older.

"They understood the environment," Ávila says. "Now, they're purely young officers."

The men's interpretation blindsides a police spokesman. The department, Lt. Marc Mikulski says, has done sensitivity training with a local outreach group to better understand Wallingford's Hispanic community.

"I wish someone at that time would have come in and talked to us," Mikulski says.

At this party, though, Jackie and the boys have vanished. The rest of the Mexican community recedes into the darkness.

This story was the first part in a three-day series, "The Reluctant Americans," that explored the cultural identity of a Mexican community in Wallingford, Conn. To read the other stories in the series, go to www.poynter.org/bnw2009/resources.

BEHIND theSTORY

Lessons Learned

By Monica Polanco

When I first arrived in Wallingford, Conn., to suss out a possible immigration story, I expected to find a vibrant Mexican community: children riding bikes or walking through town with their friends, and grandmothers walking to the corner store.

Instead, I saw a tidy town that was bereft of pedestrians and clearly inhabited by private people. I remarked to Patrick Raycraft, the photographer who had asked me to look into the story, that writing about this community would be like writing about the wind.

We started with a visit to the town hall, where the mayor gave us a quick profile of Wallingford and told us about a steel mill that employed a large group of Mexicans. That was our first important clue about this hidden community.

The then-president of the steel mill, Gus Porter, became our unofficial facilitator, introducing us to the workers who happily told us about their beloved Lagunillas. Once we learned the workers were from the same town in Mexico, we knew that would be the focus of the story.

At the time, groups on both sides of the immigration debate were protesting across the country, and lawmakers in Washington, D.C., were considering criminalizing illegal immigration.

That controversy was nonexistent in Wallingford. The Mexicans I talked to were more concerned with raising their children than with a fiery debate. Their answers to my immigration questions were brief and detached. Clearly, I was on the wrong track.

I also made the mistake of thinking that the Mexicans would not only tell me about their lives, but also interpret their experiences and help me add context to the story. But years had passed since they had come to Wallingford, and their answers weren't particularly introspective, so I found sociologists to help me understand their experience.

I stopped asking immigration questions and began asking the Lagunillans about their lives. I went from the big picture to the pointillistic, inquiring about their childhoods, their first jobs in the United States and the origin of their children's names.

I limited my time at the steel mill, a loud, hot and dangerous place for the uninitiated, in favor of a quieter setting more conducive to interviews. I tagged along with the workers' wives to their jobs at the Choate boarding school. There I learned about their culture shock in arriving in New England during the dead of winter, the camaraderie they enjoyed because of their shared hometown and the challenges they had overcome.

My Spanish skills were essential because most of the Mexicans I talked to were not comfortable speaking in English—even when they spoke it well. The Spanish language connected them to their homeland and allowed them to speak from the heart.

I had envisioned spending long, informal stretches with the Lagunillans, but their time was limited. The men worked irregular 12-hour shifts, and several of the teenagers I wanted to shadow worked after school, arriving home as late as midnight. I spent time with them when I could and looked for other opportunities to meet with members of the community.

Some months, I traveled to Wallingford several times, attending community events and watching Jackie Serna's dance practices. During other periods, I conducted research and relied on phone interviews.

I worried that those time constraints would weaken the story, but by the end of the project, I had collected a box full of reporter's notebooks, reports and recordings.

All along, I had thought this story would unfold in dramatic ways, but when that didn't happen, I began to panic. How was I going to write a three-day series with no drama?

My editor, Stephen Busemeyer, talked me down from the ledge, telling me that this story was no less interesting than one punctuated by conflict and suspense. Steve helped me take the little details, like the fact that Jackie Serna's chambelanes twirled her with upturned pinkies during her birthday dance routine, and incorporate them into the larger picture.

Steve drew on the mental associations conjured by Ellis Island and Norman Rockwell's paintings to help readers understand how the Lagunillans resembled previous generations of immigrants and how they were different.

Though I initially thought I would work on this story for about a month, I ended up spending nine months on it while covering my city hall beat. I experienced many ups and downs during that time, which taught me that progress isn't always linear.

Some days, I felt that the Lagunillans trusted me and would surely reveal something illuminating. Other days, I was sure they would grow tired of my questions and turn me away. I'm grateful the Lagunillans didn't close their doors to me, and I credit them with a lot of patience and generosity.

Monica Polanco began her journalism career in 1999 as a rotating intern for Knight Ridder, working at newspapers in St. Paul, Minn.; Fort Worth, Texas; and Belleville, Ill. She went on to cover public safety for the Austin American-Statesman *for about five years, and she now writes about New Britain's city hall and schools for* The Hartford Courant.

The Palm Beach Post

Finalist: Diversity Writing

Christine Evans

America's New Main Street: Life on K Street

NOV. 4, 2007

Soon the cafeteria at the little elementary school on South K Street will fill up with children: black ones, white ones, brown ones, pasty pink ones, a squirmy rainbow of young readers and writers who plop down their spaghetti-laden trays and chatter away in three languages—sometimes even four.

Soon, the affable guidance counselor whom everybody calls Mr. O will run upstairs to his big, airy office with the New Kids, his "little ambassadors."

They will have questions, problems, desires and quandaries. But it is too early for all that now.

Too early to say to the fourth-grader from Haiti, "How long has it been since you've seen your mother? You must miss her very much."

Too early to hear about the Mexican boy who got lost for three days in the desert.

Too early for drama, but here it comes, anyway.

It's kindergarten sign-up day at South Grade Elementary, and a 5-year-old has just arrived holding her mother's hand. She wears purple barrettes in her bouncy pigtails and a pink "It's Magical!" backpack that swings jauntily from her shoulder.

Her name is Karla.

Just a few weeks ago, she arrived, dirty and tired—no pigtails at all—after traveling 1,800 miles by bus and foot from El Salvador in the company of her two (only slightly) older sisters, an aunt and a tag team of coyotes—human smugglers—who hid the girls in stash houses when *la migra* got too hot.

Fifth-grader Midler Alexis, 11, makes a toast during Rebecca Hinson's class at South Grade. Hinson, an art instructor, is teaching her students the British custom of high tea. "Thank you, Miss Hinson, for this wonderful day," says the Haitian-born Midler, who has lived here eight years. (Photograph courtesy of Richard Graulich/*The Palm Beach Post*)

How was it?

A shrug.

Hot? Scary?

Yes, that's right, she says, taking a pencil and wide-ruled paper from the backpack.

Now look at me write my letters.

Back in El Salvador, a hired driver had escorted Karla and her siblings to school, a luxury the family could afford only because the girls' parents, already in the States, wired money home.

But Karla's mother had "cried and cried and cried" at the absence of her children, so finally she and her husband settled on the only solution they could find, since "at home it was five dollars a day for 12 hours in the clothes factory," and returning did not seem to be an option.

They "crossed" the kids.

The trip cost $6,500, *per child,* but it was worth it.

Because here's Karla. Ready to start kindergarten.

Mr. O consults his paperwork.

"Name?"

Karla's mother gives it.

"Address?"

Check.

"Social Security number?"

A pause.

Mr. O leans down the table to inquire softly of a colleague: "What if the family has no Social?"

"Just put *no tiene uno*." Doesn't have one.

He squints. Reviews the fine print. Finds what he is looking for.

"It says right here," he tells Karla's mother, who gives him a relieved smile, "that your Social is not required."

So that's it. Karla's in.

It is 11 a.m. and another entirely typical morning on K Street.

"Some days," Mr. O says, "it's hard to tell what country you're in."

This Is Not Your Mother's K Street

If you want to know what it's like to live in a place that has been radically transformed by the latest immigration wave, you might want to drop by Alphabet City.

Plant your feet at the bottom of K Street.

And look around.

This is not the famous K Street up in Washington, D.C., where for the past two years the lobbyists and lawyers have earned the big bucks trying to find ways to "fix" the nation's immigration problems.

No. This is the other K Street, where the immigrants actually live.

On a clear evening, before dusk, when the light is just right, you can stand on the schoolhouse steps and look all the way up—through the umbrella of shade trees that droop low from the 1950s homes, over the heads of tiny Guatemalan mothers strolling toddlers and carrying babies in colorful slings, past the stately silhouettes of older Haitian women, a few of whom still balance the day's shopping atop their heads, just as they did on the island.

Past tight knots of middle-schoolers who discuss homework in a rapid Creole-English mix, and past their parents, who leave dinner in a pot on the stove and carry their books to English class.

Past the lopsided, three-wheeled bicycles, the same kind used as taxis to carry people and chickens on the dirt roads that wriggle around the Suchiate River in dusty Guatemalan border towns.

Past the schoolhouse door where the sign says *Welcome,* in four languages.

Past the police officer who needs a translator to figure out what's going down.

Past the mother who takes care of somebody else's children while hers wait back in Honduras.

You never know whom you will meet or how they got here, and you cannot make assumptions based on looks. How about the curly-haired blonde at the morning parents' meeting?

She's the spitting image of a suburban soccer mom—except she's a train jumper who a few years ago slipped across the Mexican border from Guatemala to climb aboard a parked cargo train, where she hid in the dark hollows of a grain car and rode hundreds of miles north toward the U.S. line.

With her 7-month-old daughter strapped to her chest.

Forget CNN. All the latest headlines.

Forget the raids at meat packing plants in Minnesota and Texas. The boycotts and rallies and protests across the land. The anti-immigrant laws passed and appealed and tossed out in scores of cities and counties. The Pennsylvania mayor who got himself on *60 Minutes* when he tried to chase the "illegal aliens" out of his small town. The slaughterhouse raid that separated an Iowa mother from her children.

The Florida farmers who can't find pickers. The pickers who disappear in the middle of the night. The fence going up at the border.

The border that has a hole. The chicken-plucking factories that cannot fill their jobs.

The jobs that do not exist in the "sending" countries of Latin America and the Caribbean.

No—forget all that, people around here say. No more shouting heads on cable TV debating the fine points of immigration beyond the wall or the welcome mat.

The people who live in the little rows of alphabet streets—A and B and C to the west; L and M and N to the east—in this 6-square-mile town don't need the news, thank you.

They're living it.

This is the broadcast from Alphabet City.

Big Changes for 'Little Ambassadors'

11:10 a.m. at the pale peach school on K Street.

The cafeteria is filling up with the squirmy rainbow, so Mr. O runs upstairs to his big, airy office, where around a horseshoe-shaped table, six children wait.

Parishioners carry a San Miguel statue into Sacred Heart Catholic Church for Mass during the weekend of a festival in the saint's honor. (Photograph courtesy of Bill Ingram/*The Palm Beach Post*)

He does a quick count.

Four boys. Two girls.

Two Guatemalans. One Mexican. Three Haitians.

"Hello, my little ambassadors!" he begins. "How is everybody today?"

Everybody is well, *bien, bon, gracias, merci.*

This is because everybody is from someplace else.

"Small improvements," Mr. O says. "We're going to learn a little bit every day."

The slogan on the white board says, "Focus: The ability to become comfortable with new surroundings."

Javier Ortolaza is all about adapting. As a boy, he bounced back and forth between Puerto Rico and the States, so he knows a thing or two about feeling out of place. But not as much as these kids or their parents know.

In the mornings, the front lobby is abuzz with chatter, and anybody who wants to decipher it would do best to bring an interpreter—in Spanish, Creole or the Guatemalan Indian languages of Kanjobal and Mam.

A few years ago, when he took the job, the Irish American principal, Mike Riley, was shocked to find out that some of his fourth-graders had never seen the Atlantic Ocean, even though it's only a mile away.

"They might have seen the Pacific in Guatemala," he says. "But they had never been to the beach. I thought that was just incredible."

When standardized testing season begins, the silver-haired assistant principal, Goldie Stopek, sets up her teal "war room," posting color-coded charts and sticky notes on the white board in a compulsive attempt to keep track of students and translators and teachers. Of the school's 756 students, 457 began the year as "English language learners." Meaning, they lack the basics.

"I don't think," Stopek says, "that anybody can really imagine what goes on here."

She's right.

Up in the big, airy office, Mr. O passes out papers for the *Who I Am* bingo game.

Inside each square is a word, and if the word applies to you, you color the square.

For example, if you live with your mother, you fill in the square that says "mother."

A boy raises his hand.

"What if you live here and your mother lives in Haiti? Can you still say, 'Yes, I live with my mother?'"

"Let's see," Mr. O, the diplomat, says. "You are here, and your mother is in Haiti, right? So I don't think you would color in that square."

Everyone looks sad, for just a moment.

War and Disasters Push People North

How did this happen?

How did Little Lake Worth, as the locals so fondly call it, morph from a gateway to the tropics into precisely the reverse? A place where more people seem to be coming up from the south than heading down?

Duvalier and Aristide in Haiti. Civil war in Guatemala. Flooding in Honduras.

This is how the city inherited her immigrants, one by one; it is impossible to separate the reasons people come, crossing deserts, hiding children, washing away at sea, from the long, sad timelines of their homelands.

Roberto Tomas can tell you.

He is one of the "Original 23."

Like thousands of other indigenous Guatemalans caught up in the country's 36-year civil war, he fled north in the 1980s as the leftist guerrillas battled brutal government soldiers and the poorest and simplest people—the

Maya Indians—got stuck in the middle, suffering torturous deaths and disappearances.

"I saw 48 people killed. I was 10 or 11. The soldiers bashed the peoples' heads with AK-47s. One was my uncle, one my sister-in-law. They put everybody in a wood house while they were still alive and then they took the matches and burned it down."

And so he came.

Crossed at Mexicali, stitched Levis in California, picked strawberries in Michigan. Moved to New York City. Thought it was too cold.

Flew to Miami and asked the Cuban taxi driver where he should go.

Well. (The Cuban had to make a phone call to find out.) Here.

To Boynton Beach, where farmers needed good pickers cheap. From there, it was just a hop to Lake Worth, which already was attracting Guatemalans who had migrated down from Indiantown.

That is how it happened.

He is middle-aged now, a successful entrepreneur, an advocate for his homeland and one of thousands of Guatemalans who have settled here.

"In 1984, when I first came, I did my own little survey. Nothing official. But I counted 23 Guatemalans, including me.

"I was in the first wave, a war refugee. The people coming now, they flee not the war but the poorness. They have nothing to eat down there, so they come here.

"Now there are so many, I get lost with them."

Immigrants Undercounted in Overcrowded City

So does everybody else.

The city's official population of 35,000 is so in doubt—because of all the shadow people—that managers have asked the U.S. Census Bureau for permission to do a special count.

"I don't mean to laugh," assistant city manager Laura Hannah says, "but we really have no idea how many people we have. Though we do know we have a severe undercount."

By rough estimate, some 12 million undocumented immigrants are living in the U.S. Only a tiny fraction, perhaps 5,000 to 12,000, live here, city officials say. But it's enough to fret about.

Longtime residents grow frustrated with crime, gangs, sinking property values and what some view as an undesirable transformation of a sweet Old Florida city built by hardy Midwesterners almost 100 years ago. All those letters along the alphabet streets used to spell something special, they say: S-M-A-L-L-T-O-W-N U.S.A. But no longer.

It is possible, of course, to live tucked away in the far-north part of the city, where the homes are bigger, the grass is greener and the street signs bear distinguished names: Princeton and Harvard, not A and B and C. But for most folks, the burdens and joys of living in an immigrant city are keenly felt.

"Lake Worth comes in 31 flavors, and the diversity is a great thing for the city as a whole," Mayor Jeff Clemens says. "But it does present certain challenges."

To wit, overcrowded apartments, code violations, strained city services, trash and beer bottles tossed to the street—just as they would be in Guatemala—and a day-labor line that has a habit of snaking along Lake and Lucerne avenues and jamming up traffic in the trendy heart of town.

The other day, 28-year-old Jorge Diaz was standing in that line.

People like Roberto Tomas have made their fortunes, but Diaz might not.

The construction industry is down the tubes. Jobs are drying up faster than water in the desert.

"I don't know what is going to happen," Diaz said. Neither does anybody else.

You Won't Find This in Any Guidebook

The Haitian kids came by plane.

"It was easy," a boy in a red shirt says. "Just sit down in the cool air and look out the window."

This report draws envious stares from the children who crossed the desert to get here.

"I did Texas," announces the boy from Guatemala. He turns to a girl. "Did you do Texas?"

The girl does not know if she "did Texas"—it's not as if she had a map. She is glassy-eyed and would rather not talk about it.

The Mexican boy, though? Boy, does he have a story!

First, a few technical difficulties.

The Haitian boy would like to hear the Mexican boy's story, but he doesn't speak Spanish. The Mexican boy speaks Spanish and some English, but he doesn't speak Creole. The Guatemalan girl speaks only Kanjobal and Spanish and a bit of English; the Haitian girl is doing a good job learning English, but her Creole is better.

The bilingual Mr. O can take the Spanish to English, but he cannot take the Spanish to Creole or the Creole to English; still, at this point everybody just wants to hear the story.

Which goes something like this:

The Mexican boy's guide got lost in the desert.

They all walked in circles for three days.

The boy wore hard-soled shoes, but still the cactus thorns found his feet.

His drinking water boiled over.

For meals, he peeled the lids off cans.

And then—somebody found them.

"And we came here."

Everybody nods. Of course he did. So did they.

Mr. O looks at the clock.

It's time to go.

"Goodbye, my little ambassadors," he calls out as the fourth-graders trickle away to their next Tuesday afternoon class.

In America.

From Dusty Hometowns to the Lights of D Street

This is how it begins.

The dozen men standing on the train tracks wear jeans, heavy boots, freshly washed T-shirts; they carry plastic bags with maps, extra socks; they hide their money in their cuffs; leave their wives and girlfriends back home; slip out without telling their mothers.

Why make them worry? Better to reach their destination first, then make the call, say, *Mami, I'm sorry, but we need the money, don't we?*

Back home, in Guatemala, Honduras, El Salvador, where the land is dust and the cities throb with crime but not work, they languished. But in their hoped-for destination—glittering Lake Worth—they already have roofing jobs lined up.

"Yes, yes, we are leased," one man says. "The employer says come, they need us."

So this is how it begins, down on the tracks in southern Mexico. Three times, some of these men have made this same trip; the gateway to the tropics is not yet a dot on the horizon, but already they can picture the shuffleboard courts.

The little *cafeterias* up and down Dixie.

The labor vans idling at el Tropical.

Ah!

The train comes howling.

The men hop on, climb the orange ladders, lie flat and hide. On the way they will dodge electrical wires, tree branches and bandits.

They know just where they are going.

D Street.

In two months' time or 12, if they're lucky, they will arrive to start new lives in Alphabet City.

Just like the curly-haired blonde who cinched her baby to her chest and fled north to F Street.

A Gripping Story but Not So Unusual

A couple of years later, she settles onto a bench in the school cafeteria.

"Shh," she says, putting a finger to her lips. "Do not use my name. I asked my husband, can I tell my story?"

How he came first, with their older daughter. How she was pregnant and had to wait. How the baby turned 7 months, and she decided it was time.

How she was scared.

How they made it to Texas, but an agent caught them; the baby went to one city, she to another, a mix-up. The Border Patrol was *muy agradable*, very pleasant. She got her baby back, obtained a visa, only temporary. Any day now, there could be a knock at the door.

What she did, the trip, the train, the secret life in a country to which she does not belong, and which does not belong to her, all this was under the law wrong. But even though she is an educated woman and once had a good job in the city in Guatemala, once she became middle-aged, they just wanted younger women in those jobs; her husband, less educated, had even less luck. Their children needed an education—this is what drove them, she says. Because in Guatemala, "we had schools, yes, but small ones, and so many children, they sit like this," shoulder pressed to shoulder, "and it is so hard to learn."

"I wanted her to have a chance," she says of the curly-haired daughter, now 3, who rode the train tops with her toward the border.

"Plus, it was a matter of food on the table."

Almost nobody notices when she tells this story.

What's to notice?

Quaker Lace and Manners Fit for a Queen

High tea in Alphabet City.

The nervous fifth-graders file in, sweaty palms lodged in pockets, girls twisting long braids around index fingers, and take their places at the long table with the Quaker lace cloth and the plated silver and porcelain plates. Pluck delicate finger sandwiches from the three-tiered tray and remember

Lake Worth, which officially has 35,000 residents, wants federal approval to do a special count because so many immigrants live there—one official estimates about 12,000. (Photograph courtesy of Bill Ingram/*The Palm Beach Post*)

which fork to use and how to put their silverware in the "resting" position and what to do with the linen napkin when you have to go to the bathroom.

"Thank you, Miss Hinson, for this wonderful day," the boy who was born in Haiti but has lived here eight years says when he leads off the toasts. Brave boy. Both ways.

Rebecca Hinson is the art teacher.

Once she showed them slides of the White House and asked them who owned it.

They said George Washington or maybe George Bush, and she told them no, "The people own it. You own it."

She did not get into details about legal residency or citizenship, which some of the children have and some—obviously not.

Once she brought in a wooden sled and said, "This is why you want to get a good education. So you can get a good job. Then one day, you can fly your families up to New England on a winter holiday and let them sled down the big, snowy hills."

And today?

High tea, as in Britain.

She bought the silverware at Kmart.

She uses her own fine pitcher.

She taps the CD player and out comes Dan Troxell on the piano: *In a Cottage Garden.*

The PTA ladies help sponsor the tea.

Carole Douglass is an old "Lake Worthy" who grew up on K Street. She went to South Grade in the '60s, back when it was an all-white school—and she still has the first-grade class picture to prove it. Margarita Spooner? She came from Cuba at the age of 8.

An immigrant.

When she looks down the tea table, she thinks, "That's me 40 years ago."

The Technicolor Cinema in Alphabet City

Like any immigrant town, this one has its own lexicon, and it's not always pretty. Guatemalans, especially the new arrivals, are "walking ATMs," counted on to carry the day's pay in their pockets or tucked into their shirt sleeves and pants hems.

No matter how they hide it, somebody usually tries to take it—and this is "Guat bashing."

Visually, the place is a movie, shimmering with cinematic moments and full-out chase scenes.

Sometimes, on the south end of town, it seems half the population runs when a certain model green truck cruises through.

It is possible, too, though hard to believe, that you can be stopped, questioned and escorted back to your mother's home to retrieve your birth certificate—even when you are Puerto Rican, a citizen, and simply on your way to Walgreens to pick up your blood pressure medication.

"True story," says Carmen Munoz, 49, who was cutting down Sixth Avenue near J Street when the Border Patrol popped out.

"I had just picked up my groceries, steak and instant mashed potatoes. They made me feel just like a criminal."

As for cinema?

Try a Sunday at the Sacred Heart Catholic Church up on North M, where a priest on loan from Guatemala packs the house during the 1 p.m. Spanish Mass—and after every homily, a Kanjobal speaker scurries up front to provide an interpretation to the indigenous faithful.

When Mass ends, hundreds of worshippers file out—and hundreds more file in.

For the 3 o'clock in Creole.

Three New Words: 'I Like America'

6 p.m. Put dinner in a pot on the stove. Time for English class.

Outside, a brilliant evening sky, a robin's egg. Inside the school, the whir of a pencil sharpener, the whisper of Creole, the slang-twang of Spanglish.

Walk blocks to get here. Look over your shoulder after the big shooting on B Street. Haitian gangs, the police said. Everybody's scared, the insiders and the outsiders, too. The American-borns and the foreigners. All the people who live along the alphabet streets.

Downstairs, it's Beginning class. Say "Hello." Say, "How are you?" Listen to the teacher's big voice boom, "TV! English! Not just Telemundo or *telenovelas!*"

Upstairs, it's harder. The teacher says read the fine print, don't just sign anything, know what you are supposed to do on the job, be a good employee, don't make crude jokes, don't say "yes" if you don't understand the question.

After a while, the stories pour out. Somebody walked the desert while pregnant. Somebody came 25 years ago on a boat. Somebody fled a *katye cho,* a "hot" neighborhood in Haiti.

Somebody has papers, and somebody does not. Somebody has a good job as a nurse's aide, somebody sweats in the fields. Somebody—no—everybody—needs English. To get ahead. Here, in this small city where 44 percent of the population speaks something else, English is a blessing.

Could be you go to the grocery store, can't find the special cleaning liquid, can't ask for it, go home empty-handed. Could be your kids speak English but you don't. Could be you feel stupid going to the high school conferences, hoping the translator is telling you everything, thinking maybe he's not, thinking maybe your son is interested in gangs, getting talked up by the leaders, and you want to ask the school, "How do I stop this?"

But you don't have the words, which is why you are here.

Beginning class: Toilet bowl. Clean. Toothbrush.

Advanced class: Do you like America? Yes! I like America!

The Hidden People and the Hurricane

It's night.

The cafeteria thumps, pounds, buzzes. Kids and parents, a May evening, an important gathering about hurricanes. Yes, Lord, they remember Wilma. Never again, please God. So here they are, the Creole speakers, the Kanjobal speakers, the Mam speakers, the Spanish speakers, the English speakers, the school staff, the hurricane experts, the health experts, the translators.

The city's fire chief stands. It won't happen again, he says. Not like Wilma.

Next time, the city will be ready. Next time, it won't take so long to get the basics: water, ice, canned food, electricity. Because—frankly—we didn't know you were here.

And this is true. Carolyn Waite will tell you.

She runs the Beacon Center outreach programs based at the school— English classes, computer classes, parenting seminars and a teen program—and since she is an immigrant herself, having come here during the turbulent '60s from Jamaica with her minister father, she knows what it is to be an outsider: "I still remember what my alien card looked like. That's what they called it. 'Alien.'"

Now she's an insider.

After Hurricane Wilma swept through in 2005, she picked up her cell phone and tried to call her families. So did a school guidance counselor, Diana Regalado-Borges, and the principal, and anybody else who had access to a phone list.

The lights were out, the city sealed shut.

And where were the families? Sealed shut, too, inside their homes, supplies dwindling, lights out, plumbing down, outsiders in.

"They were too afraid to come out," Waite says. "They wouldn't even go to the church for the Red Cross supplies. So we got the Beacon bus and we went to the fairgrounds and we loaded it up, and then we came back and rounded that corner—and just then, one of the ladies peeked out from the pink house, and she saw us.

"We barely had time to park the bus before they came running. They were coming from everywhere. These people, they had no way of getting anywhere, and nobody knew they were here—this whole hidden population—and they came up to the bus and took their babies out of their strollers, and loaded the strollers up with ice, and then they pushed the strollers home and carried their babies on their shoulders.

"It was a refugee scene."

He Finds His Voice in the Land of Starbucks

Now, two years after Wilma, the hidden people are not so hidden anymore, even in the heart of town on a sunny day.

Up at Starbucks—Lake and L—it's busy.

Nobody notices the ponytailed blonde with the pink cell phone and the (very) short shorts that say, by way of status symbol or advertisement, Trump Spa. She heads for the counter, orders, pushes out again, passing a tall guy carrying an expensive briefcase and speaking what sounds like perfect Parisian French.

And then the line advances.

"I like an icee coffee."

"Iced coffee?"

"Yes, icee coffee."

He is a small, brown-skinned man, immediately identifiable as Guatemalan, and by entering Starbucks and giving his order to the front counter, he has successfully navigated foreign territory. Or, looked at another way, he has just invaded the homeland.

Whatever the case, he might have walked away, defeated, without his iced coffee, as so many immigrants do when tongue-tied, but this man is a successful transcultural traveler, a nervous fellow, surely, wiping his sweating hands on his workday khakis, but still, when he leaves, victorious, his step springs with confidence as he walks home through the alphabet streets.

A, B, C, J, K, L.

And so on.

That's the broadcast from Alphabet City. You can't turn it off.

This is the first story in a five-day series that explored the changing face of Lake Worth, Fla. To read more, go to www.poynter.org/bnw2009/ resources.

BEHIND the STORY

Lessons Learned

By Christine Evans

Well, somehow I always have to learn the same old lessons over again: Be persistent, never give up, don't call or write when you can just show up.

Believe in your story. Wear your soles down. Go for one more interview, read one more report, find one more person who will tell you how it is.

All that's true, and if I were a quicker study I might not have to keep learning the same stuff over and over again. But for this series on immigration—specifically, the impact it has had on one small American town, Lake Worth, Fla.—I came back to a lesson I learned years ago while growing up in a racially sensitive time on the edge of the South.

It is this: If you want to know how somebody lives, ask.

If you want to know who they are and where they came from and what they care about, ask them that, too. And if you want the truth, you cannot dance around the delicate topics—race and culture and background—and buff up the questions until they have a high sheen. You have to lay everything on the line.

Rule No. 1 for this kind of reporting is to just show up. Early, late, often, always. Don't call ahead unless absolutely necessary; simply slip in the back door with a notepad in your pocket.

For this story and others in the series, I dug so deep into town life that my family thought I had moved there. I sat through meetings, hung out on street corners, took my place in the pews. I even got myself invited to Miss Leona White's 76th birthday party.

In the business, they call this immersion reporting, but I prefer to think of it as throwing yourself out into the world with your notebook open. In the early stages, it does not pay to be too discerning; you have to be wide-eyed and interested in nearly everything. Later, you can narrow the chase.

A few tips for the road:

Do a lot of "parking lot" interviews. These are infinitely more useful than office interviews or official interviews or press conference interviews. The parking lot interview doesn't have to be held in a parking lot. It might happen spontaneously on a sidewalk or at a bus stop. It is that glorious moment when, after you have dutifully interviewed the subject in a sit-down chat, you wander together to your cars and suddenly the other person blurts out something like, "When I was a boy in Guatemala, I saw a head on a stick."

Carry a picture of your kid/spouse/partner/pet. I usually carry wallet photos of my kids, and even though a voice in the back of my head reminded me to keep a certain reportorial distance, during this project I was not beyond pulling them out when somebody asked me about my family. People want to know who you are when they tell you stuff. It seems only fair.

Never assume the blonde woman at the PTA meeting is a soccer mom when she could be a Guatemalan immigrant who jumped trains to come north. This is a true story—and she did it with her 7-month-old baby strapped to her chest. When I attended a morning PTA meeting to scout for newly arrived immigrants to interview, she was about the last person I would have picked for a train jumper. But the world can be a small place and so it happened that she had read a story I wrote the year before about train jumping in southern Mexico. If she hadn't introduced herself to me that morning (or if I had slept in), I would have missed out on her first-person account.

When all else fails, go for coffee. But make sure the coffee shop is on location. You never know when a lady in Trump Spa shorts is going to order a vanilla latte while talking on her pink cell phone and just like that you have your first-day kicker.

Finally, take your editor to lunch—dinner if you're desperate. Before you write, you need somebody to talk to. Writing is a terrible business, so try to transfer some of your pain. You will find yourself going back again and again to your editor because producing a project is not unlike raising a child. The little beast will change and grow and rebel, and you will need help taming it.

Christine Evans got her start in journalism by interviewing Norman Mailer for a student newspaper at Amherst College. In her 10 years with The Miami Herald, *Evans shared one Pulitzer Prize and was a finalist for another. As a projects reporter for* The Palm Beach Post, *she has won two Robert F. Kennedy Journalism Awards for team investigations of pesticides and migrants.*

Chicago Tribune

Finalist: ASNE Batten Medal
Finalist: Pulitzer Prize for National Reporting

Howard Witt

Racial Demons Rear Heads

MAY 20, 2007

JENA, La.—The trouble in Jena started with the nooses. Then it rumbled along the town's jagged racial fault lines. Finally, it exploded into months of violence between blacks and whites.

Now the 3,000 residents of this small lumber and oil town deep in the heart of central Louisiana are confronting Old South racial demons many thought had long ago been put to rest.

One morning last September, students arrived at the local high school to find three hangman's nooses dangling from a tree in the courtyard.

The tree was on the side of the campus that, by long-standing tradition, had always been claimed by white students, who make up more than 80 percent of the 460 students. But a few of the school's 85 black students had decided to challenge the accepted state of things and asked school administrators if they, too, could sit beneath the tree's cooling shade.

"Sit wherever you want," school officials told them. The next day, the nooses were hanging from the branches.

African-American students and their parents were outraged and intimidated by the display, which instantly summoned memories of the mob lynchings that once terrorized blacks across the American South. Three white students were quickly identified as being responsible, and the high school principal recommended that they be expelled.

"Hanging those nooses was a hate crime, plain and simple," said Tracy Bowens, a black mother of two students at the high school who protested the incident at a school board meeting.

After some black high school students in Jena, La., sought permission from school administrators to sit under a shade tree on the "white" side of campus in September 2006, nooses were found hanging from it the next day. That summoned memories of the lynchings that once terrorized blacks across the South. Then, in late November, arsonists set fire to the central wing of the school, adding to the mounting racial tensions. (Photograph courtesy of Chris Graythen/*Chicago Tribune*)

But Jena's white school superintendent, Roy Breithaupt, ruled that the nooses were just a youthful stunt and suspended the students for three days, angering blacks who felt harsher punishments were justified.

"Adolescents play pranks," said Breithaupt, the superintendent of the LaSalle Parish school system. "I don't think it was a threat against anybody."

Yet it was after the noose incident that the violent, racially charged events that are still convulsing Jena began.

First, a series of fights between black and white students erupted at the high school over the nooses. Then, in late November, unknown arsonists set fire to the central wing of the school, which still sits in ruins. Off campus, a white youth beat up a black student who showed up at an all-white party. A few days later, another young white man pulled a shotgun on three black students at a convenience store.

Finally, on Dec. 4, a group of black students at the high school allegedly jumped a white student on his way out of the gym, knocked him unconscious and kicked him after he hit the floor. The victim—allegedly targeted because he was a friend of the students who hung the nooses and had been taunting blacks—was not seriously injured and spent only a few hours in the hospital.

But the LaSalle Parish district attorney, Reed Walters, opted to charge six black students with attempted second-degree murder and other offenses, for which they could face a maximum of 100 years in prison if convicted. All six were expelled from school.

To the defendants, their families and civil rights groups that have examined the events, the attempted murder charges brought by a white prosecutor are excessive and part of a pattern of uneven justice in the town.

The critics note, for example, that the white youth who beat the black student at the party was charged only with simple battery, while the white man who pulled the shotgun at the convenience store wasn't charged with any crime at all. But the three black youths in that incident were arrested and accused of aggravated battery and theft after they wrestled the weapon from the man—in self-defense, they said.

"There's been obvious racial discrimination in this case," said Joe Cook, executive director of the Louisiana chapter of the American Civil Liberties Union, who described Jena as a "racial powder keg" primed to ignite. "It appears the black students were singled out and targeted in this case for some unusually harsh treatment."

That's how the mother of one of the defendants sees things as well.

"They are sending a message to the white kids, 'You have committed this hate crime, you were taunting these black children, and we are going to allow you to continue doing what you are doing,'" said Caseptla Bailey, mother of Robert Bailey Jr.

Bailey, 17, is caught up in several of the Jena incidents, as both a victim and alleged perpetrator. He was the black student who was beaten at the party, and he was among the students arrested for allegedly grabbing the shotgun from the man at the convenience store. And he's one of the six students charged with attempted murder for the Dec. 4 attack.

The district attorney declined repeated requests to be interviewed for this story. But other white leaders insist there are no racial tensions in the community, which is 85 percent white and 12 percent black.

"Jena is a place that's moving in the right direction," said Mayor Murphy McMillin. "Race is not a major local issue. It's not a factor in the local people's lives."

Still others, however, acknowledge troubling racial undercurrents in a town where only 16 years ago white voters cast most of their ballots for

David Duke, the former Ku Klux Klan leader who ran unsuccessfully for Louisiana governor.

"I've lived here most of my life, and the one thing I can state with absolutely no fear of contradiction is that LaSalle Parish is awash in racism—true racism," a white Pentecostal preacher, Eddie Thompson, wrote in an essay he posted on the Internet. "Here in the piney woods of central Louisiana...racism and bigotry are such a part of life that most of the citizens do not even recognize it."

The lone black member of the school board agrees.

"There's no doubt about it—whites and blacks are treated differently here," said Melvin Worthington, who was the only school board member to vote against expelling the six black students charged in the beating case. "The white kids should have gotten more punishment for hanging those nooses. If they had, all the stuff that followed could have been avoided."

And the troubles at the high school are not over yet.

On May 10, police arrested Justin Barker, 17, the white victim of the Dec. 4 beating. He was alleged to have a rifle loaded with 13 bullets stashed behind the seat of his pickup truck parked in the school lot. Barker told police he had forgotten it was there and had no intention of using it.

BEHIND the STORY

Lessons Learned

By Howard Witt

Let's be honest: As newspaper storytellers—especially storytellers usually confined to 1,000 words—we love concise narratives with virtuous good guys and evil bad guys, sympathetic victims and vicious attackers, dramatic causes with ensuing effects.

Such clear-cut morality plays abounded on the civil rights beat across the American South in the 1950s and 1960s, when rabid Klan members were murdering civil rights workers, Jim Crow sheriffs were unleashing dogs on peaceful marchers and Rosa Parks refused to give up her seat on a Montgomery, Ala., bus.

Half a century later, America is still struggling with civil rights and racial justice. But the stories today are often much more subtle, nuanced and complex. And neither the good nor the evil is quite so unvarnished.

That was certainly what I discovered in the small central Louisiana town of Jena when I first journeyed there in early May 2007. Alan Bean, a Baptist preacher and Texas civil rights activist, had seen an earlier story I had written about racial injustice in the town of Paris, Texas, and suggested I check out what was happening in Jena. What Bean told me sounded too outrageous—and too beguilingly simple—to be true.

Some white students at the high school had threatened black students by hanging nooses in a tree at the high school, Bean related. Some black students had responded by jumping a white student. And now the local prosecutor had charged the black students with attempted murder.

Those were, indeed, some of the dots, as I learned over the course of my reporting. But connecting them—for the first nationally published account of the Jena story—was not nearly so simple.

The nooses, it turned out, had been hung three months before the beating incident, suggesting that the events weren't necessarily related. Moreover, school administrators had determined that the nooses were a harmless prank. Witnesses to the school beating indicated that the white youth had been attacked by at least six black students, knocked unconscious and kicked while he was down. And Jena officials universally insisted that there were no racial tensions anywhere in the remote lumber and oil town of 3,000, which is 85 percent white and 12 percent black.

What had appeared to be a straightforward civil rights story was looking decidedly muddy. Midway through my reporting visit to Jena, I glumly returned to my hotel room one evening, second-guessing my entire trip. "Some black kids beat up a white kid and face punishment for it in an anonymous southern town," I thought. "Why is this a story that would interest the nation?"

The answer lay in more reporting. And embracing, rather than avoiding, the complexities.

In the course of more than three dozen interviews and a review of records at the local courthouse, I learned that the school beating was indeed connected to the nooses—not directly, but as one of a series of racial fights that kept breaking out after the nooses had been hung. When whites attacked blacks, the local authorities rarely pursued the cases aggressively. But when blacks attacked whites, the offenders faced the most serious possible felonies.

The attempted-murder charges brought against the six black youths implicated in the school beating looked particularly excessive, considering that the white victim didn't have to be hospitalized for his injuries and felt well enough to attend a school ceremony just a few hours after the incident.

As for the nooses, they appeared a day after an African-American student had asked school administrators for permission to sit beneath a shade tree traditionally used only by whites. Black parents did not regard those nooses as a mere youthful prank. They felt the white students who hung them should have been expelled from school for resurrecting a symbol so resonant of the lynchings that once terrorized blacks across the South. But when parents tried to address the school board about the issue, they were ignored.

And the town itself, far from being a placid backwater, was a simmering cauldron of racial animus.

For example, when I sat in my car in the high school parking lot (the principal would not grant me permission to enter school buildings), I witnessed the de facto segregation of the school courtyard during the lunch hour—blacks on one side and whites on the other.

My interviews with black Jena residents revealed how deeply they resented the fact that many local businesspeople would not hire them and followed them around when they came into their stores. Meanwhile, some white residents freely peppered their conversations with racial epithets.

And a bit of Web searching revealed that a majority of those whites once voted for a former Ku Klux Klan leader who ran unsuccessfully for Louisiana governor.

The story I finally wrote worked because of those many nuances, not in spite of them. And my account, relayed on hundreds of Internet blogs and in thousands of e-mails, was clear enough to help inspire more than 20,000 demonstrators to march through Jena in September 2007, in the largest U.S. civil rights protest in decades.

Howard Witt is the Southwest bureau chief of the Chicago Tribune, *based in Houston, Texas. He joined the paper as a summer intern in 1982, and during his 25-year career there, he has been a national corre-spondent, foreign correspondent and editor. He also was editor-in-chief of* Washington City Paper *for two years. For his 2007 stories on racial injustice, Witt was named a finalist for the Pulitzer Prize in national reporting and won the Nieman Foundation's Taylor Family Award for Fairness in Newspapers and the American Judicature Society's Toni House Award for coverage of the American legal system.*

PART 7

Looking Beyond Conflict: Reporting on Human Connections

Looking Beyond Conflict

Conflict often drives journalism. And though critics complain about too much negative news, journalists are trained to look for conflict, whether the topic is the city budget, factory layoffs or a murder.

The stories in this chapter, though, cause us to reconsider. They are not about fighting or opposition, even though two of them were written in a war zone. On the surface, not a lot happens in these stories—there's no "gotcha," no big, breaking news. Instead they focus on how people treat each other: how they go out of their way to help and honor others, even putting themselves at risk to do so.

At first, such stories may appear too small to write about. As *Washington Post* reporter David Finkel said of his stories from Iraq, "Reduced to budget lines at a news meeting, they would have seemed pretty boring: A U.S. soldier in Iraq wonders what to do about a body in a septic tank. An Iraqi father seeks help for his injured daughter."

Likewise, for Lane DeGregory's story in the *St. Petersburg Times*: A mailman cuts people's lawns.

And for Kevin Cullen's columns in *The Boston Globe*: A mentally disabled man tries to help people who lost their homes in a fire. A man who was once blind goes to a party for his eye surgeon.

Yet these stories are powerful and memorable, perhaps because they focus on small actions so often overlooked—things that appear mundane and insignificant, but reveal something essential to our humanity.

The first challenge with stories like this is to find them. The second, to write them in a way that reflects their significance. In the essay that follows his stories, Finkel told me some of his methods for identifying and reporting them:

"Go along. See what happens. Let the story emerge. Look for moments of human decency," he said, "and when writing about them, try to write about them with decency in mind."

—Steve Myers, co-editor of *Best Newspaper Writing*

The Washington Post

■ Finalist: Nondeadline Writing

David Finkel

A Grisly Problem, Grateful Iraqis and a Grim Outlook

APRIL 25, 2007

BAGHDAD—The soldiers called him Bob, and for the past several weeks, until Tuesday morning, he was the biggest obstacle to the success of an important mission in a small but crucial corner of the Iraq war.

"We can't get anybody to get Bob out. No one wants to do it," Army Maj. Brent Cummings, executive officer of the 2nd Battalion, 16th Infantry Regiment, 4th Infantry Brigade Combat Team, 1st Infantry Division, said with worry one recent morning as Bob's story began unfolding. Cummings was looking at an aerial photograph of an area in east Baghdad called Kamaliya, where there was an abandoned spaghetti factory with a hole in the courtyard, a hole in which some of his soldiers had discovered Bob.

Bob: It's shorthand for "bobbin' in the float," Cummings explained.

Float: It's shorthand for "two to three feet of raw sewage," he further explained.

Bobbin' in the float is shorthand, then, for yet another lesson in the comedy, absurdity and tragedy that is any moment in this war.

Bob was found as a result of the new strategy of trying to secure Baghdad by temporarily increasing the number of troops and moving them into neighborhood outposts. After the soldiers identified the spaghetti factory as the best place from which to secure poor, rough, dirty, insurgent-ridden Kamaliya, they began clearing the factory in order to move in.

One day, in one area, they found 16 rocket-propelled grenades, three antitank grenades, 11 hand grenades and 21 mortar shells. Another day, they found 14 more mortar shells. Another day, they found the makings of three roadside bombs. Another day, they found a square metal cover in the courtyard that they thought might be booby-trapped. Ever so carefully, they lifted it and found themselves peering down into the factory's septic tank at Bob.

The body, floating, was in a billowing, once-white shirt. The toes were gone. The fingers were gone. The head, separated and floating next to the body, had a gunshot hole in the face.

The body, it was quickly decided, would have to be removed before the 120 soldiers could move in. "It's a morale issue. Who wants to live over a dead body?" Cummings said. "And part of it is a moral issue, too. I mean he was somebody's son, and maybe husband, and for dignity's sake, well, it cheapens us to leave him there. I mean even calling him Bob is disrespectful. I don't know. It's the world we live in."

He paused.

"I'd like to put him in a final resting place," he said, "as opposed to a final floating place."

But how? That was the problem. No one wanted to touch Bob. Not the soldiers. Not the Iraqi police. No one.

Days passed. The need for the soldiers in Kamaliya increased. Bob floated on. One day the skull sank from view. Another day a local Iraqi speculated that there might be more bodies in the septic tank, that Bob might simply be the one on top.

Finally, with no easy solution in sight, Cummings decided to go see Bob for himself.

How easy is anything in Iraq, such as a short drive to a spaghetti factory? A combat plan was drawn up, just in case. A convoy of five Humvees was assembled. Body armor was strapped on. Earplugs were pushed in. Protective eyeglasses were lowered into place. Off the convoy went, slowly, never exceeding 15 mph, because slow and steady is the best way to find a roadside bomb before it explodes, unless it is a bomb with a particular kind of trigger that is best defeated by flying pedal to metal. Yard by yard, decision by decision, the convoy advanced, past trash bags that might be hiding bombs, along dirt roads under which might be buried bombs, and now past something unseen that, just after the last Humvee in the convoy passed by, exploded.

No damage. No injuries. Just some noise and smoke in the air. The convoy kept going, now past a dead water buffalo, on its back, grossly swollen, one more thing in this part of Baghdad on the verge of exploding, and now the Humvees stopped against a high wall, on the other side of which was a yellowish building topped by a torn tin roof banging around in the wind.

"The spaghetti factory," Cummings announced. Soon he and Capt. Jeff Jager, commander of the company that would be moving to the factory, were staring into the septic tank, and suddenly Cummings had an idea.

"Lye and bleach and sanitize and cover it up," he said. "We bring our chaplain here, and we'll say some words and mark it."

Easy. Done.

Jager shook his head. "I think you gotta clean it out," he said. "I mean we're gonna have some heartache moving into a building that's got a dead body in a sewage septic tank."

"Yeah," Cummings said, realizing Jager was right. "We want to do right."

"Arabic culture, you know?" Jager said. "They bury their dead in 24 hours."

"I mean someone has disgraced him as bad as you can possibly disgrace a human being," Cummings said. "And there's not a playbook that we can go to that says when you open it up: Here's how you remove a body from a septic tank."

"The one contractor I brought up here, he was willing to do everything here, but he wanted nothing to do with that," Jager said. "I asked him how much it would take for him ┐   t of there, and he said, 'You couldn't pay me ┐

"The Army h   our body," Cummings said.
"If it were a U.S.   here in a heartbeat."

"We could dr┐   ut ourselves," Jager said.
"But—"

"But what soldie┐   re to do that?" Cummings said.

They continued t┐

"Lye and bleach,"┐   ɔ that, and then he and
Jager went on a tour ɔ   ger explained that the
factory had been aban┐   he owner—a Sunni—
was apparently murder┐   told them by phone
that he had tried to com┐   ɔm his home in west
Baghdad and had been s┐   , that "we know the
militia has used this as a t┐ e are "reports that
they used this for torture ɛ   bors have told his
soldiers about "the screams┐   eing beaten."

This is where the dining f┐   Cummings. This
is where the soldiers would s┐

They stepped outside the front gate, onto the street. Surrounded by soldiers and engineers, they walked down the street to plot a route for concrete blast walls that would be brought in by truck to encircle the factory. They turned a corner to keep plotting the route, and that was when Cummings saw a mud-brick hovel practically attached to the factory wall like a barnacle, and a shirtless man outside the shack who struggled to cover himself as the soldiers came through his gate.

Through an interpreter, Cummings began to explain why they were there, that U.S. soldiers would soon be moving into the spaghetti factory, that a wall was going to be built.

I will leave, the man interrupted, shaking.

"No," Cummings said, asking the interpreter to explain again what he had said.

I will leave, the man said again, explaining that he and his family had come to this little bit of land because they had been uprooted, that they had been here two years, that they meant no harm, that they had nowhere else to go, and then, at last hearing the interpreter, he said, I don't have to leave?

"No," Cummings said.

I don't have to leave? the man said again, and then, as his shaking subsided, and his rush of words slowed, his family emerged from the shack. Child after child. An old woman. More children. And finally, a young woman, very pregnant, who stood in the doorway, trying to push her dirty hair off her dirty face with her dirty hands as she looked at the soldiers, at first breathing nervously, then easing into a slight smile as she heard the man saying thank you for saving them from the terrorists, for enclosing them in a wall, for allowing them to stay.

"You're welcome. And thank you for allowing us in," Cummings said, and soon after that, with the gratitude of a living Iraqi as fixed in his mind now as the horror of one who had been tortured and killed, his visit to see Bob ended.

There is such decency in the country, he said, back in his office. That was why, more than ever, he wanted Bob removed and given some kind of proper burial. "I would hope someone would do the same for my body. And for any human being," he said. "Otherwise, we're not human."

That was Monday.

And then came Tuesday, and a phone call in the morning from Jager, who had received a call from the factory owner's brother, who had received a call from someone who lived near the factory.

Cummings hung up.

"The spaghetti factory has been blown up," he said.

It was only a first report, he cautioned, but the report said that there were a dozen men, and they were armed, and they wore masks, and the explosion was huge.

"Gone."

Throughout the day, there were attempts to verify this, but even in Iraq some days are harder than others. The wind was up, so much so that most helicopters were grounded, as was most aerial surveillance, other than a fighter jet, circling high, whose pilot reported that some of the factory appeared to have been destroyed.

How extensive was the damage?

As of Tuesday night, no one was able to say for sure.

What about the nervous man in the flimsy house?

Nothing.

And his dozen children?

Nothing.

And the pregnant woman who was able to finally manage a smile?

Nothing.

And the plan to move into Kamaliya? Would the factory still become the outpost?

"I hope so," Cummings said.

And Bob?

Cummings shook his head. Bob, he said, was no longer the biggest obstacle.

'Izzy?…Bring Your Daughter Here'

JULY 27, 2007

By David Finkel

BAGHDAD—An hour after a car bomb exploded in downtown Baghdad on Thursday, killing at least 25 people, wounding at least 110 and destroying an apartment building, a phone call begging for help came to an Army officer in eastern Baghdad. It was from a man named Izzy who works as an interpreter for the U.S. military and whose calm voice was now filled with panic.

His apartment was in ruins, he said. One of his two daughters had been badly injured. Something had pierced her head when their apartment disintegrated. He had taken her to a hospital filled with the injured, but overwhelmed doctors had said there was nothing they could do, that she needed more help than they could give, and so he was standing on a street with his bleeding daughter at his side, afraid that she was going to die.

"The only hope you have is to get her to an American hospital?" said Maj. Brent Cummings, executive officer of the 2nd Battalion, 16th Infantry Regiment, 1st Infantry Division, for which Izzy is an interpreter. He was repeating what Izzy had just said. Izzy started to answer. The cell phone went dead. "Izzy?" Cummings said. "Izzy?"

How do moments of decency occur in a place such as Baghdad, in a war such as this war? Perhaps by what several officers on an Army base in eastern Baghdad decided to do next.

"Izzy," Cummings said after dialing 5, 10, 15 times and finally getting through. "Bring your daughter here."

It was a simple idea. The base where Izzy works has a first-rate medical facility.

"Oh, thank you, sir. Thank you, sir," Izzy said.

And that's when things got complicated.

Any Iraqi hurt by the American military is eligible for American medical care. But this wasn't an American bomb, and so none of the injured was entitled to American care—including, it seemed, Izzy's daughter.

But what Cummings had in mind was Izzy's previous life, before he was an interpreter. He had lived in New York City. He had worked there. And he had had a daughter.

A daughter who is an American citizen.

Could an American citizen living in Baghdad, who was injured by a non-American bomb, receive medical care in an American military medical facility?

Cummings didn't know. Neither did several doctors he got in touch with. He wasn't even sure which of the daughters was injured—the one born in New York, or the one born in Baghdad, who wasn't an American citizen. He tried to call a lawyer, but there was no answer.

So he called Izzy back.

"Izzy—okay—where is your daughter that is from the United States?" Again the phone went dead.

"Is your daughter from the United States with you right now?... Is she hurt?... Which daughter is hurt?... Is she on the street with you?... Okay, is your U.S. citizen daughter with you?... You can't what?... What?" Next he called one of the officers in charge of the base, whose approval would be needed for someone not in the military to get onto the facility.

"Yes. I'm sure we can produce a birth certificate," he said, wondering about a report that the bomb had set the apartment building on fire.

Next he called the battalion's physician and told him to be ready to treat one female, or possibly two females, ages unknown, one an American citizen, in a matter of minutes.

Next he called Izzy to see how close he was to the base, and Izzy, his voice even more panicked than before, said he wasn't close at all, that he was still on the street, still next to his daughter, trying to find a taxi.

And then began a series of calls to Cummings from people who had heard through the grapevine that the battalion had injured soldiers from the downtown bombing; no, make that dead soldiers; no, make that a roadside bomb.

"No," Cummings said to every caller. "There are no injured coalition forces. It is an Iraqi—an Iraqi American—who was hurt. It is the interpreter's daughter."

Back to Izzy.

Still trying to find a taxi.

Back to another caller: "I don't know the extent of the injuries.... I don't know if he's even in a cab yet.... I don't know if they're going to make it here before curfew."

Now Izzy was calling. They were in a taxi. They were on the bridge, two minutes from the base.

Cummings hurried to the gate. It was dark now. The base ambulance pulled up. The guards said there's no way a taxi could get any closer than it had gotten, which was somewhere out of sight. "Get a litter," Cummings called to the ambulance crew. Sprinting, he went out the gate, passing coils of razor wire and blast walls, and then stopping when he saw Izzy walking toward him, illuminated by the headlights of the ambulance.

Izzy's clothing was filthy.

Next to him was his wife, who was crying.

On his other side was one of his daughters, the one born in New York, who appeared to be uninjured.

And in front of them all, walking slowly, was a young girl with shiny purple sandals, blood on her bluejeans and a bandage over the left side of her face.

This was the non-American daughter, the one born in Baghdad, who began crying as she was carried into the medical facility. In Arabic, she cried out for her father, who had to remain in the waiting area.

"Was it a car bomb?" Cummings asked.

"No, sir," Izzy said. "It was two car bombs."

And then he said nothing more, not until one of the doctors came into the waiting area to tell him that his daughter was going to be all right.

"Thank you, sir," he managed to say, and when he was unable to say anything else, he bowed his head, and then sat, and then wiped his eyes, and then followed the doctor into the treatment area, where his Iraqi daughter was surrounded by American doctors and medics.

What do the rules say?

At that moment, anyway, no one seemed concerned one way or another: not the doctors, not the family, and not Cummings, who stood at the very same spot he had been at a few weeks before when the patient was a soldier of his who had been injured by a roadside bomb and had died in front of Cummings' eyes.

Again, Cummings found himself watching.

The injuries to the girl were serious. There was a deep cut across her cheek, and, worse, something that had gone into the left side of her fore-head and was embedded in her skull. Her father held her hand until the doctors swaddled her in a sheet, making sure to wrap her arms tightly. Her mother closed her eyes. The doctors leaned in. It took a while, and at the worst of it the little girl couldn't remain quiet, but then the doctors were showing her what they had found—a solid piece of glass that was nearly two inches long—and soon after that she was smiling.

The glass was part of an apartment that no longer existed, in a part of Baghdad where the sounds Thursday night were of mourning.

But in this part of Baghdad, the sounds were of a mother who no longer had a home kissing her Iraqi daughter's cheek, and a father who no longer had a home kissing his Iraqi daughter's hand, and a little girl who no longer had a home saying something in Arabic that caused her parents to smile, and Cummings saying quietly in English, "Man, I haven't felt this good since I got to this hellhole."

BEHIND the STORY

Finding the Quiet Tales

By Steve Myers

David Finkel went to Iraq and found kindness.

He didn't go looking for it, and he didn't find it everywhere—mere moments among the horrors of war. But as he followed a U.S. Army battalion to Iraq as part of the "troop surge" in early 2007, he took note of what moved him, and he wrote about it.

That's how he got the story about "Bob" and the abandoned spaghetti factory. That's how he described the efforts of an Army major to get medical help for an Iraqi man's daughter.

David Finkel

Finkel was in Iraq under unusual circumstances. He was on leave from *The Washington Post* to work on a book about the battalion, but he agreed to write occasional stories for the paper if something arose.

His stories stand out because they don't focus on counterinsurgency strategy or the battleground, though war is the backdrop. They highlight how people treat one another in such an environment.

"What surprised me," Finkel said in a telephone interview, "was the things that I had emotional reactions to over there. And the reactions were strong enough that I wanted them to guide my writing.... In the middle of the worst—the very worst place I've ever been in—just the small moments of normalcy, or intensive normalcy, or decency or intensive decency."

"These were small moments," he said, "but they're moments that felt very large to me because they represented the very best and the very worst of human behavior."

Finkel described how he reported these stories: He tagged along with soldiers as something unfolded, not knowing if a story would emerge. While he was reporting, he looked and listened for things that piqued his interest—an insightful comment, a smile, even the name "Bob." He didn't divorce his reporting from his emotions.

The story about the spaghetti factory came about because Finkel was listening to Maj. Brent Cummings talk about someone or something named "Bob" and asked about it. "Once I heard the phrase 'bobbin' in the float,'" Finkel said, "I laughed and I was sort of attracted to the idea of following this through based on that."

Before the Army could set up an outpost at the spaghetti factory, Bob would have to be removed. Cumming's explanation struck Finkel as interesting, coming from an Army commander tasked with calming a violent Baghdad neighborhood: "It's a morale issue. Who wants to live over a dead body?" Cummings said. "And part of it is a moral issue, too. I mean he was somebody's son, and maybe husband, and for dignity's sake, well, it cheapens us to leave him there."

So when Cummings went to check out the factory and the anonymous, headless corpse, Finkel asked if he could come along. "Off we went on this strange journey where I got to show how difficult anything is to do in Baghdad."

A scene from that day stayed with Finkel. The soldiers came across a hovel attached to the outside of the factory wall, and to the surprise of the Iraqi man who had settled his family there, Cummings told him to stay. As the man thanked the soldiers—and Cummings thanked the man in return—a young, pregnant woman revealed a slight smile.

At the end of the day, Finkel had interesting notes, but no real story. There was no ending—until the next day, when Cummings got a phone call and told Finkel the factory had been blown up.

"When he said that," Finkel said, "I was wondering about the woman in the doorway, wondering what had happened to them—wondering what had happened to the whole thing. And what had been funny and absurd suddenly just in a second had become so seemingly tragic."

"Why did it take that final event to make it seem like a story?" he wondered in an e-mail. "I'm not exactly sure, but I suspect it had to do less with the violence of the final act and more with all that had preceded it."

His story relies on those things that gave him pause.

"What I thought I would try to do, then, is to see if I could write a story not only that would include [those moments], but through the structure, they would be moments to arrive at—so that the reader might have the same reaction in reading about it as I did while observing it."

Finkel's tactics were similar in reporting the story about Izzy's daughter. The story shows the aftermath of a car bomb, not on the macro level with a casualty count or a description of the disaster, but by chronicling the efforts to help one person.

All those quotes in the story? Finkel listened as Cummings got the first call and made all the others. Finkel followed the major as he went out to meet Izzy's family and watched the family emerge, illuminated by headlights.

"The turning point for me was when Brent Cummings asked, 'Was it a car bomb?' and Izzy answered, 'No, sir. It was two car bombs,'" Finkel said in an e-mail. He was struck by the man's desire to give the correct answer even in those circumstances.

"It's hard to explain, but the quiet and respectful way he said that caused a strong and immediate emotional reaction. I guess it's because we're not moved by the sad event itself as much as the dignified ways that people in such moments sometimes react and behave."

These stories were not the news of the day from Iraq—they weren't intended to be. "Not exactly the stuff of classic war stories," he said in an e-mail. "Nothing gigantic or world-altering happened.

"But their success shows that there's plenty of room for quieter stories in between the loud extremes that we often look to and rely on."

David Finkel has worked at The Washington Post *since 1990, reporting from Africa, Asia, Central America, Europe, Iraq, Afghanistan and throughout the United States. His awards include a 2006 Pulitzer Prize for explanatory reporting for stories about U.S.-funded democracy efforts in Yemen, a Robert F. Kennedy Journalism Award in 2001 for a series about worldwide patterns of illegal migration and a Sigma Delta Chi award in 1999 for his reporting from Kosovo. Before joining the* Post, *he was a staff writer for the* St. Petersburg Times *and the* Tallahassee Democrat.

St. Petersburg Times

Winner: Nondeadline Writing

Lane DeGregory

Special Delivery

DEC. 11, 2007

On his day off, the mailman returns to his route.

He drives a beat-up Cherokee with a homemade trailer hitched to the bumper, parks in front of a little blue house on a corner lot tangled with weeds.

He carries no mailbag. He has nothing to deliver. Except his time.

The mailman unlocks his trailer and rolls a red lawn mower onto the yard. He tugs a battered ball cap over his sandy hair and wades into the weeds.

"This is Jack's house," says the mailman. It all started at Jack's house.

Eric Wills' postal route takes him on a 10-mile hike through the center of the city.

He starts with businesses along Central Avenue, but most of his route is residential. The neighborhoods are mixed, racially and economically. Immaculate two-story homes tower over boarded-up bungalows.

Wills, 30, has been walking the same streets for six years. When he was offered a better route, closer to his home in the Northeast Park area of St. Petersburg, he refused. Somewhere along these cracked sidewalks he found his path.

These are his people: all 480.

He knows who's on vacation, whose in-laws have moved in, who gets the best catalogs, the most bills. When mail starts coming addressed just to Mrs., he knows there's no longer a Mr.

He delivers directly to each house—climbs those steps, stands on those porches. Elderly residents call their thanks through mail slots.

For some, Wills is the only person who ever comes to the door.

While dispatching the mail two summers ago, Eric Wills decided it was time to dispatch with the overgrown grass. (Photograph courtesy of Willie J. Allen Jr./*St. Petersburg Times*)

Ask him about the people on his route and he'll tell you about Miss Lucille, 86, who worked on Navy ships during World War II; and Miss Betty, 83, whose Irish wolfhound weighs more than she does.

And he'll talk about Jack and his overgrown lawn.

* * *

Iron banisters flank the front steps of Jack's little blue house. Two summers ago, they were strangled with vines. To get the mail to the front door, Wills had to fight through a jungle.

The mailman didn't know much about Jack, except that he was old and seldom got out. A frail-looking girlfriend who didn't seem to speak English lived with him.

For weeks, the mailman struggled through the thicket, silently cursing the man who wouldn't mow his yard. One day, he heard a voice. His conscience? God?

Someone should mow that yard!

Me.

When Wills' letter bag was empty, he drove home and loaded the lawn mower into the back of his Cherokee.

Then he returned to the middle of his mail route.

He knocked on Jack's door, said he wanted to cut the yard. Just to help. No charge. "That yard is the least of my worries," the old man barked.

So Wills mowed that corner lot. Two weeks later, he mowed it again. Even after the old man moved into a nursing home, the mailman kept mowing his yard. As long as Jack's girlfriend was getting the mail, the mailman would look after the lawn.

For two years, Wills has been cutting Jack's lawn. That yard led to another, and another, and another....

* * *

On the Monday after Thanksgiving, Wills pours gas into the push mower in Jack's yard and bends to pull the cord. The ancient engine chokes to life.

Wills is tall, with broad shoulders. His calves are thick knots from hiking his route, from pushing that mower on his day off. He longs for a rider, or at least a commercial-grade push model. But with the price of gas these days, he can barely afford to fill his tank.

He turns the mower to the sidewalk, shoves his wire-rim glasses higher on his nose. As he starts to cut, a car pulls up and a dark-haired woman gets out.

"Aren't you the mailman?" she asks.

Wills nods and shuts off the mower.

"My mother lives here. Jack's girlfriend?" says the woman. "Didn't you get her note?"

* * *

In time, word spread about the mowing mailman. Much of it, Wills spread himself.

Once he started seeing overgrown yards not as eyesores but as a sign someone needed help, he began knocking on doors along his route. He told churches about his service. Other letter carriers sent referrals.

Wills cuts 15 yards now—for free. In the winter, he comes every two weeks; in summer, he tries to make it weekly. His record is eight yards in a day.

He works alone, in silence, except for the hum of the mower. No iPod or headphones intrude. He says he thinks about nothing. Everything. Mowing, he says, gives him peace.

Several years ago, Wills hurt his foot playing pickup basketball. Every step was agony. He worried he'd have to give up his postal route. So he prayed. And God healed him, he says.

Eric Wills turns from the mail to the lawn this day at the home of Elizabeth Krupa in the Euclid–St. Paul neighborhood of St. Petersburg. (Photograph courtesy of Willie J. Allen Jr./*St. Petersburg Times*)

He had been searching for a way to give back. But until he got engulfed in Jack's yard, he wasn't sure how. Now he knows: His calling smells like grass.

"It's just my little way of making a difference," he says. Some of these folks wish they could get out and mow; many can't afford $100 a month for a lawn service. They sit at home, watching through their windows while things get worse.

"A yard is a reflection of the person who lives there," Wills says. "So why not help them feel better?"

Lucille Formanek, 86, calls Wills "a blessing from heaven." A self-described old maid, she has lived alone since her mother died. "He's such a nice, strong young man."

Wills and his brother built a trailer to haul lawn gear. They painted a stick man on the side, mowing around a huge brown cross. Sprayed-on letters say, "Lawns for the Lord."

But the mailman's ministry includes more than mowing.

He rented a bush hog to clear an aged man's five lots; carried out garbage for a retired nun—then paved a path to her garbage bin; dug up azaleas for a single mom; moved heavy planters for a widow; brought his 7-year-old daughter to play piano for a lonely old lady. Recently he replaced a lightbulb for an elderly woman who said she hadn't been able to read her thermostat for weeks.

"In all that time, I was the only person who'd come to her door," Wills said. "What if I hadn't come?"

* * *

The little blue house has a postage stamp porch. Shaggy shrubs fan across the mailbox. Usually, Jack's girlfriend is good about bringing in the mail.

But just before Thanksgiving, letters started piling up.

All those holiday fliers buried the note.

It's folded in the bottom of the mailbox, written on torn paper. Wills fishes it out and walks across the yard. He smooths the message over the handle of his mower.

To: Mr. Mailman

Thank you for your help cutting the grass. Jack died last night and I will be moving out. Again, thank you very much.

The note was signed Zaida. Wills had never known her name.

More of Lane DeGregory's stories and an interview with her are printed in Part 4.

Writer's Workshop

Talking Points

1. Lane DeGregory's story "Special Delivery" begins with this description: "On his day off, the mailman returns to his route. He drives a beat-up Cherokee with a homemade trailer hitched to the bumper, parks in front of a little blue house on a corner lot tangled with weeds. He carries no mailbag. He has nothing to deliver. Except his time." Why do you think DeGregory keeps the mailman anonymous at first? What do we learn about the mailman from the first few details?

2. In an interview with Poynter's Butch Ward (see pages 287–293), DeGregory says that the story about Eric Wills is really about "giving." Identify the details and anecdotes in the story that support that statement.

3. In organizing "Special Delivery," DeGregory brings the mailman to Jack's house in the first section, introduces the question about a note in a middle section and then doesn't reveal what's in the note until the end of the story. Why do you think DeGregory chose to tell the story in this way? How does DeGregory use the note at the end of the story in a similar way as David Finkel uses the factory explosion in his story about "Bob"?

Assignment Desk

1. DeGregory says she often gets story ideas from people she has written about. For example, she kept in touch with the mother of a terminally-ill girl she wrote about. About four years later, the mother called DeGregory and said: You should do a story about our postman; he's making a difference in a lot of lives here in our neighborhood. As an exercise, contact three or four people you have written about and ask them for an update—as well as any new story ideas they might have.

2. DeGregory writes in a conversational style and sometimes sprinkles her paragraphs with one-, two- or three-word sentences. For example: "He

knocked on Jack's door, said he wanted to cut the yard. Just to help. No charge." Try experimenting with your approach to sentence structure and length. Read your sentences aloud and listen to the rhythm.

3. At first, what Eric Wills does for the people on his route seems ordinary, but DeGregory shows just how important his contributions are. In the course of a week, keep an eye out for seemingly insignificant things that may have a story behind them—perhaps someone who looks after his neighbors or a local business that treats its customers as if they are family. Think about how you would learn whether there is an untold story behind those actions.

The Boston Globe

Winner: Batten Medal

Kevin Cullen

No Time for Tears

NOV. 5, 2007

When he was born, James Elleyby's eyes were so messed up he could barely see anything.

Then, when he was 6, the lights went out. It was pitch dark, and he was blind as could be.

It was a jail sentence for a little boy.

"The worst part wasn't being blind, it was being forced to stay inside all the time," Elleyby, 24, was saying, sitting in the Oak Bar at the Copley Plaza.

His mother, Shirley, did the best she could. They would sit on the couch in their Brooklyn apartment, watching cartoons, and Shirley would hold two fingers behind his head and have him feel her fingers so he could imagine what Bugs Bunny looked like.

But mostly he was alone, listening to the shrieks of other kids playing outside, rocking in the darkness.

He went to a special school for blind children. He was 15 and Ivory was 14 when they met. She towered over him. It didn't matter. Five years later, they married.

"The only good thing about being blind is that I met my life partner at that school," James said.

Ivory was blind from eye cancer, and they knew there was a good chance their children would be blind.

"Some people said, 'Why have kids?' We're still people. We still want a family," James said.

Tammy is 3, Joanne less than a year. Both are blind.

James had the most severe form of corneal disease. While there is no hope for his wife and daughters to gain their sight, he never gave up trying to regain his.

James underwent a half-dozen corneal transplants, but they failed.

Two years ago, he and Roger Harris, a friend who can see, were fooling around on a computer, using a search engine to look for anything they could call hope.

"I was always good on the computer," James said. "I just couldn't see the screen."

They found the name of Dr. Claes Dohlman, a doctor at the Massachusetts Eye and Ear Infirmary who had developed a technique in which he places artificial corneas in the eyes of those for whom transplants don't work.

James reached out and Dohlman reached back.

Last January, after surgery, Dohlman ripped the patch off and James instinctively covered his face with his hands. Then he blinked and pulled his hands away and realized he could see his fingers. He looked around the room and saw colors, the names of which he hadn't a clue.

He took the bus back to New York and found that Ivory and his little girls were more beautiful than he had imagined. He sat on a couch, snapped his fingers, and watched Joanne crawl toward the sound, toward her daddy.

He got a job—telemarketing, working with computers. He wants to go to law school. He wants to do everything. He believes he can do anything.

A while ago, he got an invitation to come back to Boston, because Dohlman's friends had organized a dinner. Of course, he would come. But what would he bring?

"I don't have any money," James said. "What do you give a man who gave you your sight?"

A few weeks ago, James stepped outside his home in the Bronx. He looked up into the sky and saw something twinkling. He didn't know what it was and asked a neighbor. The neighbor thought James was kidding.

"It's a star, James," the man said. "It's a star."

As he gazed upon a star for the first time, James decided that the best way to show his gratitude was to rent a car and drive 200 miles to Boston, because he could.

And so he did. Dohlman had no idea he was coming. On Friday night, when Claes Dohlman spied James Elleyby sitting at a table in the Copley Plaza, the two men, doctor and patient, embraced.

There was no time for tears because they were so glad to see each other.

A Gift for Compassion

DEC. 24, 2007

By Kevin Cullen

It's a long drive up from the Cape, but Mary Quin does it without complaint. Eddie is her oldest, her baby, and she loves him the way only a mother can love her firstborn.

"Hi, Ma," Eddie said, climbing into the car.

Eddie is 50 years old, mentally retarded, and smarter than a lot of people. He lives in a group home in Wakefield and works as a janitor at a workshop in Woburn.

Mother and son have a little tradition this time of year. She picks him up, they have lunch, and she takes him to the stores, so he can buy Christmas presents for his brother and sisters.

They were sitting in the China Moon, in Stoneham, waiting for their lunch, when Mary noticed Eddie wasn't himself.

"What's the matter, Eddie?"

"I seen it on TV, Ma," he said. "There was a fire, in Everett, and everybody's house got burned up. There was an oil truck and it crashed and it burned." Eddie couldn't stop thinking about the people in Everett since he saw it on the news.

"I've got a lot of clothes, Ma," Eddie said. "I've got clothes at my house, and I've got clothes at your house down the Cape. I want to give some of my clothes to those people."

Mary Quin told Eddie that it wasn't clothes that the people in Everett needed. She had heard they needed other things, like money and gift cards. Eddie thought for a moment. Then he pulled a dog-eared bank book from his back pocket.

"Ma," he said. "Can you take me to the bank?"

At the bank in Wakefield, Eddie told the teller he wanted a check for $25. The teller said she could give him an American Express check, but that it would cost a few dollars extra for the check.

"What do you want the check for?" the teller asked.

And so Eddie told her and then the teller walked over to the bank manager. When the teller came back to the window she told Eddie she wouldn't charge him for the check.

Mary Quin called a telephone number that had been set up to help the people who got burned out in Everett. After she explained what her son had done and that they didn't know where to bring the check, the guy on the other end of the line didn't say anything for a while. Then he asked Mary to wait for a week and to bring Eddie to the Everett Recreation Center at a certain time. Mary asked why they had to wait a week and the guy said he needed to talk to some people first.

So a week went by and Mary drove back up from the Cape, to Wakefield, to get Eddie and they headed to Everett. Mary took Eddie to Sweetser Circle. They got out of the car and stood in front of some rubble that used to be the homes of 13 families.

Eddie turned his head from side to side. He didn't say anything for the longest time. It was freezing.

"Ma," he finally said, "how many people died?"

"Eddie," Mary Quin said, turning to him, grabbing his arm. "Don't you remember? Nobody died. Nobody at all died. It was a miracle."

Eddie brightened.

"Oh, yeah," he said. "A miracle."

When they got to the rec center, there were a lot of people standing around, waiting. They had come to see this man, this wise man, bearing a gift. They had come to see Eddie.

Eddie handed the check to Carlo DeMaria, the mayor-elect, and DeMaria shook his hand, and then Eddie looked up and realized everybody was looking right at him. He knew he had to say something, and so he said the only thing that felt right.

"Merry Christmas, everybody," Eddie Quin said.

More of Kevin Cullen's columns and an interview with him are printed in Part 2.

Writer's Workshop

Talking Points

1. In "No Time for Tears," Kevin Cullen quotes James Elleyby, who talks about his doctor: "I don't have any money. What do you give a man who gave you your sight?" Besides his sight, what else did Elleyby get from Dr. Claes Dohlman? And what did Dr. Dohlman get in return? How does Cullen show this?

2. In "A Gift for Compassion," Cullen writes: "Eddie is 50 years old, mentally retarded, and smarter than a lot of people." What does Cullen mean by "smarter"? As the story unfolds, how does he reveal that Eddie is smarter than a lot of people?

3. One similarity between Kevin Cullen's columns and David Finkel's stories is the backstory—everything that precedes the action that they highlight. Go back through each of these stories and circle the paragraphs that give significance to the final action (Izzy's daughter being treated by the doctors, the factory being blown up, James Elleyby visiting his doctor, Eddie Quin making the donation). How are the stories influenced by the way the writers let them unfold?

Assignment Desk

1. In "No Time for Tears," Cullen describes James Elleyby's relationship with his mother by telling a little story: She would hold two fingers behind his head to help him imagine what Bugs Bunny looked like. Later, Cullen describes how Elleyby, with his sight regained, snapped his fingers and watched his baby girl crawl toward him. Cullen got those stories through good interviewing. Write down a list of questions that you think Cullen asked to get such vivid descriptions.

2. Cullen shows rather than tells. In "A Gift for Compassion," in order to convey Eddie's sadness, Cullen writes: "They got out of the car and stood in front of some rubble that used to be the homes of 13 families. Eddie turned his head from side to side. He didn't say anything for the

longest time. It was freezing. 'Ma,' he finally said, 'how many people died?'" In your next few stories, try to write descriptive scenes that evoke emotions, rather than telling the reader about those emotions.

3. Journalists often get phone calls from people suggesting that they write about acts of charity. Imagine that someone told you about what Eddie Quin did. Write a list of questions that you would ask to learn whether this is something you should write about.

PART 8

Community Service
Photojournalism

Mona Reeder

Mona Reeder has a sixth sense for finding high-impact stories.

The Dallas Morning News photojournalist was finishing a project on the homeless when she came upon information that suggested another project. A social worker had given her a set of statistics comparing Texas with other states in public safety, education, health care, teen pregnancy, pollution, voter apathy and poverty.

"The statistics were embarrassing to the state, in my opinion, and I was stunned at seeing how lopsided the public policies seemed and the disparity between the haves and have-nots," Reeder said in an interview with Poynter's Kenny Irby.

"We had done stories on all of these issues individually, but when I saw all the numbers and issues grouped together, it sparked the idea that all of these issues painted a grim picture of Texas and they needed to be presented together for maximum impact," she said.

"For me, it was almost an immediate reaction that these statistics had to be a photo essay of vignettes that represented where Texas ranked by the numbers, to portray in pictures—real faces, real lives—how the priorities and disparities affected the citizens of Texas."

The Dallas Morning News

Through black-and-white documentary photography, Reeder human-ized a wide range of social issues by spending time with pregnant teens, children born into poverty, families living without health insurance and young people incarcerated in Texas' juvenile prison system.

For "The Bottom Line" project, Reeder won the ASNE Community Service Photojournalism Award and was a finalist for the Pulitzer Prize in feature photography.

Reeder has been with the *News* since 1999. She has covered the war in Iraq and presidential elections in Mexico and has traveled to southeastern Turkey to cover the Kurds. In 2002, she went to Afghanistan to chronicle the war on terrorism and its effects on people who have lived with war for more than two decades.

The "Bottom Line" project was three years in the making. Reeder pro-posed it in 2005, but then Hurricane Katrina hit, and she was sent to the Gulf Coast to cover the storm and its aftermath. In 2006, she spent sev-eral weeks covering low-income families in border communities, but the pro-ject was delayed again because of newsroom buyouts. She finally got the green light to focus on the project in 2007.

"It's important to put at least as much of yourself into the work as you expect from your subjects," Reeder said. "Compelling, intimate docu-mentary photojournalism demands honesty, patience and sincerity from the photographer, and I believe you should approach it with empathy and compassion.

"To gain access to a family's most intimate situations, they need to trust you and feel comfortable with you in their lives, and that kind of relation-ship comes by spending time with them, sometimes a great deal of time, and allowing them to get to know you. I spend a lot of time not even tak-ing pictures, but just listening to people."

—Thomas Huang, co-editor of *Best Newspaper Writing* and Assistant Managing Editor for Sunday and Enterprise, *The Dallas Morning News*

Texas has the most teen births and the most repeat teen births in the nation.
Barely 1 day old, Jasmine Williams has no way to know that she will soon leave the arms of her mother to be placed in the care of her grandmother. Shortly after Jasmine's birth, mother Kimberly Williams was back in shackles—in the custody of the Texas Youth Commission, where she will remain until 2008. Both of Jasmine's parents were 15 when she was born.

About "The Bottom Line"

Texas politicians celebrate the virtues of small government by touting the state's thriving economy, low cost of living and business-friendly government. But there's another side to the story, and photographer Mona Reeder carefully gathered images to tell it. She focused her camera on forgotten Texans—the working poor struggling to survive even during "good times."

The result was a stunning photo essay that showed how frayed we've allowed our social safety net to become. Her photographs were so strong and so moving that they drew an outpouring of empathy from readers, online viewers, politicians, advocates and bloggers.

All photographs courtesy of Mona Reeder/*The Dallas Morning News*

A quarter of Texas' children are born in poverty.
Three-year-old Hector Cabada patiently waits for the dribble of water to reach him in the family's shower, enclosed by hastily built walls of plywood, corrugated tin and the camper trailer they call home in the Salida Del Sol colonia near Penitas in Hidalgo County. Texas is home to the three poorest counties in the U.S.

Reeder overcame obstacles mounted by state agencies and gained the trust of people who normally would be wary of baring their lives to outsiders. Reeder tracked down the parents of inmates in the state's juvenile prison system, obtained parental release forms and gained unprecedented access to photograph the young prisoners.

Scores of readers wrote to say her pictures had touched their hearts. One wrote: "The entire section's review of statistics regarding the two-tiered racist culture of this state, which is so dear to most of us, was uncomfortable to read, but was most effective because it matched cold statistics with heart-wrenching photographs of real people in real life suffering from the basic disregard of their fellow Texans."

Reeder's powerful photographs have put an unforgettable human face on the ongoing debate over priorities in Texas.

—Adapted from *The Dallas Morning News* ASNE contest entry

BEHIND the STORY

Winner's Q&A

An Interview with Mona Reeder

This edited e-mail interview was conducted by Kenny Irby, Poynter's Visual Journalism Group Leader and Diversity Program Director, with Mona Reeder, winner of ASNE's Community Service Photojournalism Award.

KENNY IRBY: Photographic essay projects of this depth are not very commonplace. What value do such projects have?

MONA REEDER: You're right, unfortunately. I think a lot of newspapers get caught up in the tried-and-true, conventional ways and forget there are underutilized options to telling stories. But in the harsh realities of smaller budgets and staffs, it's difficult to get the amount of time necessary to produce in-depth photo essays. Most photographers who are working on these types of projects do a great deal of the work on their own time because documentary photography is a passion for them.

Generally, major newspaper projects are long, in-depth, 200-plus-inch stories that run as a series over several days, and newsrooms throw all their resources into one or two great projects for the year. I often wonder who really has time to read all that copy, no matter the interest in the topic. Sometimes a picture really is worth a thousand words—if you'll pardon the cliché. If you can make your point quickly and effectively with photos and graphics, why not do it?

To me "The Bottom Line" project embodies what our managers have been saying the last several years as newspapers experience shrinking readership and news holes. This project represented a well-researched, in-depth piece about serious issues affecting the entire state of Texas, and it was presented in an innovative manner that even the busiest person could get through and absorb in a relatively short amount of time.

Photo essays are the bread and butter of major news magazines, and our world is increasingly focused on visual mediums. It seems to follow that newspapers would gravitate to cleaner designs utilizing compelling, in-depth photo stories to attract and keep readers.

Texas tops the nation in cancerous emissions into the air and toxic chemicals released into the water.
Just moments after Yola Barriere (lying on bed) died of cancer, family members joined hands and sang "Amazing Grace." Ms. Barriere's sister Dorothea La Barrea (sitting on bed), who suffers from chronic obstructive pulmonary disease and asthma, has lived within blocks of the Port Arthur refineries and chemical plants since she was a tiny child. After Yola died, Dorothea, struggling to breathe, put her sister's oxygen tubes into her own nose. She's never had medical insurance despite working her entire life and can't afford the round-the-clock oxygen she needs.

How did this photo project originate, and how long have you done this kind of work?

As I was wrapping up a project about homelessness in Dallas, a social worker who had helped me with contacts on the streets handed me a set of statistics issued by the state comptroller's office ranking Texas with the other states in the U.S. in more than 15 categories such as public safety, education, health care, teen pregnancy, pollution, voter apathy and poverty.

The statistics were embarrassing to the state, in my opinion, and I was stunned at seeing how lopsided the public policies seemed and the disparity between the haves and have-nots. We had done stories on all of these issues individually, but when I saw all the numbers and issues grouped together, it sparked the idea that all of these issues painted a grim picture of Texas and they needed to be presented together for maximum impact.

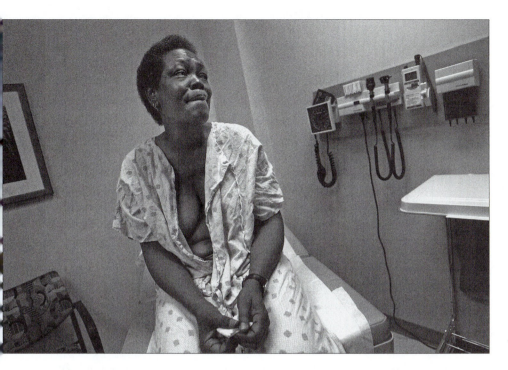

Texas has the highest number of uninsured people in the country.
Veronica Sue Prescott, 51, cries after being examined by her doctor at Houston's M.D. Anderson Cancer Center. Sue has inflammatory breast cancer, a rare and aggressive form of the disease. She was turned away from three hospitals before doctors at M.D. Anderson agreed to treat her despite her lack of medical insurance. In the meantime, her cancer had spread to her brain. The chemotherapy she now receives is mainly to keep the cancer from spreading further. Her doctor told her that if she stopped the treatments, she would probably die within a matter of months. Her sister, Yola Barriere, died in October 2007 of cancer. Both sisters believe they got cancer from living near the Port Arthur refineries.

For me, it was almost an immediate reaction that these statistics had to be a photo essay of vignettes that represented where Texas ranked by the numbers, to portray in pictures—real faces, real lives—how the priorities and disparities affected the citizens of Texas.

My first thoughts were: "How can this be? Are these numbers/statistics correct?" So I started researching and verifying the numbers to confirm the rankings and discovered that everything I'd been given was accurate. Not only were the numbers embarrassingly bad, but some of the statistics had been bad for more than a decade.

I've been working on documentary picture stories for 18 years, but this was a completely different tack—a different way to approach all of the issues I'm passionate about. In essence, "The Bottom Line" is several picture stories under one umbrella. Generally, photo essays cover one subject or one issue in-depth—they seem to flow naturally that way. A broader, multiple-subject, vignette approach is very difficult to put together in a slide show or multimedia presentation, because the common thread is generally the text.

Where and how did you gather information and identify your sources to make such intimate connections?

The research and source-gathering for this project was an enormous task and quite time-consuming. I made countless phone calls to numerous agencies, rode along with Meals on Wheels, contacted community activists and social workers and spent countless hours online reading other newspapers in various parts of the state. Every spare moment I had, both in Dallas and on the road, was spent reading, researching or contacting sources.

How do you go about gaining access and building relationships with the people that you document?

It's important to put at least as much of yourself into the work as you expect from your subjects. Compelling, intimate documentary photojournalism demands honesty, patience and sincerity from the photographer, and I believe you should approach it with empathy and compassion.

To gain access to a family's most intimate situations, they need to trust you and feel comfortable with you in their lives, and that kind of relationship comes by spending time with them, sometimes a great deal of time, and allowing them to get to know you. I spend a lot of time not even taking pictures, but just listening to people.

It took two trips to Port Arthur to spend time with the Barriere family before they really felt comfortable having me around. During the past year, I must have explained the project hundreds of times, over the phone and in person with potential subjects and sources.

How did the focus for the project come about?

After weeks of research, we looked at all the various categories and areas of statistics and determined which were the most critical, of the most interest to us and our readers, and what we could accomplish in a year. We were looking for sharp contrasts between the haves and have-nots, the human costs of such negligent public policies and which categories were the most visual.

Tell me about the editing and selection process that you followed. How many images did you choose from?

I shot literally thousands of images, working on eight or nine picture stories throughout the year, some simultaneously. Chris Wilkins, deputy director of photography, and I edited all of the images together. It was a very smooth process with absolutely no disagreements on a single image. We had talked so much about the project and had such a solid plan, that we both knew exactly the kind of images we needed to make this body of work really sing. And both of us agreed that the work had to rise above good daily work for the project to be strong with intimate and compelling images.

Who was included in your editing process and what role, if any, did a picture editor play?

Our director of photography, Leslie White, played an absolutely pivotal role by supporting the project from the beginning, even when the idea was panned by midlevel editors in our newsroom. Chris Wilkins attended every meeting and helped shape the scope of the project, in addition to editing every frame I shot. He helped pave the way, getting me time away from daily assignments when I needed to shoot something critical for the project.

This project might never have been published without all the hard work and dedication from photo editor Brad Loper. He came on board with the project later in the year and put together the initial design of the project. He helped with final picture editing and was instrumental in the production and design of the multimedia presentation. He served as a talented coordinator between the photo department and our graphics and design staff.

Did you have a writing colleague to work with along the way? If so, how did that collaboration evolve?

No, I wrote the introduction and a short story to accompany the photos for pollution and health care. And we felt the strength of the project was based on the simplicity of presenting compelling, dramatic photos accompanied by only stark statistics and very little copy. It seemed a fresh and innovative way to present these issues without a 200-inch story—a presentation that we believed would have more impact and all of our readers could get through, no matter how busy.

It seems that many hard-hitting photographic projects are presented in black and white, when in fact they were documented in color and the world that we live in is color. So why black and white?

Each image is different, just as each project is different, and I think photographers have to determine what format is best for the particular image or project as far as color or B&W.

Texas is first in the nation in executions.
Kenneth Foster prays inside a visitation cell on death row at the Texas Department of Corrections' Polunsky Unit in Livingston, one week before his scheduled execution. His sentence was commuted to life in prison by Gov. Rick Perry hours before his scheduled execution.

Twelve-year-old Matthew Clark stands crying in the rain outside The Walls unit of Huntsville Prison moments after his stepfather, John Joe Amador, was executed in August 2007. The execution of Amador was the second of three that week. He was convicted of robbing and murdering San Antonio taxi driver Mohammad Reza Ayari 13 years ago.

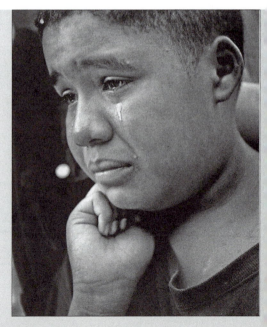

Texas has the nation's second-widest gap in income between rich and poor.
Teeka Hemphill just heard the bad news: She and her partner, Mark Spurlock (not pictured), are being evicted from the Budget Motel in McKinney that they call home. A city inspector has declared the property substandard. At the door, Amanda, who did not want her last name used, is just as depressed. Not only will she lose her home when the dilapidated motel is leveled; she will also lose her job of cleaning and running errands for the motel's managers. Both women are pregnant, making the search for a new home even more daunting.

Surrounded by clutter, dirty dishes and trash, 2-year-old Abby Henderson takes a bath in the kitchen sink of the manager's apartment at the Budget Motel. Abby and her three brothers were forced to move into their grandmother's two-room motel unit when their mother went to jail for a probation violation.

I've presented projects both ways and have had success using both color and B&W. For me, the major factor is the content of the images and the type of light present when you're shooting. It's nearly impossible to shoot intimate pictures in difficult situations with a flash jarring people. So it follows that the best way to be unobtrusive is to keep yourself and your gear very low-key.

Also, if you're working in several different types of settings and different lighting situations, the images don't seem to flow together as well. Bright colors, like red or yellow, sometimes overpower the content in the image, and for this project I knew I was going to be all over the state of Texas, shooting in institutions, outdoors, in homes and in lots of low-light situations. We made the decision at the beginning of the process that this project would be in B&W.

I believe strongly that ideas are the currency of the newsroom and that photojournalists are equal reporters in the newsgathering process with their writing colleagues. What is your reaction to this statement?

Absolutely! Too bad more newsrooms don't get it. I graduated from California State University, Sacramento, and it didn't have a photojournalism program, so in order to get a degree in journalism, I took every course that was required of students looking to graduate and work as reporters.

If anything, I was at a disadvantage when trying to find work as a photographer. My first job out of college was as a general assignment reporter at a small, three-times-weekly newspaper in Northern California, and when I did manage to find a photography job, it was only part-time.

Most newspaper photographers have had to take several writing classes and other curriculum required of reporters in addition to photojournalism classes to get their degrees.

On the flip side, most reporters I know have never taken a photography or design course. Consequently, most great photo staffs know that educating the newsroom about photojournalism is a big part of their job, and one they work at constantly. Photo departments are sometimes regarded merely as "service" departments. If more newsrooms looked at photographers as journalists—photojournalists—they could be making maximum use of their resources.

How did you interact with your online staff? Was the Web presentation very different from the newspaper's presentation?

We have a small but very talented and hardworking online staff within our photo department that is actually separate from the overall newspaper's online department. The three of us worked together nearly night and day to produce the multimedia presentation in time for publication. It was distinctly different from our print version of the project. We were able to break down each issue into separate picture stories with the accompanying statistics. We produced eight different slide shows with audio. (Editor's note: A link to the multimedia package can be found at www.poynter.org/bnw2009/resources.)

Are the goals for the online presentation different from the print edition?

The goals for both the print version and the multimedia presentation are essentially the same—you need strong, compelling content that flows together in both formats, and everything still has to be accurate and presented with a clean design. I think the print edition and the multimedia presentation need to complement each other, and having the multimedia option allows you to include additional images and information that you might not have space for in the print edition.

What are your thoughts about the role of photographic reporting and multimedia?

It's a brave new world! Just run with it. Multimedia and online presentations give us another opportunity to get our work published and get more of it published. It's a natural medium for photojournalism, especially since we've been putting our work into slide shows for decades, but with no substantial outlet or audience for that type of presentation—if you don't count seminars and contests.

How much time did you put into the coverage?

Off and on—three years. I first proposed this idea in 2005, but Hurricane Katrina hit and we were off and running for months in New Orleans and Mississippi covering the storm and its aftermath. During our hurricane coverage, I drove from New Orleans to Huntsville, Texas, to cover a controversial execution, then returned to Louisiana and continued working.

In 2006, I spent several weeks in border communities working on one aspect of poverty in Texas, but was called back to Dallas, and the project was shelved because of newsroom buyouts and a shuffling of personnel. In 2007, Leslie White, newly promoted as director of photography, gave me the green light to resume working on "Texas by the Numbers" (our working title for the project), with the caveat that I wasn't going to be pulled off the daily shooting schedule.

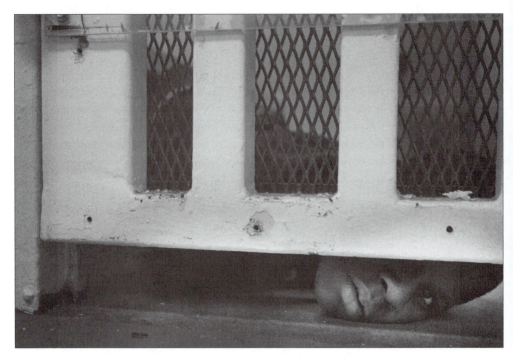

Texas is second in the nation for the number of children incarcerated.
Lying on the floor, 13-year-old Drake Swist peers out from underneath the bars on his cell door in the security unit of the Texas Youth Commission's Marlin Orientation and Assessment Unit. The facility is where kids get their first glimpse of life in custody.

Later, in September, things were really rolling and happening at a much faster pace, so I was pulled from the daily schedule until the end of the year.

What were some of the challenges that you faced? How did you overcome them?

We were breaking new ground with this project, so nearly everything about it was challenging. Selling the concept to various newsroom editors was the first hurdle, and as a photographer, being responsible for the entire content of the project was an enormous challenge and responsibility. Compiling all the research and verifying the numbers was a constant challenge, and that process was new to me. But, I knew that the success of the entire project hinged on the validity of the numbers and the thoroughness of the research.

How challenging is it to produce a powerful single image on a regular basis?

Producing powerful images on a regular basis is one of the greatest challenges that newspaper photographers face. It's important to motivate yourself and find ways to stay inspired. Even when the assignment might fall short of your expectations and you're rolling your eyes wondering why you have to shoot it, I try to remember that it may be the subject's only time in their life they get to be in the paper and it's a big deal to them. When you're shooting daily assignments, I think you try to always do a good job, and when you're working on high-profile projects, you have to kick it up a notch or two.

What are the more memorable lessons you learned during this assignment?

Organization and time management are probably at the top of that list. I was juggling a lot of hats during this project, responsible for selling the concept, compiling the research, logistics, finding all of my subjects, managing my shooting schedule, gathering all content—still photographs and audio—and then, during production, writing the intro and a short story.

There were countless meetings to attend, slide shows presented to upper management to justify space in the paper, and another grueling week of, once again, confirming the numbers (for the fourth time) immediately before publication.

I put together stacks of research folders and probably filled 10 notebooks with "to-do" lists, sources, driving directions, flight schedules, caption info, etc. And, perhaps the most important lesson I learned from this extraordinary experience is to stay determined and believe in yourself despite fierce resistance. When it seemed that no one in the newsroom was interested in the project, we didn't let that stop us, but looked for other ways to get this piece published. Our editorial department's editors loved the concept and agreed to give us space for the project.

Were there any major surprises for you while developing this project?

Probably one of the biggest surprises was having the parents of children incarcerated all agreeing to allow their kids to be photographed for the newspaper.

At one point, I was in the visiting room of the Texas Youth Commission's facility in Marlin, Texas, and actually had parents approach me and request that their children be part of the project. Many of the parents were so frustrated by the juvenile justice system that they were willing to try any avenue for help.

I traveled to the homes of each child's parent to obtain the necessary signatures on the release forms for publication, and discussed the project at length with all of them. Not one parent refused to sign after hearing about the project. Having the faces of children incarcerated appear in the newspaper was a first for Texas papers. And, perhaps another surprise was

Sixty percent of children under Texas Youth Commission supervision come from low-income homes. Joseph, 17, got a little bit of sunshine in the yard outside the security unit at Marlin; he didn't want his last name used. The facility, which once housed adult prisoners in the Texas Department of Criminal Justice, was closed in the fall of 2007.

the wonderful camaraderie and closeness that the photo and multimedia team experienced the last month of this project as we struggled and worked night and day to produce this project for publication.

What advice can you offer other photographers when it comes to being a visual reporter?

Waiting to receive a great assignment or project from the photo desk is a mistake a lot of photographers make. Some people complain that they never get anything good from the desk, but in my opinion, you make your own luck, create your own opportunities. If more photographers took the initiative and responsibility for developing stories and photo ideas, they might be happier.

Tell me about your most unforgettable photographs in the course of this past year.

The photos I took of Yola Barriere, her sisters Veronica Sue Prescott and Dorothea La Barrea, and their family will always be on my mind. Not only were those photos critical to the project, but the entire situation was deeply moving. It was a defining moment when Yola died, and Dorothea, who struggles with chronic obstructive pulmonary disease (COPD) and couldn't breathe, put her dead sister's oxygen tubes into her own nose as other members of the family sang "Amazing Grace" over Yola's deathbed.

Despite working hard her entire life, Dorothea didn't have medical insurance and couldn't afford the oxygen she needs 24 hours a day. The photo I took in that situation was one of the signature photos of the project and whenever I hear "Amazing Grace" in the future, I will forever recall those moments after Yola died.

In a way, I could have photographed nearly two-thirds of the project on just the Barriere family—if I'd found them earlier in the year. The Barrieres were a large, hard-working family that sent four sons to fight in foreign wars, yet none of them had medical insurance.

The family believes the carcinogens emitted by the area refineries and petrochemical plants in Port Arthur caused Yola's and Veronica Sue's cancers and Dorothea's COPD, although direct proof remains elusive.

And the photos of children incarcerated in the Texas Youth Commission facility will always be some of the more memorable pictures I shot this year, but it was the constant chaos and noise in that prison filled with kids that will probably haunt me.

THE PLAIN DEALER

Finalist: Community Service Photojournalism

Gus Chan

About "Johanna: Facing Forward"

On March 5, 2007, 17-year-old Juan Ruiz put a sawed-off shotgun next to the head of his former girlfriend, Johanna Orozco, 18, and pulled the trigger. Her beautiful face was virtually destroyed.

The story of the jilted boyfriend's attack made national news. Oprah wanted to interview Johanna. So did *60 Minutes* and *20/20*. But Johanna only wanted photographer Gus Chan and writer Rachel Dissell to tell her story. She allowed Chan and Dissell unfettered access for the next six months to her grueling recovery.

But why? She told them that if her story helped one girl recognize the signs of a troubling relationship, if it helped one boy realize that such obsessive behavior was wrong, then it would be worth unveiling her struggle in public.

The resulting eight-part series showed readers how Johanna overcame her fears: the fear of facing the ex-boyfriend who tried to kill her; the fear of being disfigured at an age when looks are so important; the fear of trusting a judicial system that failed to protect her when it really mattered.

Chan's photographs took us into Johanna's new world. We watched her ordeal as doctors rebuilt her lower jaw and she recovered from the trauma of the shooting. We saw her emotions as she tried on her prom dress and was voted prom queen. We saw the proud moment when she received her diploma.

The outpouring of sympathy from the community toward Johanna was remarkable. But a few of the responses meant more to her than any others, such as the e-mail from the young man who recognized himself in Juan and vowed to change his behavior.

—Adapted from *The (Cleveland) Plain Dealer* ASNE contest entry

As she sleeps in her hospital bed in spring 2007, Johanna Orozco tosses and moans. The disturbing dreams that invade the 18-year-old's sleep are part of the journey of mental healing she faces as doctors work to repair her face, damaged from a shotgun blast.

All photographs courtesy of Gus Chan/*The Plain Dealer*

On April 3, 2007, surgeons take the first major step to rebuild Johanna's shattered jaw. As she waits to be wheeled into the operating room, Dr. Michael Fritz, the surgeon who will rebuild her face, stops by to see if Johanna has any last-minute concerns. "Are you nervous?" he asks. She holds up her finger and thumb an inch apart. "A little?" he asks. She nods.

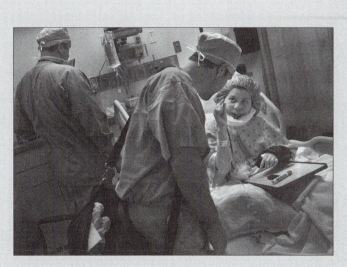

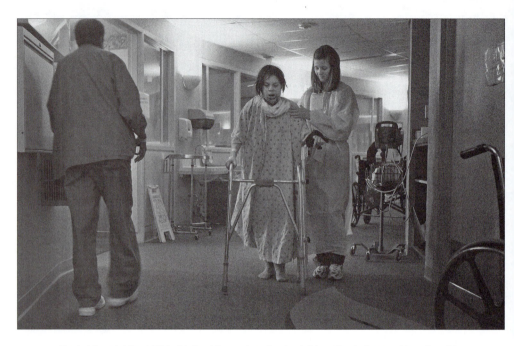

Physical therapist Crystal Schutt helps Johanna strengthen her left leg after doctors used bone from it to form her new jaw. Though she grunts and groans, Johanna is determined. If she was told to walk 30 feet, Johanna would walk 60.

After more than six weeks of recovering in the hospital, Johanna Orozco gets to put on real clothes and go home. Her grandfather Wosbely kisses her shoulder as she waits to be released.

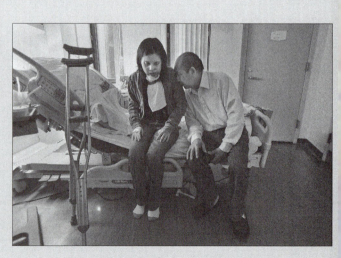

With a picture of her mother, Carmen, hanging from the wall, Johanna frets as she gets ready for prom. She worries that her friends will act weird or not accept her. But she doesn't want to miss the once-in-a-life-time event. Her surgeon, Dr. Michael Fritz, wrote a note to school officials promising she was fit to attend the dance.

The limousine stops many times on the near west side to have the prom goers photographed.

Johanna dances with prom king Zlatko Zlatanov after the two were named prom king and queen at the Lincoln West prom.

Johanna leans on her cousin, Cathy, as she waits to hear from the defense attorney whether Juan Ruiz will plead out.

Johanna twirls on the steps of the Justice Center in downtown Cleveland after her ex-boyfriend Juan Ruiz pleaded guilty on Aug. 10, 2007, to raping and shooting her. She had been nervous for months that he would go to trial and force her to testify. "It was more of a relief in my heart than anything," Johanna said.

Juan Ruiz wipes away tears before pleading guilty to all charges of rape and attempted aggravated murder in the shooting of his former girlfriend, Johanna Orozco.

BEHIND the STORY

Lessons Learned

By Gus Chan

I met Johanna Orozco in a hospital room on a March afternoon after reading about her in the paper. She had been shot by her ex-boyfriend. The family was furious as to how this could have happened, when just days earlier he had raped her. What particularly intrigued me was the outrage the family felt, and I wanted to know more. I wanted to somehow be able to tell the story from the perspective of a victim of crime. That person often fades into the background, never to be heard from.

The reporter, Rachel Dissell, and I approached the family. They understood what we were hoping to accomplish with the story, but said it was up to Johanna. When we approached Johanna about the story, she immediately saw the value in doing a piece like this. If telling her story could prevent the same thing from happening to another person, it was worth doing.

Johanna is an amazing young woman. She has a maturity about her that goes well beyond her 19 years. Sure, there are times when she acts like a teenager, but she has seen and done more in her short lifetime than most of us will ever do, and she's handled it with tremendous grace. Johanna lost her parents during her early teens—her mother to a long-term illness, and then her father to an auto accident just 10 days later.

As we followed her through the painful progress of surgery, recovery and life after the shooting, Johanna was always surrounded by a circle of friends and family. I believe they got her through those really dark times.

Johanna has moved on with her life since the trial. She has started college, though she still has a number of surgeries ahead of her to repair her jaw. She's even modeled in a fashion show. I hope to continue following her progress as she moves on to the next chapter of her life.

Three lessons:

1. **Relationship.** You need to build one with your subject. You can't take something without giving something back.

2. **Teamwork.** Find a great reporter to work with. You're going to be spending a lot of time working together, so compatibility is an issue. It's important to have the same sense of mission.

3. **Transparency.** Be upfront with your subject. If the story is going to take months to tell, let them know that in advance. Let them know they're entering into a long-term partnership with you as you tell their story.

Gus Chan has been a staff photographer for The Plain Dealer *for the past 17 years. He worked at* The Detroit News *prior to coming home to Cleveland. He received his bachelor's degree in journalism from Kent State University. In his time at* The Plain Dealer, *he has covered events ranging from the World Series to the Cleveland Orchestra's first-ever tour of Asia. In that time, he has won numerous state and national awards. His most recent coverage involved reporting on the subprime mortgage meltdown in Cleveland and how it has affected the economically depressed region.*

Seattle Post-Intelligencer

Karen Ducey

About "One Fatal Shot"

Karen Ducey's first glimpse of the Miller family's tragedy was just another daily spot-news assignment, delivered in that terse, emotionless way journalists use to put a frame around the unfathomable: Go to King County Juvenile Court, make a picture at the hearing for Jordan Jantoc, 16, who killed his stepbrother, Mikey Miller.

It was not the first grieving family Ducey had seen through the lens, or the fifth, or the twentieth. But this family was different. For one thing, it was big. For another, it was there en masse, the older children taking care of the little ones, the shock and pain radiating from them with almost unbearable force.

Ducey has had a brilliant photographic career, as well as rich life experiences outside journalism, including working on a fishing boat in the Bering Sea. She is both experienced and empathetic, and absolutely unswerving when she sees a good story.

As she sat in her car and filed her daily pictures, she resolved to do more with this story. When the Miller family came out of the courthouse, she asked the father, Tim Miller, if she could call with the hope of pursuing a larger story. He gave her his number, and everything that followed came about because Ducey was emotionally open enough to feel the family members' pain and tough enough to photograph them at the same time.

As this family strained and cracked under the combined weight of grief and guilt, Ducey was there. As mother and father wrestled with their feelings, as siblings struggled to understand why Mikey was gone, Ducey was there. Sometimes she made pictures, sometimes she recorded audio, sometimes they just talked. The result is a riveting body of work.

—Adapted from the *Seattle Post-Intelligencer* ASNE contest entry

Lena Jantoc tenderly caresses her son Michael Miller's face as she dresses him in preparation for his viewing at the Greenwood Memorial Park Cemetery in Renton, Wash., on Oct. 2, 2006.

All photographs courtesy of Karen Ducey/*Seattle Post-Intelligencer*

Sitting on the floor at his brother's service, Jordan stares at the casket as girls from Evergreen High School offer roses to Jordan and Michael's mother. The two had been the best of friends and were often referred to in unison as "Michael Jordan."

Jordan Jantoc holds the hand of his mother, Lena Jantoc, during his brother's funeral in SeaTac on Oct. 10, 2006. Jordan had accidentally shot and killed his stepbrother, Michael, while the two were playing with a handgun in the family's home almost three weeks earlier.

Jordan Jantoc appears in court in Seattle on April 25, 2007, facing eight years in jail. He turned 16 just four days after accidentally shooting his brother, and the state charged him as an adult. He was detained in adult prison twice during his year on home detention, this time for going to football practice after school without the knowledge of his social worker.

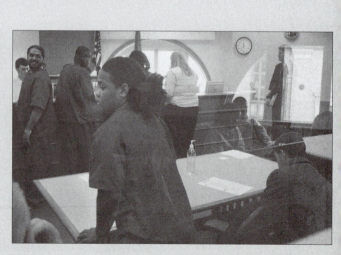

On Oct. 3, 2006, Michael and Jordan's parents, Tim Miller (left), Lena Jantoc and Jordan's biological father, Lorenzo Jantoc, react with relief in the King County Courthouse after a judge announced that Jordan would be placed under house arrest and could leave jail. Having lost Michael, they feared losing their other son, Jordan, into the adult prison system.

Under house arrest, just after arriving home from his first detention at the King County Jail, Jordan Jantoc stares out the window of his living room at family members rehearsing songs for Michael's funeral. "I was scared," he later said. "I didn't really want to see them. I didn't know what they would say or think."

Jordan Jantoc is surrounded by cousins and a sister at home, a few weeks after he accidentally shot and killed his stepbrother. "I'm pretty sure anger existed at one point or another for most of us, maybe even all of us," said one of Jordan's older brothers. "I wouldn't say it was overridden by love but it was coupled with it."

Five months after accidentally killing his brother, Jordan Jantoc jokes around with new friends. Once a student at Evergreen High School, the district made him switch schools, fearing there would be reprisals from students angry over Michael's death.

Almost a full year after fatally shooting his brother, Jordan hugs relatives after a judge spared him from doing time in prison. "This case is all too familiar," said Judge Harry McCarthy. "Instances of young offenders having easy access to the lure of firearms, and deadly consequences." He ruled that the interests of both the defendant and community would best be served by continued electronic home monitoring of Jordan for two years. After that time is served, Jordan and his father will be required to speak to youths about the dangers of firearms. "In court it's kinda scary," said Jordan. "Having my family there definitely helps because I know that they're supportive and will be with me forever."

Timothy Miller, age 18, gets a tattoo bearing his brother Michael's name at the Sin to Skin tattoo parlor. "I got my tattoo, and it's to remember Mikey, to honor him, that I love him and that I'll never forget him no matter what."

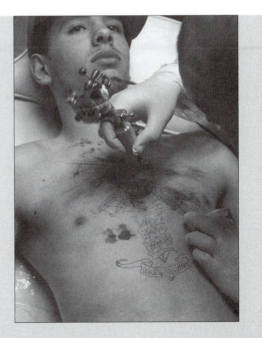

BEHIND the STORY

Lessons Learned

By Karen Ducey

Sitting in my car outside the King County Juvenile Courthouse, I tried to digest what I had just witnessed: A grieving family of more than 20 children and adults weeping in the courtroom, facing a trembling 16-year-old boy whom they could not touch, a face he could not raise because the shame and grief were so immense.

He was wearing the mandatory red jail outfit and handcuffs. The judge barred me from taking his picture. I snapped a picture of his distraught parents minutes before the hearing started. Parents both shocked and distressed—who begged the judge to allow their son, Jordan, his brother's killer, to be allowed to go home.

"We have already lost one child," said Tim Miller. "We do not desire to lose another."

I sat in my car in that parking lot on Sept. 22, 2006, and waited for them to leave. I transmitted my pictures for the daily story. Then, as the juvenile center doors opened, I went to talk to them. Tim Miller, the boys' father, did not tell me to get lost. Instead he gave me his phone number and asked that I wait a few days before coming to see them—giving the family some time to grieve.

But I didn't. I showed up outside their house late that evening and took the first picture for this project, a photograph of Michael and Jordan's mother, Lena, wearing a T-shirt in memory of her deceased son.

I was transfixed. Who are these boys and how can this happen? How did this tragic situation come to be?

What I discovered was a story of a family's love and forgiveness of one son, all the while never forgetting the tragic loss of the other son. Through this family, I knew I could address the issue of teenagers playing with guns.

This project took almost a year to complete, all the while taking daily assignments. Hence, my reporting for this story often took place on Sundays at 1:30 p.m., after the family arrived home from church and I was free from obligations at work.

Sometimes I took pictures, sometimes I made recordings, other times we just talked. As I learned more about them, they came to trust me.

I felt that stretching the multimedia technology to its maximum potential could convey a very powerful message. Online, I created six multimedia stories coupled with an interactive family portrait consisting of 17 audio clips.

I believe that kids listen to kids, parents listen to parents and police listen to police. By giving each of these three groups their own voice, I felt we could cut across all social, economic, age and gender groups and drive home the point that irresponsible gun use can have deadly consequences, no matter how bulletproof you think you and your family might be.

Picture editor Rob Sumner's intrepid belief and commitment to the story got it published across five newspaper pages. Writer Claudia Rowe's story was enticing, suspenseful and sensitive. But multimedia gave me the journalistic freedom to tell the story I had witnessed with greater depth. It enhanced the color, life, dimension and emotion of a very complex storyline.

This was the first project I ever produced in multimedia and the learning curve was tremendous. It was far more time-consuming than I imagined. I had attended a couple of multimedia seminars over the years, but for the most part, the programs were self-taught and all the audio equipment was mine. Needless to say, the process was frustrating, many mistakes were made and there were too many nights of only a couple hours of sleep. But I was committed to telling the story by making full use of the audiovisual storytelling tools I had on hand.

The night before this story was published I was petrified. This family had given me so much. I had been there for some very emotional moments and we had spent a lot of time together. I didn't want to jeopardize their dignity. I wanted them to be proud of who they were, the family I saw them to be. Would opening their hearts add to their grief? How far was too far?

After it was published, they would thank me over and over for memorializing Michael in such a special way and telling Jordan's story so he wasn't just another statistic. Reader response spanned from opinions on the family tragedy to public opinions on guns.

Almost a year after Jordan accidentally and fatally shot his brother Michael, I was once again in court witnessing the Miller-Jantoc family's grief. This time Jordan was being sentenced, facing eight years in adult prison. As the hearing went on I heard the judge make references that seemed like they were lifted from the newspaper story and online presentation. We tried hard to be fair and unbiased in our reporting in the course of a year. But when the judge let Jordan go on home detention, I knew we had done something very special. We provided the knowledge and perspectives he needed to make an informed decision.

At Jordan's sentencing that day, in a crowded King County courtroom, Judge Harry McCarthy said, "This case is all too familiar…instances of young offenders having easy access to the lure of firearms, and deadly consequences." McCarthy ruled that the interests of both the defendant and community would best be served by continued electronic home monitoring of Jordan for two years. He further ordered Jordan and his stepfather to speak to youths about the danger of firearms once the sentence has been completed.

Three lessons:

1. **When you find a good story, pursue it.** Don't wait for access to open up. Don't wait for a more convenient time. Pursue it right away.

2. **Follow your instincts.** People will try to lead you in different directions, along different story angles or discourage you altogether. Stick with it. Be true to yourself.

3. **Be true to your subjects.** Really listen to them. Try to understand what they're telling you and interpret it as best you can.

Karen Ducey is a staff photographer for the Seattle Post-Intelligencer, *joining the newspaper in 2003 after working four years at* The Indianapolis Star. *Ducey's path to photojournalism went through Alaska, where she worked for 12 years in commercial fishing. The money she made there helped fund her photographic education. Ducey graduated from the University of Wisconsin at Madison with a bachelor's degree in political science, enrolling two years later in the M.F.A photography program at New York City's School of Visual Arts. Once out of school, between fishing seasons, she worked as a freelance photographer, finding a worldwide audience for her pictures.*

Suggested Readings

RECENT RESOURCES

Adam, G. Stuart and Roy Peter Clark. *Journalism: The Democratic Craft.* New York: Oxford University Press, 2005. Poynter authors Adam and Clark narrow the gap between the classroom and the profession with this collection of classic readings, writing instruction, study guides and exercises.

Boynton, Robert S. *The New New Journalism.* New York: Vintage Books, 2005. Conversations with some of America's best nonfiction writers on their craft.

Clark, Roy Peter. *Writing Tools: 50 Essential Strategies for Every Writer.* New York: Little, Brown and Company, 2006. Easy-to-remember tips to sharpen your writing talents.

Goldstein, Norm, ed. *The Associated Press Stylebook and Briefing on Media Law.* New York: Perseus Books Group, 2007. AP's rules on grammar, spelling, punctuation, capitalization, word usage and more.

Harrigan, Jane and Karen Brown Dunlap. *The Editorial Eye.* 2nd edition. New York: Bedford/St. Martin's, 2003. This updated edition deals with both the technical and management elements of professional editing.

Harrower, Tim. *Inside Reporting.* Boston: McGraw-Hill, 2007. A well-illustrated introduction to the craft of journalism.

Hart, Jack. *A Writer's Coach: An Editor's Guide to Words That Work.* New York: Pantheon Books, 2006. Practical advice and a step-by-step approach to the writing process.

Hennessy, Brendan. *Writing Feature Articles.* Burlington, Mass.: Focal Press, 2006. An introduction to feature writing.

Hutchison, Earl R. *The Art of Feature Writing.* New York: Oxford University Press, 2007. Sensible advice for students about writing and freelancing.

Irby, John, Kenton Bird, Susan English and David Cuillier. *Reporting That Matters.* Boston: Pearson Allyn and Bacon, 2007. This university textbook expands the traditional approach to public affairs reporting.

Kennedy, George and Daryl R. Moen, eds. *What Good Is Journalism?* Columbia: University of Missouri Press, 2007. A compilation of essays about positive trends in journalism.

Kessler, Lauren and Duncan McDonald. *When Words Collide.* Boston: Thomson/Wadsworth, 2008. A media writer's guide to grammar and style.

Kramer, Mark and Wendy Call, eds. *Telling True Stories.* New York: Plume, 2007. The Nieman Foundation's nonfiction writers' guide.

McKane, Anna. *News Writing.* Thousand Oaks, Calif.: SAGE Publications, 2006. McKane's book is designed for new and inexperienced writers.

McLellan, Michele and Tim Porter. *News, Improved.* Washington, D.C.: CQ Press, 2007. A report on how America's newsrooms are learning to change.

Morgan, Arlene Notero, Alice Irene Pifer and Keith Woods. *The Authentic Voice: The Best Reporting on Race and Ethnicity.* New York: Columbia University Press, 2006. In addition to the book, a DVD and Web site offer comprehensive multimedia tools on the coverage of race and ethnicity.

Scanlan, Christopher. *Reporting and Writing: Basics for the 21st Century.* New York: Oxford University Press, 2000. A practical guide to professional journalism skills.

Sims, Norman. *True Stories.* Evanston, Ill.: Northwestern University Press, 2008. Sims traces more than a century of literary journalism.

Standring, Suzette Martinez. *The Art of Column Writing.* Oak Park, Ill.: Marion Street Press, Inc., 2007. Useful tips on becoming a newspaper columnist.

Stein, M.L. *The Newswriter's Handbook.* Ames, Iowa: Blackwell, 2006. An introduction to journalism.

Uko, Ndaeyo. *Story Building.* Lanham, Md.: University Press of America, 2007. Narrative techniques for news and feature writers.

Weingarten, Marc. *The Gang That Wouldn't Write Straight: Wolfe, Thompson, Didion, Capote, and the New Journalism Revolution.* New York: Three

Rivers Press, reprint edition, 2006. A look at the origins and rise of New Journalism.

WRITING AND REPORTING ANTHOLOGIES

American Society of Magazine Editors. *The Best American Magazine Writing 2007.* New York: Columbia University Press, 2007. A wide-ranging collection of National Magazine Award winners.

Clark, Roy Peter and Christopher Scanlan, eds. *America's Best Newspaper Writing.* 2nd edition. New York: Bedford/St. Martin's, 2006. A collection of ASNE Distinguished Writing Award-winning stories and classic news reports.

Fairstein, Linda, ed. *The Best American Crime Reporting 2007.* New York: Harper, 2007. An annual anthology of nonfiction crime stories originally published in magazines.

Flippin, Royce, ed. *Best American Political Writing 2007.* New York: Thunder's Mouth Press, 2007. This sixth volume in a series focuses on magazine writing.

Garlock, David, ed. *Pulitzer Prize Feature Stories.* Ames: Iowa State Press, 2003. Twenty-five Pulitzer Prize-winning feature stories published from 1979 to 2003.

Harrington, Walt. *The Beholder's Eye.* New York: Grove Press, 2005. A collection of some of America's finest personal journalism.

Levy, Steven, ed. *The Best of Technology Writing 2007.* Ann Arbor: University of Michigan Press, 2007. These stories explore a wide range of intriguing technology-related topics.

Maraniss, David, ed. *The Best American Sports Writing 2007.* Boston: Houghton Mifflin, 2007. Examples of excellent sports writing.

Mills, Eleanor, et. al., eds. *Journalistas: 100 Years of the Best Writing and Reporting by Women Journalists.* New York: Carroll & Graf, 2005. A collection of stories written by women during the 20th century.

Orlean, Susan, ed. *The Best American Travel Writing 2007.* Boston: Houghton Mifflin, 2007. This anthology includes well-written stories about travel.

Preston, Richard, ed. *The Best American Science and Nature Writing 2007.* Boston: Houghton Mifflin, 2007. Some of the year's finest writing on a wide range of scientific topics.

Sloan, Wm. David and Laird B. Anderson. *Pulitzer Prize Editorials: America's Best Writing, 1917–2003.* 3rd edition. Ames, Iowa: Iowa State Press, 2003. Historical and recent Pulitzer Prize-winning editorials.

Wallace, David Foster, ed. *The Best American Essays 2007.* Boston: Houghton Mifflin, 2007. This series has become a showcase for the country's finest writing.

CLASSICS

Blundell, William E. *The Art and Craft of Feature Writing.* New York: Plume, 1988. A step-by-step guide to reporting and editing.

Brande, Dorothea. *Becoming a Writer.* Los Angeles: J.P. Tarcher; Boston: distributed by Putnam Publishing, 1981. Reprint of 1934 edition. Timeless writing advice.

Clark, Roy Peter and Don Fry. *Coaching Writers.* 2nd edition. New York: Bedford/St. Martin's, 2003. Guidelines on how to improve communication between editors and reporters.

Franklin, Jon. *Writing for Story.* New York: Plume, 1994. Lessons about how to write dramatic nonfiction.

Harrington, Walt. *Intimate Journalism: The Art and Craft of Reporting Everyday Life.* Thousand Oaks, Calif.: Sage, 1997. Award-winning articles are used to describe the process of combining traditional feature writing with in-depth reporting.

Murray, Donald M. *Writing to Deadline: The Journalist at Work.* Portsmouth, N.H.: Heinemann, 2000. Murray helps journalists understand the writing process.

Snyder, Louis L. and Richard B. Morris, eds. *A Treasury of Great Reporting.* New York: Simon & Schuster, 1962. Historical examples of great reporting and writing.

Stewart, James B. *Follow the Story: How to Write Successful Nonfiction.* New York: Simon & Schuster, 1988. Stewart illustrates the techniques of compelling narrative writing.

Strunk, William, Jr. and E.B. White. *The Elements of Style.* Illustrated edition. New York: Penguin Press, 2005. A classic reference book on the
rules of usage and the principles of composition.

Zinsser, William. *On Writing Well.* New York: HarperCollins, 2006. The
30th anniversary edition of a respected writing guide.

*This list of suggested readings was compiled by David Shedden, direc-
tor of the Eugene Patterson Library at The Poynter Institute.*